Her mon mæg giet gesion hiora swæð

ANGLO-SAXON ENGLAND

10

Edited by
PETER CLEMOES
University of Cambridge

MARTIN BIDDLE
Winchester Research Unit

JULIAN BROWN
University of London

RENÉ DEROLEZ
Rijksuniversiteit-Gent

HELMUT GNEUSS
Universität München

STANLEY GREENFIELD
University of Oregon

LARS-GUNNAR HALLANDER
Stockholms Universitet

SIMON KEYNES
University of Cambridge

MICHAEL LAPIDGE
University of Cambridge

JOHN LEYERLE
University of Toronto

PAUL MEYVAERT
Mediaeval Academy of America

BRUCE MITCHELL
University of Oxford

FRED ROBINSON
Yale University

CAMBRIDGE UNIVERSITY PRESS

CAMBRIDGE

LONDON   NEW YORK   NEW ROCHELLE

MELBOURNE   SIDNEY

Published by the Press Syndicate of the University of Cambridge
The Pitt Building, Trumpington Street, Cambridge CB2 1RP
32 East 57th Street, New York, NY 10022, USA
296 Beaconsfield Parade, Middle Park, Melbourne 3206, Australia

First published 1982

Printed in Great Britain at the
University Press, Cambridge

British Library Cataloguing in Publication Data
Anglo-Saxon England. – 10
1. Great Britain – History – Anglo-Saxon period,
449–1066 – Periodicals
942.01'05   DA152   78-190423
ISBN: 0 521 24177 4

Contents

Contents

*Abbreviations listed before the bibliography (pp. 245–7) are used throughout the
volume without other explanation*

Mrs Janet Godden's help with the editing is gratefully acknowledged

Illustrations

ACKNOWLEDGEMENTS

By permission of the Trustees of the British Museum the design on the cover is taken from the obverse of a silver penny issued to celebrate King Alfred's occupation and fortification of London in 886

All the photographs for the plates are from the collection of the Committee for Aerial Photography, Cambridge University: the copyright is reserved

Material should be submitted to the editor most convenient regionally (Australasian contributions to Bruce Mitchell), with these exceptions: an article offered from North America should be sent to Peter Clemoes if concerned with Old English literature, and an article offered from any source should be sent to Martin Biddle if concerned with archaeology, to Julian Brown if concerned with palaeography, to Simon Keynes if concerned with history and to Michael Lapidge if concerned with Anglo-Latin. Whenever a contribution is sent from abroad it should be accompanied by international coupons to cover the cost of return postage. A potential contributor is asked to get in touch with the editor concerned as early as possible to obtain a copy of the style sheet and to have any necessary discussion. Articles must be in English.

The editors' addresses are

Mr M. Biddle, The Winchester Research Unit, Historic Resources Centre, 75 Hyde St, Winchester, Hampshire SO23 7DW (England)

Professor T. J. Brown, Department of Palaeography, King's College, University of London, Strand, London WC2R 2LS (England)

Professor P. A. M. Clemoes, Emmanuel College, Cambridge CB2 3AP (England)

Professor R. Derolez, Rozier 44, 9000 Gent (Belgium)

Professor H. Gneuss, Institut für Englische Philologie, Universität München, 8000 München 40, Schellingstrasse 3 (Germany)

Professor S. B. Greenfield, Department of English, College of Liberal Arts, University of Oregon, Eugene, Oregon 97403 (USA)

Dr S. D. Keynes, Trinity College, Cambridge CB2 1TQ (England)

Dr M. Lapidge, Clare Hall, Cambridge CB3 9AL (England)

Professor J. Leyerle, Office of the Dean, School of Graduate Studies, University of Toronto, Toronto, Ontario M5S 1A1 (Canada)

Mr P. Meyvaert, 8 Hawthorne Park, Cambridge, Massachusetts 02138 (USA)

Dr B. Mitchell, St Edmund Hall, Oxford OX1 4AR (England)

Professor F. C. Robinson, Department of English, Yale University, New Haven, Connecticut 06520 (USA)

Identifiable books from the pre-Conquest library of Malmesbury Abbey

RODNEY THOMSON

In memory of Richard Hunt

The Benedictine abbey at Malmesbury in Wiltshire was one of that select group of English houses which could trace its history back to the golden age epitomized and chronicled by Bede.[1] To Bede's older contemporary Aldhelm (*ob. c.* 709) belongs most of the credit for setting the recently founded community on its feet and for making it a by-word throughout the British Isles for the pursuit of divine and secular learning.[2] During his abbacy Malmesbury eclipsed the reputations of the Irish schools and of Hadrian's Canterbury. At only one other point in its long history did the abbey attain a comparable reputation for learning, when it housed the monk William (*c.* 1095–1143), whose career, intellectual interests and writings were consciously modelled upon the examples of Bede and Aldhelm.[3]

To judge from the quotations in his own works, Aldhelm's library – in secular literature at least – was more extensive than Bede's.[4] One assumes that

[1] On the early history of Malmesbury, see A. Watkin, *Victoria County History of Wiltshire* III, 230; D. Knowles, C. N. L. Brooke and V. London, *The Heads of Religious Houses, England and Wales 940–1216* (Cambridge, 1972), pp. 54–5; and William of Malmesbury, *De Gestis Pontificum Anglorum*, ed. N. E. S. A. Hamilton, Rolls Ser. (London, 1870), pp. 345–57 and 361–443 (henceforth cited as *GP*).
[2] M. L. W. Laistner, *Thought and Letters in Western Europe*, 2nd ed. (London, 1957), pp. 151–6; M. R. James, *Two Ancient English Scholars* (Glasgow, 1931), pp. 9–15; C. J. Godfrey, *The Church in Anglo-Saxon England* (Cambridge, 1962), pp. 201–6; P. Riché, *Éducation et culture dans l'occident barbare*, 2nd ed. (Paris, 1961), pp. 421–6; and M. Winterbottom, 'Aldhelm's Prose Style and its Origins', *ASE* 6 (1977), 39–76. On the dating of Aldhelm's career, see now M. Lapidge and M. Herren, *Aldhelm: the Prose Works* (Cambridge, 1979), pp. 1–10.
[3] On William, see William of Malmesbury, *De Gestis Regum Anglorum*, ed. W. Stubbs, 2 vols., RS (London, 1887–9) I, ix–lxv and cxv–cxlvii, and II, xv–cxlii, and my 'William of Malmesbury as Historian and Man of Letters', *JEH* 29 (1978), 387–413. For a bibliography, see my 'The Reading of William of Malmesbury', *RB* 85 (1975), 362–94 (henceforth 'Reading'), at 394–6, and for supplement, see my 'The Reading of William of Malmesbury; Addenda et Corrigenda', *RB* 86 (1976), 327–35, at 334–5. My study of William's books is completed in 'The Reading of William of Malmesbury; Further Additions and Reflections', *RB* 89 (1979), 313–24.
[4] On Bede's library, see M. L. W. Laistner, 'The Library of the Venerable Bede', *Bede: his Life, Times and Writings*, ed. A. H. Thompson (Oxford, 1935), pp. 237–66, repr. *The Intellectual Heritage of the Early Middle Ages*, ed. C. G. Starr (Cornell, 1957), pp. 117–49, and now P. Hunter Blair, 'From Bede to Alcuin', *Famulus Christi*, ed. G. Bonner (London,1976), pp. 239–60. On Aldhelm's reading, see *Aldhelmi Opera*, ed. R. Ehwald, Monumenta Germaniae Historica, Auct. Antiq. 15 (Berlin, 1919),

Aldhelm brought books to Malmesbury for his teaching and that some of them remained at the abbey after his death. In 1931 M. R. James tried to show that one or two of Aldhelm's books were still available to William of Malmesbury.[5] Some of the books, too, which John Leland found at Malmesbury in the first half of the sixteenth century, must have been ancient, to judge from their titles.[6] There can in fact be little doubt that, from the twelfth century on, Malmesbury's was one of the great monastic libraries of England. Can we learn anything of its prehistory? In other words, is there any possibility of reconstructing the abbey's pre-Conquest collection, or at least of compiling a list of early manuscripts which could at one time or another have been found at the house? This is a hazardous undertaking and at first sight the prospects of success look bleak: only five Malmesbury manuscripts earlier than the twelfth century find a place in Ker's *Medieval Libraries of Great Britain*;[7] works quoted by Aldhelm need not have been known to him from books at Malmesbury; demonstrably ancient manuscripts used by William could have come, and often did come, from elsewhere, sometimes to be returned after copying;[8] and Malmesbury books listed by Leland, however early they might be, could have entered the library there at any time before the sixteenth century. More fundamentally, there is little evidence that institutional libraries involving corporate ownership of books and standardized procedures for their housing, borrowing and maintenance existed in England prior to the late eleventh century. Before that time books seemed to have been more readily attached to persons and to have changed hands and places much more freely than was the case from *c.* 1100 until the Reformation.[9] Malmesbury itself had a chequered history between the times of Aldhelm and William, even becoming a college of secular clerks between *c.* 950 and *c.* 965.[10] Thus the chances of a book used by Aldhelm still being

---

11–537, *passim*; J. D. A. Ogilvy, *Books known to the English, 597–1066*, Med. Acad. of America Publ. 76 (Cambridge, Mass., 1967), *passim*, but esp. under Cicero (*Cat.* and *Verr.*), Claudian, Donatus, Gellius, Juvenal, Lucan, Orosius, Ovid, Persius, Phocas, Pliny, Pompeius, Priscian (*Inst. de Nom.* only), Seneca(?), Servius, Solinus, Suetonius and Terence. But both Ehwald's and Ogilvy's information is to be regarded critically. On both Bede and Aldhelm, see M. Manitius, 'Zu Aldhelm und Beda', *Sitzungsberichte der phil.-hist. Klasse der kaiserlichen Akademie der Wissenschaften zu Wien* 112 (1886), 535–634, also separately ptd (Vienna, 1886), and M. Roger, *L'Enseignement des lettres classiques d'Ausone à Alcuin* (Paris, 1905), pp. 290–301.

[5] James, *Two Ancient English Scholars*, pp. 12–14.

[6] See below, pp. 3–14.

[7] N. R. Ker, *Medieval Libraries of Great Britain*, 2nd ed. (London, 1964), p. 128. But two, perhaps three, additions can now be made to this; see below, pp. 6–10 and 14.

[8] This is true, for instance, of his use of London, British Library, Cotton Tiberius A. xv, a Canterbury book dated *c.* 1000, of the version of the *Anglo-Saxon Chronicle* from Canterbury and of a lost exemplar for the second part of his manuscript of John Scotus Eriugena's *Periphyseon*; see Thomson, 'Reading', pp. 367 and 389–90; and R. M. Thomson, 'William of Malmesbury and the Letters of Alcuin', *Medievalia et Humanistica* n.s. 8 (1977), 147–61.

[9] Cf. the remarks by M. B. Parkes, *ASE* 5 (1976), 170–1.   [10] *GP*, p. 403.

available to William need to be carefully considered. And *e converso*: King Athelstan (924–39) was a generous donor to the abbey and, although William does not mention books among his gifts, the king certainly gave them to other houses and one would expect him to have given them to Malmesbury as well.[11]

Such a formidable array of pitfalls enforces caution; and yet, when we examine Leland's lists, the manuscripts known to William and internal evidence in a few extant manuscripts, and when we consider these sources of information in conjunction with Aldhelm's quotations and other background material, the connections that can be made enable us to draw up an unexpectedly long and interesting list of ancient, rare and important books which were, or may have been, at the abbey in pre-Conquest days. The list will, of course, constitute no more than an unrepresentative fragment of the total collection as it was at any particular time, but it seems worth offering as a basis on which more may yet be built.

SURVEY OF THE SOURCES
Malmesbury books known to Leland

In his *Collectanea* John Leland listed twenty-four books which he found at Malmesbury, giving the author and usually the title of the first or main item of contents. Five of these books are mentioned again in his *De Scriptoribus*, evidently for their exceptional rarity and possibly for their age, for Leland describes them as 'multo praestantiora' than Aldhelm's relics and refers to a psalter 'literis Saxonicis longiusculis scriptum', which he was shown during his visit.[12] The latest dateable items of the twenty-four contained works by twelfth-century authors: Faricius of Abingdon, William of Malmesbury, Robert of Cricklade and Grossolanus of Milan. There are six of these, including one mentioned in the *De Scriptoribus*, and we may exclude them from our enquiry. The other eighteen are all worthy of consideration and I proceed roughly in the order of Leland's list.

He begins with Juvencus, an author certainly more popular before the Conquest than later and much used by Aldhelm.[13] Of eight surviving Insular manuscripts there is one each from the seventh, eighth and ninth centuries,

---

[11] *Ibid.* pp. 396–403. Cf. J. J. G. Alexander, 'The Benedictional of St Æthelwold and Anglo-Saxon Illumination of the Reform Period', *Tenth-Century Studies. Essays in Commemoration of the Millennium of the Council of Winchester and 'Regularis Concordia'*, ed. D. Parsons (London and Chichester, 1975), pp. 169–73.

[12] J. Leland, *De Rebus Britannicis Collectanea*, ed. T. Hearne, 2nd ed., 6 vols. (London, 1770–4) IV, 157, and *Commentarii de Scriptoribus Britannicis*, ed. A. Hall (Oxford, 1709), I, 100–1.

[13] Ed. J. Huemer, Corpus Scriptorum Ecclesiasticorum Latinorum 24 (Berlin, 1891); see also E. Dekkers and A. Gaar, *Clavis Patrum Latinorum*, 2nd ed. (Steenbrugge, 1961), no. 1385. On knowledge of Juvencus in Anglo-Saxon England, see Ogilvy, *Books known to the English*, p. 190.

two are from the tenth century, one is from *c.* 1000 and there is one each from the eleventh and thirteenth centuries.[14] Three, including the single post-Conquest example, have known provenances. The earliest, Cues, Hospitalbibliothek, 171, a mere fragment, may have been written in Northumbria, but, if so, it doubtless passed early to the continent. It was certainly there well before Leland's time.[15] Of the two remaining possibilities, one is the most important of all Juvencus manuscripts, Cambridge, Corpus Christi College 304. This copy, assigned to the early eighth century, was written in uncials, probably in Italy.[16] M. R. James tentatively identified it with the 'Juvencus in Romana scriptura' which figures in the twelfth-century library catalogue from Christ Church, Canterbury.[17] This, however, bore a distinguishing mark resembling HL, probably on its opening leaf, and, as James noted, there is no trace of such a mark in the Corpus Juvencus.[18] At the head of its 1r is an erased early inscription consisting of a single word of about eight to ten capitals. James distinguished *S* at the end and *A* at the beginning. Were he right, ALDHELMVS would be an attractive conjecture which would fit the space well enough. The *S* at the end seems fairly clear, but my own examination left me unconvinced about the *A* at the beginning, and, since then, Drs R. I. Page and M. Lapidge have studied the inscription under ultra-violet light and reported that James's initial letter is more likely to be a *V* and is in any case the *second* letter, not the first.[19] Thus the inscription is more likely to have read IVVENCVS. The book was certainly in England *c.* 1000, when annotations were made both in Anglo-Caroline and in Anglo-Saxon minuscule, but its exact provenance is still a mystery. The other possible candidate for identification with Leland's Malmesbury book is Cambridge, University Library, Ff. 4. 42.[20] It was made in the ninth century

---

[14] Cues, Hospitalbibliothek, 171 (?Insular, s. vii); Cambridge, Corpus Christi College 304 (?Italy, s. viii); Cambridge, University Library, Ff. 4. 42 (Wales, s. ix); London, British Library, Royal 15 A. xvi (continental, s. ix; in England by s. x²); Oxford, Bodleian Library, Barlow 25 (?English, s. x); Paris, Bibliothèque Sainte-Geneviève, 2410 (English, s. x/xi); ULC Gg. 5. 35 (St Augustine's, Canterbury, s. xi med.); and Oxford, Bodleian Library, Bodley 527 (Waverley, s. xiii).

[15] E. A. Lowe, *Codices Latini Antiquiores*, 12 vols. (Oxford, 1934–71) VIII, no. 1172; left to the Cues Library by Nicholas of Cues (*ob.* 1464).

[16] *CLA* II, no. 127; M. R. James, *A Descriptive Catalogue of the Manuscripts in the Library of Corpus Christi College, Cambridge*, 2 vols. (Cambridge, 1909–12) II, 101; and F. A. Rella, 'Continental Manuscripts acquired for English Centres in the Tenth and Early Eleventh Centuries', *Anglia* 98 (1980), 107–16, at 110. To Rella's list should be added Oxford, Bodleian Library, Marshall 19 (see below, p. 16).

[17] M. R. James, *The Ancient Libraries of Canterbury and Dover* (Cambridge, 1903), p. 11, no. 152, and cf. pp. xxxii–iii; see also H. Thoma, 'The Oldest Manuscript of Juvencus', *Classical Rev.* 64 (1950), 95–6.

[18] Marks survive in this position in CCCC 260, Cambridge, Trinity College B. 14. 3 and R. 15. 22, and New Zealand, Wellington, Turnbull Library 16; and in many other manuscripts not included in the surviving fragment of the twelfth-century catalogue.

[19] I am grateful to these two scholars for undertaking this examination on my behalf, when I was in Australia, and to Dr Lapidge for reporting their findings.

[20] T. A. M. Bishop, 'The Corpus Martianus Capella', *Trans. of the Cambridge Bibliographical Soc.* IV.4 (1967), 258.

at an unidentified centre in Wales but may later have come into the possession of an English centre, for it has Latin glosses in Anglo-Caroline script of *c*. 1000 by a scribe whose writing is found in other English manuscripts.[21] At present a Malmesbury provenance cannot be demonstrated for either of these manuscripts; it seems inherently less likely for the Welsh book, for there is no evidence of any significant cultural links between Wales and Malmesbury.

Next on Leland's list is 'Opera Fortunati carmine scripta', an entry which he repeated in the *De Scriptoribus*. This copy was probably early, since most of those extant were written between the ninth and eleventh centuries,[22] and since in England Fortunatus was well known – and probably best known – for at least a century and a half before the Conquest.[23] There is some positive evidence that William of Malmesbury did not know his verse.[24] This seems odd, for William was an omnivorous reader with pronounced antiquarian interests, and the Fortunatus may therefore have been a late-comer to the abbey. On the other hand, Fortunatus's *Vita S. Paterni*, a work noted by Leland, was known to William,[25] and Leland's reference is probably to the copy once in London, British Library, Cotton Vitellius D. xvii, burnt in the fire of 1731. This manuscript was originally bound up with Oxford, Bodley 852, written at Jumièges in the mid-eleventh century but at Malmesbury after 1106, probably acquired by William.[26] The relics of St Paternus had been given to Malmesbury by Athelstan.[27]

Of the next item, 'Beda super Canticum Abacuc', Laistner and King comment that 'MSS of it are few and it rarely appears in medieval catalogues'.[28] They list twelve manuscripts, of which six are English. All of these except one have known provenances, and all are of the twelfth century except for Cambridge, Pembroke College 81, a ninth-century book with Corbie connections, at Bury abbey by the mid-twelfth century.[29] The one English manuscript of uncertain origin is London, Lambeth Palace Library, 237, a post-medieval make-up of three volumes. Bede, *Super Habacuc*, is in the first volume, from the twelfth century. There is no positive evidence to

---

[21] BL Cotton Vespasian D. xv, fols. 102–21, and BL Harley 3376; see Bishop, *ibid.*

[22] *Fortunati Opera*, ed. F. Leo, MGH, Auct. Antiq. 4.1 (Berlin, 1881), v–xiv.

[23] Ogilvy, *Books known to the English*, p. 140, is now thoroughly superseded by R. W. Hunt, 'Manuscript Evidence for Knowledge of the Poems of Venantius Fortunatus in Late Anglo-Saxon England', *ASE* 8 (1979), 279–95.

[24] Thomson, 'Reading, Additions and Reflections', p. 317.

[25] *GP*, p. 399.

[26] R. M. Thomson, 'The "Scriptorium" of William of Malmesbury', *Medieval Scribes, Manuscripts and Libraries: Essays presented to N. R. Ker*, ed. M. B. Parkes and A. G. Watson (London, 1978), pp. 121–3.

[27] *GP*, pp. 398–9.

[28] M. L. W. Laistner and H. H. King, *A Hand-List of Bede Manuscripts* (Ithaca, N.Y., 1943), pp. 43–4.

[29] The suggestion that the manuscript was copied from a Corbie exemplar was made to me by Dr D. Ganz. The manuscript bears the Bury *ex-libris* of *c*. 1200 and figures in the earliest part of its composite library catalogue from the second half of the twelfth century.

connect this volume with Malmesbury. Even less can be said of the next entry in Leland's list, 'Bedae allegorica expositio super Leviticum et Tobiam'. Laistner and King comment that the popularity of *De Tobia*, 'especially in the twelfth century, is astonishing' and they list seventy-four manuscripts of it.[30] None of the surviving English ones includes (pseudo-)Bede on Leviticus.[31]

I deal next with a group of items, 'Claudii tres libri super Mattheum', 'Cassiodorus de Anima', 'Exameron Basilii' and 'Gregorius Nicenus de conditione hominis', which can be connected with Malmesbury only on Leland's testimony. To judge from other library catalogues and surviving copies all of these were especially popular in the twelfth century, and probably the Malmesbury examples were typical stately folios of that date. Aldhelm quotes Basil's work,[32] but the *Hexaemeron* was too common for that to be significant. Gregory of Nyssa is included in the twelfth-century section of Lambeth 237.

Interspersed with this group are some items which look more promising. 'Sententiae Xysti, interprete Rufino, qui contendit hunc fuisse Xystum pontificem Romanum' denotes Rufinus's translation of the *Sentences of Sextus*, a rare work surviving in twelve manuscripts of which no fewer than six, interestingly enough, are from England.[33] Glastonbury had a copy in 1247 and Leland records two others, at Faversham and the London Carmelite priory.[34] No less than five of the extant manuscripts from England are later than the twelfth century (two being of known provenance), so that we might well think that not much can be made of this item of Leland's. The remaining English manuscript is the third part of Lambeth 237, dating from the early tenth century. It was written on the continent but was in west or south-west England by the middle of the same century.[35] It may therefore be the copy recorded in the thirteenth-century Glastonbury catalogue. Leland's rendering of the alleged pope's name as 'Xystus', rather than 'Sixtus' or 'Sextus', seems at first sight against the connection; since this form occurs in only two of the extant manuscripts, Paris, Bibliothèque Nationale, lat. 2676 and 113, both continental and of the ninth and eleventh centuries respectively, it might indicate that Leland saw an early continental manuscript at Malmesbury. But

---

[30] Laistner and King, *Hand-List*, pp. 78–82.

[31] Pseudo-Bede, *Super Leviticum* (F. Stegmüller, *Repertorium Biblicum Medii Aevi*, 7 vols. (Madrid, 1940–61), no. 1649).

[32] Ed. Ehwald, p. 263 (*De Virg. Prosa*), in the version of Rufinus.

[33] Rufinus, *The Sentences of Sextus*, ed. H. Chadwick, Texts and Stud. n.s. 5 (Cambridge, 1959); repr. Corpus Christianorum Series Latina 20 (Turnhout, 1961), 257–9; see also *Clavis*, no. 198h. Cambridge, St John's College 168 is from Witham; Cambridge, Sidney Sussex College 94, from York Franciscans. Unassigned are Cambridge, University Library, Add. 584, Cambridge, Gonville and Caius College 351, BL Royal 2 F. ii and London, Lambeth Palace Library, 237.

[34] For the Glastonbury catalogue, see T. W. Williams, *Somerset Medieval Libraries* (Bristol, 1897), p. 63, and, for the manuscripts seen by Leland, see *Collectanea* IV, 6 and 53.

[35] Rella, 'Continental Manuscripts', p. 113, no. 22, and T. A. M. Bishop, *English Caroline Minuscule* (Oxford, 1971), no. 3.

Lambeth 237 remains a possibility for he renders the name thus for the Faversham and London copies also. Leland follows this entry with 'Questiones Albini super Genesim. parvus libellus', meaning Alcuin's *Interrogationes et Responsiones in Genesim*. Thirteen manuscripts of this work are known, five each from the ninth and tenth centuries, two from the twelfth century and one from the thirteenth.[36] The two English examples are late: Lambeth 148, twelfth-century from Lanthony, and BL, Royal 8 E. xvi of the early thirteenth century. But it is the description of the book rather than its contents that arouses our interest, for Leland's words suggest that it contained *only* the item he mentions. Such a book would resemble Malmesbury's extant ninth-century copy of Jerome, *De Nominibus Hebraicis*, of which more later. It might not have been as early as that, but early it would almost certainly have been. By the twelfth century a single volume would scarcely have been wasted on this work alone. It is followed in Leland's list by another ninth-century author, 'Dionysius, interprete Ioanne Scoto', referring to the standard collection of pseudo-Dionysius's works in John Scotus Eriugena's translation, accompanied by the glosses and preface of Anastasius the Librarian and other matter.[37] This collection does not seem to have reached England before *c.* 1100, after which it became very popular.[38] William of Malmesbury had it[39] and one imagines that Leland's volume must have had some connection with William. Two other books containing works of Alcuin appear in the *Collectanea* list and we may mention them to dismiss them. One, 'Albinus super Ecclesiasten', is probably Oxford, Merton College 181, containing this work and others, made for William of Malmesbury in the 1120s or 1130s.[40] The other, 'Epistolae Albini', from which Leland quotes elsewhere in the *Collectanea*, refers to the apograph of BL Cotton Tiberius A. xv, made by William of Malmesbury, now lost.[41] In other words, the

---

[36] Stegmüller, *Repertorium*, no. 1085; Migne, Patrologia Latina 100, cols. 515–66; prologue MGH, Epist. 4 (Berlin, 1895), 122 ff. (Ep. 80).

[37] MGH, Epist. 7 (Berlin, 1928), 430–4; see J. Cappuyns, *Jean Scot Erigène* (Brussels, 1933), pp. 150–61 and H. F. Dondaine, 'Le Corpus dionysien de l'université de Paris au XIIIe siècle', *Storia e Letteratura* 44 (1953), esp. 35–66.

[38] The earliest known English manuscript, from which all others seem to derive, is Oxford, St John's College 128, from the first quarter of the twelfth century, provenance unknown. Collation with William's quotation suggests that his manuscript too derived from this one. I have examined the St John's College manuscript for a possible Malmesbury connection, but could find no positive evidence. The historiated initial on 9v might assist in localizing the manuscript. It is an *O* enclosing *Christus super aspides*, in tinted outline style, the drapery showing 'nested V-folds'. Later English manuscripts are Cambridge, Trinity College B. 2. 31; Oxford, Bodleian Library, Laud misc. 639, Ashmole 1526 and e Mus. 134.

[39] The evidence is set out Thomson, 'Reading, Additions and Reflections', pp. 318–19; cf. E. Jeauneau, 'Guillaume de Malmesbury, premier éditeur anglais du "Periphyseon"', *Sapientiae Doctrina, Mélanges de théologie et de littérature médiévales offerts à Dom Hildebrand Bascour* (Louvain, 1980), pp. 148–79.

[40] Thomson, 'The "Scriptorium"', pp. 139–41.

[41] Thomson, 'William of Malmesbury and the Letters of Alcuin', pp. 147–50. Cf. Ker, *Medieval Libraries*, p. 128, identifying Leland's manuscript with Oxford, Bodleian Library, Wood Empt. 5, of the early thirteenth century.

manuscript seen by Leland almost certainly dated from the early twelfth century.

There remain four works in Leland's list and they are the most interesting of all. I begin with one already studied by James, 'Junilius ad Primasium papam', noted again by Leland in *De Scriptoribus* as 'fragmenta Junilii et Primasii'. The work meant is Junilius's *Institutes* or *De Partibus Divinae Legis*, dedicated to Primasius, bishop of Hadrumetum.[42] James noted that this work was quoted by Aldhelm,[43] who also made Leland's mistake as to the office held by Primasius: 'Iunillius, instituta regularia...Primasio, sedis apostolicae pontifici scribens'.[44] James thought that this error must stem from Aldhelm's manuscript of Junilius, and that this manuscript was the one seen by Leland. This suggestion, in itself plausible, can be supported with additional evidence. Twenty-one of the twenty-three known manuscripts of Junilius are early, dating from the seventh to the eleventh century. But we may even have the remains of the Malmesbury copy.

BL Cotton Tiberius A. xv, fols. 175–80, is a fragment of Junilius in early-eighth-century Anglo-Saxon minuscule, written, according to Lowe, 'probably in a southern centre'.[45] The six leaves, containing *Inst.* 1.9–11.17 and 22–4, were much damaged in the fire of 1731 and are now mounted separately. Their correct order is fols. 177, 179, 180, 176, 175 and 178 and they now measure *c.* 230 × 160 mm. There are two obstacles to be tackled before considering some positive arguments for identifying these leaves as the remains of the Malmesbury book. First of all, Lowe compared the script of the present manuscript with that of BL Cotton Charter Augustus ii. 18, dated 704–5 and now proved to have been written in London.[46] The resemblance is not however close and we can with greater justice assign the script of Cotton Tiberius A. xv to south-west England. In a recent article Malcolm Parkes has studied the handwriting of St Boniface and of an associate whom Parkes calls 'Glossator B', describing him as 'a kind of

---

[42] See James, *Two Ancient English Scholars*, p. 13. The work is ptd PL 68, cols. 15–42; for bibliography, see *Clavis*, no. 872, and Stegmüller, *Repertorium*, no. 5328. There is a critical edition by H. Kihn, *Theodor von Mopsuestia und Junilius Africanus als Exegeten* (Freiburg, 1880), 467–528, based on thirteen manuscripts. Another ten were added by M. L. W. Laistner, 'Antiochene Exegesis in Western Europe', *Harvard Theol. Rev.* 40 (1947), 19–31. For the dates of the earliest manuscripts, see *CLA* II, no. 189 (addition), III, no. 348 (s. viii/ix), and VII, no. 965 (s. vii/viii). Cf. also Avranches, Bibliothèque Municipale, 109 (s. xi), fols. 138–50, Laon, Bibliothèque de la Ville, 273, and Oxford, Bodleian Library, Laud Misc. 159 (Lorsch), ninth-century manuscripts containing Wicbod, *Questiones in Octateuchum ex Dictis Sanctorum Patrum Augustini, Ambrosii, Hilarii, Eucherii et Junilii* (on which see J. Contreni, *The Cathedral School of Laon from 850 to 930* (Munich, 1978), pp. 37–8 and 45).

[43] James, *Two Ancient English Scholars*, p. 13; Laistner, 'Antiochene Exegesis', pp. 26–7.

[44] Ed. Ehwald, pp. 81–2 and n. 1 (*De Metris*). [45] *CLA* II, no. 189.

[46] Earlier transcriptions and discussions are now superseded by P. Chaplais, 'The Letter from Bishop Wealdhere of London to Archbishop Brihtwold of Canterbury', *Medieval Scribes, Manuscripts and Libraries*, ed. Parkes and Watson, pp. 3–23.

amanuensis...working under supervision, amplifying the glosses of Glossator A' (whom Parkes identifies as Boniface).[47] This man and the scribe of the Spangenberg Servius[48] form a group which Parkes connects with south-west England. Dr Parkes himself suspects Malmesbury as a likely place of origin for the Servius;[49] it is a pity that Aldhelm's quotations from Servius are not extensive enough to permit a comparison. Characteristics of the handwriting of this group are: an upright **g** with a long, horizontal head-stroke, the tail occasionally brought back to form a loop; **tio** in a ligature; **fi** ligature with the **i** traced across the head-stroke of **f**; and **g** in ligature with a following letter at the beginning of a word. The Cotton Junilius fragment has Glossator B's form of **g** and his **g** and **tio** ligatures, but not the others. It has the form for **fi** used by Glossator A (**f** plus **i** subscript).

Another consideration is that a copy of Junilius, described as 'vetustus', appears in the Glastonbury library catalogue of 1247.[50] One has therefore to make a case for identifying the Cotton fragment with Leland's Malmesbury book rather than with the Glastonbury one. The compiler of the Glastonbury catalogue distinguished between books which were 'vetustus' and those which were 'vetustissimus', which suggests that the local Junilius was perhaps not as old as the eighth century. Nor is there any evidence that this book survived until the Dissolution, as was the case with the Malmesbury example. But what tips the scales decisively in favour of Malmesbury, I believe, is the fact that Leland called what he saw there 'fragmenta' and the Cotton leaves were in that state even before the fire of 1731. In his catalogue entry for Cotton Tiberius A. xv Thomas Smith described a 'Fragmentum theologicum, characteribus uetustis, et a festinante scriba exaratis'.[51] That this was the Junilius is proved by Wanley's annotation of 'Saxonicis cursoriis' after 'characteribus' in Oxford, Bodleian Library, Gough Lond. 54, his copy of Smith's *Catalogus*.

Aldhelm's quotation from Junilius does not tell us much. Collation with Kihn's edition shows that Aldhelm's exemplar was not related to A, D, E or L, but that leaves another nine possibilities. Kihn did not use the Cotton fragment, which does not overlap with Aldhelm's quotation. It is not related to A, D or L either (it does not overlap with the excerpts in E), nor to B, H, M, P or R. Thus all that can be said is that there are no insuperable textual obstacles to its identification with Aldhelm's manuscript and that there is a

---

[47] M. B. Parkes, 'The Handwriting of St Boniface; a Reassessment of the Problems', *Beiträge zur Geschichte der deutschen Sprache und Literatur* 98 (1976), 161–79, esp. 177.

[48] *CLA* Suppl., no. 1806.

[49] So Dr Parkes informs me.

[50] Williams, *Somerset Libraries*, p. 75.

[51] T. Smith, *Catalogus Librorum Manuscriptorum Bibliothecae Cottonianae* (London, 1696), p. 21.

balance of probability in favour. It was apparently written early in the eighth
century, by which time Aldhelm was an old man; unfortunately the *De Metris*,
in which Aldhelm quotes Junilius, cannot be closely dated.[52] To sum up:
there is good if not conclusive evidence that the Cotton Junilius is a fragment
of the Malmesbury copy, and some reason to connect it with Aldhelm.

The next work, mentioned in both of Leland's books and therefore
thought by him particularly noteworthy, is the *Peri Hermeneias* doubtfully
ascribed to Apuleius. The two most recent editors of this work[53] together
list ten manuscripts, all continental, four from the ninth century, two from
the tenth, three from the eleventh and one from the twelfth. Again this gives
us grounds for presuming that the book which Leland saw was an ancient
one. Neither editor mentions CCCC 206, a tenth-century copy written in a
puzzling mixture of continental Caroline script with many Insular abbreviations. It contains (in addition to the *Peri Hermeneias*) the fourth book of
Martianus Capella's *De Nuptiis*, Boethius, *De Trinitate*, and Alcuin,
Dialectica.[54] The opening leaf of this manuscript was rewritten in England
c. 1100, in a fine hand uninfluenced by newly introduced continental fashions
but accompanied by a striking 'Norman' initial outlined in red, tinted with
violet, red and green and displaying a lion and dragon, foliage and interlace.
This was obviously done in a well-established scriptorium and at this date
one thinks of Canterbury. It is perhaps worth noting that William of
Malmesbury certainly knew Boethius's Trinitarian works, although they were
not uncommon at the time, and probably knew Alcuin's *Dialectica*, much
rarer.[55] There is therefore a possibility that CCCC 206 was the manuscript
that Leland saw at Malmesbury, but it is a remote one.

The next item, 'Grammatica Euticis', survives in thirty manuscripts dating
from the ninth century to the eleventh.[56] The only specimen of English
provenance is one of the ninth-century sections of St Dunstan's 'Classbook'
from Glastonbury,[57] and even that originated in Brittany. Leland records
another copy at St Augustine's, Canterbury.[58] In 1247 Glastonbury had two
copies of this work, both described as 'vetustissimi',[59] but it was evidently
not well known in England, nor thought useful after the early eleventh

[52] Lapidge and Herren, *Aldhelm*, pp. 12–13.
[53] A. Goldbacher, 'Liber περὶ ἑρμηνείας qui Apuleii Madaurensis esse traditur', *Wiener Studien* 7 (1885), 253–77, and P. Thomas, *Apuleii Opera* III (Leipzig, 1908), 176–94.
[54] James, *Catalogue of Manuscripts in Corpus Christi College* I, 495–8, and C. Leonardi, 'I Codici di Marziano Capella', *Aevum* 34 (1960), 21–2, no. 29. Neither notices the rewritten first recto.
[55] Thomson, 'Reading, Addenda et Corrigenda', pp. 328–9.
[56] C. Jeudy, 'Les Manuscrits de l'*Ars de Verbo* d'Eutychès et le commentaire de Rémi d'Auxerre', *Études de civilisation médiévale IXᵉ–XIIᵉ siècles: mélanges offerts à E.-R. Labande* (Poitiers, 1974), pp. 421–36.
[57] Oxford, Bodleian Library, Auct. F. 4. 32; ed. R. W. Hunt, *St Dunstan's Classbook from Glastonbury*, Umbrae Codicum Occidentalium 4 (Amsterdam, 1961).
[58] Leland, *Collectanea* IV, 7.
[59] Williams, *Somerset Libraries*, p. 75; also Leland, *Collectanea* IV, 154, though this is Dunstan's book yet again.

century.[60] We may be fairly confident, therefore, that the book which Leland saw was part of the pre-Conquest library at Malmesbury, that it was continental and probably not older than the ninth century. Ogilvy credits Aldhelm with a reference to Eutyches, but it is a dubious one.[61]

I have left until last the most complicated case of all, yet also the most important and interesting. In his *Collectanea* Leland refers to an item as simply 'Tertullianus'. M. R. James was misled, and has misled others, into thinking that this referred to a collection containing Tertullian's *Apology* and some works of Lactantius put together by William of Malmesbury and known from late manuscripts.[62] Had James looked at Leland's *De Scriptoribus*, however, he would have seen that this was wrong, for there Leland refers to a 'Tertulliani librum de Spectaculis, de Ieiunio'. The two references enable the manuscript to be identified as another example of the 'Corpus Corbiense' of Tertullian's works, originally compiled in the fifth century and containing *De Resurrectione Mortuorum*, *De Trinitate* (now attributed to Novatian), *De Spectaculis*, *De Praescriptione Haereticorum*, *De Pudicitia*, *De Monogamia* and *De Ieiunio*.[63] This collection is known to have existed in two manuscripts: one, probably of the ninth century, described in two eleventh-century catalogues from Corbie, the other listed in the early-ninth-century (833) catalogue of Cologne cathedral library. Two folios from the second of these manuscripts were not long ago discovered doing duty as endleaves in the sixteenth-century register of a German baronial family. The script apparently resembles the work of the scribes under Hildebald, bishop of Cologne (785–819).[64]

The Cologne manuscript, dismembered by *c.* 1563, was probably used by the second editor of Tertullian, Mesnart (1545), and perhaps by the third, Ghelen (1550).[65] However, on his title-page Ghelen claimed to have had recourse to 'complures veteres e Gallicanis Germanisque bibliothecis con-quisitos...codices, in quibus praecipuus fuit unus longe incorruptissimus in ultimam usque petitus Britanniam'. On the verso he added further details of this manuscript: 'Tandem ex ultima Britannia Ioannes Lelandus, uir antiquarius et feliciori dignus ualetudine, communicauit exemplar in Mas-burensi coenobio gentis eius uetustissimo repertum.'[66] It is astonishing that the modern editors of Tertullian and Novatian have, because of Ghelen's

---

[60] Ogilvy, *Books known to the English*, pp. 137–8.

[61] Ed. Ehwald, p. 195 (*De Metris*); cf. Roger, *L'Enseignement*, p. 329, n. 4.

[62] James, *Two Ancient English Scholars*, p. 20; cf. Thomson, 'Reading', pp. 365–6. The 'Codex Luganensis', to which William's text of Tertullian's *Apology* is related, is now Oxford, Bodleian Library, Lat. theol. d. 34.

[63] *Tertulliani Opera* I, ed. E. Dekkers *et al.*, CCSL 1 (Turnhout, 1954), vii and n. 3.

[64] G. Lieftinck, 'Un Fragment de *De Spectaculis* de Tertullien provenant d'un manuscrit du 9e siècle', *Vigiliae Christianae* 5 (1951), 193–203, esp. 196, and E. Dekkers, 'Note sur les fragments récemment découverts de Tertullien', *Sacris Erudiri* 4 (1952), 372–83.

[65] Lieftinck, 'Fragment', pp. 198–9, and Dekkers, 'Fragments', pp. 379–82.

[66] *Novatiani Opera*, ed. G. F. Diercks, CCSL 4 (Turnhout, 1972), 3.

generally untrustworthy editorship, from time to time doubted the very existence of this manuscript, without checking Leland's works.[67] But let us proceed further.

In 1579 Jacques de Pamele (Pamelius) published the third edition of the works of Tertullian and Novatian, using, *inter alia*, 'liber manuscriptus Anglicus quidam, quem thesauri loco penes se adseruabat Ioan. Clemens Anglus'.[68] In the *Notarum Explicatio* he refers to 'Anglicus codex antiquissimus Ioan. Clementis Angli, e quo VII castigati sunt libri'. The seven works are those in the 'Corpus Corbiense' and Pamele, using this manuscript, was able to correct some faults of Mesnart and Ghelen. The latest editor of Novatian says: 'On ne saurait rien dire avec certitude sur le rapport mutuel de ces trois manuscrits, ne serait-ce que parce que nous ne savons pas exactement de quelle manière les éditeurs se sont servis des ressources qui étaient à leur disposition.'[69] Again, it is astonishing that the continental editors of Tertullian and Novatian have not troubled to identify the Englishman John Clement. He is not hard to track down. A distinguished Oxford graduate, protégé of Sir Thomas More and royal physician, he was the owner of a fine library,[70] which was catalogued in 1554–5 as part of proceedings to recover property seized during his exile from England in the reign of Edward VI. Among the authors listed in this catalogue is Tertullian.[71] Since these books were sequestrated in England, they must have been in Clement's possession before his first flight to the continent, which was in July 1549. In the autumn of 1560 or thereabouts he transferred to Antwerp and then to Malines, where he died in 1572. I assume that his ancient copy of the 'Corpus Corbiense' of Tertullian's works was Leland's, passed on to him either by Leland himself or by Ghelen after he had finished with it. For one thing, the only alternative interpretation, that *two* ancient English manuscripts of this rare collection were owned by two contemporary English scholars who lent them to successive continental editors, seems remote and unlikely. Secondly, Leland and Clement had for a time at least been friends. They were at St Paul's School together under Lily and, when in 1526 Clement married Thomas More's step-daughter, Leland, then in the Duke of Norfolk's household, composed

[67] Dekkers, 'Fragments', p. 381, and *Novatiani Opera*, ed. Diercks, p. 3.

[68] Dekkers, 'Fragments', pp. 374–5, and *Novatiani Opera*, ed. Diercks, pp. 4–7.

[69] *Novatiani Opera*, ed. Diercks, p. 7.

[70] A. B. Emden, *A Biographical Register of the University of Oxford, A.D. 1501–1540* (Oxford, 1974), pp. 121–2; *Dictionary of National Biography* IV, 489; E. Wenkelbach, *John Clement: ein englischer Humanist und Arzt des sechzehnten Jahrhunderts*, Studien zur Geschichte der Medizin 14 (Leipzig, 1925); G. Mercati, 'Sopra Giovanni Clement e i suoi Manoscritti', *La Bibliofilia* 28 (1926), 81–99, repr. Mercati's 'Opere Minori' IV, *Studi e Testi* 79 (Rome, 1937), 292–315; and A. W. Reed, 'John Clement and his Books', *The Library* 4th ser. 6 (1926), 329–39.

[71] Reed, 'John Clement', p. 339. But Reed says that 'in all instances the books appear to be printed editions unless they are described as written' (p. 337).

an appropriate epithalamium.[72] After 1530, certainly, one assumes that relations between the two men must have become somewhat strained, since Leland supported the religious policies of Henry VIII, while Clement remained faithful to the principles of his benefactor. What happened to their copy of Tertullian after Pamele had used it is not known.

In other words, Ghelen's 'codex Masburense' did in fact exist and did contain the 'Corpus Corbiense', and we have the word of Ghelen and Pamele that it was very ancient. Can we find out any more about it? The copy of the 'Corpus Corbiense' which appears in the Cologne catalogue apparently did not contain any authors' names ('sed auctorem ignoramus' runs the entry) and Novatian, *De Trinitate*, and Tertullian, *De Spectaculis*, were lumped together under the title 'De Fide'.[73] John Clement's manuscript, which I take to be Leland's from Malmesbury, distinguished the two works as in the tables of contents reproduced by the Corbie catalogues.[74] So the Malmesbury manuscript was, in this respect at least, more closely related to the Corbie copy than to the Cologne one. Were the manuscripts from Malmesbury and Corbie indeed one and the same? The two Corbie catalogues in which the Tertullian appears date from the first half and third quarter of the eleventh century respectively. But Tertullian is absent from a third Corbie catalogue of *c.* 1200.[75] One assumes that it left the house (if it was not destroyed outright) during the intervening period and there is therefore a real possibility that it came to England and thus to Malmesbury. One is tempted to see it as yet another of William of Malmesbury's continental acquisitions, although there is no evidence for his knowing these particular works of Tertullian. The most likely alternative hypothesis would be that the Malmesbury manuscript was a *gemellus*, early copy, or even the ancestor of the Corbie book and that it was at Malmesbury well before the Conquest.

With this we leave Leland's list, but it does not include all the notable manuscripts that he found at Malmesbury. Elsewhere in the *Collectanea* and also in *De Scriptoribus* he quotes a series of verse inscriptions ascribed to Bede and others, which he says he found in an ancient volume from Malmesbury abbey.[76] Michael Lapidge was able to show that William of Malmesbury knew this collection, which was originally made in the eighth century by Bishop

---

[72] Wenkelbach, *John Clement*, pp. 17–18 and 55–8 and n. 55.

[73] Dekkers, 'Fragments', pp. 374–5.

[74] *Ibid.*

[75] L. Delisle, *Le Cabinet des manuscrits de la Bibliothèque Impériale*, 3 vols. (Paris, 1858–81) II, 428 (first catalogue), 428–32 (second) and 432–40 (third). On their dates, see C. de Merindol, *La Production des livres peints à l'Abbaye de Corbie*, 3 vols. (Lille, 1976) I, 70–1. Dr D. Ganz informs me that the titles of works in the second catalogue were taken from tables of contents apparently written in the ninth century.

[76] Leland, *Collectanea* III, 114–18; and *De Scriptoribus*, p. 134. See the full discussion of these verse inscriptions by Patrick Sims-Williams, below, pp. 21–38.

Milred of Worcester.[77] Recently a bifolium from the Malmesbury manuscript came to light in the library of the University of Illinois, Urbana.[78] It is written in tenth-century Anglo-Saxon square minuscule and is annotated by Leland.[79] How long it had been at Malmesbury before William's time cannot as yet be determined; it may have been another of his acquisitions.[80]

Let us sum up before proceeding to other kinds of evidence. In the Cotton Junilius fragments we have perhaps identified the remains of one of Aldhelm's books. Several others, Juvencus, Fortunatus, Rufinus, Alcuin *Super Genesim*, Apuleius and Eutyches, were probably ancient and part of the pre-Conquest library at Malmesbury, although this cannot be proven. The Tertullian was certainly ancient, probably from the ninth century, perhaps written and for a time kept at Corbie, in which case it came to Malmesbury during the twelfth century. Finally, a tenth-century copy of Bishop Milred's collection of epigrams by English and other authors was at Malmesbury by William's time. To William we turn now.

Pre-Conquest Malmesbury books known to William of Malmesbury

In the lecture in which he connected Aldhelm's quotation from Junilius with the Malmesbury copy seen by Leland M. R. James drew attention to William's copy of the rare *Breviarium Alaricum*.[81] He noted that Aldhelm claimed to be teaching Roman law at Malmesbury and asked what text he could have used, concluding that at this period it could hardly be other than the *Breviarium*.[82] Thus he conjectured that William copied an ancient manuscript available to Aldhelm. As I have pointed out elsewhere,[83] the textual evidence supports James's suggestion, for William's copy, in spite of its comparatively late date and William's heavy editing, is the closest to the lost archetype of the 'classis melior', which must have predated the second half of the seventh century, the date of its earliest surviving descendant. The question arises: how is it that, in spite of the existence of many early continental copies of the *Breviarium*, William's should be the closest of all to the archetype? That this archetype left the continent early, having had time

[77] M. Lapidge, 'Some Remnants of Bede's Lost "Liber Epigrammatum"', *EHR* 90 (1975), 798–820.

[78] L. Wallach, 'The Urbana Anglo-Saxon Sylloge of Latin Inscriptions', *Poetry and Poetics from Ancient Greece to the Renaissance: Studies in honor of James Hutton*, ed. G. M. Kirkwood, Cornell Stud. in Classical Philol. 38 (Ithaca, N.Y., 1975), 134–51, and D. Schaller, 'Bemerkungen zur Inschriften-Sylloge von Urbana', *Mittellateinisches Jahrbuch* 12 (1977), 9–21.

[79] The annotations are visible on the photograph reproduced Wallach, 'Urbana Sylloge', p. 135. See D. Sheerin, 'John Leland and Milred of Worcester', *Manuscripta* 21 (1977), 172–80, and also my 'William of Malmesbury's Edition of the *Liber Pontificalis*', *Archivum Historiae Pontificiae* 17 (1978), 100–4.

[80] Lapidge, 'Some Remnants', p. 820, and Thomson, 'Reading, Addenda et Corrigenda', pp. 330–1.

[81] James, *Two Ancient English Scholars*, pp. 13–14.

[82] See also A. S. Cook, 'Aldhelm's Legal Studies', *JEGP* 23 (1924), 105–13.

[83] Thomson, 'Reading, Addenda et Corrigenda', pp. 329–30; cf. Thomson, '*Liber Pontificalis*', pp. 104–5.

to produce only one or two descendants there, is certainly an attractive hypothesis. The late seventh century and Aldhelm's lifetime would suit admirably.

I mentioned earlier William's copy of Tertullian's *Apology* and three works of Lactantius.[84] The *Apology* had some circulation in England after *c.* 1100,[85] but the only other trace of these particular Lactantius items in pre-Conquest England is Aldhelm's quotation from one of them, the *De Opificio*.[86] The extreme rarity of Lactantius manuscripts makes it likely that William's exemplar was, or was derived from, the manuscript used by Aldhelm. This is not contradicted by the meagre textual history of William's copy, which shared a common ancestor with Paris, BN lat. 1664, of the twelfth century, and Monte Cassino, Archivio della Badia, 595, *c.* 1100.[87]

A more certain relic of the pre-Conquest Malmesbury library was the old copy of Aldhelm's *De Metris* described by both Faricius and William in their Lives of the saint.[88] Faricius called it 'quodam antiquissimo codice in eiusdem [*scil.* Malmesburiae] ecclesiae reperto'. Ehwald suggested that it must have resembled extant early manuscripts containing the *De Metris* alone, such as Brussels, Bibliothèque Royale, 9581/95, of the tenth century. In his *Gesta Pontificum* William mentions a bible in the possession of his church, allegedly once owned by its patron.[89] Not knowing the basis for this attribution one has to be sceptical of it, although we can at least accept William's testimony that it was a venerable book. The *De Metris*, bible and *Breviarium* are the only works known to William through ancient manuscripts of certain Malmesbury provenance. The handful of other early and interesting manuscripts which it can be demonstrated he knew could have come from elsewhere, since he visited many other libraries, some more than once.[90] We do, however, possess one of William's own ancient books. This is CCCC 330, his edition of Martianus Capella.[91] It consists of two volumes bound together

---

84 Above, p. 11; Thomson, 'Reading', p. 366 and nn.

85 Three English Tertullian manuscripts are known apart from the copies of William's collection (Oxford, Balliol College 79 and the German Gotha, Forschungsbibliothek, membr. I. 55): Oxford, Bodleian Library, Lat. theol. d. 34 (see above, n. 62); BL Royal 5 F. xviii (*c.* 1100); and Oxford, Bodleian Library, Add. C. 284 (s. xii). Ogilvy, *Books known to the English*, p. 250, produces virtually no evidence for knowledge of Tertullian's works before the Conquest, though to argue from Ogilvy's silence is dangerous.

86 James, *Two Ancient English Scholars*, p. 20; Ehwald, p. 197 (*De Metris*). Lactantius was listed by Alcuin among the authors in the library at York (Ogilvy, *Books known to the English*, p. 191).

87 *Lactantii Opera* i.i, ed. S. Brandt, CSEL 19 (Berlin, 1890), xlvii–liii. The Paris manuscript gives accents and breathings to the Greek passages, a remarkable feature in a twelfth-century western manuscript. They must surely have been present in the archetype and are a fair guarantee of its antiquity.

88 *Acta Sanctorum Maii* vi, 84–93 (25 May), esp. 87 and *GP*, p. 344; see R. Ehwald, 'De Aenigmatibus Aldhelmi et Acrostichis', *Festschrift Albert von Bamberg* (Gotha, 1905), pp. 1–26, esp. 13–14.

89 *GP*, p. 378.   90 For this evidence, see Thomson, 'Reading', pp. 392–4.

91 Bishop, 'The Corpus Martianus Capella', pp. 267–8, and Thomson, 'Reading', p. 381, and 'The "Scriptorium"', pp. 124–5.

by William himself. The first, which does not interest us, is the text of Martianus written *c.* 1100, with Remigius's gloss added by William; the second contains commentaries on Martianus in late-ninth-century Carolingian minuscule. It was in England by the tenth century, but, again, where William found it cannot be said. The odds are that it was a local book.

Extant manuscripts containing evidence of pre-Conquest Malmesbury provenance

This brings us to the third class of evidence, features in extant books. Oxford, Bodleian Library, Marshall 19 is the ninth-century copy of Jerome, *De Nominibus Hebraicis*, mentioned earlier.[92] It was written by one Theudbert for the church of St Medard in Soissons, but it was at Malmesbury by the late tenth century, for a hand of that date has inscribed at the head of the first folio the opening line of the *ex-libris* verses, mentioning Aldhelm, found in CCCC 23, also from the house. The line was repeated just below by a hand of the late eleventh century. The book, however, has the thirteenth-century pressmark of Christ Church, Canterbury. It is one of the two certain attributions to the pre-Conquest Malmesbury library. CCCC 23, a splendid, illustrated copy of Prudentius's works written *c.* 1000, is the other.[93] The verses at the beginning show that it was given to the house by Abbot Æthelweard (*c.* 1033–44). Two other manuscripts with claims, BL Cotton Otho B. x, fol. 51 + Otho C. i, part 1 (gospels in English)[94] and CCCC 361 (Gregory, *Pastoral Care*),[95] date from the first half and middle of the eleventh century respectively. The first, badly burnt in the 1731 fire, is connected fairly firmly with Malmesbury from early on by the addition to it *c.* 1050 of an Old English translation of Pope Sergius's confirmation of Aldhelm's foundation. The second bears annotations possibly by William as well as a fifteenth-century *ex-libris*.

Finally I must discuss the recent attribution to Malmesbury by Dr P. Lucas of another great illustrated Anglo-Saxon manuscript, Oxford, Bodleian Library, Junius 11 (the 'Caedmon Genesis').[96] This manuscript has been traditionally assigned to Christ Church, Canterbury, on stylistic grounds, and because it fits the entry of 'Genesis anglice depicta' in Prior Eastry's early-fourteenth-century library catalogue.[97] The stylistic parallels are, how-

---

[92] Above, p. 7; Thomson, 'The "Scriptorium"', pp. 120–1; *Summary Catalogue of Western Manuscripts in the Bodleian Library*, no. 5265.

[93] Thomson, 'The "Scriptorium"', p. 121; E. Temple, *Anglo-Saxon Manuscripts 900–1066* (London, 1976), no. 48, with bibliography.

[94] N. R. Ker, *Catalogue of Manuscripts containing Anglo-Saxon* (Oxford, 1957), no. 181.

[95] Thomson, 'The "Scriptorium"', p. 121.

[96] The attribution is argued in his edition of the Old English *Exodus*, Methuen's Old Eng. Lib. (London, 1977), pp. 1–6. Cf. Temple, *Anglo-Saxon Manuscripts*, no. 58. Some of my criticisms of Lucas are also made by D. Jost, *Speculum* 54 (1979), 829–30.

[97] Dr Temple has been criticized for her tendency, in *Anglo-Saxon Manuscripts*, to attribute a number of manuscripts to the Canterbury scriptoria or libraries on insufficient evidence; see L. Brownrigg,

ever, in themselves not compelling and Lucas argues that the catalogue description suits just as well a manuscript such as BL Cotton Claudius B. iv. (This suggestion would carry more weight if Claudius B. iv had been at Christ Church rather than at St Augustine's in the later Middle Ages.[98]) Lucas then mounts four positive arguments for a Malmesbury origin and provenance for Junius 11. Firstly some of its illustrations are by the artist of CCCC 23. 'This identification makes it likely that both manuscripts were produced at one place...Since the provenance of the "Corpus Prudentius" is Malmesbury...it seems most probable that the two manuscripts were produced there.' Both these inferences are questionable. Considering the peripatetic operations of illuminators in the twelfth century at least, one cannot assume a single scriptorium for two manuscripts simply because they were illustrated by the same artist. The work of the 'Alexis Master' of the St Albans Psalter or of the artist of the Lambeth Bible are cases in point.[99] And then, a Malmesbury *origin* is not proven for CCCC 23. Since it was donated by the abbot *c.* 1033–44 its presence is guaranteed only from that time and it may have come from elsewhere. Secondly, Lucas notes a 'very close and exclusive correspondence between features of some of the illustrations in MS Junius 11 and features of some of the carved medallions (*c.* 1170–80) on the voussoirs of the entrance arch of the south porch of Malmesbury abbey'. He does not give the details of this correspondence, foreshadowing a further publication in which he will study the problem in detail, but Dr Malcolm Parkes tells me that two medallions in the porch's Genesis cycle (Noah's ark and Adam and Eve hiding from God) show iconographical details otherwise found only in Junius 11. Any conclusions from this, however, must be exceedingly muted, because of Lucas's double 'some of', because of the late-twelfth-century date of the carvings and because some of them show iconographical affinities with BL Cotton Claudius B. iv, CCCC 23 and other manuscripts.[100] The most that this evidence could be expected to support would be the presence of Junius 11 at Malmesbury in the twelfth century. But I think it more inherently likely that the carvers' team used a pattern-book containing an eclectic repertoire of Old English iconographical schemes. Thirdly the 'Ælfwine' whose portrait was added to p. 2 of Junius 11 is identified as the abbot of Malmesbury *c.* 1043–6, although Lucas admits that 'this name was

'Manuscripts containing English Decoration 871–1066, Catalogued and Illustrated: a Review', *ASE* 7 (1978), 258–66.

98 Temple, *Anglo-Saxon Manuscripts*, no. 86.

99 F. Wormald, C. R. Dodwell and O. Pächt, *The St Albans Psalter* (London, 1960), pp. 165–8; C. R. Dodwell, *The Great Lambeth Bible* (London, 1959), pp. 16–18; and C. M. Kauffmann, *Romanesque Manuscripts 1066–1190* (London, 1975), nos. 29–34 and 70–1, and the important review of this book by A. Stones, *Speculum* 53 (1978), 586–90.

100 On the correspondences, see now M. Q. Smith, *The Sculptures of the South Porch of Malmesbury Abbey* (Malmesbury, 1975), based on, and sometimes correcting, K. J. Galbraith, 'The Iconography of the Biblical Scenes at Malmesbury Abbey', *JBAA* 3rd ser. 28 (1965), 39–56.

quite common among the Anglo-Saxons'. It so happens that an Ælfwine was prior of Christ Church, Canterbury, at some time between 1052 and *c.* 1074.[101] Finally Lucas notes that the book was exposed to thick smoke before it was sewn and bound, that is, earlier than *c.* 1050.[102] He connects this with the fire which destroyed 'totum coenobium' at Malmesbury 'in the time of Edward the Confessor', that is, between 1042 and 1066.[103] But his authority on this point, William of Malmesbury, speaks of two fires 'quæ totum coenobium temporibus Elfredi et Æduuardi regum consumpserunt'.[104] Had William meant the Confessor he would have said so; an Edward paired with Alfred can only mean the latter's son who reigned 899–924 and this puts both of the Malmesbury fires earlier than the manufacture of Junius 11.[105] Again, however, one thinks of the fire at Christ Church, Canterbury, in 1067, which Osbern says destroyed Latin writings on Dunstan, although some in Old English escaped.[106] The dating of eleventh-century bindings is surely not certain enough to rule out this alternative.[107] Four weak arguments do not support each other or constitute a single strong one. These particular arguments do not make much of a case for a Malmesbury provenance for Junius 11 and no case at all for its origin there. On the contrary, some of the new facts adduced by Lucas add support to the case – such as it is – for Christ Church, Canterbury.

CONCLUSIONS

William and the extant books add a few items to the pre-Conquest abbey library. The *Breviarium* used by William was certainly venerable and possibly Aldhelm's ; so perhaps was William's Lactantius exemplar, and the copy of Aldhelm's *De Metris* still at the abbey in the twelfth century could have dated from the eighth century or the ninth. Oxford, Bodleian Library, Marshall 19 is the best-attested case of an ancient manuscript which was also at the abbey early on and the Corpus Prudentius shows that the house was acquiring splendid books during the period of monastic reform. Some of the other old

---

[101] Knowles, Brooke and London, *Heads of Religious Houses*, p. 33.
[102] Lucas ed., *Exodus*, p. 4, based on the opinion of the late G. Pollard. Interesting details of the manuscript, not affecting the question of its provenance, are given by P. Lucas, 'On the Incomplete Ending of *Daniel* and the Addition of *Christ and Satan* to MS Junius 11', *Anglia* 97 (1979), 46–59 (the binding is discussed, pp. 50–1).
[103] Lucas ed., *Exodus*, p. 4.
[104] *GP*, p. 363.
[105] On the date of Junius 11, see Brownrigg, 'Manuscripts', p. 255, n. 2. Moreover William says that a beam, miraculously lengthened by Aldhelm, was not harmed by the fires, although since then 'annis et carie uicta defecit'. This seems to imply a substantial lapse of time between the later fire and William's day.
[106] *Memorials of St Dunstan*, ed. W. Stubbs, RS (London, 1874), p. 70.
[107] G. Pollard, 'Some Anglo-Saxon Bookbindings', *The Book Collector* 24 (1975), 130–59, unfortunately not treating Junius 11. Note especially his cautionary comments, p. 137.

and valuable books available to William may have been local, such as the second part of CCCC 330, but this cannot be proven.

Few generalizations can be made on the basis of such a brief list of sometimes uncertain attributions, but the variety of important and interesting books which we have discovered is noteworthy: rare patristic works, late antique secular literature, early copies of English and Carolingian writings. The possession of such works was due to a number of factors: the early origins of the house, the learning of Aldhelm and William, and probably Malmesbury's relative provinciality after the early twelfth century, permitting the survival of books which would have been discarded as outdated in centres with a more continuous intellectual vitality. Had we more evidence, we would probably find the Malmesbury library to have been most like those at Durham and Glastonbury, comparable ancient centres. The loss of nearly all of its books has undoubtedly deprived us of one of the greater libraries of pre-Reformation Europe.[108]

[108] In the preparation of this article I am beholden to several scholars: Drs N. R. Ker, M. Lapidge and M. B. Parkes read complete drafts of it, and I hope that I have benefited from their criticisms. For specific information on Corbie I am indebted to Dr D. Ganz. The essay is dedicated to the late Dr R. W. Hunt, in token of many kindnesses and in humble acknowledgement of his *magisterium* (which will long continue to be felt) in the field of medieval books and learning. I intended the article to be a tribute to him in his lifetime and so attempted to keep its preparation a secret from him, but of course he found out, and it is consequently enriched with some of his own incomparable learning. Any infelicities or errors are my responsibility.

Milred of Worcester's collection of Latin epigrams and its continental counterparts

PATRICK SIMS-WILLIAMS

Milred, who was bishop of Worcester from 743 × 745 to 774 × 775, is almost as shadowy a figure in the history of Anglo-Latin literature today as he was in the sixteenth century when John Leland recorded in his *Commentarii de Scriptoribus Britannicis*: 'invidiosa vetustas *Milredi* monumenta destruxit'.[1] The only composition by Milred that has come to light, in a single ninth-century continental manuscript, is the letter of consolation that he sent to Lull of Mainz after St Boniface's martyrdom. Apart from its inherent interest, this letter, with its elegant use of Vergilian echoes, is a valuable indication of Milred's literary interests and aspirations. Better still, it ends with a tantalizing glimpse of the literary world in which Milred lived: a postscript in which he apologizes for failing to send a copy of the picture poems of Optatianus Porphyrius because Cuthbert, the archbishop of Canterbury, had failed to return them. It was perhaps this very copy of Porphyrius that served as the model for the decoration of the Codex Aureus (Stockholm, Kungliga Biblioteket, A. 135), which may have been produced at St Augustine's, Canterbury, during Cuthbert's time.[2]

Two pieces of English evidence add to this slender knowledge of the poetic interests which Milred shared with many of the higher clergy of eighth-century England. Both were known to Leland but have been neglected by modern scholars until very recently. The first was noted by Daniel J. Sheerin.[3] The

---

[1] Ed. Anthony Hall (Oxford, 1709) I, 114. Abbreviations used in the course of this article are: *CLA* = E. A. Lowe, *Codices Latini Antiquiores* (Oxford, 1934–72); *ICUR* = vol. II, pt 1, of *Inscriptiones Christianae Urbis Romae*, ed. Giovanni B. de Rossi (Rome, 1857–88); *ICUR* n.s. = *Inscriptiones Christianae Urbis Romae* n.s., ed. Angelo Silvagni (Rome, 1922–); *ILCV* = *Inscriptiones Latinae Christianae Veteres*, ed. Ernst Diehl, repr. with *Supplementum*, ed. J. Moreau and H. I. Marrou (Dublin and Zürich, 1967–70). I should like to acknowledge the help I have received at various points from Professor Bernhard Bischoff, Herr Helmuth Domizlaff and my colleagues David Dumville, Michael Lapidge and Neil Wright.

[2] References to discussions of this point and of the letter are given in my 'Cuthswith, Seventh-Century Abbess of Inkberrow, near Worcester, and the Würzburg Manuscript of Jerome on Ecclesiastes', *ASE* 5 (1976), 16. I have discussed in detail the letter and the material mentioned in my next paragraph in a book on the dioceses of Worcester and Hereford in the seventh and eighth centuries, to be published by Cambridge University Press.

[3] 'John Leland and Milred of Worcester', *Manuscripta* 21 (1977), 178–80.

mid-tenth-century manuscript of Bede's Lives of St Cuthbert probably written at St Augustine's (London, British Library, Cotton Vitellius A. xix) contains four epigrams and a prose note on the Six Ages of Man, added by a later tenth-century hand. The epigram on 8r, as Leland noted in the margin, contains Milred's name, severed by tmesis:

> Hos tibi . mil . lyrico . red . feci carmine uersus
> Suscipe care deo quæso uice muneris illos
> Et felix inter felices uiue per aeuum.

Milred of Worcester had no monopoly over the name Milred, but it seems likely, in view of his known interests, that he is the *Mil-red* named here and that the late-tenth-century scribe was copying from a collection of epigrams etc. which was available at St Augustine's and which had been assembled in Milred's day. Whether it was assembled *by* Milred or *for* Milred depends on whether one takes *Mil-red* with *feci* or with *tibi*. I should like to conjecture that the unnamed party – whether author or recipient of the poem – was Archbishop Cuthbert himself.

Attention was drawn to the second piece of English evidence by Michael Lapidge.[4] Leland, in his brief notice of Milred in the *Commentarii*, remarks:

Legi præterea in antiquissimo codice epigrammaton, quæ ecclesiastica spectabant ornamenta, hos versiculos in ipsa libelli fronte scriptos:

> Hunc proprie librum *Milredus* possidet ipse,
> Antistes sanctus, magno qui dignus honore:
> Est etenim dapibus scripturæ plenus & actu.[5]

These *versiculi* must have been written in the lifetime of 'Milredus' (*possidet* cannot be an error for *possedit*, for the latter would not scan), though one cannot assume that the ancient codex Leland saw was the original 'liber' rather than a later copy. Fortunately we have a good idea of the contents of Leland's codex because he made extracts 'ex antiquissimo codice epigrammaton', beginning with the above *versiculi* 'ex primo libri epigrammate', in his *Collectanea* in Oxford, Bodleian Library, Top. gen. c. 2 (S.C. 3118). pp. 111–15. (I shall refer to these as L1, L2, etc., according to the numbering in Lapidge's edition of the extracts.[6]) On the basis of the items of English interest in Leland's extracts Lapidge argued convincingly that the extracts as a whole represent some of the contents of a collection of epigrams made at Worcester in the time of Bishop Milred, the only known *antistes* of that

[4] 'Some Remnants of Bede's Lost *Liber Epigrammatum*', EHR 90 (1975), 798–820.
[5] I, 113.
[6] Lapidge, 'Some Remnants'. This in most respects supersedes the edition in John Leland, *Collectanea*, ed. Thomas Hearne, 2nd ed. (London, 1774) III, at 114–18; but see below, nn. 15 and 60.

name.[7] I should like to add no more than one further argument here, as I discuss the English poems in detail elsewhere.[8] L18 is an epitaph on

Cð et Sigbertus, dominumque deumque colentes.

Cð is surely for *Cuð*, which would scan, rather than an abbreviation of a dithematic name such as *Cuðbertus*.[9] Now the only occurrence of the name *Cuð* known to me is in the title of a hexameter creed in BL Royal 2 A. xx (s. viii[2]), 40r: *versus cvð de sancta trinitate*.[10] It is surely no coincidence that the latter manuscript is known to have been at Worcester in the twelfth century and may well have been written there during Milred's episcopate.[11]

If the collection of epigrams was of Worcester origin, it is nonetheless clear that the ancient codex which Leland saw was at Malmesbury when he saw it. William of Malmesbury, in his *Gesta Pontificum*, quotes two poems 'nuper mihi visi' by Cuthbert, the eighth-century bishop of Hereford, which correspond to L20–1.[12] Now Leland, both in his *Collectanea* and in his *Commentarii*, quotes from William, and adds that he found the same verses at Malmesbury 'in vetustissimo codice sacrorum carminum' and 'in vetustissimo libro sacrorum epigrammatôn'.[13] Moreover, in quoting from William he introduces some emendations (sometimes silently) from the *codex epigrammaton*; where, for instance, the manuscripts of the *Gesta* (including William's autograph) read 'Hec veneranda crucis Christi *veneranda* sacratæ',[14] Leland silently restores Cuthbert's original *vexilla*, as in L20. Conversely, in his extracts from the *codex epigrammaton* Leland interlineates variants to L20–1 which correspond to the readings given in the *Gesta*.[15] All this agrees very well with Leland's marginal note to his extracts from the *Gesta*: 'Hos versus, sed corruptos, alias legi in vetustissimo codice sacrorum carmine Melduni sed sine autoris nomine.'[16] There can be no doubt, then, that the Milred codex was of Malmesbury provenance. It was probably at Malmesbury as early as *c.* 1125 since, as Lapidge and R. M. Thomson have argued, it is likely to have

---

[7] 'Some Remnants'; but in view of the adjective *sanctus* it is unlikely that the verses are by Milred himself (*ibid.* p. 802), and, for evidence that the manuscript was later than the eighth century, see below, p. 26.

[8] In the book mentioned above, n. 2.

[9] *Cuð* (which is distinct from *Cudd*) is not listed in William George Searle, *Onomasticon Anglo-Saxonicum* (Cambridge, 1897).

[10] *The Book of Cerne*, ed. A. B. Kuypers (Cambridge, 1902), p. 218.

[11] See *CLA* II, no. 215, and N. R. Ker, *Catalogue of Manuscripts containing Anglo-Saxon* (Oxford, 1957), no. 248.

[12] *Gesta Pontificum*, ed. N. E. S. A. Hamilton, Rolls Ser. (London, 1870), p. 299. As to whether Cuthbert of Hereford was the same as the archbishop mentioned earlier, see my 'Cuthswith', p. 16, n. 5.

[13] Leland, *Collectanea* III, 265, and *Commentarii* I, 134–5.

[14] *Gesta Pontificum*, ed. Hamilton, p. 629.

[15] Lapidge prints only the interlineated readings ('Some Remnants', p. 812, n. 4), not what Leland originally wrote; for the latter one must return to Hearne's edition (cited above, n. 6).

[16] *Collectanea* III, 265.

been used by William of Malmesbury himself;[17] but, if so, it is unlikely to have been of Malmesbury origin, for William would hardly have said 'nuper mihi visi' about poems present in his own monastic library all along – the phrase suggests rather that he had found them somewhere else (say, Worcester or Canterbury).

It might be supposed that the Milred codex which Leland saw perished when many Malmesbury manuscripts were destroyed and, as Aubrey describes, their leaves 'flew about like butterflies'.[18] Fortunately that seems not to have been entirely the case. The Library of the University of Illinois at Urbana possesses an uncatalogued bifolium in quarto (375 × 230 mm), which, written in Anglo-Saxon square minuscule, contains sixteen poems on ecclesiastical subjects, mostly copies of inscriptions. (I shall refer to these as U1, U2 etc., following the numbering in Luitpold Wallach's edition.[19]) Sheerin has pointed out that U14–15 correspond to L9–10 and are both accompanied by marginalia, indicating their subject matter, in a hand which he identifies as Leland's.[20] U14/L9 is a poem by an unknown Irishman on a chapel dedicated to St Patrick, which Traube, who edited it from the only manuscript previously known, attributed to Cellanus of Péronne (d. 706), on the basis of inadequate evidence.[21] U15/L10 is an otherwise unknown poem by Bede on a cathedral church built by Cyneberht, bishop of Lindsey.[22] There are some differences between the readings of L and those of U (including the erroneous attribution of the Patrick verses to Bede in L), but Sheerin attributes them all to Leland's errors or 'improvements' in copying from U. His textual arguments are convincing; I would modify them only in respect of the last two lines of the Patrick poem (lines 6–7):

> Calpurnus genuit istum, alma Brittania [*sic*] misit,
> Gallia nutriuit, tenet ossa(q*ue*) Scottia felix.

---

[17] Lapidge, 'Some Remnants', pp. 813 and 820, and Rodney M. Thomson, 'The Reading of William of Malmesbury: Addenda and Corrigenda', *RB* 86 (1976), 330–1, and 'William of Malmesbury's Edition of the *Liber Pontificalis*', *Archivum Historiae Pontificiae* 16 (1978), 100–4 and 110. Their discussions of the variant readings of William and Leland need modification in view of the point made above, n. 15, but further enquiry vindicates both Lapidge and Thomson and supports the main thesis of this paper, as I show in 'William of Malmesbury and "La Silloge Epigrafica di Cambridge"' (forthcoming).

[18] *Natural History of Wiltshire*, ed. John Britton (London, 1847), p. 79.

[19] 'The Urbana Anglo-Saxon Sylloge of Latin Inscriptions', *Poetry and Poetics from Ancient Greece to the Renaissance: Studies in honor of James Hutton*, ed. G. M. Kirkwood, Cornell Stud. in Classical Philol. 38 (Ithaca, N.Y., 1975), 134–51. Cf. Dieter Schaller, 'Bemerkungen zur Inschriften-Sylloge von Urbana', *Mittellateinisches Jahrbuch* 12 (1977), 9–21.

[20] 'Leland and Milred', pp. 173–8. There are further marginalia, illegible in my microfilm, on 1v–2r.

[21] Ludwig Traube, *Vorlesungen und Abhandlungen*, ed. Franz Boll (Munich, 1909–20) III, 95–119. Cf. Edmondo Coccia, 'La cultura irlandese precarolingia: miracolo o mito?', *SM* 3rd ser. 8 (1967), 318–20, and Lapidge, 'Some Remnants', p. 805.

[22] Re-edited by Schaller, 'Bemerkungen', pp. 17–21. Was Leland's *premia vitae* (for *pignora uitę*) suggested by the same cadence in Damasus, *Epigram* I (discussed below, pp. 33–4), or in *ILCV*, no. 1804 (where the word *pignora* also occurs)?

In the ninth-century manuscript (probably from Monte Cassino) which Traube edited (Florence, Biblioteca Medicea Laurenziana, lat. plut. LXVI 40) there is an eighth line to end the poem ('Ambo stelligeri capientes praemia caeli'). Sheerin supposes that U and L agree in omitting line 8. In fact, however, this cannot be regarded as a shared error; rather the text of U and L confirms Paul Grosjean's conjecture that the poem properly ends with line 7 and that Traube's eighth line is a fragment of a separate poem.[23] I would add that there is further confirmation in the fact that the *last* line of a poem on St Modwenna, which is clearly an imitation of the Patrick poem, runs

Felix Burtonia virginis ossa tenet.[24]

Rather more significant is Sheerin's observation that U and L agree in reading *ossaque* in line 7 against the *ossa* of the Florentine manuscript and that the *-que* in U is a later addition, possibly by the annotating hand (of Leland). The emendation in U was evidently inspired by unwarranted dissatisfaction with the scansion of *ossă*. It is thus perhaps significant that when Leland quotes the Patrick poem 'ex Bedæ (nisi fallor) epigrammatibus desumpto' elsewhere he gives the reading *artus* instead of *ossa*;[25] this looks like another attempt on his part at a metrical improvement of *ossă* and so fits in well with the supposition that the emendation in U is indeed due to him.

I have not been able to trace much of the history of the Urbana bifolium. It was clearly used for a book binding at some stage, but whether that happened at Malmesbury, where 'all musick bookes, account bookes, copie bookes, &c. were covered with old manuscripts',[26] or after Leland or some other carried it off, one cannot say. It did not reappear, as far as I can discover, until about 1934, and that was in Berlin.[27] Then in November 1957 the Berlin firm of Gerd Rosen sold it to Helmuth Domizlaff, Antiquariat, of Munich, who in turn sold it to the New York firm of H. P. Kraus in July 1958. Kraus

---

[23] 'Les Inscriptions métriques de l'église de Péronne', *AB* 78 (1960), 369–70.

[24] Edited from thirteenth- and fourteenth-century manuscripts by Mario Esposito, 'Conchubrani Vita Sanctae Monennae', *Proc. of the R. Irish Acad.* 28, Sect. C (1910), 246 (cf. pp. 205–6).

[25] *Collectanea* III, 276. Sheerin's statement ('Leland and Milred', p. 175) that 'Leland encountered this poem in two other MSS at Glastonbury' is based on a misunderstanding of this passage. For the lengthening of *-ă* before *sc-* see *Aldhelmi Opera*, ed. R. Ehwald, Monumenta Germaniae Historica, Auct. Antiq. 15 (Berlin, 1919), 755, and Dag Norberg, *Introduction à l'étude de la versification latine médiévale*, Studia Latina Stockholmiensia 5 (Stockholm, 1958), 8.

[26] 'One may also perceive by the binding of old bookes how the old manuscripts went to wrack in those dayes' (Aubrey, *Natural History of Wiltshire*, p. 79).

[27] Professor Bernhard Bischoff writes to me: 'Etwa 1934, jedenfalls kurz nachdem Karl Christ Direktor der Berliner Handschriftenabteilung geworden war, arbeitete ich in Berlin. Dabei zeigte mir Christ oder Albert Boeckler das Fragment, das – wie ich glaube, von dem Erben eines Dr Amt(?) in Quedlinburg, eines Sammlers – soeben der Bibliothek zum Kauf angeboten worden war. Damals war man noch sparsam, und so konnte Christ sich nicht zum Ankauf entschliessen...Wie [das Fragment] in den Besitz des Quedlinburger Sammlers gekommen ist, ist mir unbekannt.' The fragment was no. 1731 in Gerd Rosen's catalogue no. XXIX, 2 Teil (pp. 42–3), which I have seen only in a photocopy kindly sent me by Herr Domizlaff.

published three of the four sides in facsimile in a catalogue that year.[28] The manuscript was bought by the University of Illinois at Urbana and was eventually edited there in 1975, elaborately but inaccurately, by Wallach. Fortunately, as Wallach included a facsimile of the remaining side, his errors may easily be corrected from the facsimiles.

There has been much confusion about the date of the fragment. Bischoff was quoted in the Rosen catalogue as placing it at the end of the ninth century; the Kraus catalogue gave 'late IXth – early Xth century'; Wallach dates it to 'the latter part of the tenth century, if not the beginning of the eleventh' on non-palaeographical grounds, which have been rightly rejected by Sheerin and Schaller.[29] Sheerin himself gives the date as '*s*. viii *ex.* – *s*. ix *in.*', strangely citing the Kraus catalogue for this dating, while Schaller offers a tenth-century date. I would accept a mid-tenth-century date myself.[30] It is at any rate clear that the manuscript was later than Milred's day and should probably be regarded as a copy of one written for him, in view of the verses 'in ipsa libelli fronte scriptos', which appear to have been the work of Milred's scribe or librarian or some other contemporary well-wisher.[31] One cannot prove that the collection has not been expanded somewhat in copying, but it is significant that none of the new poems that have come to light in U appears to be later than Milred's time. There are a couple of indications that poems in the collection were known in Milred's Worcester. The *Epitaphium Cð et Sigberti* (L18), which we have some reason to connect with Worcester, shows in the line quoted above ('...dominumque deumque colentes') a clear echo of the Patrick poem ('Hic nobis Christum dominumque deumque colendum / Iussit').[32] Again the cadence of U16 (a single line, breaking off at the foot of 2v) –

Hoc tibi Christe, deus *uitæ spes unica terris*

recurs, to my knowledge, only in the *Versus Cvð de Sancta Trinitate* discussed above.[33]

Leland's twenty-nine extracts (L) give the impression that the Milred codex was of mainly English interest. That this is a false impression is shown by the fact that he passed by all sixteen poems in U save the two which he annotated (on Patrick and Cyneberht), evidently because they had no obvious English or historical interest for him. To judge by U the complete codex was

---

[28] *Catalogue 88: Fifty Mediaeval and Renaissance Manuscripts* (New York [1958]), pp. 8–10 and 124.

[29] *Ibid.* p. 8; Wallach, 'Urbana Sylloge', p. 151; Sheerin, 'Leland and Milred', p. 172 and n. 2; and Schaller, 'Bemerkungen', pp. 9 and 13.

[30] I rely here on the advice of my colleague D. N. Dumville.

[31] Cf. above, n. 7.

[32] Lapidge, 'Some Remnants', p. 811. Mr Neil Wright points out that *dominumque deumque* originates in Juvencus (I, 24).

[33] Wallach gives less exact parallels and overlooks *uitae spes unica* in Juvencus (III, 521).

as much of Roman as of English interest. In fact the title given to U in the Kraus catalogue will suit the whole collection rather well: *Sylloge Inscriptionum Latinarum Christianarum*. Milred's collection is comparable to other syllogae which circulated in the early Middle Ages,[34] with the important exceptions that it is the first to have been discovered that was certainly put together in Anglo-Saxon England and the only one to contain large numbers of English compositions. It bears witness to Anglo-Saxon devotion to Rome and to the Christian Latin poetry upon which Anglo-Latin epigraphic and epigrammatic verse was modelled as early as Bede's time. It suits very well with what little we know of Milred's interests that this collection should go under his name.

I shall not seek to trace the source of every poem in the Milred collection but seek simply to determine its relation to certain continental syllogae. Similar enquiries have already been pursued in the case of L by Lapidge and in the case of U by the editors of the Kraus catalogue, by Wallach and by Schaller; but now that Sheerin has shown that L and U represent a single collection it is worth reopening the discussion.

The Urbana bifolium was not the innermost bifolium of its gathering, so there must be a break of four sides or more between fol. 1 (U1–9) and fol. 2 (U10–16). Assuming that Leland copied his extracts in the order of the manuscript, the most probable sequence of items (in which the items from L would not normally be consecutive, as Leland made only a selection) is L1–8, U1–9; U10–13, U14–15 (= L9–10), U16, L11–29; but it is possible that some of L2–8 came between fols. 1 and 2 of U.[35] The break between the two folios is reflected in their contents. Most of U1–9 can be paralleled in other early syllogae of Italian inscriptions, whereas U10–16 is a more disparate and unusual group of English and continental interest for which there is no trace of a continental source. I suspect that U10–16 were assembled in England from diverse sources, perhaps by Milred himself.[36] U1–9 are more homogeneous. U1 and U3 are inscriptions from the church of St Peter *ad Vincula* in the middle of Rome and U2 (quoted below) is headed 'uincula Petri'. After U4 (a couplet from Vergil which was perhaps used as a caption to a mural[37]) come two inscriptions from the church of St Laurence without the Walls (U5–6) and an inscription from St Mary beyond Tiber (U7). U8 is Pope Damasus's epigram on St Felix, which was inscribed either at Rome or (more probably) at Nola,[38] and U9 is a copy of the epitaph of St

---

[34] Most of these are printed in *ICUR*. For a useful survey with tables, see *ICUR* n.s. 1, xvii–xxviii.

[35] If fol. 2 came earlier than fol. 1 the order would be L1–8, U10–13, U14–15 (= L9–10), U16, (some of L11–29?), U1–9, (the rest of) L11–29.

[36] On the evidence of the Codex Bertinianus, see, further, below.

[37] So Wallach, 'Urbana Sylloge', p. 149; cf. Schaller, 'Bemerkungen', p. 11, n. 5.

[38] The location is discussed in *ICUR* n.s. II, at 121–2, and *Epigrammata Damasiana*, ed. Antonio Ferrua (Vatican City, 1942), at pp. 213–15. If, as Silvagni argues in the former, it refers to the basilica on the Via Portuensis, it is perhaps significant that in U it stands next to the verses from St Mary over Tiber.

Augustine's mother, Monica, a fragment of which was rediscovered at Ostia in 1945.[39] Wallach, followed more cautiously by Schaller, thinks that this group of epigrams is related to the so-called *Sylloge Laureshamensis Quarta* (*SLQ*), a seventh-century sylloge which is preserved (along with three others) in a ninth-century Lorsch manuscript (Vatican, Pal. lat. 833).[40] This opinion would be especially interesting in view of A. Silvagni's theory that *SLQ* derives from a mid-seventh-century sylloge possibly put together by an Anglo-Saxon;[41] but I regret that I can see no relationship between U and *SLQ*. Wallach states erroneously that U1–3 and U5–8 are all found in *SLQ*, but Schaller reduces the total to U1–2 and U5–6, corresponding to *SLQ* 64, 82, 46 and 47.[42] U2 cannot be equated with *SLQ* 82, however. U2 is the couplet headed 'uincula Petri':

> Solue, iuuente Deo, terrarum Petre catenas
> Qui facis ut pateant cælestia regna beatis.

It occurs also (with the classical spelling *iubente*) in the so-called *Anthologia Isidoriana*, which I discuss below, and there it is headed 'In icona sancti Petri hi duo sunt versus';[43] the picture in question may have been at St Peter's in the Vatican, since the couplet was known there in the later Middle Ages.[44] *SLQ* 82, on the other hand, is a four-line inscription by the early-fifth-century bishop of Spoleto, Achilleus, for St Peter's, Spoleto, which also occurs in another early sylloge, in both beginning, 'Solue, iuuante [*sic*] Deo...'.[45] Thus the sole overlap between U and *SLQ* is U1 and U5–6. Considering that *SLQ* is one of the most extensive syllogae, with 104 items in its extant form, this overlap seems insignificant. As it contains no less than six inscriptions from St Peter *ad Vincula* (*SLQ* 64–9), it is hardly surprising that one of them is the same as one in U (*SLQ* 64 = U1); it is more significant that *SLQ* does *not* include U3, an inscription from the same church which is included in other collections and was apparently extant until the fifteenth century.[46] The occurrence of two inscriptions from St Laurence without the Walls in both *SLQ* (46–7) and U (5–6) is also without significance, for, as they are the only known early inscriptions from this church,[47] it is not surprising that they

---

[39] See Russell Meiggs, *Roman Ostia*, 2nd ed. (Oxford, 1973), pp. 213 and 399–400 (and cf. p. 525).

[40] *SLQ* is edited, *ICUR*, pp. 95–118. Cf. Wallach, 'Urbana Sylloge', pp. 148 and 151, and Schaller, 'Bemerkungen', p. 11.

[41] *ICUR*, n.s. I, xxvii. Silvagni's theory that every sylloge derives from one or other of two archetypes (p. xxviii) is implausible and will be disregarded.

[42] Wallach, 'Urbana Sylloge', p. 148, and Schaller, 'Bemerkungen', p. 11 and n. 8.

[43] *ICUR*, p. 254.   [44] *ICUR*, pp. 80, n. 12, 114, n. 82, and 254, n. 5, *ICUR*, n.s. II, 20.

[45] *ICUR*, pp. 80, no. 12, and 114, no. 82; misprinted Migne, Patrologia Latina, Suppl. III, col. 1246.

[46] *ICUR*, pp. 134, no. 1, 157, no. 10, 286, no. 11, 290, no. 2, and nn.

[47] In *ICUR*, n.s. I at xxii a third text is noted in the *Sylloge Wirceburgensis* (no. 3); but it is not certain that it refers to the same church of St Laurence (see *ICUR*, p. 155, n. 3). See also *Le Liber Pontificalis*, ed. L. Duchesne (Paris, 1886–1957) I, 310, n. 5, and III, 92–3.

appear together in both collections. They also appear together in a sylloge which is believed to date from the mid-seventh century, the so-called *Sylloge Turonensis*.[48] The texts of the two inscriptions in U may derive from the latter or from independent transcription on the site, rather than from a sylloge related to *SLQ*.

One epigram transcribed by Leland has a parallel in *SLQ*. L16 runs:

> Vltima concludens praesentis munera vitae
> victor in hoc positus tumulo per secla quiescit,
> gratus in officiis atque omni strenuus actu.

As Lapidge notes, the probable original of this epitaph is an inscription erected in Vercelli in 528 for a certain [...]LDO (the stone is broken). There is a copy of the seven-line Vercelli text in *SLQ* 31 in which the name *Dalmatius* has been substituted.[49] Apparently, then, it was a text that lent itself to reuse. I suggest that the reason why L reads *victor in* where *SLQ* reads *presbiter* (and in the original the word(s) before 'HOC' are missing) is that it, too, is an adaptation, designed for a person called Victor, perhaps an Anglo-Saxon whose name contained the element *Sige-*. It is, of course, possible that it was inspired by a copy of *SLQ*; but Lapidge's suggestion[50] that it may reflect the movement of English pilgrims to and from Rome via Vercelli is just as likely. Independent transcription is also the most plausible explanation for the occurrence of an inscription from St Mary beyond Tiber in only the Milred collection (U7) and the *Sylloge Laureshamensis Prima*.[51] The latter sylloge, which is of uncertain date, contains no other epigram in common with U or L.

A much more promising source for Milred's collection is the tiny sylloge which de Rossi called the *Anthologia Isidoriana*, from the fact that it frequently occurs in manuscripts of Isidore's *Etymologiae*.[52] De Rossi argued that it may have been put together in Spain as early as the middle of the seventh century, although the earliest manuscripts belong to *c.* 800 (Leiden, Bibliotheek der Rijksuniversiteit, Voss. Lat. F. 82, from Saint-Germain-des-Prés, and Voss. Lat. Q. 69, from St Gall). His main reason, apart from the transmission with Isidore, was the inclusion of an epigram commemorating the gift of a veil

---

[48] *ICUR*, pp. 63–4, nos. 10 and 9 respectively.
[49] *ILCV*, no. 3360, and *ICUR*, p. 172, no. 31 and n.
[50] 'Some Remnants', p. 809.
[51] *ICUR*, p. 151, no. 22; cf. *ICUR*, n.s. 1, xxvi, no. 232. On the date of this sylloge see *ibid.* p. xix, and cf. Heinrich Fichtenau, 'Karl der Grosse und das Kaisertum', *Mitteilungen des Instituts für österreichische Geschichtsforschung* 61 (1953), 300.
[52] See *ICUR*, pp. 58–9, 250–4, 275 and 462, and *ICUR*, n.s. 1, xix–xx, nos. 15 and 19. On Voss. Lat. F. 82 (fol. 155) and Q. 69 (18v–19r), see *CLA* x, nos. 1582 and 1585, and K. A. De Meyier, *Codices Vossiani Latini* (Leiden, 1973–5) 1, 178–82, and 11, 159–63. In Q. 69 the *Anthologia* etc. is followed on 19v by a poem of Eugenius of Toledo.

to St Peter's in the Vatican by the Visigothic king Chintila (636–40); the heading 'In velo quod a Chintilane rege Romae di[re]ctum est' suggests that this epigram was written and transmitted in Spain, not copied in Rome – a conclusion which is supported by its absence from Roman and other sources.[53] Another hint of a Spanish origin for the *Anthologia* is the inclusion of the epitaph of Augustine's mother, Monica. Strangely this text is not recorded in Italian sources (perhaps the inscription at Ostia was lost early) but is first recorded, outside the *Anthologia*, in Paris, Bibliothèque Nationale, lat. 8093, a collection of poems by Eugenius of Toledo and others copied by Visigothic scribes at Lyons in the early ninth century, and in a related mid-ninth-century manuscript, BN lat. 2832, which was probably also written at Lyons.[54] BN lat. 8093 is unique in naming the author of the epitaph and does so in a manner which suggests that it was copied from an original transcribed not long after the author's death: 'UERSUS INLUSTRISSIME MEMORIE UASSI EX CONSULE· SCRIPTI IN TUMULO S*ANCTE* MEMORIE MU*NNICE* MATRIS SANCTI AGUSTINI' (32v).[55] It seems quite possible that Monica's epitaph, now rediscovered at Ostia, was known to the Middle Ages solely via Spanish intermediaries.[56]

The extant Milred collection reproduces three of the seven epigrams that make up the *Anthologia Isidoriana:*

    2. *Epitaphium beatae Monnicae genetricis sancti Augustini* (= U9)
    5. *In icona sancti Petri hi duo sunt versus* (= U2)
    7. *In velo quod a Chintilane rege Romae di*[re]*ctum est* (= L11).

---

[53] *ICUR*, pp. 250, 254, n. 7, and 462, and *ICUR*, n.s. 1, xxv, no. 200, and 11, 16. On Chintila and Rome, see *ICUR*, p. 254, n. 7, and E. A. Thompson, *The Goths in Spain* (Oxford, 1969), pp. 184–5.

[54] *ICUR*, pp. 273, no. 2, and 267, no. 16. On BN lat. 8093, see *ICUR*, pp. 271 and 292–3; Bernhard Bischoff, *Mittelalterliche Studien* (Stuttgart, 1966–7) 1, 292; and De Meyier, *Codices Vossiani Latini* 1, 235–40. (For Visigoths at Lyons, see *CLA* vi, no. 774c). On BN lat. 2832, see *ICUR*, pp. 262–5 and 460, and Charles Samaran and Robert Marichal, *Catalogue des manuscrits en écriture latine portant des indications de date, de lieu ou de copiste* (Paris, 1959–) 11 (text), 131. On the connection between the two manuscripts in the transmission of Eugenius of Toledo, see *Eugenii Toletani Episcopi Carmina et Epistulae*, ed. Friedrich Vollmer, MGH, Auct. Antiq. 14 (Berlin, 1905), xix–xx, xxii, xl–xli, xlv and xlvi; also Günter Bernt, *Das lateinische Epigramm im Übergang von der Spätantike zum frühen Mittelalter*, Münchener Beiträge zur Mediävistik und Renaissance-Forschung 2 (Munich, 1968), 142–5 and 184. Cf. above, n. 52, and below, n. 63.

[55] *ICUR*, pp. 252, n. 2, 271 and 273, no. 2. I quote from the manuscript. De Rossi says 'nomen *Vassi* (Bassi) exaratum est in litura' (*ibid.* p. 273, n. 2); but there is no sign of any erasure, merely that the manuscript is worn. He also emends *inlustrissime* to *inl*(*ustris*) (*ibid.* p. 252, n. 2).

[56] Only two other manuscripts of the epitaph (other than ones of the *Anthologia Isidoriana*) are mentioned in *ICUR*, at pp. 252, n. 2, 271 and 290, n. 7, and in PL Suppl. III, at col. 1246: 'EPITAPHIUM BEATAE MONICAE GENETRICIS BEATI AUGUSTINI' in a miscellaneous context in BN lat. 8094, at 57r (s. xi), a manuscript of Ausonius (etc.) not used in Schenkl's edition; and 'EPITAPHIUM S*ANCTI* AUGUSTINI' in BN lat. 5315, at 48v (formerly pt II, 2v), a manuscript of Victor of Vita not used in the modern editions, but printed (inaccurately) PL 58, col. 186, n. *c*, after Ruinart. The latter manuscript is dated 's. xii' in the Bollandists' *Catalogus Codicum Hagiographicorum Latinorum qui Asservantur in Bibliotheca Nationali Parisiensi* (Brussels, 1889–93) 11, at 87. I have no information about the origin of either manuscript.

The overlap is significant because these three epigrams are not widely disseminated, as we have seen. The title of no. 2 in U ('In tumulo matris sancti Agustini' [*sic*]) is intermediate between that in the *Anthologia Isidoriana* and that in BN lat. 8093. The text of U9 is interesting as well. I use it below to complete the first four lines of the above-mentioned fragmentary original, which agrees with U9 (except where U has the spelling *Agustine*) as far as it goes:[57]

> HIC POSVIT CINEres genetrix castissima prolis,
>   AVGVSTINE TVI altera lux meriti,
> QVI SERVANS PAcis cælestia iura sacerdos
>   COMMISSOS POpulos moribus instituis.
> GLORIA VOS M[*aior gestorum laude coronat*]
>   VIRTVTVM M[*ater felicior subolis*].

U agrees with BN lat. 8093 in the Vulgar Latin – or probably, in this context, Hispanic – spelling *Agustine* in line 2 but lacks its faulty *genetris, serbans* and *instituens*,[58] agreeing at these three points with the *Anthologia Isidoriana* manuscripts. De Rossi suggested that in line 2 *tui...meriti* should be emended to *tuis...meritis*.[59] The Ostia original is no help, as it is broken immediately after 'TVI'; but it may be significant that U agrees with the (Spanish?) manuscript tradition in having *tui...meriti*, if the reading posited by de Rossi was the original one.

No. 5 in the *Anthologia* corresponds to the couplet U2, which begins 'Solue, iuuente (*sic*) Deo...' and which was discussed above. Since the only early medieval sylloge to include the couplet is the *Anthologia*, it is probable that it was the source from which it reached the Milred collection. I suggest further that *iuuente* for *iubente* in U may be the result of hyper-correction by an ignorant scribe copying from a Spanish exemplar, in which he would often have had to change *b* to *u* (compare *serbans* above), rather than a reflection of the *iuuante* in the four-line version of the epigram from Spoleto. As the *Anthologia* is also the only other source for the epigram on Chintila's veil, it was probably the means by which that, too, reached England. The title, as quoted by Leland ('In velo quod a Cintilane rege Romae directum est') agrees with the *Anthologia* and, as Lapidge notes, even has the correct reading *directum* posited by de Rossi, following Ruinart.[60] We may conclude, then,

---

[57] I quote the original (in capitals) from Antonio Casamassa, *Scritti Patristici* (Rome, 1955–6) I, pl. iii (his printed text on p. 218 is misprinted). I quote U from the Kraus facsimile, as Wallach is inaccurate. The last two lines are missing from U because IV ends here; I supply them (in italics) from the *Anthologia Isidoriana*. Casamassa's *subole* has no manuscript support: see *ICUR*, p. 253, n. 2.

[58] Wallach misprints *institutis*, following the erroneous reading of *ILCV Suppl.*, p. 2. In BN lat. 5315 between the *u* and *i* of *instituis* a letter (a minim?) has been erased.

[59] *ICUR*, p. 253, n. 2, accepting the alleged reading of a lost manuscript.

[60] The manuscripts have *dictum, ductum, deductum, dicatum* (cf. *ICUR*, p. 254, n. 7, and Lapidge, 'Some Remnants', p. 808, n. 6). Note that L agrees with the *Anthologia* in the use of the dative (*Romae*)

that the Spanish sylloge known as the *Anthologia Isidoriana* or a prototype of it was one of the direct or indirect sources of the Milred collection of epigrams. In view of the minute points of spelling noted above, it is likely that it was a fairly direct source.

My other possible source for Milred's collection, or rather a reflection of a possible source, is the Codex Thuaneus, well known to classical scholars: BN lat. 8071 (hereafter P). This ninth-century French manuscript[61] has often been assigned to the Loire region, possibly Fleury,[62] though the case seems not to have been argued in detail. It is very obviously a compilation from a number of independent sources.[63] The part that is of interest here is the cento of epigrams copied, mainly as prose and with little regard for Latin grammar, on the last two leaves of the manuscript (fols. 60–1).[64] The scribe evidently copied them from an older, badly damaged exemplar in which the beginnings or ends of many lines of verse had crumbled away or been destroyed by damp; and his own work has been rendered partly illegible by stains. The exemplar appears to have been a composite collection of epigrams intended for a variety of purposes, like Milred's, but it overlaps with U and L in only two places, as we shall see. The first part of it must have been derived from Carolingian circles: after three epigrams without indication of date or place (the first of which is inscribed in part on the ninth- or tenth-century Liudger Chalice from Helmstedt[65]) and an epitaph on a certain *beatus Columbanus* come two riddles and the trace of a third, one of which contains a clear echo of one of Boniface's riddles;[66] and these are followed by a poem referring to Angilramm, archbishop of Metz (d. 791) – a fact that makes one suspect that the Columbanus of the earlier epitaph is not the famous St Columbanus, as de Rossi thought, but Columbanus abbot of Saint-Trond in the diocese of Metz, Angilramm's associate whose life has

---

which was not used in prose in the classical period, though it occurs in Medieval Latin prose; Leland puts two points under the *-ae* (*Collectanea* III, 115, n. *d*) to indicate his surprise. (Lapidge omits these marks in his edition; see 'Some Remnants', p. 801, n. 5.)

[61] See *CLA* x, no. 1474. 'S. ix¹' is given by Bernt, *Das lateinische Epigramm*, p. 114.

[62] See, e.g., B. L. Ullman, 'The Transmission of the Text of Catullus', *Studi in Onore di Luigi Castiglioni*, ed. A. Rostagni *et al.* (Florence, 1960) II, 1028, n. 3. Facsimile in *Pervigilium Veneris*, ed. Cecil Clementi, 3rd ed. (Oxford, 1936), pp. 172–3.

[63] See, e.g., *CLA* x, no. 1474. I would not, therefore, attach much importance to the fact noted by Schaller ('Bemerkungen', p. 12) that it contains works of Eugenius, like BN lat. 8093 and 2832 (discussed above, p. 30 and n. 54; cf. *Eugenii Carmina*, ed. Vollmer, pp. xli and xlv–xlvi) and the Valenciennes manuscript of the *Anthologia Isidoriana*.

[64] Edited in two halves in *ICUR*, at pp. 56–7 (§v) and 244–9 (§xxi). Cf. *ICUR* n.s. I, xix. no. 14. It is not clear where the cento begins. The only large initials are at xxi.2 and 6 and v.13 and 18b. A little more is legible than de Rossi prints.

[65] *ICUR*, p. 244 (xxi.1). Victor H. Elbern, 'Der eucharistische Kelch im frühen Mittelalter', *Zeitschrift des deutschen Vereins für Kunstwissenschaft* 17 (1963), 3–12, 63–6, 68–9 and 123.

[66] Line 8 of xxi.4 ('Horridum hoc animal genuit Germa[nic]a tellus') echoes Boniface, *Aenigmata*, IX, line 4 ('Ob quod semper amauit me Germanica tellus'), ed. F. Glorie, Corpus Christianorum Series Latina 133 (Turnhout, 1968), 339.

been studied recently by Lapidge.[67] After part of a poem by Optatianus Porphyrius[68] there is a long series of poems which all come from Italy, so far as one can tell, and mostly refer to the churches of Rome and the monuments in the Vatican. It is this second, apparently Italian, part of P that may be related to the Milred collection.

The more significant of the two parallels is an untitled poem in four elegiac couplets on Jerome's eighteen books of commentary on Isaiah.[69] The only other text of this poem is a three-couplet version among Leland's transcripts (L2), which is headed 'Versus Bedae de tractatu Hieronymi in Esaiam'. Schaller, who discovered this correspondence, maintained that the ascription to Bede was mistaken and incompatible with the non-English context in P.[70] It is true that Leland attributed the Patrick poem (L9 = U14) to Bede on his own initiative (probably because it preceded a poem attributed to Bede in U)[71] and that in the present case he may have wrongly connected the verses with a lost work of Bede mentioned in the list at the end of the *Historia Ecclesiastica* (v.24): 'In Isaiam, Danihelem, XII prophetas et partem Hieremiae distinctiones capitulorum ex tractatu beati Hieronimi excerptas.' On the other hand it is quite possible that the Bedan attribution was already present in the manuscript Leland saw at Malmesbury. We cannot rule that out merely because of the context in P, for in P the poem is not entirely surrounded by Roman inscriptions. It follows a quotation about Adam and Eve from Avitus of Vienne's epic (perhaps regarded as a description of a picture),[72] a Roman inscription and Damasus's famous poem on St Paul, which was often inscribed in manuscripts of the bible or of the Pauline epistles.[73] (One

---

[67] Michael Lapidge, 'The Authorship of the Adonic Verses "Ad Fidolium" attributed to Columbanus', *SM* 3rd ser. 18 (1977), 249–314. The Angilramm poem is re-edited by P. von Winterfeld and K. Strecker, *Poetae Latini Aevi Carolini* IV, MGH, Poetae Latini 4 (Berlin, 1899–1923), 1043. The epitaph mentioning Columbanus is reprinted PL, Suppl. IV, col. 1611. Note that it is textually related to the epitaph of Chrodegang *of Metz* (*Poetae Latini Aevi Carolini*, I, ed. Ernst Dümmler, MGH, Poetae Latini I (Berlin, 1881), 109–10) and to the latter's model by Fortunatus.

[68] Traube (*Vorlesungen* III, 89) identified XXI.6 as Porphyrius, *Carmina*, XXV, lines 1, 3, 2 and 4. These lines were often transmitted separately.

[69] Note Traube's correction, *ibid.* p. 89, to the text in *ICUR*, at p. 248 (XXII.13).

[70] 'Bemerkungen', p. 21, n. 49. But note that L2 seems to be echoed in lines 1534–6 of Alcuin's poem on York (*Poetae* I, ed. Dümmler, p. 203). Moreover L2's last line ('cernit apostolicis equiperata tubis') is modelled on line 386 of Venantius Fortunatus, *Carmina* VIII.iii ('quod dat apostolica Paulus ab ore tuba'), a poem much quoted by Bede (see Michael Lapidge's appendix to R. W. Hunt, 'Manuscript Evidence for Knowledge of the Poems of Venantius Fortunatus in Late Anglo-Saxon England', *ASE* 8 (1979), 291). Compare also the last line of Bede's elegiacs on Cuthbert: 'Cum tremet angelicis, mundus ab axe tubis' (*Two Lives of Saint Cuthbert*, ed. and trans. Bertram Colgrave (Cambridge, 1940), p. 294). I owe all these parallels to Mr Neil Wright.

[71] See Sheerin, 'Leland and Milred', p. 175, and above, pp. 24–5.

[72] Identified by Traube, *Vorlesungen* III, 89. See *Aviti Opera*, ed. R. Peiper, MGH, Auct. Antiq. 6, ii (Berlin, 1883), 224 (bk III, lines 12–19). The text in P agrees with his α group of manuscripts (Gallicani) against his β group (Germanici); cf. *ibid.* p. 200.

[73] Cf. *ICUR*, p. 441, and *Epigrammata Damasiana*, ed. Ferrua, no. 1.

surmises that the poem on Jerome's commentary was placed after Damasus's poem because of their similar function as epigraphs for books.) Although Damasus's poem is, in a sense, Italian, it was widely disseminated. In England Aldhelm knew it in the seventh century[74] and we have an eighth-century manuscript of it, Cambridge, Corpus Christi College 173, fol. 81, written 'probably in a Kentish centre'.[75] Moreover in line 17 (*profundum penetrare maris noctemque diemque*) the Corpus text has the impossible reading *nocteque diem*que (*sic*) which is found in exactly the same form in P.[76] This gross and uncorrected error suggests that the P text had either come from eighth-century England or had passed there in the eighth century. The former alternative is supported by its *uisus* for *iussus* in the preceding line (16), which is doubtless miscopied from an exemplar with *iusus*, a typically Insular spelling which is found in the Corpus text.[77] These points are very far from confirming Bede's authorship of the Jerome poem, but they show that P may reflect material which could have been available in eighth-century England.

The other poem common to Milred's collection and P is Damasus's inscription on St Felix (U8), which comes from Nola or Rome.[78] In P it precedes the Avitus extract.[79] Great stress cannot be laid on the appearance of the Felix poem in both U and P, for it is extant in six other texts. On the other hand five of these texts are late medieval and descend from a defective lost common exemplar and only the sixth is early: a sylloge of Nola inscriptions in BN nouv. acq. lat. 1443, at 76v, a ninth-century manuscript of Cluny provenance, whose text is cognate with the lost exemplar mentioned above.[80] Thus U8 was not a common text in the early Middle Ages, so far as we know. If it was inscribed at Nola rather than Rome, that is not incompatible with English knowledge of it as early as the seventh century in view of the well-known Campanian influence on early English liturgy, which is usually associated with Hadrian of Canterbury, who came from that region.[81]

---

[74] *Epigrammata Damasiana*, ed. Ferrua, pp. 83–7.

[75] *CLA* II, no. 123. On this manuscript, see M. B. Parkes, 'The Palaeography of the Parker Manuscript of the *Chronicle*, Laws and Sedulius, and Historiography at Winchester in the Late Ninth and Tenth Centuries', *ASE* 5 (1976), 149–71. I quote from the manuscript as Ferrua's collation is incomplete.

[76] *ICUR*, p. 248, prints *nocteque diemque*, failing to note that the second *-que* is abbreviated. These seem to be the only examples of *nocteque*.

[77] This spelling occurs also in London, BL, Harley 1772 (s. ix), 4r; see *The Epistles and Apocalypse from the Codex Harleianus*, ed. E. S. Buchanan (London, 1912).

[78] See above, n. 38.

[79] It is XXI.9 (*ICUR*, p. 247) and is edited *ibid.* p. 190; *ICUR* n.s. II, 120–2; and *Epigrammata Damasiana*, ed. Ferrua, no. 59.

[80] See the variants and discussion in the three editions noted above, n. 79. Cf. Bernt, *Das lateinische Epigramm*, p. 81.

[81] Klaus Gamber, 'Die kampanische Lektionsordnung', *Sacris Erudiri* 13 (1962), 326–52, and G. G. Willis, *Further Essays in Early Roman Liturgy* (London, 1968), pp. 214–19. Cf. Wilhelm Levison, *England and the Continent in the Eighth Century* (Oxford, 1946), p. 143, n. 2.

I have suggested that Milred's collection drew on the *Anthologia Isidoriana* or a prototype[82] of it and on some lost sylloge that was used also in the compilation of the exemplar of P. There are also three continental syllogae which seem to have shared sources with the Milred collection or even to have drawn on the Milred collection itself.

The *Sylloge Wirceburgensis* (*SW*) in Würzburg, Universitätsbibliothek, M. p. misc. f. 2, at 75v–76r, is a short collection of ten items written at Würzburg in the mid-ninth century.[83] Although all ten are copied in the same hand (which is different from that of the main contents of the manuscript, Cicero's *Rhetorica ad Herennium*), de Rossi rightly argued that *SW* 1–5 are different in origin from the remainder, which is the part that interests us.[84] *SW* 6–10 are all Roman inscriptions. Of these *SW* 9 corresponds to U5 (from St Laurence without the Walls) and *SW* 10 corresponds to U3 (from St Peter *ad Vincula*). This overlap between *SW* and U could easily be due to chance, were it not that in line 10 of the Laurence inscription they share the error *celerasse* for *celebrasse*,[85] which points to a textual relationship between them. We do not know the age of the exemplar(s) of *SW* 6–10. *SW* 6 was composed *c.* 821 for the church of St Cecilia over Tiber; but it could easily be an accretion between *SW* 1–5 and *SW* 7–10, which include no inscriptions later than the seventh century. It seems probable that *SW* 7–10, or at least *SW* 9–10, derive from a source used also for Milred's collection. A direct connection between Milred and Würzburg is not impossible in view of his recorded visit to Germany and the history of the Cuthswith Codex.[86]

My other two continental sources are both connected with Alcuin. Their relation to U has already been discussed by Schaller, but the discussion may be carried a little further, for instance by taking L into consideration.[87]

All we known about the Codex Bertinianus (hereafter B), a lost manuscript from the Saint-Bertin library, has to be deduced from the 272 poems from it printed in the 1617 edition of Alcuin.[88] Many of these poems, though not by Alcuin, were known to him and influenced his authentic poetry; thus B is regarded as his poetic *Nachlass*, probably put together soon after his death. B2–17 are Aldhelm's *Carmina Ecclesiastica* and B25, 27–45 and 47 are epigrams by Rusticus Helpidius.[89] The table below (p. 36) shows how the intervening

---

[82] The latter possibility is supported by the title of Monica's epitaph in U (see above, p. 31).

[83] *ICUR*, pp. 154–7; see Bernhard Bischoff and Josef Hofmann, *Libri Sancti Kyliani* (Würzburg, 1952), pp. 20, 36, 43, 133–4, 171 and 199.   [84] *ICUR*, pp. 154–5.

[85] *Cebrasse* in the *Sylloge Turonensis* (manuscripts of s. xii) is presumably an independent error. *SLQ* 46 has the correct reading. See *ICUR*, pp. 64 and 106.

[86] See Sims-Williams, 'Cuthswith', pp. 1–21.

[87] Schaller, 'Bemerkungen', pp. 13–17. Cf. Thomson, 'William of Malmesbury's *Liber Pontificalis*', p. 103.

[88] *Alcuuini Opera*, ed. A. Quercetanus [Duchesne] (Paris, 1617), cols. 1673–746.

[89] See Schaller, 'Bermerkungen', p. 14; *Poetae* I, ed. Dümmler, p. 164. B1 = *ibid.* p. 349, no. cxxi. On Rusticus see Bernt, *Das lateinische Epigramm*, pp. 74–5.

items correspond with Milred's collection; the references to de Rossi and Dümmler refer to the items they reprint from B.[90]

B	U	L	de Rossi	Dümmler
18			—	344 I
19		6?	—	345 II
20	1		1–2	345 III
21			3	345 IV
22	10		4	345 V
23	12		5	345 VI
24	11		—	346 cxviia
26			—	347 cxviib
46		3	—	—

The correspondences between B and fol. 2 of U (U10–16) are particularly striking, seeing that B22–4 are found only in these two sources. All three could refer to churches in Rome, but that is not at all certain.[91] B20 is an extract from Arator's *De Actibus Apostolorum*, bk 1, lines 1070–6, but the title 'Ad uincula *sancti* Petri' in U and the occurrence of the same extract in *SLQ* make it probable that the passage was actually inscribed on a wall of St Peter *ad Vincula*, where Arator had first recited his epic in 544.[92] U and B are better texts than *SLQ* 64 (which has *uincta* for *cuius* in line 1073) except that for line 1071 B inadvertently substitutes the penultimate line of a fifth-century Vatican inscription, which refers to St Peter's power to loose chains and is found in several syllogae.[93] This error suggests that B derives from a source which included both epigrams, probably because both referred to *uincula Petri*. As we have already seen, U begins with three epigrams on *uincula Petri* and so it is quite likely that the fourth one, which contaminated B20, was also part of the Milred collection and preceded U1 on the lost page before 1r. It is thus interesting to note that one of the syllogae which contain the contaminating Vatican inscription is P, whose relation with the Milredian collection has already been discussed.[94]

B46 corresponds to the 'Epitaphium Poetae' (L3), given as follows by Leland

Vivere post obitum vates vis nosse, viator?

quid[95] legis ecce loquor: vox tua nempe mea est.

[90] *ICUR*, pp. 285–6, and *Poetae* 1, ed. Dümmler, pp. 344–7.

[91] *ICUR*, pp. 281 and 285–6, nn. 3–5.

[92] *ICUR*, p. 110, n. 64. Cf. *Aratoris De Actibus Apostolorum*, ed. A. P. McKinlay, Corpus Scriptorum Ecclesiasticorum Latinorum 72 (Vienna, 1951), xxviii, and F. J. E. Raby, *A History of Christian-Latin Poetry*, 2nd ed. (Oxford, 1953), pp. 118–19 (quoting the relevant lines). In his note on bk 1, line 1076, McKinlay notes that Alcuin was influenced by this line in his own verse.

[93] *ILCV*, no. 981, and *ICUR*, pp. 55, no. 12, 56, no. 17a, 80, no. 8, and 144, no. 3.

[94] *ICUR*, p. 56 (v.17a).   [95] An error (by Leland?) for *quod*.

Lapidge points out that this distich probably derives from Possidius's *Vita Augustini*, ch. 31, where it is quoted and ascribed to 'a certain secular poet'.[96] He notes that Possidius correctly reads *vatem*, not *vates* as in L3. It is surely significant that B46 agrees with L in reading *vates*; as far as I know, the only other example of this reading is in Vatican, Reg. lat. 421, fols. 21–5 (a mid-ninth-century French manuscript of canons), which has the epigram, with another from Possidius, as an addition (s. ix²) on 21r.[97] Presumably the reading *vates* crept into some branch of the manuscript tradition of Possidius, or of the epigrams abstracted from his *Vita*, and so reached L and B, probably not independently.

If Leland had given us more than the titles of some of the poems in the Milred codex, we might be able to equate more of them with the poems in B; for instance, L6 ('Epigramma Bedae ad S. Michaelem') may correspond to B19, which is addressed to Michael. Yet even on the available evidence it is clear that B is closely related to U and L and that Alcuin had either a copy of Milred's collection of epigrams or a copy of a lost collection which was used to compile that collection.

Schaller has drawn attention to a possible connection between U and another manuscript of Alcuiniana.[98] Munich, Bayerische Staatsbibliothek, Clm 19410, a mid-ninth-century miscellany from Passau, Bavaria,[99] contains a series of short poems on pp. 51–4. The first half of the series consists mostly of poems or fragments by Alcuin, though there is a piece by Eugenius of Toledo among them.[100] The scribe continued without a break to copy a series of Roman inscriptions, obviously derived from some sylloge.[101] Schaller suggests that this whole body of Alcuiniana on pp. 51–4 reached Bavaria via Alcuin's friend, Arn of Salzburg.[102] If we follow him in treating the whole group of poems as part of Alcuin's *Nachlass*, like B, it is doubtless significant that one of the Roman inscriptions in it[103] is the same as U3 ('ad uincula'), even though it is recorded in other syllogae as well.[104] The Alcuinian

---

[96] 'Some Remnants', p. 803; PL 32, col. 64, and 95, col. 1531; *ICUR*, pp. 277 and 279; and Dieter Schaller and Ewald Könsgen, *Initia Carminum Latinorum Saeculo Undecimo Antiquiorum* (Göttingen, 1977), no. 17464.

[97] *ICUR*, p. 279, no. 4. Cf. PL 81, col. 838, and A. Wilmart, *Codices Reginenses Latini* (Vatican City, 1937–) II, 513–14. (In the text in *ICUR*, at p. 277, de Rossi prints *vate(m)*; presumably the manuscript has *uate* for *uatē*.)

[98] 'Bermerkungen', pp. 16–17.

[99] See Bernhard Bischoff, 'Paläographische Fragen deutscher Denkmäler der Karolingerzeit', *FS* 5 (1971), 125–6.

[100] Nearly all are ptd *Poetae* I, ed. Dümmler, pp. 266–8 (on the manuscript, cf. p. 168).

[101] *ICUR*, p. 286 (cf. p. 281).

[102] 'Bemerkungen', p. 17. His suggestion is perhaps supported by the recurrence of the first poem on p. 51 in a manuscript written for Arn. See *Poetae* I, ed. Dümmler, pp. 166 and 266 (n. on no. LV, 1).

[103] *ICUR*, p. 286, no. 11.   [104] See above, p. 28 and n. 46.

collection, on which the Passau manuscript may have drawn, was perhaps derived partly from material of English provenance related to Milred's collection. If so, the last, acephalous epigram on p. 54 (though it has attracted no attention from modern scholars) is of special interest:

> Lector adesto vigil pagina queque canit.
> Beda dei famulus scripsi versusque notavi.
> Pro [quo] quisque legis obsecro funde preces.[105]

I suggest that it was with these lines that Bede concluded his lost *Liber Epigrammatum*. If so, our discussion has come full circle, for it was in the context of a search for remnants of that lost *Liber* that Lapidge, in 1975, reawakened interest in Milred of Worcester's collection of epigrams.[106] In this article I have not tried to settle the relation of Milred's collection to Bedan and other English sources but have attempted only to show its connection with certain earlier and later syllogae preserved on the continent. Although mainly concerned with textual matters the investigation has filled out our knowledge about the reception and transmission of Christian Latin poetry in England between the age of Bede and the age of Alcuin. Milred's collection, with its mixture of native and Roman inscriptional verse, is fresh testimony to Rome's impact on the Anglo-Saxon imagination.

---

[105] Printed *ICUR*, p. 286, n. 13. Cf. 'obsecro quisq*ue* legis' in Bede's poem on Cyneberht's church (see Schaller, 'Bemerkungen', p. 21) and Bede's prefatory epigram to his *De Natura Rerum* (ed. C. W. Jones, CCSL 123A (Turnhout, 1975), 189):

> Naturas rerum uarias labentis et aeui
> Perstrinxi titulis, tempora lata citis,
> *Beda Dei famulus.* Tu fixa, *obsecro*, perennem,
> *Qui legis*, astra super mente tuere diem.

[106] See his valuable study cited above, n. 4. On Bede's *Liber Epigrammatum*, see, further, Bernt, *Das lateinische Epigramm*, pp. 164–71, and Bruno Luiselli, 'Sul perduto "liber epigrammatum" di Beda', *Poesia latina in frammenti: miscellanea filologica*, Publicazioni dell'Instituto di Filologica Classica dell'Università di Genova 39 (Genoa, 1974), 367–79. It is interesting to note that one of the earliest manuscripts of Bede's poetry is BL Royal 2 A. xx (discussed above, pp. 23 and 26), which contains two of his poems in elegiacs on fol. 26, immediately before the *Versus Cuð de Sancta Trinitate*. They are edited J. Fraipont, *Bedae Venerabilis Opera*, Pars iv, CCSL 122 (Turnhout, 1955), pp. 445–6 and 449. They may have formed part of the *Liber Epigrammatum*, despite Luiselli, who thinks it entirely lost.

The prefix *un-* and the metrical grammar of *Beowulf*

CALVIN B. KENDALL

Two rules of the metrical grammar of the *Beowulf* poet are the subject of this paper. One concerns the variation of stress on the prefix *un-*; the other pertains to the alliteration of compounds. The two are correlated. The paper rests on the premise that the 'metre' of an Old English poem is only one function of a set of regularities that make it something we call verse rather than prose. Separately these regularities may be described as 'rules'; taken as a group, the rules comprise a metrical grammar. Each Anglo-Saxon scop absorbed such a grammar during the course of long immersion in the poetic tradition of his culture. No two scops' metrical grammars could have been exactly alike; in addition to individual differences, there must have been regional and dialectal variations, although the poetic tradition ensured remarkable uniformity over a wide area and a considerable period of time, and only at the end of the Old English period, with let us say *The Battle of Maldon*, are significant changes manifest. Further investigation would therefore be needed to determine to what extent the rules here described apply to other grammars.

Many of the rules of the scop's metrical grammar corresponded nearly or exactly to the grammatical rules of his native language. A few differed markedly. Some, and in particular those relating to the arrangement and distribution of certain sounds (alliteration) and stresses (metrical ictus), were unique. From these last we abstract our notions of metre as it is commonly understood. The scop internalized the rules of metre along with the other rules of his metrical grammar in the course of learning his craft. The chances are that he was never conscious of metre as a separate entity, especially if he had not received schooling in the metres of Latin. If we could return to the seventh century and Abbess Hild's monastery at Whitby for the purpose of quizzing Cædmon, we would probably find him as tongue-tied in the face of questions about his metre as he would certainly be about the way in which he constructed his sentences. Parry and Lord, working with illiterate singers of tales in Yugoslavia, discovered that they had no conception of so basic a notion as a line of poetry.[1] For this reason, it is unlikely that the scop ever

---

[1] Albert B. Lord, *The Singer of Tales* (1960; repr. New York, 1965), p. 25.

39

consciously bent the rules of his metre for poetic effect. His poetic utterance was governed by the metrical grammar he had acquired. To speak poetically was to speak metrically, because metre was an integral part of that grammar. Of course he might mis-speak in rapid oral composition, or blunder on parchment, and thereby produce a metrically anomalous line. This is quite different from playing with the expectations set up by metre, as a modern poet might do. It is true that we sometimes find alliterative stress placed on a normally unaccented word for what looks like rhetorical emphasis, e.g.:

on þǽm dæge þýsses līfes.[2] (*Beowulf* 197)

But this is a formula in *Beowulf* (see 790 and 806) that belongs to the poetic tradition.[3] Similar 'violations', which have likewise been attributed to rhetorical emphasis, fall into fairly predictable categories and can probably be accounted for within the rules of the metrical grammar.

The view, which has had some currency, that Old English metre was so accommodating that it routinely permitted similar half-lines to be variously scanned to suit the exigencies of alliteration or the rhythmical whims of the poet is simply untenable.[4] By and large the scansion of the half-line is internally determined without reference to context. I do not mean to suggest that the scop lacked flexibility, that he could not vary his lines to suit his contextual purposes. Of course, he could. The *Beowulf* poet for one was enormously skilled at attaining an almost infinite variety in the shape and sound of his lines. But flexibility was provided by the formal properties of his metrical grammar rather than by liberties that he might take with its implementation. Because of this comparative rigidity,[5] a special interest attaches to those few areas where his metrical grammar permitted him to make certain 'choices'. Here, where we can watch him plying his craft as it were,

---

[2] This study is based on Fr. Klaeber's text, *Beowulf and The Fight at Finnsburg*, 3rd ed. with first and second supplements (Boston, 1950). All references to *Beowulf* are to this edition unless otherwise noted. Other Anglo-Saxon poems are cited according to the texts in The Anglo-Saxon Poetic Records, ed. George Philip Krapp and Elliott Van Kirk Dobbie, 6 vols. (New York and London, 1931–53). Macrons have been added to quotations from ASPR to mark vowel length.

[3] For *on þǽm dæge* with alliterative stress on *þǽm*, see *Christ* 1096b and 1371b (ASPR 3, 33 and 41); for *þysses līfes* with alliterative stress on *þysses*, see *Genesis* 1120b, 1600b and 2452b (ASPR 1, 36, 49 and 73), *Guthlac* 74b (ASPR 3, 51), *Phoenix* 151b (ASPR 3, 98), *The Gifts of Men* 19b (ASPR 3, 137) and *Solomon and Saturn* 242b (ASPR 6, 40). Cf. the formulaic system ...*þēos/þās woruld* with alliterative stress on *þēos/þās*, *Genesis* 1126b (ASPR 1, 36), *Christ* 1583b (ASPR 3, 47), *Guthlac* 125b (ASPR 3, 53), *The Phoenix* 501b (ASPR 3, 108), *The Wanderer* 58b (ASPR 3, 135) and *Deor* 31b (ASPR 3, 179).

[4] The view can be illustrated *passim* in the papers of Marjorie Daunt, 'Old English Verse and English Speech Rhythm', *TPS* 1946, 56–72, and Paull F. Baum, 'The Meter of the *Beowulf*', *MP* 46 (1948), 73–91 and (1949) 145–62.

[5] *Pace* Baum: 'And we are, accordingly, to expect not a rigid meter but rather a loose and easy manner, a sort of talking style...' ('The Meter of the *Beowulf*', p. 76).

we may gain a fresh insight into the nature of the metrical grammar he was responding to.[6]

One such area, in the case of the *Beowulf* poet, involves the negative prefix *un-*. The prefix occurs seventy times in the poem,[7] exclusive of its possible appearance in the proper name *Unferth*.[8] It is evenly distributed between the *a* verse (34 times) and the *b* verse (36 times). Though the fact that *un-* was not originally a verbal prefix suggests that it should be accented, it is clear from the evidence of *Beowulf* (and elsewhere) that an unstressed form existed side by side with the stressed prefix.[9] This is demonstrated – as the line alliterations confirm – by the contrasting pairs:

 únmurnlīce (449b) sē þe unmúrnlīce (1756a)

and

úndyrne cūð (150b) Þæt is undýrne. (2000a)

If we assume that an unstressed alternative existed for every compound with the stressed form of *un-*, it follows that the poet had a choice to make whenever he wished to use the negative prefix. In sixty of the seventy verses, neither option generates an unacceptable metrical contour.[10] Consider the

---

[6] It will become apparent, from what follows, that I regard these 'choices' as largely illusory. That is, the poetic tradition and the rules of the metrical grammar determine the outcome here as they do elsewhere. But in order to develop the argument I speak as though the poet were consciously deciding between alternatives freely available to him.

[7] In the *a* verse: 111a, 287a, 413a, 444a, 498a, 573a, 744a, 833a, 932a, 960a, 987a, 1097a, 1129a, 1238a, 1254a, 1389a, 1655a, 1734a, 1756a, 1865a, 2000a, 2188a, 2214a, 2291a, 2443a, 2548a, 2564a, 2624a, 2739a, 3012a, 3031a, 3059a, 3135a and 3168a. In the *b* verse: 120b, 127b, 130b, 150b, 276b, 410b, 449b, 468b, 602b, 727b, 741b, 876b, 885b, 1072b, 1308b, 1410b, 1792b, 2068b, 2089b, 2120b, 2140b, 2268b, 2413b, 2420b, 2435b, 2578b, 2721b, 2728b, 2821b, 2863b, 2881b, 2908b, 2911b, 2921b, 3138b and 3148b. 357a (MS, *eald 7 un hár*; Klaeber, *eald ond anhár*) is not included because *un-/an-* is the intensive rather than the negative prefix.

[8] One of the working assumptions of this study is that proper nouns in *Beowulf* behave differently from common nouns. I have systematically excluded proper nouns from consideration where they directly impinge on the question being investigated. Thus I have nothing to say about the proper noun *Unferth* or about proper nouns that might be or are compounds. On the other hand I cite as evidence lines which contain proper nouns when they themselves are not at issue.

[9] A. Campbell, *Old English Grammar* (1959; corrected repr. Oxford, 1964) asserts: 'The negative prefix *un-* was not originally used with finite verbs (though freely added to participles...), and so should always be accented. Occasional unaccented uses, however, occur, e.g. *unclǣne* impure, beside *únclǣne*' (§75). With respect to *Beowulf* 1756a and 2000a cited below, W. P. Lehmann and Takemitsu Tabusa, *The Alliterations of the Beowulf* (Austin, 1958) observe: 'we may account for these two unstressed forms of un- by considering them metrical survivals of past practices, here of proclitic negative prefixes' (p. 8). A. J. Bliss, *The Metre of Beowulf* (1958; revised, Oxford, 1967) says simply, 'stress on compounds with *un-* is variable' (§44). Neither Bliss nor anyone else has attempted to isolate the rules governing this variability.

[10] For the purposes of this paper, an acceptable metrical contour is one of the Sievers types as analysed and catalogued by John Collins Pope, *The Rhythm of Beowulf: an Interpretation of the Normal and Hypermetric Verse-Forms in Old English Poetry* (1942; rev., New Haven, 1966), and by Bliss, *Metre*. I give the types according to the following modified system, where unraised 1 = a single syllable

four half-lines just cited. Only 1756a becomes 'unmetrical' if the stress is shifted. Presumably in the other three cases the poet was free to choose the stressed or unstressed form, depending on his desire for vocalic or consonantal alliteration, or on his preference for one metrical contour over another.

It is rare to find half-lines in an Old English poem for which alternative scansions are real possibilities; rarer still to find half-lines which can legitimately accommodate two different alliterative patterns. In the *a* verse twenty-six of the thirty-four half lines have acceptable contours whether they are read with or without the stressed prefix;[11] in the *b* verse thirty-four of thirty-six.[12] Of the remaining ten verses, one (*ungedēfelīce*, 2435b) cannot be scanned normally whether or not the prefix is stressed. Only nine are metrically unambiguous as they stand.

Let us take a closer look at these nine. 1756a can only be scanned:

$$\times \quad \times\times \quad / \quad \backslash\times$$
sē þe unmurnlīce.   (type C)

Putting the stress on *un-* would generate a type D[1] with unbound disyllabic anacrusis, which is unparalleled in *Beowulf*. 2188a, 2214a and 2564a must be scanned, e.g.:

$$/ \times \quad / \times$$
eldum uncūð.   (2214a; type A1)

The alternative $* \angle \times \times \times \angle$, although rare examples of it can be adduced, is to my mind unquestionably anomalous.[13] Similar, 2443a must be scanned:

$$/ \times\times \quad / \quad \backslash \times$$
æðeling unwrĕcen.[14]   (type D*1)

between the final two metrical stresses, unraised 2 = two (or three) syllables between the final two stresses, and D2 is short for D1² (varieties which do not come up in the discussion are not listed):

A1 = ´⌣x × ´⌣x ×	D1 = ⌣x ⌣x × ×
A2 = ´⌣x (×) × × ⌣x ×	D*1 = ´ (×) × ´⌣x `× ×
A3 = (…×) × × ⌣x × [*a* verse only]	D2 = ⌣x ⌣x × ×
B1 = (…×) × ⌣x × ⌣x	D2² = ⌣x ⌣x × × ×
C = (…×) × ⌣x ⌣x ×	E1 = ´⌣x `× × ´⌣x

[11] The metrical type produced by the unstressed form is given first. A1 or D[1]: 444a, 498a, 833a, 960a, 1129a and 3012a; A2 or D*[1]: 987a, 1097a, 1865a and 3031a; A3 or C: 111a, 932a, 1655a, 1734a, 2000a, 2291a and 3059a; B1 or E1: 573a; C or A1: 1238a and 1254a; C or D[1]: 744a, 1389a and 2548a; and E1 or A1: 287a, 2624a and 3135a.

[12] A1 or D[1]: 120b, 127b, 727b, 741b, 885b, 2068b, 2120b, 2413b, 2578b, 2821b, 2881b, 2921b and 3148b; A2 or D*[1]: 2863b; A2 or D2²: 1792b, 2420b, 2721b and 2728b; B1 or E1: 130b, 150b, 276b, 410b, 602b, 876b, 1072b, 1410b, 2140b and 2268b; and C or D[1]: 449b, 468b, 1308b, 2089b, 2908b and 3138b.

[13] I agree with Pope's reservations about the possible instances; see *Rhythm*, p. 372 (F3), and Preface, p. xxxi.

[14] The uninflected formative element *-ing* can hardly take secondary stress in this position. Otherwise one might argue for the possibility of type E1 here and in 2188a. See Julian Huguenin, *Secondary Stress in Anglo-Saxon* (Baltimore, 1901). pp. 3–11.

413a, 2739a and 3168a must be scanned, e.g.:

$$/ \times \times \quad / \quad \times$$
īdel ond unnyt,   (413a; type A2)

to avoid the alternative $* \underset{\smile}{} \times \times \times \underset{\smile}{}$.[15] and 2911b must be scanned:

$$\times \quad \times \quad / \quad \backslash \quad \times$$
syððan under[ne],   (type C)

since putting the stress on *-dérne* would generate a type A3, which is unacceptable in the *b* verse. In all nine cases, the alliterative pattern of the whole line either confirms, or does not conflict with, the unequivocal scansion of the half-line.[16]

Of course many of the half-lines cease to be ambiguous as soon as the alliterative pattern of the whole line is taken into account. Here we must distinguish. First there is the group of half-lines in which the word prefixed by *un-* bears the sole alliterating stress. For example:

únbyrnende   (2548a)   únblīðe sæt.   (130b)

In this group the prefix in the *a* verse alliterates nine times (111a, 744a, 932a, 1389a, 1655a, 1734a, 2291a, 2548a and 3059a); the stem on̩ce (2000a; cf. 1756a). In the *b* verse the prefix bears the alliteration in every case (sixteen times: 130b, 150b, 276b, 410b, 449b, 468b, 602b, 876b, 1072b, 1308b, 1410b, 2089b, 2140b, 2268b, 2908b and 3138b; cf. 2435b and 2911b).

Next there are three *a* verses with double alliteration in which the word prefixed by *un-* receives the first alliterating stress. In each case it is the prefix which alliterates. Certainty here derives from a comparative knowledge of the alliterative practice of the *Beowulf* poet. A fundamental principle of his metrical grammar is this: in any half-line the stressed syllable of the leftmost word of high alliterative rank[17] always bears the first metrical ictus, which

---

[15] Bliss, *Metre*, §84, discusses the sequence $\underset{\smile}{} \times \mid (\times) \times \underset{\smile}{}$, where (|) stands for a word boundary. I cannot accept his conclusion that the 'caesura' (word boundary) suffices to make this 'the simplest and most fundamental variety' of type E. For a critique of Bliss's view, see Thomas Cable, *The Meter and Melody of Beowulf*, Illinois Stud. in Lang. and Lit. 64 (Urbana, 1974), 45–64.

[16] Contrary to some current views (e.g. Cable, *Meter and Melody*, p. 67, 'stress, and not alliteration, is the basic element of Old English meter'), I regard alliteration as an integral part of metre. Alliteration in one half-line is not determined by the alliteration of the other half-line, but by the rules of the metrical grammar. Once we know, for example, that the initial ictus in 1756a falls on *-múrn-*, a fact that we derive from the rules of the metrical grammar, we know that the half-line alliterates on *m*. Comparison with 1756b merely confirms that fact. The group of lines with alternative scansions is interesting precisely because the stress rules of the metrical grammar allow two realizations and we cannot know which the *Beowulf* poet chose until we compare the corresponding half-line or apply other rules. The alliteration and scansion were still determined internally by his choice.

[17] Words of high alliterative rank are, by my definition, initially stressed compounds with two fully meaningful elements; nominals (nouns, descriptive adjectives and most other adjectives, infinitives and participles); a few other classes and specially marked words (e.g., forms beginning with *ǽg-*, the pronoun *self*); and other parts of speech raised to high alliterative rank by transformation rules. See

is marked by alliteration. Hence (vocalic alliteration being demanded by the head-stave):

> únfǽgne eorl.   (573a; likewise 1238a and 1254a)

We come now to the remaining group of thirteen *a* verses, in which the word prefixed by *un-* follows a word bearing alliterative stress. These must be considered together with a similar group of seven *a* verses which are not metrically ambiguous (the latter already discussed[18]). The combined group of twenty may be subdivided. Seventeen half-lines (ambiguous: 287a, 444a, 960a, 987a, 1097a, 1129a, 1865a, 2624a, 3031a and 3135a; unambiguous: 413a, 2188a, 2214a, 2443a, 2564a, 2739a and 3168a) display vocalic alliteration, e.g.:

> éafoð uncūþes.   (960a)

If the prefix is stressed, the entire sub-group of seventeen is characterized by double alliteration. In no case does this create an impossible metrical contour. But the seven unambiguous half-lines become unmetrical if the prefix is not stressed. The assumption that the remaining ten are similarly stressed seems plausible. Its likelihood is increased when we notice that in the *a* verse the combination of finite verb qualified by stressed adverb, where the finite verb alliterates and is not preceded by any unstressed syllables, always in *Beowulf* (seven times) displays double alliteration. Thus we should stress:

> ēodon únblīðe.[19]   (3031a)

Furthermore all the indisputable cases of type E1 of the form disyllabic compound plus iamb ($\frac{\prime}{\smile\times} \underset{\smile\times}{\overset{\backprime}{-}} | \times \frac{\prime}{\smile\times}$) display double alliteration.[20] This argues against reading

> *ómbeht unfórht.   (287a; likewise 2624a and 3135a)

In short there is no compelling argument against, and one or more in favour of, stressing the prefix in all seventeen cases.

The other three half-lines, all metrically ambiguous, are ones in which the word prefixed by *un-* does not alliterate whether the stress falls on the prefix or the stem. These are:

> dúguð unlȳtel   (498a)   tórn unlȳtel   (833a)
>
> góld unrīme.   (3012a)

Eduard Sievers, *Altgermanische Metrik* (Halle, 1893), pp. 22–46; Andreas Heusler, *Deutsche Versgeschichte mit Einschluss des altenglischen und altnordischen Stabreimverses* 1, Paul's Grundriss der germanischen Philologie 8 (Berlin and Leipzig, 1925), 105–13; and D. Slay, 'Some Aspects of the Technique of Composition of Old English Verse', *TPS* 1953, 1.   [18] Above, pp. 42–3.

[19] The seven verses are 307a, 402a, 560a, 702a (where, however, double alliteration depends on an emendation of the Thorkelin transcript), 905a, 1501a and 3031a. The alliterative stress on the finite verb may be ornamental. If so, these would be 'light verses'. See below, n. 24. The stress in 3031a falls on *un-* in any case.

[20] 477a, 548a, 633a, 667a, 1077a, 2469a, 2487a, 2508a, 2566a, 2748a and 2792a (Pope's types E3, 6, 12 and 15; Bliss's type 2E2a).

In the group of twenty verses with the word prefixed by *un-* in second position, these are the only three that do not display double alliteration. The only other occurrence of *unlȳtel* in *Beowulf* is in the *b* verse where it is also metrically ambiguous (*dōm unlȳtel*, 885b).[21] There are three other occurrences of *unrīm*; the prefix, as we saw in the previous two paragraphs, must be stressed in all three (1238a, 2624a and 3135a). One could suggest several hypotheses to account for the fact that there is no double alliteration in 498a, 833a and 3012a. The simplest, based on the assumption that the prefix should always be stressed in this position, would be that the pattern of double alliteration is dominant, but not obligatory (17 out of 20). Pope and Bliss implicitly adopt this hypothesis; both scan all three as type D¹.[22] Or, accepting the first hypothesis as true for most forms, one might postulate that *unlȳtel* is specially marked with a weak prefix, at least in the metrical grammar of the *Beowulf* poet.[23] Or one could argue that the absence of double alliteration in these three verses indicates a shift to the unstressed form of *un-* in both words (*unlȳtel, unrīme*).

The third hypothesis must be adopted, for reasons which I will try to make clear. A pattern of double alliteration which exists in seventeen out of twenty cases is striking, but not in itself decisive. The *Beowulf* poet might have found the pattern pleasing, without feeling obliged to produce it at every opportunity. Fortunately there is a way to cross-check his intentions. Words with the stressed form of the prefix *un-* immediately followed by the stem comprise a sub-group of the class of compounds with clashing stress – that is, compounds with the metrical contour $\overset{\prime}{\underset{\smile}{\times}} \overset{\backslash}{\smile}$ (××). If in the three verses in question we take *un-* to be stressed, as Pope and Bliss do, we have a stressed simplex (*dŭguð, torn, gold*) followed by a compound with clashing stress (*unlȳtel, unrīme*), or a metrical type D¹. What is the *Beowulf* poet's regular practice with such verses? Only six of the twenty verses with *un-* can be so classed: the three in question with the stress put on *un-* for the sake of the argument, plus

ĕtan unforhte   (444a)   ĕafoð uncūþes   (960a)

[ea]l unhlitme.   (1129a)

But in addition to these six there are fifty-eight *a* verses with stressed simplex followed by clashing-stress compound that can be scanned as type D¹,[24] e.g.:

21 See below, p. 51, for its determination.
22 See Pope, *Rhythm*, line index (his types D1 and D2), and Bliss, *Metre*, index to the scansion (his type 1D1).
23 Elsewhere in Old English poetry *unlȳtel* appears unambiguously both with the prefix stressed (*Genesis* 1614a, 2407b and 2552b: ASPR 1, 50, 72 and 76) and unstressed (*Riddle 40* 75a: ASPR 3, 202).
24 21a, 31a, 54a, 160a, 163a, 165a, 288a, 322a, 398a, 436a, 449a, 487a, 551a, 554a, 592a, 598a, 692a, 732a, 742a, 816a, 868a, 936a, 1109a, 1409a, 1641a, 1845a, 1847a, 1895a, 1897a, 1919a, 1927a, 1948a, 1954a,

$$\text{léof lándfrùma} \quad (31a) \qquad \text{éft éardlùfan} \quad (692a)$$
$$\text{bétst bĕadorinca.} \quad (1109a)$$

A variety of syntactic patterns is represented: verb + subject, verb + direct object, infinitive + adverb, noun + dependent adjective, adjective + dependent noun, noun + dependent noun, infinitive + dependent noun, and noun or adjective + complementary noun or adjective. In every case we find double alliteration (58 out of 58). When we add the six verses with *un*- the figure becomes 61 out of 64.

Here then are two different but partially overlapping groups of *a* verses: (*a*) the twenty verses of various metrical types in which a word prefixed by *un*- follows another word bearing alliterative stress and (*b*) the sixty-four verses of type D^1 in which a clashing-stress compound follows a stressed simplex. It would be difficult to believe that in both groups double alliteration tends to be found, though with exceptions, and that by chance the exceptions to the tendency happen to be the same (498a, 833a and 3012a). The third hypothesis provides the solution. The three problematic half-lines are not members of either group. Double alliteration characterizes all true members of (*a*) and (*b*), and the three half-lines, all containing the unstressed form of *un*-, must be scanned as type $A1$:

$$\text{dŭguð unlytel} \quad (498a) \qquad \text{torn unlytel} \quad (833a)$$
$$\text{gold unrime.} \quad (3012a)$$

Two related propositions *concerning the a verse* can immediately be derived. (1) The stressed prefix *un*- always alliterates. A necessary corollary is that when *un*- does not alliterate, it is not stressed.[25] (2) In type D^1 an initially stressed compound in which the second element is semantically meaningful[26] must alliterate. (It will be remembered that such compounds in initial position alliterate according to the fundamental alliterative principle.[27]) There are no exceptions in *Beowulf* to either proposition.

2025a, 2042a, 2090a, 2112a, 2118a, 2226a, 2239a, 2263a, 2266a, 2271a, 2273a, 2315a, 2368a, 2408a, 2414a, 2476a, 2517a, 2557a, 2563a, 2582a, 2642a, 2827a, 2902a, 2915a and 2950a. Included in this list are certain verses which in my view are not genuine type D^1's, but light verses of type C. Since the rescansion automatically places alliterative stress on the first element of the compound, it does not affect the present argument except by reducing somewhat the size of the list.

[25] Only compounds consisting of *un*- + stem beginning with vowel or diphthong (there is none in *Beowulf*) could not be correctly stressed at sight, although compounds in second position theoretically remain ambiguous. That is, if *góld unríme* is properly so scanned, then 960a, for example, could be scanned **éafoð uncúþes*, ignoring the vocalic alliteration of *un*-, without violating proposition (1). But, since double alliteration in these cases *always* fits an acceptable metrical contour and single alliteration sometimes does not, the theoretical possibility can be ignored.

[26] Cf. Campbell, *Grammar*, §§87 and 88.

[27] See above, pp. 43–4.

Although these two propositions may seem limited in scope they have broad implications. In order to see what they are it is necessary to take up the eighteen remaining ambiguous half lines, all in the *b* verse. These are half-lines in which the word prefixed by *un-* follows the word bearing alliterative stress:

Wiht unhǣlo	(120b)	wyrd ungemete nēah	(2420b)
gumum undyrne	(127b)	bāt unswīðor	(2578b)
lēoht unfǣger	(727b)	þegn ungemete till	(2721b)
slāt unwearnum	(741b)	dēað ungemete nēah	(2728b)
dōm unlȳtel	(885b)	guman unfrōdum	(2821b)
Gēat unigmetes wēl	(1792b)	seah on unlēofe	(2863b)
Denum unfǣcne	(2068b)	fȳr unswīðor	(2881b)
Wīf unhȳre	(2120b)	milts ungyfeðe	(2921b)
Weard unhīore	(2413b)	Higum unrōte	(3148b)

Since double alliteration is precluded from the *b* verse, we lack evidence of the sort that enabled us to classify similar half-lines in the *a* verse. Nevertheless some conclusions can be reached.

Consider the eighteen half-lines in isolation, that is, without the knowledge of the alliterative pattern supplied by the *a* verse. The fundamental alliterative principle correctly assigns alliterative stress to fifteen, each of which begins with a word of high alliterative rank (a noun). But three half-lines (741b, 2578b and 2863b) begin with a finite verb. A finite verb acquires high alliterative rank only under certain conditions. Normally this does not happen when it is followed by another word of high alliterative rank.[28] However in the *b* verse, if the stressed syllable of the word of high alliterative rank is necessarily restricted to the second, non-alliterating, metrically stressed position (N), leaving the first, alliterating, metrically stressed position (A) open, promotion of the finite verb to high alliterative rank occurs.[29] Suppose that *un-* is stressed in the three half-lines. The adverbs *unwearnum* and *unswīðor* become words of high alliterative rank by virtue of the stress on the initial element.[30] The nominal *unlēofe* has high alliterative rank by definition whether or not the prefix is stressed. The initial stressed syllable of a trisyllabic compound is not restricted to the second (N) position. It can alliterate. So, for example, 741b could be scanned:

$$\overset{\times \ \text{A} \ \ \text{N} \ \ \times}{\text{*slāt unwearnum.}} \qquad (\overset{\times \ \prime \ \backslash \ \times}{- \ -}; \text{ type C})$$

---

[28] A verb which has been displaced from the first dip of the verse clause is assimilated to the stressed elements of the clause and does have high alliterative rank. The verbs in 741b, 2578b and 2863b have not been displaced. See Bliss, *Metre*, §16.

[29] Proof of the statements made in this paragraph must await another occasion.

[30] See above, n. 17.

Compare 640b:

$$\text{x x A N x}$$
ēode goldhroden.　　($^{\text{x x}}$ $\underline{}$ $\smile$ ^{x} ; type C)

In neither case can the finite verb be promoted and alliteration of the first element of the compound is required. On the other hand, if *un-* is not stressed, the base element of the compound must occupy the second (N) position, because the metrical contour represented by type A3 is not permitted in the *b* verse. Now the necessary condition for the promotion of a finite verb to high alliterative rank has been met and alliteration on the initial consonant of the verb is required by the fundamental alliterative principle. Since we know from the corresponding *a* verses that the three verbs do alliterate, it follows that the prefix is unstressed in all three cases:[31]

$$\text{A x N x}$$
slāt unwearnum　　(type A1)

$$\text{A x N x}$$
bāt unswīðor　　(type A1)

$$\text{A x x N x}$$
seah on unlēofe　　(type A2)

Pope scans *milts ungyfeð*e (2921b) as type D^1 (his D5) with resolution of the secondary stress. That would be the only instance of such resolution in type D^1 in *Beowulf*.[32] Bliss is surely right to prefer reading the verse with the unstressed prefix:[33]

$$\text{′ x ′x x}$$
milts ungȳfeðe.　　(type A1)

Four half-lines contain some variant of the adverb *ungemete*. All have the form *wyrd ungemete nēah* (2420b). Pope's scansion,

$$\text{′ x x ′x x}$$
wyrd ungemĕte nēah,　　(type A2; his A47)

may with some hesitation be accepted. It applies equally to 1792b, 2721b and 2728b.[34]

Pope and Bliss agree that the ten verses like *gumum undyrne* (127b; similarly 120b, 727b, 885b, 2068b, 2120b, 2413b, 2821b, 2881b and 3148b) should be scanned as type D^1s. Their scansions assume stress on *un-*. But, as we have seen,[35] the *a*-verse half-lines corresponding to these are type A1, with the

---

[31] Bliss, *Metre*, §44, arrives at the same scansion of 2863b on different grounds. See also E. G. Stanley, 'Verbal Stress in Old English Verse', *Anglia* 93 (1975), 307–34, esp. 309–10. Bliss stresses the *un-* in 741b and 2578b. Pope, *Rhythm*, stresses the *un-* in all three cases.

[32] In fact, Pope expresses a strong reservation about this scansion: 'the stressing of *un-* [in 2921b] may be questioned, because there is evidence on both sides. To read this verse as type A would therefore be legitimate, and the rhythm would be smoother' (*Rhythm*, p. 77).　　[33] *Metre*, §61.

[34] The alternative, type $D2^2$ with a three-syllable drop, is 'barely possible', according to Pope, *Rhythm*, p. 331. Bliss, *Metre* §86, objects that '*ungemete(s)*, though unusually long, is an adverb of degree, and must be proclitic on the adjective it qualifies'. He relegates the four half-lines to the group of unclassifiable 'remainders'. Although Bliss's objection is weighty, Pope's scansion has the merit of keeping the verses, whose authenticity is vouched for by the repetition of the pattern, within the compass of the normal metrical contours.　　[35] See above, p. 46.

prefix unstressed. I argue that this group of *b*-verse half-lines must have the weakly stressed form of *un-* as well.

If the prefix were stressed, 127b would exhibit an initially stressed two-element compound in the second (N) position of the *b* verse. That the *Beowulf* poet normally avoided such a placement when the second element of the compound was fully significant[36] can hardly be doubted. The generalization holds strictly true for type A. In the *a* verse I count 122 occurrences of type A with compounds in the second position, all with double alliteration, e.g.:

> wyrm ofer weallclif   (3132a; type A2)
> swancor ond sadolbeorht.   (2175a; type A2)

There is none in the *b* verse. With respect to type D the situation is less clear-cut. Here too compounds are common in the *a* verse: 247 by my count, all with double alliteration, e.g.:

> scearp scyldwiga   (288a; type D^1)
> lāc ond luftācen.   (1863a; type D^{*1})

However the restriction against their use in the *b* verse appears to have been slightly relaxed. Leaving to one side the ten half-lines with *un-* under discussion, I find a possible maximum of twenty-one *b* verses with an initially stressed compound in the second (N) position. Let us group these according to the nature of the compound (all are type D^1 unless otherwise indicated):

> *Full compound*
>
> Samod ǣr-dæge   (1311b and 2942b)
> Fæder al-walda   (316b)
> swȳn eal-gylden   (1111b)
> þēod eal-gearo   (1230b)
> Beorh eall-gearo   (2241b)
> segn eall-gylden   (2767b)
> hroden ealo-wǣge   (495b)
> eafor hēafod-segn   (2152b; type D^2)
> fēond man-cynnes   (164b)
> hider wil-cuman   (394b)

---

[36] When the stress on the second element was weakened as a result of the fusion or near-fusion of the two elements into a single form, the restriction seems to have been relaxed. Thus, not only compound proper nouns but also forms like *ǣghwylc* (621b, 984b and 2887b), *missēra* (153b, 1498b, 1769b and 2620b) and *ōrettu* (2538b) appear in the second (N) position of the *b* verse, as do compounds composed of stem + suffix like *innanweard* (991b and 1976b).

Prefix + stem

æf-:	micel æfþunca	(502b)
and-:	Godes andsaca(n)	(786b and 1682b)
	grim andswaru	(2860b)
	him on andsware	(1840b, with alliteration on *him*; type D*¹)
on-:	firen' ondrysne	(1932b)
	hil*d* onsæge	(2076b)
	gūð onsæge	(2483b)
or-:	smiþes orþancum	(406b)
ūð-:	feorh ūðgenge.	(2123b)

We now have before us every non-alliterating compound (excluding proper names) in the *b* verse in *Beowulf* of which it might be claimed that the first element is stressed and the second is fully significant.³⁷ Both lists could be reduced. Line 2152b is troublesome on other grounds and some editors prefer to read it as a triple compound,³⁸ *eaforhēafodsegn*. Bliss argues that the compounds in 1111b, 1230b, 2241b and 2767b should be divided and the verses scanned as type A,³⁹ e.g.:

$$\text{swȳn eal gylden.} \qquad (1111\text{b})$$

Line 1840b violates the fundamental alliterative principle. The expected scansion of the half-line is exhibited by *Elene* 642:

> Élene maðelade   him on óndsware.   (ASPR 2, 83)

There is almost certainly some disturbance in the received text here.

Some of the remaining half-lines in both lists can probably be set aside on the grounds that the stress on the second element of the compound has been reduced. This is Bliss's solution to the problem. He gives several conditions for stress reduction – among them fusion of the elements of the compound, the obsolescence of one of the elements and the presence of a prefix with full stress.⁴⁰ So he scans the compounds *al-walda* (316b), *wil-cuman* (394b) and *ár-dǽge* (1311b and 2942b) in the half-lines in the first list, as well as all the compounds in the half-lines in the second list, with reduced stress on the second element.⁴¹

---

37 With the addition of *brūnfāgne helm* (2615a), we have every non-alliterating compound in *Beowulf* in either half-line. Line 2615a violates the fundamental alliterative principle, according to which *brūn-*, not *helm*, should alliterate; it is clearly anomalous. Max Reiger proposed reading *byrnan bringde* (2615b), which solves the problem very neatly ('Die alt- und angelsächsische Verskunst', *Zeitschrift für deutsche Philologie* 7 (1876), 21).

38 E.g. Dobbie (ASPR 4, 66); cf. Bliss, *Metre*, §63.   39 *Metre*, §§61, 62, 77, 78.   40 *Ibid.* §32.

41 *Ibid.* index to the scansion. Evidence of phonological weakening would strengthen Bliss's case, which apparently rests entirely on metrical criteria. Some evidence can be found. For example, phonological weakening accompanies the stressed prefix *æf-*: *æf-ēst* > *afst*. On the other hand, I think it possible that the true explanation of certain forms in these lists may prove to be that the second element is more heavily stressed than the first.

The number of exceptions (not counting the ten verses with the prefix *un-*) to the generalization that fully stressed, two-element compounds are excluded from the second position of the *b* verse can reasonably be put at nearer two – *fēond mancynnes* (164b) and *hroden ealowǣge* (495b) – than twenty-one. Granted the exceptions, the accumulated evidence makes it possible not only to extend proposition (2)[42] to the *b* verse but also to broaden it to apply to all relevant metrical types. Certainly the *Beowulf* poet avoided placing compounds in the second position in the *b* verse – a placement which freely occurs in the *a* verse, always with double alliteration. The reason is apparent. His metrical grammar marked all fully stressed compounds for alliteration. It also required initial nominals to alliterate. The combination in the *b* verse of nominal plus fully stressed compound brings the two requirements into conflict. As for the ten verses in question. I think there can be little doubt that the *Beowulf* poet would have utilized the unstressed form of *un-* to avoid a metrical solecism:

$$\acute{\times} \times \times \acute{\times} \times$$

gŭmum undyrne.   (127b; type A1. Similarly 120b, 727b, 885b, 2068b, 2120b, 2413b, 2821b, 2881b and 3148b)

This being so, proposition (1)[43] can also be extended to the *b* verse.[44]

Far from being a rarity, it is clear, if my arguments are sound, that the unstressed prefix *un-* was a common feature of the *Beowulf* poet's metrical grammar. As many as twenty-three of the seventy occurrences of the prefix, or more than 30 per cent, were unstressed.[45]

That most of the unstressed forms appear in the *b* verse ought not to cause surprise. It is one reason why this phenomenon has gone unnoticed. Without alliteration to guide us, the unstressed form is nearly invisible. Even in the *a* verse it may be overlooked. So, to take an example from outside *Beowulf*, D. G. Scragg assumes that the stressed prefix occurs in *Andreas* 1371:[46]

unfyrn faca   feorh ætþringan.   (ASPR 2, 41)

[42] See above, p. 46.

[43] *Ibid.*

[44] Bliss, *Metre*, §32, gives the prefix *un-* as an example of a stressed prefix which causes stress reduction in the following stem. Thus he would exclude all verses with *un-* from the category of fully stressed, two-element compounds. There seem to me to be two objections to his solution. (1) The prefix *un-*, unlike some of those that occur in the list of verses above, p. 50, has been an active and productive feature of the language in every period. One would expect to find abundant evidence of phonological weakening. So far as I know, there is none. (2) Two unrelated explanations are required to account for the evidence of the text – stress reduction and the alternation of stressed and unstressed *un-*. But alternation alone suffices to account systematically for the distribution of the forms when the alliterative patterns are taken into account.

[45] To recapitulate, I have argued for five instances of the unstressed form in the *a* verse out of thirty-four: 498a, 833a, 1756a, 2000a and 3012a; and for eighteen out of thirty-six in the *b* verse 120b, 127b, 727b, 741b, 885b, 1792b, 2068b, 2120b, 2413b, 2420b, 2578b, 2721b, 2728b, 2821b, 2863b, 2881b, 2921b and 3148b.

[46] 'Accent Marks in the Vercelli Book', *NM* 72 (1971), 703.

This would constitute a violation of the fundamental alliterative principle. Instead, the *a* verse must be scanned:

$$\overset{\times}{\text{un}}\overset{\prime}{\text{fyrn}} \; \overset{\prime}{\text{fa}}\overset{\times}{\text{ca.}} \quad \text{(type C)}$$

The stressed form readily fits both strong metrical positions in the *a* verse and the first strong metrical position in the *b* verse. (This is precisely the distribution of all other fully stressed compounds.) The preference for the stressed form in these positions may reflect contemporary spoken usage, though it is difficult to be certain of this. Only in the second position in the *b* verse would it be necessary to employ the unstressed form to meet the demands of the metrical grammar. The statistics generated by the arguments I have put forward are perfectly consistent with this conclusion. Forms with *un-* are evenly distributed between the *a* verse and the *b* verse. Only five unstressed forms appear in the *a* verse (twice in the first position; three times in the second). In the *b* verse the forms are evenly distributed between the first and second positions. They are always stressed in the former (eighteen times); always weak in the latter (eighteen times).

Propositions (1) and (2) as generalized can now be restated as rules of the metrical grammar of the *Beowulf* poet, which apply to both halves of the line:

(1) The stressed prefix *un-* alliterates. If the prefix does not alliterate, it is not stressed.

(2) An initially stressed compound in which the second element is semantically significant is marked for alliteration. That is to say, the first element of every such compound normally alliterates in *Beowulf*.

It follows from (2) and from the fundamental alliterative principle that any *a* verse which contains such a compound in second position (that is, following a metrically stressed word) displays double alliteration. It also follows that these compounds are normally excluded from the second position in the *b* verse. These rules affect the scansion of a number of lines in the poem. More importantly, they suggest that there is a greater degree of regularity in the distribution of single and double alliteration in the *a* verse than is usually realized.[47] This too is a function of the metrical grammar of the *Beowulf* poet.[48]

---

[47] Bliss, *Metre*, §§33 and 61–5, implicitly arrives at a similar conclusion by somewhat different means.

[48] I am most grateful to Professor Pope for a meticulous critique of a first version of this article. I am grateful also to Professor Greenfield for helpful comments.

Hrothgar's 'sermon' in *Beowulf* as parental wisdom

ELAINE TUTTLE HANSEN

Until fairly recently modern commentators seem to have agreed that the gnomic sayings in *Beowulf* carry us away from the main current of the poem into the 'doldrums of didacticism'.[1] Now, however, at least two critics have suggested that these apparently trite old saws are in fact central to the epic and that they reflect a way of thinking about the aims and methods of literary composition that we no longer share. Instead of merely cataloguing their appearances, as earlier readers had done, Robert B. Burlin has persuasively shown us how the *Beowulf* poet uses at least some of the gnomic sayings effectively and skilfully to 'give both shape and scope to his utterance... relating the actuality of his fiction to familiar universals in the appreciation of which his audience can easily concur'.[2] Burlin himself does not set out to question the prevailing assumption that the gnomic sayings are 'not in the same artistic league with the obliquity of the "digressions"',[3] but T. A. Shippey has gone on to point out that 'they have power and beauty in their own right'. He also argues that the *Beowulf* poet was not especially original in his use of the gnomic sayings but in fact depended on their traditional function: 'the poet was rightly but only exploiting... qualities incomprehensible to those who see them as linguistic phenomena devoid of social content'.[4] Building on his own earlier work and on Burlin's analysis, Shippey suggests that the maxims in *Beowulf* reflect cultural ideals and that 'they bind the characters, the poet, and the audience together in common assumptions too precious to be threatened, establishing what Professor Burlin calls "societal interdependence", a theme very close to the heart of the poem'.[5]

Speaking generally of gnomic sayings in a narrative context, Shippey further notes: 'Indeed, if the poems help us to understand the maxims, the

---

[1] The phrase is W. W. Lawrence's in 'The Song of Deor', *MP* 9 (1911–12), 23.

[2] Robert B. Burlin, 'Gnomic Indirection in *Beowulf*', *Anglo-Saxon Poetry: Essays in Appreciation for John C. McGalliard*, ed. Lewis E. Nicholson and Dolores Warwick Frese (Notre Dame, 1975), p. 42.

[3] *Ibid.* pp. 41–2.

[4] T. A. Shippey, 'Maxims in Old English Narrative: Literary Art or Traditional Wisdom?', *Oral Tradition Literary Tradition*, ed. Hans Bekker-Nielsen *et al.* (Odense, 1977), p. 31.

[5] *Ibid.* p. 42.

maxims also give us clues about some of the most difficult features of the poems.'[6] In this essay I offer support for his claim by suggesting how a new appreciation of the nature and function of the gnomic sayings in *Beowulf*, especially as it emphasizes their conventional character and their reflection of the social function of certain types of literature, can lead us to a better understanding of a crux in the epic: Hrothgar's 'sermon', 1700–84. Hrothgar's 'sermon' and the gnomic sayings, two apparently distinct problems, trouble modern readers for the same reason: both are more or less alien to contemporary preferences in poetry because of their didactic nature, the blatant sententiousness with which they interrupt the narrative action of the poem and tell us what to make of it. But we are learning to be wary of basing our critical appraisal of Old English poetry solely on modern preferences; in Shippey's words, 'simply denouncing proverbs as over-general, superficial, clichéd, innately inadequate, is at worst patronising and at best anachronistic'.[7] Similarly, Betty S. Cox, in her discussion of Hrothgar's 'sermon', has reminded us 'that they [the king's words] are moralistic... unpalatable to modern taste; but what is unpalatable to modern taste should not be confused with what is unfitting to the poem'.[8]

Both the 'sermon' and the gnomic voice throughout *Beowulf* have seemed to us 'unpalatable' and 'unfitting', I suggest, because they do reflect and depend on the conventions of wisdom literature, a now unfamiliar and unpopular type of literary activity whose dimensions and importance modern readers are only beginning to explore.[9] Our understanding of both these 'difficult features' of the poem can and should be grounded in a recognition of their conventional character, and, with our emerging appreciation of the tradition of wisdom in Old English poetry, we are able to clarify the function and significance of Hrothgar's 'sermon': Hrothgar's longest speech is, I will argue, primarily intended to be read as a parental instruction or wise father's advice poem. The 'sermon' is anything but an interpolation; Hrothgar is specifically characterized as the wise father of Beowulf, his speech is carefully

---

[6] *Ibid.* p. 30.   [7] *Ibid.* pp. 45–6.

[8] Betty S. Cox, *Cruces of Beowulf* (The Hague, 1971), p. 143.

[9] For the original suggestion that the term 'wisdom literature' should be used to describe a number of didactic and 'minor' Old English poems, see Morton Bloomfield, 'Understanding Old English Poetry', *Annuale Mediaevale* 9 (1968), 5–25. T. A. Shippey first uses the term 'wisdom literature' in ch. 3 of his *Old English Verse* (London, 1972), pp. 53–79, and further explores the topic in *Poems of Wisdom and Learning in Old English* (Cambridge and Totowa, 1976). Other recent articles concerned with the social function of poetry in the Anglo-Saxon period, with or without specific discussion of the concept of wisdom literature, include Robert P. Creed, 'Widsith's Journey through Germanic Tradition', *Anglo-Saxon Poetry*, ed. Nicholson and Frese, pp. 376–87; Stanley B. Greenfield and Richard Evert, '*Maxims II*: Gnome and Poem', *ibid.* pp. 337–54; Loren C. Gruber, 'The Agnostic Anglo-Saxon Gnomes: *Maxims I* and II, *Germania*, and the Boundaries of Northern Wisdom', *Poetica* 6 (1976), 22–47; Neil D. Isaacs 'Up a Tree: to See *The Fates of Men*', *Anglo-Saxon Poetry*, ed. Nicholson and Frese, pp. 363–75; Jeff Opland, '"Scop" and "Imbongi" – Anglo-Saxon and Bantu Oral Poets', *Eng. Stud. in Africa* 14 (1971), 161–78; and Lynn L. Remly, 'The Anglo-Saxon Gnomes as Sacred Poetry', *Folklore* 82 (1971), 147–58.

structured on themes and techniques commonly used by wise speakers in Old English poems and what he says plays an integral part in the dramatic structure of *Beowulf*. Before I illustrate and defend this reading of the 'sermon', however, it may be useful to review the ways in which the gnomic sayings, summoning up as they do the traditional concerns and techniques of wisdom upon which Hrothgar's speech also depends, are used in the epic as a whole.

It has long been recognized that many of the two dozen or so gnomic sayings in *Beowulf* come from a traditional Old English gnome-hoard with numerous analogues in Old English, Old Norse, Old Welsh and Old Irish,[10] and all of the gnomic passages are readily identifiable by those formal and thematic characteristics which, in accord with what we know from other extant works, conventionally signal the gnomic mode. Formally the sayings in *Beowulf* depend on a conventional gnomic vocabulary and syntax: the specialized use of the verb forms *sceal*, *biþ* and *mæg*, organizing experience into what is and what ought to be; the adjectives *gedefe* and *gemet*, designating what is proper or fitting, and the comparative *selre* and the superlative *selast*, pointing out what is better and best; adverbs of generalization and frequency, such as *a*, *oft*, *oftost* and *hwær*; and the *se þe* or *se þæm* construction, used to invoke the unspecified and representative individual. Thematically the gnomic sayings in *Beowulf* share proverbial and sententious concerns found repeatedly in gnomic matter in Old English and elsewhere, including the celebration of heroic virtues such as generosity, courage and loyalty; the condemnation of cowardice, indiscretion and treachery; and the acknowledgement of the power of God or fate, on the one hand, and of the limits of human knowledge on the other. Underlying the gnomic world view in *Beowulf*, as in all wisdom literatures, is a bipolar view of the moral universe: experience offers us *wel* and *wa* (183b–8),[11] *leof* and *laþ* (1061a), *god oþþe yfel* (*Precepts* 45b); consequently the ability to distinguish wisely in words and to act on the perception of differences is imperative.

The number, range and structural and thematic importance of the gnomic sayings in *Beowulf* suggest that aphoristic didacticism is embraced by the epic for a serious and pervasive purpose: the speaker's extensive and emphatic display of his gnomic repertoire – akin, as we shall see, to Hrothgar's display of his parental wisdom in the 'sermon' – affords him an authoritative, generalizing (and inherently pessimistic) voice with which to establish the epic's prevailing attitude towards the nature and meaning of the human

---

[10] My discussion of gnomic poetry in general is indebted to P. L. Henry's work in ch. 5, 'The Gnomic Manner and Matter of Old English, Irish, Icelandic, and Welsh', of his *The Early English and Celtic Lyric* (London, 1966), pp. 91–132.

[11] All quotations from *Beowulf* are from *Beowulf and the Fight at Finnsburg*, ed. Fr. Klaeber, 3rd ed. (Boston, 1950). All other Old English quotations are from The Anglo-Saxon Poetic Records, ed. George Philip Krapp and Elliott Van Kirk Dobbie (New York, 1931–42).

experience it narrates. If we consider one group of gnomic passages on a conventional topic, fame (*lof, dom*) and how to get it (or lose it), we can specifically and clearly see how the gnomic formulations in *Beowulf* typically function both as integral parts of their immediate contexts and as generalized and unifying commentary, unmistakably distinguished by formal differences from the rest of the discourse and together used to underline and develop the major themes and attitudes which the poet intends his narrative structure to support. The first and perhaps best known of these passages, only twenty lines into the poem, interrupts the eulogy of Scyld Scefing and his son to call our attention to what is characteristic and fitting in their behaviour:

> Swa sceal (geong g)uma   gode gewyrcean,
> fromum feohgiftum   on fæder (bea)rme,
> þæt hine on ylde   eft gewunigen
> wilgesiþas,   þonne wig cume
> leode gelæsten;   lofdædum sceal
> in mægþa gehwære   man geþeon.[12]   (20–5)

The heroic virtues of generosity and the performance of deeds deserving praise are of course celebrated elsewhere in Old English gnomic verse; the appearance of these familiar gnomic generalizations at the onset of *Beowulf* immediately signals the prevailing heroic and aristocratic ethos of the epic. The gnomic passage, moreover, ironically relates the initial focus on two Danish heroes to the central narrative to follow. Beowulf, like Scyld Scefing and his son, will live up to these explicitly stated standards of kingly generosity and praiseworthiness. But in the second half of the epic he will rightly expect, and then tragically fail to receive, the reciprocal loyalty and support of his companions, when adversity comes to him in old age. In one sense Beowulf's final lot belies the neat alignment of good deeds and just deserts predicted in lines 24–5; however, the survival of the reputation his *lofdæda* have won in the memories of those who mourn him (and in the fact of the epic itself) suggests that we consider extended senses of the verb *geþeon*. For Beowulf, as for other heroes of Old English literature, 'to prosper' is not merely to achieve limited earthly success but more importantly to do those 'praiseworthy deeds' with which he simultaneously accepts and defies death.[13]

---

[12] 'Thus should the young warrior do good, with splendid dispensing of treasure, while under his father's care, so that in his old age dear companions will still stand beside him, his people support their chief; with praiseworthy deeds, in all races, a man shall [should] prosper.' Cf. *Maxims II* 14–15: 'Geongne æþeling sceolan gode gesiðas / byldan to beaduwe and to beahgife.' *Maxims I* puts it more succinctly: 'gold mon sceal gifan' (155a); 'Dom biþ selast' (80b). See also *Widsith* 11–13.

[13] Another possible interpretation of this ironic reversal of heroic expectation and justice is suggested by Robert W. Hanning's brief discussion of the rôle of time and perspective in early medieval narratives in *The Individual in Twelfth-Century Romance* (New Haven and London, 1977), pp. 140 ff.

In the second gnomic passage on fame Beowulf is the speaker, as he prefaces his vow to track down and kill Grendel's mother with this gnomic consolation for the grieving Hrothgar:

> Selre bið æghwæm,
> þæt he his freond wrece, þonne he fela murne.
> Ure æghwylc sceal ende gebidan
> worolde lifes; wyrce se þe mote
> domes ær deaþe; þæt bið drihtguman
> unlifgendum æfter selest.[14] (1384b–9)

The hero's words remind us not only that he embodies what is the 'better' and 'best' course of action for all brave men to choose, in the light of human mortality, but also that Beowulf himself is not simply a symbol of youthful *fortitudo* in contrast to Hrothgar's *sapientia*. Even in his youth Beowulf understands and can authoritatively articulate the heroic principles that motivate his actions throughout the poem. And less than two hundred lines after Beowulf's own gnomic observation on the need to win *dom* before death the narrator comments on the struggle between the hero and Grendel's mother with this gnomically formulated praise of Beowulf's decision to trust to the strength of his bare hands when his sword fails:

> Swa sceal man don,
> þonne he æt guðe gegan þenceð
> longsumne lof; na ymb his lif cearað.[15] (1534b–6)

The transitional *swa sceal* formula here serves precisely the same function as it does in line 20: it moves the speaker from the immediate action or narrative

Hanning argues that 'The *Beowulf* poet is attempting in his epic to recapture the virtues of the heroic age while putting it in perspective as a time when men were ignorant of God's purposes' (p. 143). He illustrates this argument with a discussion of the poet's 'digressions' when Beowulf is given the necklace (1192–1214a). Similarly, we might say that through his use of a plot whose outcome denies in some senses the validity of the gnomic commentary, the *Beowulf* poet attempts to give us a 'double perspective' on the heroic values of *lof* and *dom*. From the limited point of view of Beowulf and his age the hero's behaviour is exemplary, admirable and right, while in the poet's age the inevitability of betrayal and death suggests the need for a higher perspective on human existence. This deployment of the gnomic commentary with respect to the plot would further illustrate, then, Hanning's theory of 'the inevitable...disjunction between the characters' involvement in time and our own, larger involvement' (p. 144). A similar argument for the poet's double perspective on the heroic past is offered by Patrick Wormald, 'Bede, *Beowulf* and the Conversion of the Anglo-Saxon Aristocracy', *Bede and Anglo-Saxon England*, ed. Robert T. Farrell, BAR 46 (1978), 32–90. In Wormald's words (p. 67). 'As a member of the warrior-classes himself, the poet must have admired – perhaps he even imitated – the virtues in which his work glorifies. As a Christian, he knew, and perhaps he lamented, that heroic virtues are not enough.'

[14] 'It is better for each man that he avenge his friend, rather than mourn him greatly. Each of us must live to see the end of worldly life; let him who may endeavour to win glory before death; that is to dead warriors afterwards the best.' Cf. *Precepts* 7 and 47. *Widsith* 142, *The Seafarer* 72 ff., *The Battle of Maldon* 258–9 and *Hávamál*, stanzas 77–8.

[15] 'Thus should a man do, when he expects to obtain longlasting praise at battle; not be anxious about his life.'

to a generalized observation and again enables the poet to point out the rightness and propriety of this exemplary behaviour and to suggest that it is a mode of conduct that all who seek *lof* should adopt. The delay in the action here may serve one or two narrative purposes: for one thing it may heighten our suspense; we are waiting to learn how Beowulf wins despite the odds against him and the poet may mean to tantalize his audience by pausing for a moralizing reflection before proceeding to the victorious climax of this fight. While we wait, moreover, we have time to catch our breath and regain perspective on the scene, to interpret the superhuman struggle not only as an exciting and suspenseful episode, needed to keep us interested in the hero's adventures, but also as an exemplary heroic feat, needed to round out the picture of any hero's life, and as an archetype of the kind of conduct that in this society wins *lof* and *dom*.

The final gnomic words on the subject of fame, near the end of the poem, are appropriately enough spoken by Wiglaf, the only surviving hero of the story. Wiglaf has been rebuking the disloyal and cowardly companions who deserted their lord in his last struggle, and, in keeping with the mood of the second half of *Beowulf*, the heroic ideal is inversely reflected in his parting proverbial shot at the deserters: 'Deað bið sella / eorla gehwylcum þonne edwitlif' (2890b–1).[16] Wiglaf's probably familiar, even commonplace, words poignantly and emphatically recall the positive standards of conduct celebrated in gnomic sayings and enacted in narrative events in the first half of the poem, and the crime of the deserters is ironically heightened when set against those standards in that very type of utterance previously used to underline the unfailing rightness and blamelessness of Beowulf's acts. Wiglaf's saying also reminds us of the meaning of Beowulf's death in the light of the wisdom and understanding which have been defined by the gnomic voice throughout: the hero's fall embodies the fitting choice of *lof* and *dom* over the base and futile instinct of self-preservation, his consistent though doomed willingness both to perceive and to choose the 'better' path.

These four gnomic passages on fame epitomize the way in which the gnomic matter of Anglo-Saxon wisdom, the expression of traditional beliefs in a conventional style, is used throughout the epic. On each gnomic occasion a speaker, always a figure of cultural authority – most frequently the narrator, but sometimes the hero or a minor heroic character – shares his wisdom with his listeners by uttering a formally and thematically conventional summary of what is characteristic, fitting or right (or wrong) about the specific incident or subject under discussion. In each case the gnomic observation explicitly

---

[16] 'Death is better for each warrior than a life of disgrace.' Cf. the Irish proverb *Ferr bás bithanim*, 'Death is better than a blemish', cited by Roland Smith, '*The Senbriathra Fithail* and Related Texts', *Revue Celtique* 45 (1915), 27.

elevates the individual incident to the representative or universal concept of fittingness or inevitability that it embodies and asks us to measure the immediate experience against the ideal.[17] This tendency to abstract general truth from individual experience, to align and judge observed phenomena according to a schematic system, is a given of the gnomic voice. The poet thus chooses the gnomic saying as an apt and efficient way of encoding the significance of his narrative for an audience accustomed to and presumably interested in hearing wise men pass on commonly accepted truths in a spare, pithy and (to us at least) cryptic form. The gnomic sayings are never digressive or inconsequential platitudes; they are essential signposts intended to direct us towards the ethical framework according to which Beowulf's actions have meaning and worth.

Without necessarily arguing with Professors Burlin and Shippey, who suggest that the gnomic sayings 'comfortably evoke the ideal norms of their society and their world',[18] I also suggest that it is not necessary to assume that the poet and his audience shared all of those values that are upheld throughout the poem in the gnomic sayings; perhaps they did, and the gnomic sayings then might be said to establish the moral nexus between story and audience, between heroic legend and contemporaneous Anglo-Saxon Christians. Or perhaps they did not; perhaps the audience simply recognized that the poet was using the well-known sayings of the dying or dead heroic world, sometimes Christianized, in order to evoke that world most fully and appropriately, to set his retrospective epic in its proper ethical and stylistic frame. In either case (and the 'right' answer probably lies somewhere between these alternatives), it is necessary to assume that audience and poet alike understood and still respected the power of the gnome.[19] At one point in the search for meaning and order in human experience and natural phenomena the gnomic saying was conventionally and widely used to record and pass on certain accumulated and accepted perceptions about the truths

---

[17] As Hanning notes (*The Individual*, p. 143), 'The nature of oral culture is such that all deeds can only be evaluated by comparing them with the legacy of stories about past deeds. Thus the measure of tribal reality in such a culture is not the individual but the body of tradition into which the individual and his deeds must be fitted.'

[18] Burlin, 'Gnomic Indirection', p. 42.

[19] Again, for a discussion of the historical relationship between the *Beowulf* poet and the heroic past of which he writes, see Wormald, 'Bede, *Beowulf* and the Conversion'. Wormald argues that the ambivalent attitude of the poet towards pagan heroes (see above, n. 13) reflects the domination of aristocratic values in the English church and he concludes (p. 67) that 'the baffling discrepancy in the poem between pagan practice and Christian sentiment is decisive evidence that, although the Anglo-Saxon aristocracy was willing to accept a new God, it was *not* prepared to jettison the memory or the example of those who had worshipped the old...Literature like Beowulf was important to Anglo-Saxon noblemen not because these Scandinavian tales described any part of their real past (so far as we know) but because they encapsulated, and indeed identified, the social and cultural values of the class.'

of life as they were then understood. If we are aware of this ancient and serious function of gnome and precept, we may begin to understand how a poet writing in the Old English period about an earlier native culture might have used gnomic sayings and how they might have worked. We may begin to perceive that gnomic sayings can fittingly and naturally come out of the mouths of the narrator, the hero and the sage as the narrative unfolds, while at the same time they may clearly stand out, in their elegantly terse and traditional form, to reinforce the structural and thematic unity of the epic with recurrent and appropriately varied soundings of its central ethical concerns.

The relationship between Hrothgar's 'sermon' and the gnomic sayings has already been suggested by at least one critic, Betty S. Cox, when she argues that the 'sermon' is not an interpolation: its sententiousness, she notes, is obviously not alien to the poet who uses the numerous gnomic passages we find throughout the poem. To the question 'If the passage, though, is not unduly sententious, nor unduly long, and not a reflection upon Beowulf, what is it?'[20] she provides a number of interesting answers and concludes: 'I believe that the most important function of the entire 84 lines – over contrast, didacticism, a natural outgrowth of patristic and biblical instruction – is its place as an expected speech by a king in his court on an occasion honoring a distinguished warrior.'[21]

To these arguments I would add that if we look around at the wider tradition to which the gnomic mode itself belongs, the tradition of wisdom literature, we discover the existence of another now unfamiliar literary mode, the parental instruction, which seems to explain something more about Hrothgar's 'sermon'. In ancient Near Eastern traditions, for instance, we note that most Egyptian instructional wisdom literature was set in the father–son framework, and, moreover, on many occasions the father was a king or high counsellor addressing a prince who would some day rule. The convention of parental wisdom, thought perhaps to reflect the origins of wisdom literature in family and clan wisdom, survives in the opening 'My son' address of many Old Testament proverbs. Nearer to home Old Irish instructional literature includes a number of *tecosca* or 'instructions to princes', collections of gnomic sayings and instructions given by kings or foster-fathers to their sons and heirs or by tutors to their noble pupils.[22] And in Old English itself we have one extant indication that the parental

---

[20] Cox, *Cruces*, p. 143.

[21] *Ibid.* pp. 151–2.

[22] See Roland M. Smith, '*The Speculum Principum* in Early Irish Literature', *Speculum* 2 (1927), 411–45, and my discussion of this genre, '*Precepts*, an Old English Instruction', *Speculum* 56 (1981), 1–16.

instruction was known to Anglo-Saxon poets: the short poem *Precepts*, in the Exeter Book, records ten instructional occasions on which a wise father passed on proverbial advice to a beloved son. Unlike the Irish texts *Precepts* is more than a string of formally related sayings or a set of questions and answers; the Old English father combines gnomic sayings with homiletic advice and personal reflections. The more list-like quality of the Irish prose works is evoked, perhaps, in the precise numbering of the occasions in *Precepts*, each of which (from the second on) is introduced by the formula *on þa* ×-*an syþan*.

When we turn back to *Beowulf* itself we find telling internal evidence that the *Beowulf* poet meant Hrothgar's 'sermon' to be recognized as the conventional admonitory address of a wise king and father to a young prince, a 'set piece' of wisdom literature. In the first place we note that Hrothgar the king is characterized both inside and outside his speech as an archetypal wise man. The familiar terms *snottor, frod* and *wis* (also used to describe other Old English wise men and their teachings, as in *Precepts*, *Vainglory* and *The Wanderer*) are repeatedly applied to the Danish king.[23] Moreover, three times during his 'sermon' Hrothgar mentions his wide experience, his age and his memory – those qualities upon which the wise man traditionally depends for his authority (see also 1057b–62); in 1700–3a he bases his judgement of Beowulf as the 'better' man on his own long and just rule and his far-reaching memory; again in 1723b–4a he explicitly relates his rôle as speaker and teacher to the wisdom acquired with age; and at the end of his speech he again summons up the long period of his reign and his experience of 'gyrn æfter gomene' (1775a).

Furthermore, three times before the 'sermon' itself Hrothgar is identified as Beowulf's surrogate father. In 946b–8a, congratulating the hero on his defeat of Grendel, Hrothgar says 'Nu ic, Beowulf, þec, / secg betsta, me for sunu wylle / freogan on ferhþe.' At the feast of celebration which follows, Wealhtheow comments on his new relationship as she speaks to her husband: 'Me man sægde, þæt þu ðe for sunu wolde / hereri[n]c habban' (1175–6a). And yet once more, almost as if to draw our attention to the fact lest we, too, forget, Beowulf reminds Hrothgar, before the young hero sets out to rid the land of Grendel's mother, of his promise to stand 'on fæder stæle' (1479b) to the Geatish prince. This relationship reminds us of the tradition of foster-fathers in aristocratic heroic cultures and it may also explain

---

[23] Hrothgar is called *snotor hæleð* (190b), *snotor guma* (1384a), *snot(t)ra fengel* (1475a and 2156a), and *se snotera* (*snottra*) (1313b and 1786b); he is also referred to as *frod* (279a, 1306b, 1724a and 2114a) and *þone wisan* (*se wisa*) (1318a and 1698b). In *Precepts* the father-speaker is called *modsnottor* (2a), *þoncsnottor* (21b) and *frod* (1a, 15b, 53a and 94a); he speaks *wordum wisfæstum* (3a). The speaker in *Vainglory* tells us that he learned *snottor ar* (2a) from a *frod wita* (1a); the speaker in *The Wanderer* is *snottor on mode* (111a).

something about Hrothgar's intense grief when Beowulf leaves his kingdom, his tears and his 'dyrne langað' (1879b).

The themes and techniques used in Hrothgar's speech also provide us with some persuasive evidence that the conventions of wisdom literature are of influence. As Cox and Klaeber read the 'sermon', it has four major divisions: (*a*) introduction (1700–9a), (*b*) second Heremod episode (1709b–24a), (*c*) homily proper (1724b–68) and (*d*) concluding observations (1769–84).[24] But this analysis of the structure of the speech obscures its unity. The fact that Heremod has already been mentioned in the poem, for instance, is less central to an understanding of the way the 'sermon' works than the observation that the example of Heremod is one of three different types of illustration Hrothgar uses to embody his advice to Beowulf. I would suggest a slightly different view of the structure of the passage which calls attention to the fact that Hrothgar uses each of the three kinds of narrative example or illustration commonly used by wise speakers in Old English poetry – one from legend or 'history', one from hypothetical or fictional material and one from personal experience. The illustrations are held together by transitional passages combining the two kinds of instructional devices found in a less complex parental instruction poem like *Precepts*: admonitory, imperative sentences and longer gnomic observations. I would describe the structure of the speech in this way: (1) introductory link (1700–9a), (2) first illustrative narrative (Heremod) (1709b–22a), (3) first admonitory advice and gnomic observation (1722b–7), (4) second illustration (the arrogant man) (1728–57), (5) second admonitory advice and gnomic observation (1758–68), (6) third illustration (personal experience) (1769–78a) and (7) conclusion (1778b–84).

By my reading the introductory link (1700–9a) reminds the audience that Hrothgar's authority, as I have already suggested, is that of the traditional wise man and king; it is based on his age ('eald eþelweard', 1702a), his long memory ('feor eal gemon', 1701b) and his experience as a wise and just ruler ('se þe soð ond riht / fremeð on folce', 1700b–1a). Secondly these lines link the 'set piece', the father's advice poem, with its narrative occasion and with the events of the narrative as a whole: Hrothgar speaks of the *blæd* Beowulf has won (1703b), praises his conduct as a hero who wears his gifts well ('mægen mid modes snyttrum', 1706a), promises to carry out their vows of friendship and loyalty and prophesies the noble career as a ruler which Beowulf is destined to have 'to frofre... / ...leodum þinum, / hæleðum to helpe' (1707b–9a).

This brief praise of Beowulf leads quickly and directly into Hrothgar's first illustration, by means of antithesis: 'Ne wearð Heremod swa' (1709b). Like

---

[24] Cox, *Cruces*, p. 132.

the speaker in *Deor* Hrothgar alludes to a well-known historical or legendary figure, here the archetypal anti-hero who is used elsewhere in the poem as a foil to Beowulf. In 1709b–22a the Danish king reminds his listeners of Heremod's arrogant and malicious behaviour and his ignominious end. The obvious application of this illustration is made explicit in direct address to the hero, 'Ðu þe lær be þon, / gumcyste ongit' (1722b–3a), and then Hrothgar reminds us of his right and capacity, because of his age and experience, to undertake the instruction of a prince such as Beowulf: 'Ic þis gid be þe / awræc wintrum frod' (1723b–4a). A gnomic observation on the power of God follows:

> Wundor is to secganne,
> hu mihtig God   manna cynne
> þurh sidne sefan   snyttru bryttað,
> eard ond eorlscipe;   he ah ealra geweald.[25]   (1724b–7)

The generalization follows logically from the earlier reference to Heremod as one of the race of men to whom God gave special powers:

> ðeah þe hine mihtig God   mægenes wynnum,
> eafeþum stepte,   ofer ealle men
> forð gefremede.[26]   (1716–18a)

And since Beowulf himself has already been described as a man specially endowed by his creator, the gnomic observation by this implicit logic links the immediate and larger contexts, the anti-hero of Germanic legend and the hero of the epic. The gnomic passage also reflects a familiar perspective on God's munificence to mankind found in other Old English poems, most notably in the catalogue poems, *The Gifts of Men* and *The Fortunes of Men*. In both of the catalogue poems gnomic observations about God's distribution of gifts and fates lead the speakers into *sum* catalogues listing the various skills or fortunes ordained by God for Anglo-Saxon men. In *Beowulf* the wise speaker moves from his gnomic observation to a single illustration, introduced, however, by a 'cataloguing' adverb, *Hwilum* (1728a). Hrothgar's second illustration offers us the story of the hypothetical individual to whom God gives a great deal of earthly power and pleasure, so much in fact that his guard slips and he is overcome, like Heremod, by pride. The use of the unnamed man as an exemplar of arrogance is also found in *Vainglory*, and in both the epic and the shorter poem the speakers associate this unfortunate man with

---

[25] 'It is a wonder to say, how the mighty God through his great spirit distributes wisdom, land and rank to the race of men: he has authority over all.'
[26] 'Although the mighty God had furthered him with the pleasures of power, with strengths above all men.'

the image of the arrow or arrows of the devil.[27] In Hrothgar's version of the familiar story *werga gast* encourages this Heremod-type to become covetous and angry and forgetful of his *forðgesceaft*; he dies and the greedily hoarded treasure he has left behind is recklessly expended by some other foolish man.

Again, at the end of this second illustration, Hrothgar explicitly points out the moral of his story to Beowulf:

> Bebeorh þe ðone bealoni∂,   Beowulf leofa,
> secg betsta,   ond þe þæt selre geceos,
> ece rædas;   oferhyda ne gym,
> mære cempa![28]   (1758–61a)

His traditional admonition to choose *þæt selre* is once more followed by a gnomic observation, here reminding Beowulf of his mortality by means of a catalogue of the possible disasters, one of which will, inevitably, bring about his downfall:

> Nu is þines mægnes blæd
> ane hwile;   eft sona bi∂,
> þæt þec adl oð∂e ecg   eafoþes getwæfe∂,
> oð∂e fyres feng,   oð∂e flodes wylm,
> oð∂e gripe meces,   oð∂e gares fliht,
> oð∂e atol yldo;   oð∂e eagena bearhtm
> forsite∂ ond forsworce∂;   semninga bi∂,
> þæt ∂ec, dryhtguma,   dea∂ oferswy∂e∂.[29]   (1761b–8)

Following the catalogue, Hrothgar moves, for a third and final time, from the generalized observation to the specific illustration, again using the linking *swa* seen elsewhere in the gnomic passages of the poem. As in *The Wanderer*,[30] a speaker's 'personal' experience leads him to better understanding – here

---

27 In *Vainglory* the arrogant man (introduced to us in a *sum* clause, 23b) is metaphorically wounded by evil weapons: 'Bi∂ þæt æfþonca eal gefylled / feondes fligepilum' (26–7a); a little later it is observed that in his ignorance he lets these *inwitflan* of the devil pierce his spiritual armour: 'laete∂ inwitflan / brecan þone burgweal, þe him bebead meotud / þæt he þæt wigsteal wergan sceolde' (37b–9). Hrothgar's example finds him in much the same loathsome predicament: his pride grows until the watch ('sawele hyrde', 1742a) sleeps; then a nearby murderer shoots him with a bow ('of flanbogan', 1744a) and he is struck in his heart 'biteran stræle' (1746a), identified as 'wom wundorbebodum wergan gastes' (1747).

28 'Protect yourself from such wickedness, beloved Beowulf, best warrior, and choose the better, eternal counsel; do not care about pride, splendid hero.'

29 'Now is the renown of your strength for a little while, but soon it will be that sickness or the sword will deprive you of strength, or the grasp of fire or the whelming of the wave or the bite of a weapon or the flight of a spear or terrible old age, or the brightness of your eyes will fail and grow dim; presently it will be, that death, hero, overcomes you.'

30 As Klaeber points out (*Beowulf*, p. 192), the specific use of *swa* by a speaker moving from a generalization to his own experience, as Hrothgar does here, parallels the usage of *swa* in *The Wanderer* 19a.

of man's need to be constantly on guard against inevitable disaster. The old king recalls his long ('hund missera', 1769b) and successful rule, whose apparent success lulled him into believing that he had no enemies. Then came Grendel, 'gyrn æfter gomene' (1775a) – the experience of alternatives which, we recall, the narrator had predicted in his earlier gnomic observation:

> Fela sceal gebidan
> leofes ond laþes, se þe longe her
> on ðyssum windagum worolde bruceð![31]   (1060b–2)

Hrothgar concludes (1778b–84) by bringing us from the sober, philosophical and pessimistic realm of his wisdom back again to the immediate context of the occasion; he thanks God for this opportunity to behold the bloody head of Grendel and he sends Beowulf back to the pleasures of feasting with the promise of more treasure to be shared in the morning.

The preceding analysis reveals both the unity of Hrothgar's 'sermon' and its dependence on techniques familiar in Old English didactic poetry, including the three different types of illustrative examples as well as the imperative admonitions and the gnomic observations which together serve a transitional function and relate the speaker's exemplary material both to a specific listener and to the universal principles it reflects. The content of the king's wise words accords with the themes and sentiments of the poem as a whole as well as with the themes and sentiments of a great deal of Old English wisdom literature, from elegy to catalogue poem to parental instruction. I infer from these correspondences, and from the emphatic establishment of Hrothgar's wisdom, experience and parental relationship to Beowulf, that what we are dealing with here would have been recognized not only as 'an expected speech by a king in his court...honoring a distinguished warrior', but also, more specifically, in the light of that warrior's age and relationship to the speaker, as a parental instruction speech, in the tradition of the wise father's advice poem which we find also in the Old English *Precepts*.

The realization that the speech has been anticipated by the earlier characterization of Hrothgar as a wise man and father should add weight to the argument that his 'sermon' is not an interpolation; moreover, an understanding of the conventions behind the sermon can, I think, alter our understanding of the narrative significance and the dramatic effect of the passage. Once again, the dictates of modern taste seem to have misled us: it has seemed inappropriate to twentieth-century readers that at this point in the action, the climax of Beowulf's heroic success, the old king whose

---

[31] 'Much shall he experience of the beloved and the hateful, he who lives for a long time here in this windy world.'

country the hero has saved spends only a few moments praising the younger warrior and then turns to 'harangue' him, as Klaeber comments,[32] with seventy-five lines of apparently irrelevant advice, ominous and unwarranted comparison and gloomy prediction. In his recent examination of the theme of 'joy in the hall', Jeff Opland has noted the lack of any expression of the conventional signals of celebration at this point in the narrative:

It is somewhat surprising that the theme does not occur in the poet's description of the joy in Heorot after Beowulf's defeat of Grendel's mother. This scene is curiously off-key, containing as it does Hrothgar's sermon to Beowulf; it is an unsettling passage because of the absence of what one has come to expect, and it sets the mood for the rest of the poem.[33]

I indeed agree that Hrothgar's 'sermon' 'sets the mood' for what is to follow in the poem; it certainly seems at first reading like an unaccountably dark moment, but it is not 'off-key' in quite the way that it is usually taken to be. With a sense of the traditional and pervasive nature of the various types and modes of didactic poetry usefully termed 'wisdom literature' and a clearer idea of how Hrothgar's speech, like the gnomic passages, depends on and evokes the audience's interest in this kind of wisdom, we can see that Hrothgar's advice is not only appropriate to the context in which it appears but also essential to the poem as a whole. Gloomy though it may seem to us, the sermon is intended in no way to obscure the glory of Beowulf's astonishing feat but rather to honour the hero with another precious gift, which, like the material treasure he gives, Hrothgar offers as a part of his *hord*, a portion of what he owes this man who has fulfilled a heroic commitment and stands as a son to him. The parental relationship and the tradition underlying it in so many wisdom literatures provide the key here: there is nothing especially harsh or the least bit 'personal' in Hrothgar's remarks; they offer the conventional wisdom, and in an age familiar and comfortable with various types of wisdom literature, including the parental advice poem, they would be taken by the younger man and the audience not as a rebuke or as a trying and badly timed scene with a boring old king but as a part of his due. The solemnity and importance of the occasion – like the power and distinctness of gnomic discourse – is again a given of the conventional format; as the narrator points out (1699b), everyone in the hall was silent when the old king stood to speak. As in the gnomic passages, the *Beowulf* poet's skill is revealed in his use of the traditional matter at the right time and for fitting effect. Here he exploits the inherent pessimism of the wise man's characteristic vision of life, which accords with the inherent pessimism

---

[32] Ed. Klaeber, p. 190.
[33] Jeff Opland, '*Beowulf* on the Poet', *MS* 38 (1977), 448.

of his poem too, to turn the emotional direction of the epic from the transitory moment of glory towards the second half of the action, in which the hero, through no fault of his own, meets defeat and his fated end, 'gyrn æfter gomene'. Hrothgar's parental instruction provides a pivotal scene in which joy is tempered and elevated by the certain knowledge of grief to be endured, and, as in the gnomic passages, an individual experience of life is absorbed into the poem's unifying and traditional conception of its universal application.

Lexical evidence for the authorship
of the prose psalms in
the Paris Psalter

JANET M. BATELY

'Forðy me ðyncð betre, gif iow swæ ðyncð, ðæt we eac sumæ bec, ða ðe niedbeðearfosta sien eallum monnum to wiotonne, ðæt we ða on ðæt geðiode wenden ðe we ealle gecnawan mægen.'[1] With these well-known words, King Alfred, in the prefatory letter to his Old English version of Gregory's *Pastoral Care*, enunciates the policy of translation he wishes to see implemented with a view to restoring wisdom and learning to his war-torn kingdom. In the last twenty years or so modern scholars have made a determined effort to define the contribution the king himself made to his scheme. Traditionally it had been accepted that he translated the *Pastoral Care*, Boethius, *Soliloquies*, Bede and Orosius.[2] But it has now been firmly established that, while the first three works are his, both Bede and Or are to be excluded as the work of others.[3] A sixth candidate, the Old English prose version of the first fifty psalms in the Paris Psalter,[4] has hitherto

---

[1] *King Alfred's West-Saxon Version of Gregory's Pastoral Care*, ed. Henry Sweet, EETS o.s. 45 and 50 (London, 1871–2; repr. 1958), 7, lines 6–8. I refer to this work henceforth as CP. See also *The Pastoral Care, edited from British Library MS. Cotton Otho B. ii*, by Ingvar Carlson, completed by Lars-G. Hallander together with Mattias Löfvenberg and Alarik Rynel, *Stockholm Stud. in Eng.* 34 and 48 (Stockholm, 1975 and 1978).

[2] *King Alfred's Old English Version of Boethius De Consolatione Philosophiae*, ed. Walter John Sedgefield (Oxford, 1899); *King Alfred's Version of St Augustine's Soliloquies*, ed. Thomas A. Carnicelli (Cambridge, Mass., 1969); *The Old English Version of Bede's Ecclesiastical History of the English People*, ed. Thomas Miller, EETS o.s. 95, 96, 110 and 111 (London, 1890–8; repr. 1959 and 1963); *The Old English Orosius*, ed. Janet Bately, EETS s.s. 6 (London, 1980). I refer to these works henceforth as Bo, Solil, Bede and Or respectively.

[3] See Dorothy Whitelock, 'The Old English Bede', *PBA* 48 (1962), 57–90; Elizabeth M. Liggins, 'The Authorship of the Old English *Orosius*', *Anglia* 88 (1970), 289–322; and Janet M. Bately, 'King Alfred and the Old English Translation of Orosius', *ibid.* pp. 433–60. Sherman Kuhn's attempts to rehabilitate Bede ('Synonyms in the Old English Bede', *JEGP* 46 (1947), 168–76, and 'The Authorship of the Old English Bede Revisited', *NM* 73 (1972), 172–80) are unconvincing, resting as they do on an attempt to explain away Mercian features, not on an assessment of the work as a whole, and presupposing direct copying without intermediate dictation. A combination of linguistic and literary/historical evidence on the other hand indicates convincingly that CP, Bo and Solil are substantially the work of one person and that this person was King Alfred; see further, below, pp. 77–95. For selective lexical differences between Bede and the genuine works of Alfred, see further, below, pp. 86–9.

[4] *Liber Psalmorum. The West-Saxon Psalms*, ed. James Wilson Bright and Robert Lee Ramsay (Boston and London, 1907). I cite this work as Ps(P) by psalm and verse; my quotations and figures are based on a partial recollection of the manuscript.

hovered on the brink of acceptance. This psalter, Paris, Bibliothèque Nationale, Fonds Latin 8824, dated mid-eleventh-century,[5] contains parallel Latin and Old English texts of the psalms, with a series of 'introductions' in Latin and, up to ps. L only, Old English.[6] The Old English text consists of a prose paraphrase of pss. I to L and a metrical version of the rest. The Latin text is not the source of either part of the Old English.[7] Although Thorpe's edition of the Paris Psalter made the text of Ps(P) accessible as early as 1835,[8] it was not until 1885 that Wülker attempted to identify this unique prose version with the translation of the psalms which, according to William of Malmesbury, King Alfred was engaged on at the time of his death.[9] Wülker's suggestion was quickly taken up by Wichmann and more recently by Bromwich.[10] However, although recent word studies have revealed general agreement in usage between CP, Bo and Solil on the one hand and Ps(P) on the other,[11] scholarly opinion, not without reason, has remained at best cautious on the subject. The existing case for Alfred's authorship is gravely weakened not only because its two main proponents have based their arguments on similarities between Ps(P) and a canon which included the now disallowed Or and Bede, but also because the likenesses which they produced are, as the Sisams have pointed out, 'not all striking; very few are shared by the Prose Psalms with more than one of Alfred's works; and dissimilarities (though some are to be expected in works by the same author) should be brought into the balance'. The material cited by Wichmann and Bromwich indeed does not entitle us to claim more than that Ps(P) is 'undoubtedly nearer

---

[5] For a facsimile, see *The Paris Psalter*, ed. Bertram Colgrave *et al.*, EEMF 8 (Copenhagen, 1958).

[6] The Old English introductions are preserved also in the margins of London, British Library, Cotton Vitellius E. xviii (cited below as MS V).

[7] I make no attempt to reassess the nature of the Latin text of the psalter used by the translator of Ps(P) or his other sources; Patrick O'Neill, of the University of North Carolina, has been studying these questions.

[8] *Libri Psalmorum Versio Antiqua Latina; cum Paraphrasi Anglo-Saxonica*, ed. Benjamin Thorpe (Oxford, 1835).

[9] Richard Paul Wülker, *Grundriss zur Geschichte der angelsächsischen Litteratur* (Leipzig, 1885), §§500–1. William of Malmesbury also claimed Alfred's authorship for Bede and Or; see *De Gestis Regum Anglorum*, ed. W. Stubbs, Rolls Ser. (1887–9), I, 132.

[10] J. Wichmann, 'König Aelfreds angelsächsische Übertragung der Psalmen I-LI Excl.', *Anglia* 11 (1889), 39–96, and J. I'A Bromwich, 'Who was the Translator of the Prose Portion of the Paris Psalter?', *The Early Cultures of North-West Europe*, ed. Sir Cyril Fox and Bruce Dickins (Cambridge, 1950), pp. 290–303. A. S. Cook was cautious: 'We have seen that Alfred must certainly have translated 1.1, pretty certainly 11.6, not improbably 23.4, and at least possibly the whole of the prose portion of the Paris Psalter. Yet against the last supposition must be set the notable discrepancies of language revealed by the parallel passages adduced above. It will require a more comprehensive and detailed examination to decide whether Alfred is really to be credited with the translation of all the prose Psalms extant' (*Biblical Quotations in Old English Prose Writers* (London, 1898), p. xl). See, further, *ibid.* pp. xxxvi–xl, and below, n. 60.

[11] E.g., Hans Schabram, *Superbia, Teil I* (Munich, 1965), and Elmar Seebold, 'Die AE. Entsprechungen von lat. *sapiens* und *prudens*', *Anglia* 92 (1974), 291–333; see also Bately, 'King Alfred and the Old English Translation of Orosius', pp. 454–6.

to *Boethius* than to Ælfric's prose or Wulfstan's'.[12] However, both these advocates of Alfred's authorship overlooked a number of points of agreement between Ps(P) and the known works of Alfred. Moreover, as Dorothy Whitelock has pointed out, Ps(P) agrees with Alfred's practice in the freedom of its renderings and in the additions made to the text,[13] while, if we take the intention of Alfred's educational plan to be the restoration of wisdom in the land,[14] a comprehensible rendering of the psalms, one of the two sapiential books of the bible and, as we know, constantly by Alfred's side, must surely have seemed to him a highly desirable undertaking.[15] It is on these grounds that I want now to reopen the question of the authorship of Ps(P), with special reference to lexical features.[16]

LEXICAL DIFFERENCES BETWEEN PS(P) AND WORKS NOT BY ALFRED

The non-occurrence in Ps(P) of mannerisms accepted as typical of Ælfric or Wulfstan[17] and the absence of words generally thought of as late West Saxon[18]

[12] Celia and Kenneth Sisam, *The Paris Psalter*, ed. Colgrave *et al.*, p. 16.

[13] 'The Prose of Alfred's Reign', *Continuations and Beginnings*, ed. E. G. Stanley (London, 1966), pp. 67–103, at 94–5.

[14] See Janet M. Bately, *The Literary Prose of King Alfred's Reign: Translation or Transformation. An Inaugural Lecture* (London, 1980), pp. 6–10.

[15] The need for comprehensibility must have been an important factor in determining the translator's methods of rendering the psalms. Close and accurate translation of this difficult devotional text would simply have transferred existing problems from Latin into English: where the thought is hard to grasp in Latin, it would have remained hard in English. What is more, for the author of Ps(P) part of the meaning of the psalms was their relevance to mankind, to the church, to the individual Christian using them: the wise man needs to appreciate this relevance to use the psalter effectively. So the translator not only made clear by expansion or alteration what otherwise might have been obscure but also spelled out the application of each psalm, whether universal or particular. As in the case of Bo and, to a lesser degree, in that of CP, the 'translation' is more explicit than the original. See, further, Bately, *ibid. passim*. For Alfred's love of the psalter, see Asser, *Life of King Alfred*, trans. *English Historical Documents* 1, ed. Dorothy Whitelock, 2nd ed. (London, 1979), 292–3. For the importance of the psalter in continental education, see, e.g., Cora E. Lutz, *Schoolmasters of the Tenth Century* (Hamden, Conn., 1977), p. 84.

[16] I am indebted to Professor Peter Clemoes for his constructive criticism of this paper and for his help in the final shaping of it.

[17] Unfortunately a number of lexical items cited as most typical of Ælfric – e.g. *gefredan*, *hreppan* and *cweartern* – not only are themselves absent from Ps(P) but also represent concepts not found there. However, Ps(P) differs from Ælfric's works in using *(ge)gearwian* (2 ×), not *gearcian*; pret. *for* (1 ×), not *ferde*; and *fremde* (2 ×) as well as *elþeodig* (8 ×), but not *ælfremed*. It never represents the concept 'despise' by *forhogian*, though it does use *forseon* (8 ×); moreover it has *earfoþ* (54 ×), not *earfoþnes* as Ælfric, and unlike Ælfric never uses *snottor(nes)*. For Ælfric's vocabulary, see *Homilies of Ælfric. A Supplementary Collection*, ed. John C. Pope, EETS 259–60 (London, 1967–8), 99–103, and for words and mannerisms typical of Wulfstan, Karl Jost, *Wulfstanstudien* (Bern, 1950), pp. 110–271. It may be noted that, unlike Wulfstan, Ps(P) has *(ge)arian* as well as *beorgan*; *gescieldan*, not *werian*; and *hælend* as well as *dryhten*.

[18] For a useful list of 'late' and 'Winchester school' words, see Helmut Gneuss, 'The Origin of Standard Old English and Æthelwold's school at Winchester', *ASE* 1 (1972), 63–83, at 76–8. Words absent from Ps(P) include *mese* (Ps(P) *beod* 1 ×), *bepæcan* (Ps(P) *beswican* 2 ×), *besargian* (Ps(P) *seofian* 23 ×, *heofan* 1 ×, etc.), *gedeorf* (Ps(P) *geswinc* 4 ×), *scrudnian* (Ps(P) *smeagan* 11 × etc.), *þæslic* (Ps(P) *cyn* 2 ×

enable us to conclude with some confidence that Ps(P) is most probably early rather than late Old English and – if vocabulary and style are any guide at all to authorship – is not attributable to either ecclesiastic. Likewise, the non-occurrence in Ps(P) of a range of words found in Bede, the Old English Martyrology and Werferth's translation of Gregory's *Dialogues*,[19] a number of them associated with the Mercian dialect,[20] justifies us in ruling out here too not only common authorship but also a non-West Saxon origin. Striking differences can be cited also between Ps(P) and psalter glosses,[21] between Ps(P) and the West Saxon Gospels[22] and, still more significantly, between Ps(P) and Or, which was apparently composed in the Wessex of Alfred's reign though not sharing certain important characteristics of Alfred's accepted works.[23] The list could easily be extended.[24] However, the following

and *gemetlic* 1 ×) and *gelaþung* (Ps(P) *gesamnung* 4 × in the sense of *ecclesia*), while present in Ps(P), but not in 'Winchester school' texts, are *altare* and *alter* (3 ×, 'Winchester school' *weofod*). See further, *The West-Saxon Gospels*, ed. M. Grünberg (Amsterdam, 1967), p. 334; Mechthild Gretsch, *Die Regula Sancti Benedicti in England* (Munich, 1973), p. 361; and *Theodulfi Capitula in England*, ed. Hans Sauer (Munich, 1978), p. 267. Ps(P) also differs from late West Saxon in its preference for *tid* (11 ×) over *tima* (1 ×), even in a general context; however, see *ibid.* p. 262. It also uses a number of words which late scribes tend to remove as (possibly) obsolete or obsolescent, e.g. *andwlita*, *cneores*, *gehat*, *sar* and *symle*; see *The Salisbury Psalter*, ed. Celia Sisam and Kenneth Sisam, EETS 242 (1959), 35.

19 *An Old English Martyrology*, ed. George Herzfeld, EETS 116 (London, 1900); *Bischof Wærferths von Worcester Übersetzung der Dialoge Gregors des Grossen*, ed. Hans Hecht, Bibliothek der angelsächsischen Prosa 5 (Leipzig and Hamburg, 1900 and 1907; repr. Darmstadt, 1965). I refer to these works henceforth as Mart and GD respectively.

20 See, however, below, pp. 81–2 and n. 77. For attempts to identify Anglian dialect forms in these and other texts, see, in particular, Richard Jordan, *Eigentümlichkeiten des anglischen Wortschatzes* (Heidelberg, 1928); Günther Scherer, *Zur Geographie und Chronologie des angelsächsischen Wortschatzes* (Berlin, 1928); Jackson J. Campbell, 'The Dialect Vocabulary of the Old English Bede', *JEGP* 50 (1951), 349–72; and Celia Sisam, 'An Early Fragment of the Old English *Martyrology*' *RES* n.s. 4 (1953), 209–20, at 216, n. 5. For valuable summaries of earlier findings, with bibliography see, further, *Theodulfi Capitula*, ed. Sauer, to which, for the sake of economy, I refer frequently below.

21 In this paper I have concentrated my attention on the Mercian glosses on the psalms in BL Cotton Vespasian A. i (*The Vespasian Psalter*, ed. Sherman M. Kuhn (Ann Arbor, 1965)), which I cite as Ps(A), since these appear to be roughly contemporary with the reign of King Alfred; I have excluded the glosses on the hymns. Where relevant I have given variants from the Junius Psalter (Ps(B)), because of the manuscript's apparent connections with the Lauderdale manuscript of Or, the Tanner manuscript of Bede, and the Parker manuscript of the *Anglo-Saxon Chronicle*; see M. B. Parkes, 'The Palaeography of the Parker Manuscript of the *Chronicle*, Laws and Sedulius, and Historiography at Winchester in the Late Ninth and Tenth Centuries', *ASE* 5 (1976), 149–71, and (for the text of Ps(B)) *Der altenglische Junius-Psalter*, ed. Eduard Brenner (Heidelberg, 1908). For some of the other psalter glosses and their relationships, see Frank-Günter Berghaus, *Die Verwandtschaftsverhältnisse der altenglischen Interlinearversionen des Psalters und der Cantica* (Göttingen, 1979); see also Helmut Gneuss, *Lehnbildungen und Lehnbedeutungen im Altenglischen* (Berlin, 1955). Since I understand that this is the subject of a forthcoming article by Richard Clement, I have not attempted to consider the possible influence of psalter glosses on Ps(P).

22 I refer to this text henceforth as WS. For convenience I have treated the four gospel translations as a unit, although I am not convinced that they are the work of a single translator. For figures for WS I have drawn on the somewhat inaccurate and misleading glossary by Mattie Anstice Harris, repr. *Word Indices to Old English Non-Poetic Texts, with a Preface by Fred C. Robinson* (Hamden, Conn., 1974); for the text, see ref. above, n. 18.

23 For lexical differences between Or and Ps(P), see below, pp. 88–93, and Bately, 'King Alfred and the Old English Translation of Orosius', pp. 454–6.

24 For some of the special characteristics of the sections of the *Chronicle* either compiled in or relating

instances taken more or less at random from Bede, GD,[25] Ps(A) and WS, with occasional variants from other texts, will suffice as illustration:

(*a*) *infirmitas*: Bede *untrumnes* (48 ×);[26] and WS *untrumnes* (12 ×); beside Ps(P) *mettrumnes* (6 ×), *untrumnes* (3 ×) and *untrymþ* (1 ×).[27] In Ps(A) and Mart *untrumnes* and *mettrumnes* occur with equal frequency (though Ps(A) has only one instance of each), while surviving manuscripts of GD show a preference for *mettrumnes*.[28]

(*b*) *iniquitas*: Bede *wohnes* (6 ×); Ps(A) *unrihtwisnes* (95 ×) and *unriht* (5 ×);[29] and WS *unrihtwisnes* (7 ×); beside Ps(P) *unriht* (19 ×) and *unrihtwisnes* (11 ×).[30] *Wohnes* is found also in GD, BlHom[31] and Ælfric's works.

(*c*) *labor* and *laborare*: Bede *gewinn* (22 ×) and *winnan* (7 ×);[32] and Ps(A) *gewinn* (16 ×) and *winnan* (4 ×); beside Ps(P) *geswinc* (1 ×) and *swincan* (2 ×).[33] *Gewinn*

---

to King Alfred's reign, see Janet Bately, 'The Compilation of the Anglo-Saxon Chronicle 60 B.C. to A.D. 890: Vocabulary as Evidence', *PBA* 64 (1978), 93–129.

[25] Figures for GD are based on the readings of MSS O and C, not on the revised version in MS H, for which, see David Yerkes, *The Two Versions of Waerferth's Translation of Gregory's Dialogues: an Old English Thesaurus* (Toronto, 1979). Where the surviving manuscripts of Bede, GD and Mart have variant readings the form cited is normally that of the base manuscript used by the editors of the work concerned; only selective variants are noted here. Normalized spellings of the head-word are given throughout, mainly following the practice of John R. Clark Hall, *A Concise Anglo-Saxon Dictionary*, 4th ed. with suppl. by Herbert D. Merritt (Cambridge, 1960). For total occurrences in Ps(P) of Old English words cited in this section, see below, pp. 87–8. Unless otherwise stated, the Latin text of the psalter I have used is that of the Paris Psalter, collated with the Latin of the Vespasian Psalter as representative of the Roman text. For Gallican and Hebrew texts of the vulgate psalms, see *Biblia Sacra iuxta Vulgatam Versionem*, ed. Robert Weber I (Stuttgart, 1969).

[26] I include here the variant *untrymnes*, which is the preferred form in MS T, with MSS B, Ca and O normally using *untrumnes*. Miller reports (Bede, pt II, p. 106) one instance of *mettrumnes* from the now mainly destroyed MS C, cited in Whelock's edition of the text.

[27] On this occasion only I have included instances in Ps(P) without equivalent in the Latin psalter, *mettrumnes* being confined to the introductions (along with one of the instances of *untrumnes*). Despite this limited distribution there is nothing in the lexical evidence taken as a whole to suggest separate authorship for these introductions.

[28] Cf. Mart, p. 180, line 14, where MS B has *untrumnes* and MS C *mettrumnes*, and GD, p. 83, line 31, where MSS C and O have *mettrumnes* and MS H *untrumnes*. In the Blickling homilies the distribution is *untrumnes* (7 ×) in homs. XI, XIII, XVII and XVIII and *mettrumnes* (1 ×) in hom. V; see *The Blickling Homilies of the Tenth Century*, ed. R. Morris, EETS 58, 63 and 73 (London, 1874, 1876 and 1880; repr. 1967), and D. G. Scragg, 'The Corpus of Vernacular Homilies and Prose Saints' Lives before Ælfric', *ASE* 8 (1979), 223–77. I refer to the Blickling homilies henceforth as BlHom and follow the numbering of Morris's edition.

[29] For Ps(A) *unriht* Ps(B) has *unrihtwisnes*.

[30] Ps(A) also has *unrihtwisnes* for *iniustitia* (4 ×), beside *unriht* (1 ×), making a total of ninety-nine instances of the Old English noun. In Ps(P) *unrihtwisnes* occurs a total of fifteen times, rendering not only *iniquitas* but also *impietas*, *insipientia* and *iniustitia* (each 1 ×). *Unriht* is used thirty-one times, rendering also *iniustitia* (3 ×) and *nequitia* (2 ×). For *impietas* Ps(A) has *arleasnes*.

[31] Twice, both in hom. X.

[32] These figures include instances of *handgewinn* and *wiþwinnan* where these correspond to *labor* and *laborare* in the Latin source. In addition Bede has five instances of *gewinn* where the Latin uses the corresponding verb.

[33] *Geswinc* and *swincan* each occur four times in all in Ps(P). *Labor* is also rendered by *broc* and *earfoþ* (each 1 ×). In Ps(A) *geswinc* occurs thirteen times and is reserved for *afflictio* and *tribulatio* along with *geswencednes* (24 ×), beside Ps(P) *earfoþ* (11 ×), *geswinc* and *(nyd)þearf* (each 2 ×) and *unrotnes* (1 ×).

and *winnan* are also the norm in GD and BlHom and are identified as Anglian by Jordan,[34] while WS agrees in its rendering of these Latin words with Ps(P).

(*d*) *sacrificium*, *holocausta* and *hostia*: Bede *onsægdnes* (7 ×) and *lac* (1 ×); and Ps(A) *onsægdnes* (23 ×);[35] beside Ps(P) *offrung* (10 ×) and *lac* (1 ×). WS has *onsægdnes* (4 ×) and *offrung* (1 ×), while *onsægdnes* is found alongside *offrung* and *lac* in GD and Ælfric's works.[36]

(*e*) *tribulatio*: Bede *costung* (1 ×); Ps(A) *geswencednes* (24 ×) and *geswinc* (11 ×); and WS *gedrefednes* (4 ×) and *geswencednes*, *gedeorf* and *costnung* (each 1 ×); beside Ps(P) *earfoþ* (11 ×) and *geswinc* (2 ×).[37]

(*f*) *umbra*: Bede *scua* (1 ×); and Ps(A) *scua* (11 ×); beside Ps(P) *sceadu* (3 ×). Ps(B) five times reads *sceadu* for Ps(A) *scua* and WS has *sceadu* (2 ×) and *þystru* (1 ×), while *scua*, identified by Rauh and Menner as an Anglian word,[38] occurs also in BlHom.

(*g*) *circumdare*: Bede *ymbsellan* (10 ×) and *ymbsettan* (1 ×);[39] Ps(A) *ymbsellan* (23 ×); and WS *betrymian* (2 ×) and *behabban* and *bestandan* (each 1 ×);[40] beside Ps(P) *ymbhringan* (7 ×), *behringan* (2 ×) and *bestandan*, *ymbstandan* and *ymbþringan* (each 1 ×). *Ymbsellan*, which is found also in GD and BlHom, is identified as an Anglian word by Rauh.[41]

(*h*) (*con*)*firmare*: Bede *getrymman* (4 ×), *trymman* (3 ×) and *fæstnian* (1 ×);[42] Ps(A) *getrymman* (26 ×) and *trymman* (2 ×); and WS *getrymman* (4 ×); beside Ps(P) *gestrangian* (3 ×) and *getrymman* (2 ×). In Ps(A) (10 ×) and WS (3 ×) *gestrangian* is reserved for *confortare*, a usage found also in Ps(P) (3 ×). In Bede

---

[34] *Eigentümlichkeiten* p. 43. See, further, Klaus R. Grinda, '*Arbeit*' *und* '*Mühe*'. *Untersuchungen zur Bedeutungsgeschichte altenglischer Wörter* (Munich, 1975), and *Theodulfi Capitula*, ed. Sauer, pp. 260–1. For GD MS H's replacement of *winnan* and *gewinn* by *swincan* and *geswinc*, see Yerkes, *Thesaurus*.

[35] Ps(B) has *offrung* (2 ×) and *bærning* (1 ×), for Ps(A) *onsægdnes*.

[36] For *offrung* as a possible West Saxon word, see Hildegard Rauh, *Der Wortschatz der altenglischen Übersetzungen des Matthaeus-Evangeliums* (Berlin, 1936), p. 28; Robert J. Menner, 'Anglian and Saxon Elements in Wulfstan's Vocabulary', *MLN* 63 (1948), 1–9, at 7; and *Theodulfi Capitula*, ed. Sauer, p. 257. For *oblatio* Ps(P) has *oflata* (1 ×), Ps(A) *oflate* and *onsægdnes* (each 1 ×) and Bede *lac* (2 ×) and *onsægdnes* (1 ×). WS has *offrung* for *victima* and *lac* for *munus*. The only instance of *onsægdnes* in BlHom occurs in hom. VI.

[37] Ps(B) has *geswinc* (11 ×) for *geswencednes*; see, further, Grinda, '*Arbeit*' *und* '*Mühe*', esp. chs. III, IV and V.

[38] See Rauh, *Wortschatz*, p. 40, and Robert J. Menner, 'The Anglian Vocabulary of the *Blickling Homilies*', *Philologica: the Malone Anniversary Studies*, ed. Thomas A. Kirby and Henry Bosley Woolf (Baltimore, 1949), pp. 56–64, at 58; also Jordan, *Eigentümlichkeiten*, p. 8, n. The single instance of *scua* in BlHom occurs in hom. VI.

[39] With MS variant *ymbhringan* and a single instance of *gegyrewan*. See also *circumstare*, Bede *ymbsellan*, and Robert J. Menner, 'The Vocabulary of the Old English Poems on Judgment Day', *PMLA* 62 (1947), 583–97, at 593. Of particular interest in Bede is the use of *ymbhringan* by MSS O and Ca in the 'duplicated' section, beside MS B *ymbsellan* 7 *ymbhabban* and MS T *ymbhabban*; see, further, Jackson J. Campbell, 'The Old English Bede: Book III, chapters 16–20', *MLN* 67 (1952), 381–6, at 385.

[40] See also WS's use of *betynan* and *scrydan* (each 2 ×) and *gecnyttan* (1 ×) for *circumdare*.

[41] *Wortschatz*, p. 16, and see Menner, 'The Anglian Vocabulary of the *Blickling Homilies*', p. 58. *Ymbsellan* is found in BlHom I and xix. Ps(P) has *ymbgittan* (2 ×) and *behringan* (1 ×) without equivalent in the Latin.   [42] See also p. 108, line 4 *geþwærede*.

confortare is rendered by *gestrangian* (2 ×) and *strangian* (1 × , in collocation with *trymman*).

(*i*) *congregare*: Bede *gesamnian* (11 ×); and Ps(A) *gesamnian* (11 ×); beside Ps(P) *gegaderian* (5 ×) and *gaderian* (2 ×). Cf. WS *gegaderian* (18 ×), *gaderian* (11 ×) and *gesamnian* (5 ×), and BlHom (*ge*)*samnian* (8 ×), and compare Ps(P)'s preference for the noun *gesamnung* (9 ×), beside *samnung* and *gegaderung* (each 1 ×).[43]

(*j*) *deficere*: Bede *aspringan* (1 ×);[44] Ps(A) *aspringan* (32 ×); and WS *geteorian* (7 ×); beside Ps(P) *geteorian* (3 ×) and *aspringan* (2 ×).[45] Cf. GD, p. 227, line 11, where *deficeret* is rendered *asprang 7 ateorode*, and p. 264, lines 5 and 6, where the verb is rendered by first *aspringan* and then *teorian*.

(*k*) *expectare*: Ps(A) *bidan* (10 ×) and *abidan* (6 ×); beside Ps(P) *hopian* (3 ×) and *anbidian* and *gebidan* (each 2 ×).[46] Bede's usage here is *bidan* (10 ×) and *gebidan* (1 ×), with MS variants including *abidan* and *onbidan*.[47] WS has *geanbidian* (6 ×), *abidan* and *onbidan* (each 2 ×) and *gebidan* (1 ×). Both *abidan* and (*ge*)*anbidian* are used by Ælfric.

(*l*) *exultare*: Bede *gefeon*, *blissian* and *wynsumian* (each 1 ×); Ps(A) *gefeon* (37 ×) and *wynsumian* (2 ×); and WS *geblissian* (4 ×) and *gefægnian* and *fægnian* (each 2 ×); beside Ps(P) *fægnian* (10 ×),[48] *blissian* (5 ×) and *wynsumian* (2 ×). *Gefeon* is also used for *exultare* in GD and is found in both BlHom and Mart (Latin equivalent unknown).[49] By late Old English this word seems to be confined mainly to Anglian texts.[50]

---

[43] Cf. *gegaderian* (1 ×) in the Vespasian Hymns. Bede and Ps(A) also use (*ge*)*samnian* for Latin *colligere* and *convenire*: in BlHom this verb is found in homs. IV, VI, VII, VIII, XIII, XV and XVII (Latin equivalents unknown).

[44] A second example of *deficere* is rendered *benumen 7 bescired* in Bede.

[45] Ps(P) also has *gedwæscan* and *forweorþan* (each 1 ×) for *deficere* and once uses the pair *geteorian 7 geendian* (XXX.11). In all it employs *aspringan* five times and *geteorian* four times. Ps(B) has *ateorian* (3 ×) for Ps(A) *aspringan*. In WS's figures I include *ungeteorod* (1 ×) for *non deficiens*. See also BlHom, where *aspringan* is found in hom. VII and *geteorian* in homs. X and XIX.

[46] *Hopian* is used in collocation with *anbidian* and *gebidan* (each 1 ×); see, further, below, n. 106. Ps(A) also uses *abidan* for Latin *sustinere*.

[47] MS Ca *abidan* (2 ×), MS B *gebidan* (2 ×) and MS B *onbidan* (1 ×). Ps(B) similarly has *onbidan* three times for Ps(A) *bidan* and twice for Ps(A) *abidan*. Cf. BlHom, with *onbidan* (6 ×) in homs. VI and XIX, *gebidan* (2 ×) in homs. XV and XVIII and *bidan* (2 ×) in homs. I and IX.

[48] Including one instance of *fægnian* where the Latin psalter has *exaltare*, suggesting an intermediate misreading *exultare*.

[49] In place of one instance of *gefeon* in Ps(A) Ps(B) has *wynsumian*, a word which it and Ps(A) normally use for *jubilare* (Ps(A) 8 ×). In Ps(P) the single instance of *jubilare* is rendered by *fægnian 7 myrgan*. See also *gaudere*: Bede *gefeon* (22 × , twice paired with *blissian*) alongside *efngefeon* (2 ×) and *blissian 7 gefeon* (1 ×) for *congaudere*; and Ps(A) *gefeon* (6 ×); beside Ps(P) *blissian* (1 ×); and see GD, p. 69, line 13, where *gaudebat* is rendered by *gefægnode* in MS C but *gefeah* in O and *geblissode* in H. In Ps(A) (*ge*)*blissian* is reserved for *laetari* and *laetificari*, while in Bede *blissian* is the normal rendering for *laetari* (9 × , twice paired with *gefeon*), though it is not confined to it. For the frequent substitution of *fægnian* for what I am assuming, rightly or wrongly, to be 'original' *gefeon* in manuscripts of Bede, see Jordan, *Eigentümlichkeiten*, p. 89. For further details of the usage in Ps(P), see below, p. 87 and no. 107. In BlHom *gefeon* is found in homs. I, VI, VII, XIII, XIV, XV, XVII, XVIII and XIX.

[50] See Jordan, *Eigentümlichkeiten*, pp. 89–90; Gretsch, *Regula*, p. 336; and *Theodulfi Capitula*, ed. Sauer, pp. 228–9.

(*m*) *habitare* and *inhabitare*: Bede *eardian* (11 ×, for both Latin words) and *oneardian* (1 ×, for *habitare*); and Ps(A) *eardian* (38 ×, for *habitare*) and *ineardian* (20 ×, for *inhabitare*); beside Ps(P) *bu(i)an* (7 ×, for both Latin words), *wunian* (5 ×, for both Latin words) and *eardian* (3 ×, for *habitare*).[51] Cf. *circumhabitare*: Ps(A) *ymbeardian* (1 ×); beside Ps(P) *ymbutan bu(i)an*. GD here agrees with WS against Bede in having occasional *wunian* beside its norm, *eardian*.

(*n*) *retribuere*: Ps(A) *geeadleanian* (14 ×) and *gieldan* (1 ×); beside Ps(P) *gieldan* (6 ×) and *forgieldan* (2 ×). Cf. WS *forgieldan* (1 ×).[52] Ps(B) has *agieldan* (4 ×) and *forgiefan* and *forlætan* (each 1 ×) for Ps(A) *geedleanian*. The corresponding noun, *retributio*, is rendered by *edlean* in Ps(A), WS and Ps(P).

(*o*) *impius*: Bede *arleas* (6 ×); and Ps(A) *arleas* (15 ×); beside Ps(P) *unrihtwis* (13 ×), *arleas* (2 ×) and *unriht* (1 ×).[53] In Ps(A) *unrihtwis* is reserved (along with *unriht* and *unrihtlic*) for Latin *iniustus* and *iniquus*, just as *rihtwisnes* is used exclusively for *iustitia*, *iustificatio* and *aequitas* and *soþfæstnes* for *veritas*. For *unrihtwisnes*, see above, (*b*). Bede's usage is *unriht* for *iniustus* and *iniquus* (2 ×) and *soþfæstnes* for *iustitia* (7 ×) as well as for *veritas*. In contrast Ps(P) uses *rihtwisnes* for both *iustitia* and (along with *soþfæstnes*) *veritas*.[54]

(*p*) *euge euge*: Ps(A) *wel þe wel þe* (3 ×) and *weolga weolga* (1 ×);[55] and WS (single *euge*) *geblissa* (2 ×) and *beo bliþe* (1 ×); beside Ps(P) *wel la wel*, *hit is la ful good* and *is þæt la well* (each 1 ×).

To these differences in the rendering of specific Latin words may be added differences in the selection of Old English words to render the same concept, or similar ones, where there is not a single Latin equivalent. For instance Bede and Mart have a marked preference for *feran* rather than *faran* and for *gangan* rather than *gan*, whereas Ps(P) has only *faran* (7 ×) (never *feran*) and prefers *gan* (9 ×) to *gangan* (5 ×, in the first person singular present indicative only).[56]

Now, as I have indicated, some of these differences may be due to differences of dialect, others to differences in date of composition, while the possibility of scribal alteration can never be ruled out.[57] But a significant

51 In Ps(A) *wunian* is found only for *demorari*, *manere* and *commorari*, while *bu(i)an* does not occur. Ps(B) has occasional *eardian*, frequent *oneardian*, for Ps(A) *ineardian*, Latin *inhabitare*. In BlHom *eardian* and *wunian* are the norm, with pp. *gebuen* (1 ×) in hom. XI.

52 *Retribuere* is not used in Bede's *Historia Ecclesiastica*; however, GD has *geeadleanian* for *remunerare*.

53 XVI.12 *þam unrihtan wisan*. *Unrihtwis* is also used in Ps(P) for *iniustus*, *iniquus*, *peccator* etc. The two instances of *arleas* occur in the same psalm, XXV. For the usage of the West Saxon Gospel of St Matthew, see ed. Grünberg, pp. 331–2 and 333.

54 *Soþfæst* is not found in Ps(P), which uses *rihtwis* and *riht* for *iustus* and *rectus*. See Jordan, *Eigentümlichkeiten*, p. 43, and *Theodulfi Capitula*, ed. Sauer, pp. 258–9. Ps(B) eight times replaces *rihtwisnes* by *efnes*.

55 Ps(B) has *gefeoh gefeoh* (1 ×) for Ps(A) *wel þe wel þe*.

56 See Bately, 'The Compilation of the Anglo-Saxon Chronicle', p. 127 and n. 2. In surviving manuscripts of the 'first' version of GD, on the other hand, *gan* is more frequent than *gangan*.

57 See Bately, *ibid.* esp. pp. 100 and 109–10. An example of deliberate revision is provided by MS H of GD, for which, see above, n. 25.

number of variants appear to be the result of choice, of a preference for one term for a given concept at the expense of current alternatives.

LEXICAL AGREEMENTS BETWEEN PS(P) AND THE ACCEPTED WORKS OF ALFRED

In certain circumstances a restriction through choice, if found in a range of works, could be the result of standardization of the kind that typifies Helmut Gneuss's late West Saxon 'Winchester school'. However, as Professor Gneuss points out in his important study, such a standardization is not to be expected in early West Saxon;[58] there restriction is more likely to be through personal preference, through idiosyncracy. If, therefore, we find 'significant' agreement between Ps(P) and other works, it is probably the result of common authorship rather than of common policy.[59] What 'significant' lexical agreement, then, is there between Ps(P) and the accepted works of Alfred? Here one is on very difficult ground, as the juster criticisms made of Wichmann and Bromwich have demonstrated.[60] These scholars were able to find numerous resemblances and points of agreement between Ps(P) and not only Bo, CP and Solil but also Or and, in Wichmann's case, Bede. Because they did not deliberately set out to look for differences, they apparently failed to notice the features which distinguish Or (and Bede) from the other works. So, before attempting to assess the evidence *for* common

---

[58] 'The Origin of Standard Old English', pp. 66–8.

[59] Attention is not infrequently drawn to the 'remarkable agreement' in the rendering of Latin words in Bede and GD; see, e.g., Simeon Potter, *On the Relation of the Old English Bede to Werferth's Gregory and to Alfred's Translations* (Prague, 1931), pp. 17–18. However, in a number of cases the translating word is the obvious one and the same equations are found in texts which have no pretensions to being of late-ninth-century Mercian origin. At the same time preferences are frequently different.

[60] Although J. D. Bruce had 'little difficulty in exposing the weakness of Wichmann's evidence' (*The Paris Psalter*, ed. Colgrave *et al.*, p. 16), some of his attacks are completely unfounded; see J. Douglas Bruce, 'The Anglo-Saxon Version of the Book of Psalms commonly known as the Paris Psalter', *PMLA* 9 (1894), 43–164, and Bromwich, 'Who was the Translator?', pp. 292–3. Unlike Wichmann, Cook made a deliberate attempt to look for significant differences between Ps(P) and the works of Alfred as well as for similarities; see above, n. 10. However, his corpus is far too small to provide results of any great value and not only do his similarities include forms found in works no longer ascribed to Alfred, namely Or and Bede, but also his differences can be explained away on stylistic grounds. For example, the presence of the expression *wolberendum setle* in both Ps(P) and CP could, but need not, be evidence of common authorship, while the fact that CP translates Lat 'Avertisti faciem tuam a me, et factus sum conturbatus' by 'Dryhten, ðu ahwyrfdes ðinne ondwlitan from me, ða wearð ic gedrefed' (ed. Sweet, p. 465, lines 19–20) whereas Ps(P) has 'þa awendest þu þinne andwlitan fram me, þa wearð ic sona gedrefed' (xxix.7) is equally non-conclusive. Indeed, underlying some of the differences are actual similarities of method. Thus CP's addition of *Dryhten* is not only contextually explicable but paralleled in a number of other verses in Ps(P) as well as CP (see, e.g., CP, p. 413, line 17, Ps(P) xxxviii.14 and Ps(P) xxii.4, where the word alliterates with *deaðes* and *ondræde*); the expression 'ðu ahwyrf(des) ðinne ondwlitan from me' is actually found elsewhere in Ps(P) (xii.1); and the addition of *sona* in Ps(P) conforms with the translator's general practice of attempting to write a balanced and poetic prose, about which, see, further, below.

authorship, I shall act as devil's advocate and do the converse – look for differences which, unless explained away, might indicate more than one author at work.

Some variations

It is to be expected, of course, that there will be some variations of usage between the works of a single author, composed, as they will have been, at different times and, quite often, in different circumstances. Thus there are a number of points of disagreement between CP and Bo, of which some may be due to variations in the influence and help of the body of scholars that Alfred collected around him, others to differences of subject matter and approach.[61] Differences of subject matter certainly account for the existence of a not inconsiderable corpus of words in Ps(P) which are absent from the accepted works of Alfred because the concepts which they represent are themselves not found there. For instance, *anhyrne* and *unicornus* occur only in Ps(P), but this is of no significance to a discussion of authorship, since the concept 'unicorn' is confined to this text. Similarly verbs such as (*a*)*cwacian*, *awindwian, gecoronian*[62] and *sceotan*, nouns such as *aliesnes*,[63] *beod, boga, cocer* and

---

[61] For Alfred's helpers, who were presumably active on numerous occasions, see the prefatory letter to CP and Asser's *Life*, chs. LXXVII, LXXIX and LXXXVIII, trans. *EHD* I, 294–8; for differences between CP and Bo, see, further, Bately, 'King Alfred and the Old English Translation of Orosius', pp. 457–8, and for differences between the various works of Ælfric, see M. R. Godden, 'Ælfric's Changing Vocabulary', *ES* 61 (1980), 206–23.

[62] For *gecoronian*, see Josef Kirschner, *Die Bezeichnungen für Kranz und Krone im Altenglischen* (Munich, 1975).

[63] Cf. CP, Bo, Solil *aliesan* and CP *aliesend*. The noun *aliesnes* is composed of verb stem + *nes* suffix, a formation usually assumed to be characteristic of Mercian, it being often said that the only verb form to which the suffix could be added in West Saxon was the past participle; see, e.g., Campbell, 'Dialect Vocabulary of the Old English Bede', pp. 367–8. According to Campbell, *ibid.* no. 40, 'The *Cura Pastoralis*, alone among WS documents, shares this Anglian peculiarity of adding -*niss* directly to the stem of the verb rather than to the participle. Hence the occurrences in the *Past* do not prove that the word *towesniss* was known in the Saxon area.' For a somewhat less extreme attitude, see Jordan, *Eigentümlichkeiten*, pp. 101–2, and *The Life of St Chad*, ed. R. Vleeskruyer (Amsterdam, 1953), p. 29; see also Sauer's summary, *Theodulfi Capitula*, p. 241, according to which the construction is Anglian or primarily Anglian but occurs 'noch gelegentlich' in early West Saxon. A study of all nouns formed from verb + -*nes* in Ps(P) yields the following:
(*a*) past participle + -*nes*: four words, one of which is found also in CP, three are found in Bo and one in Solil, with one apparent hapax legomenon, *ymbsetennes* (1 ×);
(*b*) verb stem + -*nes*: fifteen words, eight of which are found also in CP, two in Bo and two in Solil, with only five not appearing anywhere in the accepted works of Alfred, namely *aliesnes* (with MS V having the West Saxon *aliesednes* for two of Ps(P)'s five instances of this word), *gehieldnes* (apparently a hapax legomenon), *trymenes, wyrgnes* and *generennes* (if this represents an original *generenes* not *generednes*).
If Ps(P), then, is a West Saxon translation, attributable to King Alfred, the inference to be drawn from Campbell's claim is that, as in the case of CP, Ps(P)'s relative fondness for the construction verbal stem + -*nes* is to be attributed to the involvement of one or more of Alfred's Mercian helpers. However, neither frequency of occurrence nor distribution patterns will allow us to treat this construction as necessarily untypical of a king whose West Saxon dialect did not have the status of a standard language and whose wife (from whom he might have acquired some of his speech habits) was herself a Mercian. Of the thirteen Ps(P) words not in Bo the majority represent concepts not

78

drosna and adverbs and adjectives such as *forsewenlice, ofergeotol*,[64] *unwemme, wuldorfæst* and *wuldorlic* are absent from the accepted works of Alfred along with the concepts they represent and may be discarded from this discussion.[65] As for differences of approach, as I have suggested elsewhere, the character of the rendering is affected by the fact that for the Old English translator part of the meaning of the psalms was their poetic quality, their sentence rhythms, their tight and balanced structure:[66] he tried to convey something of this level of meaning. Selection of forms for the sake of their sound patterns is often the most obvious explanation of variation in this work,[67] as the following highly selective summary of the major differences of lexical usage between Ps(P) and the accepted works of Alfred will, I hope, demonstrate.[68]

(1) Ps(P) and the accepted works of Alfred use different words for the same or a closely related concept, but these words are of such infrequent occurrence that an authorial norm or preference cannot be established.[69] Moreover

found there, while the remainder occur in Ps(P) alongside the 'Boethian' usage: thus *acennes* (1 ×) beside *acennednes* (1 ×), *herenes* (1 ×) beside *hering* (1 ×) and *trymenes* (1 ×) beside *trymnes* (1 ×), *untrymnes* (1 ×), *untrumnes* (2 ×) etc.; Bo *acennednes* (1 ×), *hering* (3 ×) and *untrymnes* (1 ×), with CP using *acennes, herenes, hering, untrymnes* and *(un)trumnes, acennes* occurring also in Or and in the West Saxon genealogy prefixed to the *Anglo-Saxon Chronicle*, MS A. The conclusion must be that at least some formations of the type verb stem + *-nes* were current in early West Saxon as well as in Anglian and that their appearance in works associated with King Alfred, though possibly due to the dialect preferences of his helpers, could represent his own usage.

64 Bo and Solil, however, have the noun *ofergietolnes*.

65 I would include here Ps(P) *a/on worulde woruld* (12 ×) for *in saeculum saeculi*, since the only similar expression in the accepted works of Alfred, *a to worulde*, is in the prayer at the end of MS B of Bo, which in my opinion does not belong to the Boethius and does not represent Alfred's work, cf., e.g., this prayer's exceptional use of the preposition *toforon*.

66 Bately, *Literary Prose*, p. 14. The translator showed a remarkable restraint in the use of correlation and a remarkable sensitivity to the cadences and unexpressed relationships of the Latin; see, further, above, n. 60, and below, section (1), *passim*, and cf., e.g., XVIII.8 with III.5.

67 Cf., e.g., the use of *hær*, not *locc* or *feax*, in XXXIX.14 'Mine fynd wæran gemanigfealdode þæt heora wæs ma þonne hæra on minum heafde' with Ps(A) rendering Latin *capillos* by *loccas*, and XXXVII.8 *gesæged 7 gehnæged*, for *(in)curvatus* [Gallican *adflictus*], with Ps(A) *gebeged* and CP, p. 67, line 18 *gebiged* (a word found two verses earlier in Ps(P) for Gallican and Hebrew *(in)curvatus*, Vespasian Psalter *turbatus*). Assonance and alliteration are indeed very common, while compounds sometimes replace two or more Latin words: e.g., *sæfiscas* for *pisces maris, sæwegas* for *semitas maris, eorþcyningas* for *reges terrae* and *handgeweorc* for *opera manum*; see also *gebeorhstow* for *refugium*, and *rothwil* without equivalent in the Latin psalter. The desire for a tight and balanced structure may explain the absence of certain of Alfred's syntactical mannerisms, e.g. *swa...swa...swæþer* (though see the use of *oþer twega oþþe...oþþe* and *awþer oþþe...oþþe*, cited below, p. 90).

68 The summary is based on an exhaustive study of the lexis of Ps(P) in relation to the usage of the Latin psalter versions on the one hand and that of the accepted works of Alfred (and, selectively, other texts of the late ninth century) on the other; it is based also on a detailed study of concepts for which Ps(P) uses a range of Old English words and on a detailed examination of the adjectives and adverbs in Ps(P) and of those in the accepted works of Alfred. I have also investigated every word which occurs frequently in the latter texts but never in Ps(P), but otherwise I have not attempted an exhaustive study of the lexis of the accepted works of Alfred, either individually or as a whole.

69 A number of words in this category are verbs which occur with and without the *ge-* prefix in one or other corpus. Reference to the textual notes to Carlson's edition of CP will show how much

variation occurs within the accepted works of Alfred themselves, demonstrating a much freer and more flexible approach to translation than that found in certain other texts of the period and showing that occasional differences of rendering do not of themselves indicate differences of authorship. For example:

(*a*) *currus*: Ps(P) *rynewæn* (1 ×); beside Bo *scridwæn* (1 × in the prose text and 2 × in the list of contents in MS B) and *hrædwæn* (2 × in prose and 1 × in verse).[70] Bosworth and Toller's *Anglo-Saxon Dictionary* (cited henceforth as BT) records these compounds in -*wæn* from only these texts; the usage of Ps(A) is *cræt* and *scrid*. Alfred's selection of *hrædwæn*, 'swift chariot' or 'swift carriage', in Bo is obviously influenced by the *volucrem currum* of his verse source; in choosing *rynewæn* the author of Ps(P) appears to have been seeking a poetic rendering of *currus*, bringing out the underlying meaning of 'running' (*currere*) in order perhaps to convey something of the cause of the pleasure experienced by the chariots' owners, an exulting in their speed (thus XIX.7 'On rynewænum 7 on horsum ure fynd fægniað 7 þæs gilpað; we þonne on þæm naman Drihtnes ures Godes us micliað', corresponding to the Roman and Gallican psalters, XIX.8 'Hii in curribus et hii in equis. nos autem in nomine domini dei nostri magnificabimur [*Gallican* invocabimus]').[71]

(*b*) *clamor*: Ps(P) *gehrop* (2 ×); beside CP *geclips* (2 ×) and *hream* (1 ×). Cf. Ps(A) *clipung* and the variant readings *clipung* and *hream* in GD. BT records *gehrop* only from Ps(P) (where it is on both occasions used in close conjunction with *stemn*), through *hrop* is found in BlHom and the related *onhrop* and *hropan* are of wider occurrence. In CP *hream* occurs in the phrase *Sodomwara hream 7 Gomorwara* (p. 427, line 33), quoting from Genesis XVII.20, a verse in which *clamor* is rendered by *hream* also in Ælfric's translation, and it may be that the word has been selected because of its connotations of strong emotion (pain, terror, fear etc.; see BT Supplement, *s.v. hream*).[72] Why Ps(P) selected *gehrop* rather than CP's *geclips* or the *clipung* of texts not by Alfred must be a matter for conjecture. However, in one of its occurrences the word both

---

variation of usage could have arisen in the transmission of these forms; see also variations between the two manuscripts of Bo cited in Sedgfield's notes and see Dorothy Horgan, 'Patterns of Variation and Interchangeability in some Old English Prefixes', *NM* 81 (1980), 127–30.

[70] Like the instances from the list of contents the verse example is derived from the corresponding passage of prose and so does not strictly represent a separate usage. It should be noted that Sedgfield does not include forms from either the list of contents or the final prayer in his glossary. My figures are based partly on information in Sedgfield's glossary, partly on my own collection of references. I make no attempt to assess the extent to which the verse metres of Bo reflect Alfred's normal usage or indeed the extent of Alfred's responsibility for them.

[71] For a different explanation of *rynewæn*, see John D. Tinkler, *Vocabulary and Syntax of the Old English Version in the Paris Psalter*, Janua Linguarum, series practica 67 (The Hague, 1971), 61.

[72] CP goes on to make a distinction between 'calling' and 'shouting', using *clipian* and *hrieman* respectively (p. 429, line 1). For the expected noun to translate vulgate *clamor* WS substitutes the expression *man hrymde*.

contributes to the alliterative pattern of its verse and avoids repetition of roots and alliterative patterns used in the preceding verse: XVII.5–6 '...7 on eallum minum earfoðum ic clypige to Drihtne 7 to minum Gode ic cige. 7 he gehyrde of his þam halgan temple mine stemne, 7 min gehrop com beforan his ansyne, 7 eac on his earan hit eode.'

(c) Ps(P) *sican* (1 ×, without equivalent in the Latin psalter); beside Bo *onsican* (2 ×). Cf. CP *sicettan* (1 ×), rendering Latin *conticescere*.[73] Ps(P) here has the basic verb form and uses it in a collocation (*ic sice 7 wepe*) found also in Middle English. Cf. Ps(P) and Bo (verse) *sicettung* (each 1 ×).

(d) *annuere oculis*: Ps(P) *wincettan mid eagum* (1 ×); beside CP *biecnan mid eagum* (2 ×). Cf. CP *wincian mid...eagum* for *oculos claudere* (1 ×) and Bo *eage bepriewan* (1 × in prose), corresponding to Boethius's *unius mora momenti*. *Annuere* is rendered by *beacnian* and *biecnian* in WS and Ps(A). With *wincettan* beside *wincian* cf. *sican* beside *sicettan*, cited above, under (c). Ps(P)'s choice seems the most vivid and effective of the alternatives and provides alliteration within the verse: XXXIV.19 'For þæm þæt mine fynd ne blissien æfter me, þa þe winnað mid unrihte ongean me, and me hatiað butan scylde 7 wincettað mid heora eagum betwuh him', corresponding to the Gallican psalter, XXXIV.19 'non supergaudeant mihi qui adversantur mihi inique, qui oderunt me gratis et annuunt oculis'.[74]

(e) *corona*: Ps(P) *heafodgold* and *cynegold* (each 1 ×); beside CP *ðyrnenne beag* (1 ×, in a passage inspired by the Latin 'spinis caput supponere non recusavit') and Bo *heafodbeag* (2 × in prose, including an instance in the list of contents) and *beag* (2 × in prose). Ps(P) appears here to be deliberately using 'poetic' compounds to denote, in the one case certainly and in the other possibly, a royal crown; in Bo, in contrast, Alfred is referring merely to a victor's wreath, while in CP the reference to Christ's crown of thorns directs attention to the material, not to the symbolism.[75]

(f) *vendere*: Ps(P) *bebycgan* (1 ×); beside CP *sellan* (2 ×). *Bebycgan* is generally identified as an Anglian form, its presence in Or (as adjectival *unbeboht*) and in the Laws of Alfred usually being explained away as due to Mercian influence.[76] However, the absence of *bebycgan* from the accepted works of

---

[73] See also the gloss 'Conticiscent, silebant: Sicittan' *Anglo-Saxon and Old English Vocabularies*, ed. Thomas Wright and Richard Paul Wülcker (London, 1884) I, col. 211, line 43. *Conticescere* is rendered by *geswigian* in the Vespasian Hymns.

[74] If it had been selected, *biecnan* would, of course, have alliterated with *blissian*, but at the same time it would have directed the emphasis outside rather than inside the series of subordinate clauses in which the concept occurs. *Wincettað*, on the other hand, alliterates with *winnað*, which belongs to that series. For Gallican *supergaudeant* the Vespasian Psalter reads *insultent*.

[75] For *corona* words, see, further, Kirschner, *Kranz und Krone, passim*. *Cynegold* is found also in *The Phoenix*; *heafodgold* and *heafodbeag* both occur in the Vercelli homilies.

[76] See Jordan, *Eigentümlichkeiten*, p. 50; Scherer, *Geographie und Chronologie*, p. 13, and *The Old English Orosius*, ed. Bately, p. lxxii. Elsewhere Or has the expression *gesellan wiþ feo*. In late West Saxon tests the

Alfred does not rule out the possibility that it was current in early West Saxon.[77] That it could exist alongside alternatives in texts of the same dialect origin is suggested by its presence and by that of the expression *sellan wiþ feo* in BlHom,[78] while CP's instances of the concept 'sell' (the only two I have found in the accepted works of Alfred) occur together, in a context where the presence of *gebycgan*, 'buy', could well have prompted the rejection of *bebycgan*, 'sell': 'Hi sellað wið to lytlum weorðe ðæt ðæt hi meahton hefonrice mid gebycggan: sellað wið manna lofe' (p. 449, line 14).[79]

(2) Ps(P) uses a word not found in the accepted works of Alfred as well as a word or words that Alfred employs. For example:

(*a*) *refugium*: Ps(P) *gebeorh* (2 ×) and *gebeorhstow* (1 ×) as well as *friþstow* (3 ×); beside CP *friþstow* (1 ×) and BO *friþstow* (1 × in prose and 1 × in verse). *Friþstow* occurs also in the Laws of Alfred but is otherwise recorded by BT from only these texts; cf. *friþstol* in the Laws of Æthelred and the *Anglo-Saxon Chronicle* 1006 CDE. *Gebeorhstow*, according to BT, is found only

---

most frequently used words for 'sell' are (*be*)*ciepan* and its varients and (*ge*)*sellan* in conjunction with a phrase indicating that the 'giving' or 'handing over' is in return for money, e.g. *to ceape, wiþ weorþe* or *wiþ feo*; see further, Gretsch, *Regula*, p. 322.

[77] Indeed all arguments for provenance based on the concentration of a given word at a given period in texts of the same apparent dialect origin must be treated with a certain amount of suspicion, particularly in view of the absence of published concordances of so much of the small corpus of Old English texts that has come down to us; see, e.g., Kenneth Sisam, *Studies in the History of Old English Literature* (Oxford, 1953), pp. 119–39, and the qualifications made to the claims of earlier word-geographers, *Theodulfi Capitula*, ed. Sauer, pp. 212–76. Given the small corpus and the very restricted number of early West Saxon authors whose work we have, both personal preference and the limited opportunities afforded by the subject matter have to be taken into consideration. In this connection it should be noted that Ps(B) retains *bebycgan* in both the places Ps(A) has it.

[78] BlHom, p. 63, line 7, beside pp. 69, line 8, 69, line 13, 75, line 22, and 79, line 23. The two homilies involved, nos. v and vi, contain other allegedly Anglian features; see Menner, 'The Anglian Vocabulary of the *Blickling Homilies*', pp. 56–64. See Rushworth 1 glosses *bebygið vel sellað* and *sylle vel bebycge* (*The Holy Gospels in Anglo-Saxon, Northumbrian and Old Mercian Versions*, ed. W. W. Skeat (Cambridge, 1871–7), text of Oxford, Bodleian Library, Auct. D. 2. 19, also known as the Macregol Gospels). Of course scribal interference can never be ruled out, as variant readings in Bede, GD, Mart and psalter glosses show: e.g., Bede, p. 130, line 33; GD, p. 64, line 7; Mart, p. 94, line 16; and Berghaus, *Verwandtschaftsverhältnisse*, p. 96.

[79] Ps(P)'s use of *bebycgan* may also have been influenced by contextual considerations: XLIII.14 'Þu us bebohtest 7 bewrixledest 7 nan folc mid us ne gehwyrfdest' for Roman and Gallican, XLIII.13 'Vendidisti populum tuum sine pretio et non fuit multitudo in commutationibus nostris [*var. eorum*]'; exploiting the identical prefixes of *bebohtest* and *bewrixledest* and the trisyllabic structure of *bebohtest* and *gehwyrfdest*. *Sellan* in the sense 'give' occurs freely in both Ps(P) and the accepted works of Alfred. Other words in Ps(P) with an allegedly Anglian flavour are *stræl* (1 ×, beside *fla* and *flan* (4 ×)) and *herenes* (1 ×, beside *hering* etc.); see also *giornes* (1 ×) and cf. Jordan, *Eigentümlichkeiten*, p. 75; Menner, 'The Anglian Vocabulary of the *Blicking Homilies*', p. 58; and GD, ed. Hecht II, 147, Anm. 7. However, the form *giornes* is found in Solil and *herenes* in CP and so, even if we have to suppose the influence of Alfred's Mercian helpers, the presence of similar forms in Ps(P) does not rule out authorship by Alfred for that work. Moreover, though surviving Anglian texts may well have preferred *stræl* to *flan*, the current West Saxon word, the Middle English evidence indicates exactly the reverse. In any case in Ps(P) *stræl* may have been deliberately selected at the expense of the 'normal' form for the sake of alliteration: XVII.14 He sende his stræ[las] 7 hi tostencte.'

in Ps(P), presumably being preferred to the abstract *gebeorh* (found in Ps(A) and as the normal rendering for *refugium* in psalter glosses and texts of all periods) because of the siege element in the context: XXXI.8 'þu eart min gebeorhstow on minum earfoþum, þa me habbað utan behringed; ac þu þe eart min frefrend, ahrede me æt þam þe me habbað utan bestanden', corresponding to the Vespasian Psalter, XXXI.7 'Tu mihi es refugium a pressura quae circumdedit me exultatio mea redime me a circumdantibus me.'[80] Since the concept 'refuge' occurs only three times (effectively twice) in the accepted works of Alfred, the absence of variation there cannot be considered of itself significant. On the contrary, the fact that *friþstow* is the preferred form in both Ps(P) and the accepted works of Alfred could be taken as support for an Alfredian connection for the former.

(*b*) Ps(P) *frefrung* (1 ×) as well as *frofor* (6 ×), without equivalent in the Latin psalter; beside CP *frofor* (4 ×), Bo *frofor* (4 × in prose and 4 × in verse) and Solil *frofor* (2 ×).[81] The context seems to have influenced Ps(P)'s choice of this apparently unique form: XXII.5 'þin gyrd 7 þin stæf me afrefredon, þæt is þin þreaung 7 eft þin frefrung', with the first syllable of *frefrung* echoing the stressed second syllable of *afrefredon* and with its second syllable repeating the ending of *þreaung*.

(*c*) Ps(P) *fulian* (1 ×) as well as (*for*)*rotian* (2 ×); beside CP *rotian* (2 ×) and *forrotian* (5 ×). We have here to do with deliberate variation in Ps(P), since the two words occur together: XXXVII.5 'Min wunda rotedan 7 fuledon for minum dysige', corresponding to the Gallican psalter, XXXVII.6 'putruerunt et corruptae sunt cicatrices meae a facie insipientiae meae'.[82]

(*d*) *sperare*: Ps(P) *gehyhtan* (2 ×) as well as *hopian* (43 ×, of which thirty-two render Latin *sperare*, the remainder *confidere*, *sustinere*, *expectare* etc.); beside CP *hopian* (4 ×), Bo *hopian* (2 × in prose and 1 × in verse) and Solil *hopian* (3 ×).[83] Cf. CP *hyht* (1 ×) instead of normal *tohopa*[84] and Bo *hyhtlic* (1 × in verse). *Sperare* is rendered by (*ge*)*hyhtan* in Ps(A) and this is the preferred form

---

[80] Note also how the *b* of *gebeorhstow* connects it with *behringed* and *bestanden*, linking the opposed ideas of protection and aggression. The Gallican text of the vulgate psalms reads not *pressura* but *tribulatione*.

[81] A fifth instance of *frofor* is found in the prayer at the end of MS B of Bo. Cf. Ps(P) *bismrung* (1 ×) instead of normal *bismer* (7 ×) and *leahtor* (1 ×) instead of *leahtrung* (3 ×).

[82] Similarly *healsung* is used twice for *deprecatio* instead of normal *gebed*, because on each occasion the latter is being used in the same verse for Latin *oratio*: VI.7 '7 God gehyrde mine healsunge 7 Drihten onfeng min gebed', corresponding to the Roman, Gallican and Hebrew psalters, VI.10, 'exaudivit [*var.* audivit] Dominus deprecationem meam. Dominus orationem meam suscepit [*var.* adsumpsit *and* suscipiet]' and XXXVIII.14 'Drihten, gehyr min gebed 7 mine healsunga', corresponding to the Gallican psalter, XXXVIII.13 'exaudi orationem meam Domine et deprecationem meam'; see, further, below, p. 93.

[83] I include here instances of *hopian* with the separable prefix *to*, taken by Carnicelli and Carlson as the verb *tohopian*.

[84] For *tohopa* beside *hyht*, see below, p. 89.

in Bede and WS.[85] It is possible that Ps(P)'s choice of *gehyhtan* here, instead of its normal usage, has been influenced by contextual considerations, the verb not only occurring in conjunction with the similarly sounding *Dryhten* but also containing a high vowel sound which, at least to modern ears, is particularly appropriate to the meaning of the verses in which it occurs: XXVII.8 'Drihten is min [fu]ltumend 7 min gescyldend; on hine gehyht min heorte 7 he me gefultumað' and XXXII.18 'Sy, Drihten, þin mildheortnes ofer us, swa swa we gehyhtað on þe.'

(*e*) *exultare*: Ps(P) *wynsumian* (2 ×) as well as *fægnian* (10 ×) and *blissian* (5 ×); Ps(P) also uses *fægnian* and *blissian*, along with *gefeon*, for *gaudere* and *laetari*, agreeing in this with the accepted works of Alfred, which, however, never use *wynsumian*. The complete figures for these Old English words are: Ps(P) *fægnian* twenty-three times, *blissian* nineteen times and *gefeon* and *wynsumian* each twice;[86] CP *fægnian* twenty-two times, *blissian* ten times and *gefeon* six times; Bo *fægnian* nineteen times in prose (including three in the chapter headings) and twice in verse; and Solil *fægnian* five times. Cf. Ps(A) *wynsumian* (10 ×) for *exultare* and *jubilare* and *gefeon* (44 ×) for *exultare* and *gaudere*, with (*ge*)*blissian* (58 ×) restricted to *laetari* and *laetificari*.[87] It should be noted that both Ps(P)'s instances of *wynsumian* occur alongside the Alfredian *fægnian* and *blissian* as an additional variant: XXX.7 'Ic þonne symle hopige to Drihtne 7 fægnie 7 wynsumige 7 blissie on þinre mildheortnesse' and XXXI.13 'Blissiað for þæm on Gode 7 wynsumiað, ge rihtwisan, 7 fægniað 7 wuldriað ealra rihtwillenda heortan.'

(*f*) *retro* and *retrorsum*: Ps(P) *on bæcling* and *on earsling* (each 2 ×), as well as *under bæc* (3 ×); beside CP *under bæc* (4 ×) and Bo *under bæc* (3 × in prose). Cf. Ps(A) *on bæc*.[88] Once again Ps(P)'s commonest form is the Alfredian one.

In the cases of (*a*), (*e*) and (*f*) the greater variety in Ps(P) may well have been linked with the greater opportunity for variation afforded by the larger number of contexts provided by the text.[89] This is certainly true of one set

---

[85] Once in the group *gehyhte 7 wende*. The distribution of forms rendering Latin *sperare* is *gehyhtan* Bede (6 ×) and WS (3 ×), (*ge*)*wenan* Bede (5 ×) and WS (2 ×), *wilnian* Bede (1 ×) and WS (1 ×) and *hopian* WS (1 ×). Cf. GD, p. 27, line 23, where the *gehihte* of MSS C and O appears as *hopode* in H.

[86] See, further, above, p. 75. The pp. adj. *gefægen* is not included here.

[87] For Bede's usage, see above, p. 75. BlHom has *gefeon* (18 ×), (*ge*)*blissian* (11 ×) and *wynsumian* (6 ×), Latin equivalents unknown.

[88] Ps(B) *on bæcling* (1 ×) for Ps(A) *on bæc*. *On bæcling* is found also in Bede and BlHom.

[89] The converse is frequently also true. However, I find misleading Grinda's claim ('*Arbeit*' *und* '*Mühe*', pp. 235–6): 'In Pl besteht eine relativ feste Bindung von *earfoð* an *tribulatio*, während in Alf CP usw. eine ganze Reihe weiterer lat. Wörter durch *earfoð* übersetzt wird' and, as a result, if William of Malmesbury's statement that Ps(P) was Alfred's last work is to be believed, 'so bliebe der schematische Zug an der Wortverwendung in Pl zu erklären'. The accepted works of Alfred certainly use *earfoþ* to render a range of Latin terms (*adversa*, *adversitas*, *dolor*, *flagella*, *labor*, *pressura* and *tribulatio*), while the majority of instances of *earfoþ* in Ps(P) with equivalents in the Latin psalter do indeed render

of variants, representing the concepts 'set free', liberate', 'rescue' and 'release', Lat *liberare, redimere* etc. For these Ps(P) uses *ahreddan* no fewer than thirteen times, yet the word is absent from CP, Bo and Solil. At first sight this might seem to be a potential argument against common authorship. But in Ps(P) *ahreddan* is merely one of no fewer than four different words, occurring, in all, fifty-four times: *aliesan* (37 ×) *ahreddan* (13 ×) and *gefreogan* and *generian* (each 2 ×).[90] In contrast, CP has four words in a total of only eight possible contexts, namely *aliesan* (3 ×), *onliesan* (1 ×) and *gefreogan* and *generian* (each 2 ×); Bo, though using five words – *aliesan, onliesan, gefreogan, gefreolsian* and (in verse) *nerian* – has only one example of each; and Solil has *aliesan* (3 ×) and *gefreogan* and *gefreolsian* (each 1 ×). Since in late West Saxon *a-* sometimes replaces earlier *on-*, *aliesan* and *onliesan* may be considered as variants of the same word.[91] The absence of *ahreddan* from the accepted works of Alfred therefore is statistically non-significant and once again the commonest word in Ps(P) turns out to be also the one preferred by Alfred. So too with the different representations of the concept 'crush', 'destroy', Lat *confringere, conterere* and *conturbare*, Ps(A) *gebrecan/tobrecan, geþræstan/for-þræstan* and *gedrefan* respectively. Ps(P) agrees with Ps(A) in having *gedrefan* as the main representative of *(con)turbare* (20 ×, along with *tobrecan* and *gebrytan* each 1 ×) and this is also the usage of CP. For *confringere* and *conterere*, on the other hand, Ps(P) uses *forbrecan* (2 × and 3 × respectively), *tobrecan* (1 × and 2 ×), *gebrytan* (1 × and 2 ×) and *brecan, abrecan* and *forbrytan* (2 ×, 1 × and 1 ×, for *confringere* only). Of these words only *brecan* and its compounds (*abrecan, forbrecan* and *tobrecan*) are found in the accepted works of Alfred, along with *gebrecan*, which is absent from Ps(P), and of these only *gebrecan* is used to represent one of the Latin words in question, *confringere*. However, these figures have to be interpreted not only in the light of an almost total absence of both *confringere* and *conterere* from the Latin sources of CP, Bo and Solil – the only instance that I have found being the one of *confringere* rendered *gebrecan* in CP – but also in the light of the predilection for variation on the part of the author of Ps(P). Thus the instances of *gebrytan* and *forbrytan* for *confringere* are both used alongside their counterparts in

Lat *tribulatio*. However, Ps(P) also uses *earfoþ* for *labor* and *pressura* (see above, n. 80) and the only other Latin term in Grinda's list which occurs in the first fifty psalms is *dolor*, which is translated in Ps(P) by *sar*, the normal rendering also in Alfred's accepted works. So the relatively restricted use of *earfoþ* in Ps(P) must be attributed to the Latin source, not to the translator.

90 Ps(P) also uses *aliesan, ahreddan* and *generian* in verses where the Roman psalter has *eripere*, which it normally renders by *gefriþian*. Ps(A) has *aliesan* for *redimere, generian* for *eripere* and *eruere* and *gefreogan* for *liberare*. Rauh (*Wortschatz*, p. 35) takes *forbrytan* to be late West Saxon; however, given the relative rareness of this word, its presence in Ps(P) does not make the latter a late text; see, further, Gretsch, *Regula*, pp. 337–8.

91 Cf. A. Campbell, *Old English Grammar* (Oxford, 1959), §474. *Onliesan* and *aliesan* occur not infrequently as variant readings in the manuscripts of GD.

brecan: XXVIII.5 'Þæs Godes word brycþ cedortreowu...Drihten forbrycð 7 forbryt þa myclan cedortreowu', corresponding to the Roman, Gallican and Hebrew psalters, XXVIII.5 'Vox Domini confringentis cedros. et confringet Dominus cedros Libani', and XLV.8 'He afierð fram us ælc gefeoht ut ofer ure landgemæru 7 forbrycð ura feonda bogan 7 eall heora wæpn gebryt 7 heora scyldas forbærnð', corresponding to the Roman and Gallican psalters, XLV.10 'Auferens bella usque ad finem [*var.* fines] terrae arcum conteret et confringet arma et scuta conburet in ignem [*var.* igni].'[92] In sum, the above examples, constituting a representative sample, illustrate how there is no variation that has to be interpreted as evidence of separate authorship; on the contrary, in some cases, close examination gives an impression of an intimate connection between Ps(P) and Alfred.

Correspondences

It is now time to consider the very substantial body of material which, taken as a whole, suggests that this connection is more than accidental, is more than is to be explained by the proximity of authors in time and space, which accounts for the numerous points of agreement between the accepted works of Alfred, Or and certain sections of the *Anglo-Saxon Chronicle*.[93] Since Wichmann's detailed lists[94] demonstrate that Ps(P) and the accepted works of Alfred share the same common core of vocabulary but do not take into account the extent to which there was possibility of disagreement, I propose to concentrate here on identical selections, identical preferences, comparing, where relevant, the usage of the two other major early West Saxon texts, Or and the '890 *Chronicle*', in particular Or.[95]

(1) Ps(P) and the accepted works of Alfred agree in their representation of the concepts which have been discussed above as distinguishing Ps(P)

---

[92] Cf. WS, where *confringere* is rendered by *forbrecan*, *tobrysan* and *forbrytan* (each 1 ×), *conterere* by *tobrysan* (1 ×) and *conturbare* by *gedrefan* (3 ×).

[93] See *Two of the Saxon Chronicles Parallel*, ed. John Earle and Charles Plummer (Oxford, 1892–9; repr. 1952) I, cvi–cvii, and Bately, 'The Compilation of the Anglo-Saxon Chronicle', pp. 116–23; for my arguments for an '890 *Chronicle*', see *ibid. passim*. Unless otherwise stated, figures are based on readings from MS A, the Parker manuscript.

[94] They are not altogether accurate. For instance, a number of words said not to occur in Alfred's works are in fact there (e.g., *ofsittan*, *gesweotolian* and *geuntrumian* in CP; *fægernes*, *gehiernes*, *genealæcan*, *swiftnes* and *geteorian* in Bo; and *welwilnes* in Solil). The list of words in works of Alfred's time could be extended similarly.

[95] Cf. Bruce's criticism of Wichmann, 'The Anglo-Saxon Version of the Book of Psalms', p. 153, n. 1: 'I will refrain from discussing the laborious comparison of the vocabulary of our text with that of King Alfred's various translations which Wichmann has made...It seems to me impossible to draw any conclusions from such comparisons...At any rate...Wichmann, himself, has not made the slightest attempt to point out in what respect the results of his comparisons tell in favour of Alfredian authorship. One may say, also, of the points of phraseology and diction...that, if they prove anything, it is simply that the text was composed in the same period as those with which it is compared.'

from Ps(A), Bede, WS etc.[96] Thus both use (a) *mettrumnes* in preference to *untrumnes* etc.;[97] (b) *unriht* in preference to *unrihtwisnes*, never *wohnes*;[98] (c) *geswinc* and *swincan* for 'labour', 'toil', with *gewinn* and *winnan* reserved for 'fight', 'contend' etc.;[99] (d) *offrung* and *lac*, not *onsægdnes*;[100] (e) *earfoþ* in preference to *geswinc*, never *geswencednes*;[101] (f) *sceadu*, not *scua*;[102] (g) *ymbhringan*, *ymbstandan* etc., not *ymbsellan*;[103] (i)[104] (*ge*)*gaderian* in preference to *gesamnian*;[105] (k) (*ge*)*anbidian* and (*ge*)*bidan*, not *abidan* and *onbidan*;[106] (l) *fægnian* and *blissian* in preference to *gefeon*;[107] (m) (*ge*)*bu*(*i*)*an* as well as *wunian* and *eardian* for 'to dwell';[108] (n) *gieldan* and *forgieldan*, not *geedleanian*;[109] (o) *arleas* only very

96 Pp. 71–7. In this section I give figures for total occurrences of the Old English words, not, as before, linking them to specific Latin words.

97 *Mettrumnes* etc.: Ps(P) 6 ×, CP 24 ×, Bo 2 × in prose and 1 × in verse and Solil 2 ×; *untrumnes*: Ps(P) 3 ×, CP 9 ×, Bo 1 × in prose and Solil 2 ×; *untrymþ*: Ps(P) 1 ×.

98 *Unriht*: Ps(P) 31 ×, CP 16 × and Bo 5 × in prose and 1 × in verse; *unrihtwisnes*: Ps(P) 15 ×, CP 14 × and Bo 5 × in prose. Cf. *woh* in Ps(P), CP and Bo, a form found also in Or. Eleven of CP's fourteen instances of *unrihtwisnes* render Lat *iniquitas*.

99 *Geswinc*: Ps(P) 4 ×, CP 37 ×, Bo 8 × in prose and 3 × in verse and Solil 3 ×; *swincan*: Ps(P) 4 ×, CP 15 ×, Bo 12 × in prose and 3 × in verse and Solil 2 ×. See also below, n. 101. For *gewinn* and *winnan* in the sense 'fight', 'struggle', see below, p. 91, and cf. Bo, Lay IV, lines 55b–6, where the 'hit nu eall winð on þam yðum þisse worulde' of the prose (p. 10, line 27) appears as 'nu hi on monegum her / worulde yðum wynnað 7 swincað'.

100 *Offrung*: Ps(P) 10 × and CP 7 ×; *lac*: Ps(P) 1 × and CP 19 ×.

101 *Earfoþ*: Ps(P) 54 ×, CP 15 ×, Bo 17 × in prose and 2 × in verse; *earfoþnes*: CP 3 ×, Bo 1 × in prose. For *geswinc*, see above, n. 99. *Gedrefednes* occurs in both Ps(P) (1 ×, for *conturbatio*) and the accepted works of Alfred (CP 5 ×, Bo 9 × in prose and Solil 2 ×, with *gedrefnes* 2 × in Bo verse, Solil 1 ×). *Gedeorf* is not found in either corpus. 102 Ps(P) 5 ×, CP 1 × and Bo 6 × in prose.

103 For Ps(P)'s figures, see above, p. 74. Ps(P) also has one instance of *hweorfan ymb* where the Gallican text of the vulgate psalms has the verb *circumdare*, however, Ps(A), like the 'Hebrew' text, here uses the verb *circuire*, a word rendered by *hweorfan ymb* elsewhere in Ps(P). The usage of the accepted works of Alfred is CP *behringan, besittan, ymbhringan* and *ymbsettan* (each 1 ×) and *ymbsittan* (3 ×); and Bo *ymbstandan* (1 × in prose and 1 × in verse). Ps(P) also has *ofsittan* (2 ×), rendering Lat *obsedere*; *ofsittan* also occurs in CP (4 ×), Bo (3 ×) and Solil (1 ×), in the sense 'to beset', 'to oppress'.

104 I do not include an entry to correspond to the (h) of the first section, since equivalents of *confirmare* are absent from the accepted works of Alfred; however, *gestrangian* occurs three times in CP for *confortare* and *roborare*, while *getrymian* or *getrymman* is found sixteen times in CP and once each in Bo prose and Solil and *trymman* four times in CP and once in Solil. Similarly I omit any reference to (j) since I have found no equivalent for *deficere* in the accepted works of Alfred. However, Bo has *geteorian* in the sense 'to get tired'. For Ps(P)'s usage, see above, p. 74

105 *Gaderian*: Ps(P) 4 ×, CP 11 ×, Bo 7 × in prose and Solil 2 ×; *gegaderian*: Ps(P) 6 ×, CP 5 ×, Bo 26 × in prose and 1 × in verse and Solil 1 ×; *gesamnian*: CP 1 × and Bo 2 × in prose and 5 × in verse (the presence of the larger number of forms in the verse being quite possibly significant).

106 *Anbidian*: Ps(P) 7 × and Solil 1 ×; *geanbidian*: Bo 2 × in prose; *gebidan*: Ps(P) 3 ×, CP 1 ×, Bo 4 × in prose and 2 × in verse and Solil 1 ×; *bidan*. CP 4 ×. For *hopian*, see above, p. 83.

107 *Fægnian*: Ps(P) 23 ×, CP 22 ×, Bo 19 × in prose and 2 × in verse and Solil 5 ×; *blissian*: Ps(P) 19 ×, CP 10 ×; *gefeon*: Ps(P) 2 × and CP 6 ×. For *wynsumian* (Ps(P) 2 ×), see above, p. 84. The two instances of *gefeon* in Ps(P) correspond to the Gallican psalter, *supergaudere*, Roman *insultare*; see also Ps(P) XXXIV.19, where *blissian* corresponds to *supergaudere* in the Gallican, *laetari* in the Hebrew and *insultare* in the Roman.

108 (*Ge*)*bu*(*i*)*an*: Ps(P) 8 ×, CP 1 × and Bo 7 × in prose; *eardian*: Ps(P) 5 ×, CP 4 ×, Bo 3 × in prose and 2 × in verse and Solil 2 ×. *Wunian* is used also for 'to dwell' as well as 'to remain', 'to continue', both in Ps(P) and the accepted works of Alfred.

109 *Gieldan*: Ps(P) 13 ×, CP 6 × and Bo 5 × in prose and 1 × in verse; *forgieldan*: Ps(P) 3 ×, CP 4 × and Bo prose and Solil each 1 ×.

rarely;[110] (*p*) *wel la wel*, not *wel þe wel þe*.[111] Finally both prefer *faran* and *gan* to *feran* and *gangan*.[112]

In contrast, although Or agrees with Ps(P) and the accepted works of Alfred in its use of *unriht*, not *wohnes*, and of *geswinc*, not *gewinn*, in the sense of 'labour', 'toil', in its preference for (*ge*)*gaderian* over *gesamnian*,[113] in its use of (*ge*)*bu(i)an* as well as *wunian* and *eardian*[114] and of (*for*)*gieldan*, not *geedleanian*, in its very infrequent use of *arleas*[115] and in its preference for *faran* and *gan* over *feran* and *gangan*,[116] it disagrees in several important respects. Firstly, although it uses *offrung* (2 ×), the preferred words for 'sacrifice' are *geblot* (5 ×), *blot* (2 ×) and *blotung* (1 ×), with *tibernes* (1 ×). And in this context it may be noted that beside the Alfredian *offrian* (5 ×) it has *blotan* (8 ×) and *onsecgan* (1 ×).[117] Secondly, it never uses *behringan*, *ymbhringan*, *bestandan*, *ofsittan* or *ymbstandan* for 'to surround', 'to besiege', and, though it does have *ymbsittan*, it shows a marked preference for *besittan*.[118] Thirdly, it never has (*ge*)*anbidian*, though, unlike Ps(P) and the accepted works of Alfred, it uses *onbidan* as well as (*ge*)*bidan*.[119]

The '890 *Chronicle*' agrees with Or, Ps(P) and the accepted works of Alfred in its preference for *gegaderian* over *gesamnian*, in its use of *bu(i)an* as well as *wunian* and *eardian* and in its preference for *faran* over *feran*, with *gan*, never *gangan*.[120] For 'to surround', 'to besiege', it has only *ymbsittan* (2 ×) and *utan*

---

[110] Ps(P) 2 ×, CP 3 ×. Cf. *arleasnes*: CP 1 × and Bo 1 × in prose; and *arleast*: Bo 2 × in verse.

[111] Ps(P) 1 × and *wel la* Bo 2 × in prose, Solil 1 ×.

[112] For Ps(P)'s usage, see above, p. 76. In CP *faran* outnumbers *feran* more than 5 : 1, while Bo has *faran* some twenty-two times in prose and ten times in verse, *gefaran* three times in prose and *feran* three times in prose and once in verse and Solil has *faran* six times. *Gan* occurs in Ps(P) nine times, CP thirty-four times and Bo fourteen times in prose and once in verse; *gangan* is found in Ps(P) five times, CP ten times and Bo three times in verse, with *eode* the only form in the preterite. Ps(P)'s examples of *gangan* are all first person singular, a form never found in Bo.

[113] *Gaderian* occurs once, *gegaderian* thirty-three times and *gesamnian* five times.

[114] *Bu(i)an* occurs five times in the section dealing with Ohthere's report to King Alfred, with *gebud* once and *gebun* twice in this section and *gebudon* once and *gebun* twice elsewhere in the work. *Wunian* is used for both 'to dwell' and 'to remain', *Eardian* is found three times (including two instances in Ohthere's report).

[115] Twice, in the same sentence. Or also uses both *earfoþ* and *geswinc* (each 4 ×) and *mettrumnes* and *untrumnes* (each 1 ×).

[116] Or has nearly 200 examples of intransitive *faran*, with *gefaran* 'to go' thirty-four times and *feran* six times. *Gan* occurs three times, beside *gangan* three times and *gegan* once.

[117] In the accepted works of Alfred *blotan* occurs only once (in CP).

[118] *Ymbsittan* occurs four times and *besittan* twenty-eight times. Cf. also the range of words used to describe surrounding by water: *behabban*, *belicgan*, *ymblicgan*, *ymbhabban*, *ymbfon* and *licgan ymbutan*; and see also *uton ymbfaran*.

[119] *Bidan* and *gebidan* each occurs five times and *onbidan* occurs once. *Hopian*, which Ps(P) occasionally uses for *expectare*, is not found in Or.

[120] *Gegaderian* is found three times and *gesamnian* once, while the figures for the following section, 891–900, are 6 : 1. The single instance of *eardian* is in annal 491 in MSS A and E, MSS B, C and F reading *wæron*, while *bu(i)an* occurs also in the 891–900 section. For the distribution of *faran* (35 × in MS A) and *feran* (7 ×), see Bately, 'The Compilation of the Anglo-Saxon Chronicle', pp. 111, n. 1, and 127; *gan* occurs twice, with nine instances in the 'genealogical preface' alongside two instances of *agan*.

began (1 ×); but the following section, 891–900, agrees with Or against the other texts in preferring *besittan* to *ymbsittan* (the former 5 × and the latter 2 ×). We may compare the *Læceboc*, which prefers *untrumnes* to *mettrumnes*, *earfoþ* to *geswinc* and *gan* to *gangan*.[121]

(2) Ps(P) and the accepted works of Alfred agree in their use of a number of words which have not yet been dealt with in this paper and which can be identified as in some way or other typical of early West Saxon[122] and in their avoidance of words which are typical of other dialects or periods. For example, the use of *cræft*,[123] *gefea*,[124] *ofermetto, ofermod* and *ofermodlic(e)*,[125] *tohopa*,[126] *unþeaw*,[127] *cigan*,[128] *hatian*,[129] (*eac*) *swa ilce*[130] and *swa þer* introducing a simile.[131] Or too has *cræft, gefea, ofermetto, tohopa* and

---

[121] See *Kleinere Angelsächsische Denkmäler* 1, Bibliothek der Angelsächsischen Prosa 6, ed. Günther Leonhardi (Hamburg, 1905).

[122] I include here usages which word studies suggest may be generally restricted to Anglian dialects in the later period but which occur also in early West Saxon texts.

[123] In the sense 'power', 'strength', 'might'; cf. Gretsch, *Regula*, pp. 347–8, and *Theodulfi Capitula*, ed. Sauer, pp. 252–3. It should be noted that, while *cræft*, like *mægen*, is found in Ps(P), CP and Bo, *miht* is confined to Bo (3 × in prose and 14 × in verse). See, further, the discussions of these words by Käsmann and Gneuss, cited by Sauer, *ibid.* p. 253.

[124] Ps(P) 5 ×, CP 15 ×, Bo 4 × in prose and 2 × in verse and Solil 1 × ; beside *bliss* (Ps(P) 11 ×, CP 7 × and Bo 8 × in prose and 1 × in verse) and *bliþnes* (Bo 2 × in prose). For details of late West Saxon usage and for Ostheeren's conclusion that *gefea* is the central word for *Freude* in early West Saxon, see Gretsch, *Regula*, pp. 335–6, and *Theodulfi Capitula*, ed. Sauer, p. 228; see also *The West-Saxon Gospels*, ed. Grünberg, p. 322.

[125] *Ofermetto*: Ps(P) 2 ×, CP 35 ×, Bo 7 × in prose and 3 × in verse and Solil 1 × ; *ofermod*: Ps(P) 5 ×, CP 15 × and Bo 5 × in prose and 3 × in verse; *ofermodlic(e)*: Ps(P) 1 ×, CP 3 × and Bo 1 × in prose. Cf. *ofermodnes* (CP 4 × and Bo 1 × in prose) and *ofermedu, ofermodgung* and *ofermodig* (each CP 1 ×); beside *oferhygd* (CP and Bo prose each 1 ×) and *oferhygdig* (CP 1 ×). The usages of Ps(A) is *oferhygd*. See, further, Schabram, *Superbia, passim*, and Bately, 'King Alfred and the Old English Translation of Orosius', pp. 444, 455 and 456.

[126] Ps(P) 8 ×, CP 17 ×, Bo 2 × in prose and 1 × in verse and Solil 8 ×. Cf. *hyht* (CP 1 ×) and *hyhtlic* (Bo 1 × in verse) and (*to*)*hopian* beside *gehyhtan*, for which, see, further, above, p. 83, and see *Theodulfi Capitula*, ed. Sauer, p. 263. The normal Old English word for Lat *spes* is *hyht*.

[127] Ps(P) and CP also use *uncyst*, while Bo has *leahtor* (2 × in verse), a word which in Ps(P) occurs alongside *leahtrung* in the sense 'opprobrium', 'reproach'; see, further, Gretsch, *Regula*, pp. 343–4, and *Theodulfi Capitula*, ed. Sauer, pp. 249–50.

[128] Ps(P) 1 × and CP 4 ×, for *clamare*; beside (*ge*)*clipian* (Ps(P) 32 ×, CP 24 ×, Bo 6 × in prose and 2 × in verse and Solil 11 ×); see, further, Jordan, *Eigentümlichkeiten*, p. 93. *Cigan* is found also in the Laws of Alfred.

[129] Ps(P) 16 ×, CP 10 ×, Bo 7 × in prose and 1 × in verse and Solil 4 ×. Bo also has *feon* (1 × each in prose and verse). Cf. *feoung* Ps(P) 1 ×, CP 4 × and Bo prose 2 ×), beside 'normal' West Saxon *hete*; and see *Theodulfi Capitula*, ed. Sauer, p. 238. The usage of Ps(A) is *feon* and *feoung*.

[130] See Bately, 'King Alfred and the Old English Translation of Orosius', pp. 448, 451, 455 and 458, n. 200. For *eac swelce* in Or, see below, n. 133.

[131] This usage has caused a great deal of trouble to Anglo-Saxon scribes as well as to modern editors and commentators. All five instances in Ps(P) are obscured either by emendation by Bright or by scribal error, with confusion of *s* and *r* (a common error in Anglo-Saxon minuscule and one found elsewhere in Ps(P); e.g., XLVIII.19 *þæs* for adverb *þær*): x, Introduction *swa þes spearuwa* and XXI.5 *swa þes wyrm* (described, *The Paris Psalter*, ed. Colgrave *et al.*, p. 16 as 'a curious use of the demonstrative *þes* in similes') beside XXI.12 *swa þær weax*, XXXVI.19 *swa ðer smec* and XLV.3 *swa þer muntas* (emended by Bright to *swa þæt weax*, *swa swa smec* and *swa þa muntas*); cf. CP, p. 90, line 19

unþeaw[132] but never uses *hatian* or *swa þer*, and instead of *ofermod, ofermodlic, cigan* and *(eac) swa ilce* it selects the non-Alfredian *ofermodig* and *eac* and the Alfredian *clipian*.[133] The '890 *Chronicle*', in contrast, has *swa þer* (1 ×), removed through scribal alteration,[134] and uses *ofermede* (1 ×).[135]

(3) Ps(P) and the accepted works of Alfred agree against Or and the '890 *Chronicle*' in their use of a wide range of words for certain concepts. For example, 'to show': Ps(P) *oþiewan* and *ætiewan* (each 1 ×)[136] and *æeawed* (1 ×, for either *æteawed* or *geeawed*) and Alfredian *oþiewan* (CP 2 × and Bo 1 × in prose and 2 × in verse), *otiewan* (Bo 1 × in verse), *ætiewan* etc. (CP 21 ×) and *(ge)eowian, iewan* etc. (CP 24 ×, Bo 8 × in prose and 1 × in verse and Solil 8 ×); beside Or *oþiewan* (6 ×) and '890 *Chronicle*' *oþiewan* (4 ×).[137] Ps(P) and the accepted works of Alfred also agree in using the constructions *oþer twega oþþe...oþþe* and *awþer oþþe...oþþe*, not found in either Or or the '890 *Chronicle*'.[138]

(4) Ps(P) and the accepted works of Alfred agree against Or and the '890

swa ðer bieme MS Cii *sua ðer*, with variant *ðær* in C12, *ðes* in H and *oþer* in R5 and I2). For Dorothy Horgan ('The Relationship between the OE MSS of KingAlfred's Translation of Gregory's *Pastoral Care*', *Anglia* 91 (1973), 153–69, at 156) H's reading *ðes* 'seems to be better than that in the other manuscripts'. 'It seems likely', she says, 'that there was some difficulty in reading a primary source in which the letter *s* may have been confused with the letter *r*. The reading of H indicates that the scribe has resolved satisfactorily the difficulty presented by the spelling *ðer*...T and U [= Carlson's R5 and I2], both inheriting *r* instead of *s*, have a form which has been created to fit the context; J [= Carlson's Ju] and Cii appear to have kept the misreading, whilst the scribe of CC [= Carlson's C12] substitutes another word.' For Carlson (*The Pastoral Care* I, 150), on the other hand, Horgan's 'general line of argumentation cannot be accepted without reservations'. His tentative suggestion is that the original reading was *sua oðer bieme* and he compares the construction *swilce oðer*, described by E. Tengstrand, 'A Special Use of Old English *oþer* after *swilce*', *SN* 37 (1965), 382–92. However, if we add to the instances of *swa þer* and *swa þes* in Ps(P) and CP the four instances of *swaþer* or *swæþer* in this context in Bo (3 × in prose and 1 × in verse, with two instances altered in MS B to *swa þæt* and *swa þe* respectively) and a further instance in the '890 *Chronicle*' (473 A *swa þær fyr*, with *þær* subsequently erased), there seems no doubt at all that, whatever its ultimate origin and affiliations, the construction *swa þer* or *swaþer* is not only genuine but also associated particularly with texts of the time of Alfred.

132 Beside *cræft* it has both *mægen* and *miht*; beside *gefea* (3 ×) it has *bliþnes* (1 ×). The other figures are *ofermetto* 7 ×, *tohopa* 1 × and *unþeaw* 2 ×. Ps(A) differentiates between *miht* for *potestas* and *potentia* and *mægen* for *virtus* and *vis*.

133 For *ofermodig* (4 ×), see Schabram, *Superbia, passim*, and Bately, 'King Alfred and the Old English Translation of Orosius', p. 444; for *eac swelce* (3 ×), see Bately, 'The Compilation of the Anglo-Saxon Chronicle', p. 126 and n. 3, and *Theodulfi Capitula*, ed. Sauer, pp. 236–7. *Clipian* occurs twice. The concepts 'to hate' and 'proudly' are not found, but cf. *hete* (2 ×).

134 See above, n. 131.

135 See, further, the discussion of the distribution of *wisdom* and *snyttro*, Seebold, '*Sapiens und prudens*', pp. 291–33.

136 Used intransitively in the sense 'to appear'.

137 One of these has been altered to *ætiewan* in MS A. The first 'original' instance of *ætiewan* in this manuscript is *s.a.* 892. For Lat *ostendere, ostendi* and *(ap)parere* Ps(A) has *oteawan*, while Bede's normal usage appears to have been *æteawan* (common MS variant *ætywan*).

138 See Bately, 'King Alfred and the Old English Translation of Orosius', pp. 450–3, 455 and 457.

Chronicle' in their use of a small range of words for certain concepts. For example:

(*a*) 'to fight': Ps(P) *winnan* and *feohtan* (each 3 ×) and Alfredian *winnan* (CP 16 × and Bo 20 × in prose and 12 × in verse) and *feohtan* (CP 8 × and Bo 2 × in prose); beside Or *winnan* (over 100 ×), *gefeohtan* (59 ×), *feohtan* (35 ×) and *gewinnan* (2 ×) and '890 *Chronicle*' *gefeohtan* (50 ×), *feohtan* (22 ×) and *winnan* (5 ×). The order of preferences is also significant, Ps(P)'s equal numbers of *winnan* and *feohtan* agreeing with the Alfredian usage.[139]

(*b*) 'to help': Ps(P) (*ge*)*fultumian* (5 ×) and Alfredian (*ge*)*fultumian* (CP 11 ×, Bo 4 × in prose and 1 × in verse and Solil 8 ×); beside Or (*ge*)*fylstan* (12 ×) and *fultumian* (2 ×). The '890 *Chronicle*' agrees with Ps(P) and the Alfredian practice in using (*ge*)*fultumian* (4 ×).[140]

(5) Ps(P) and the accepted works of Alfred agree against Or and the '890 *Chronicle*' in certain preferences. For example:

(*a*) 'mercy': Ps(P) *mildheortnes* (33 ×) and *milts* and *miltsung* (each 1 ×) and Alfredian *mildheortnes* (CP 24 ×, Bo 3 × in prose and Solil 2 ×), *milts* (CP 3 × and Bo prose and Solil each 1 ×) and *miltsung* (CP 3 × and Bo 1 × in prose); beside Or *miltsung* (6 ×), *mildheortnes* (3 ×) and *milts* (1 ×).[141]

(*b*) 'to drive away': Ps(P) *adrifan* (6 ×) and Alfredian *adrifan* (CP 12 ×, Bo 9 × in prose and 2 × in verse and Solil 2 ×) and *adræfan* (CP 1 ×); beside Or *adræfan* (11 ×) and *adrifan* (10 ×) and '890 *Chronicle*' *adrifan* (5 ×) and *adræfan* (4 ×).[142]

(*c*) 'to be called', 'to be named':
(i) Ps(P) and the accepted works of Alfred agree in preferring *hatte* and *is* (*ge*)*haten* etc. to the construction (*þe*) *man hæt*: Ps(P) *hatte* (4 ×) and *is gehaten* and (*þe*) *man hæt* (each 1 ×) and Alfredian *hatte* (CP 8 × and Bo 8 × in prose and 1 × in verse), *is haten* (CP 3 × and Bo 7 × in prose and 2 × in verse), *is gehaten* (CP 6 ×, Bo 5 × in prose and 2 × in verse and Solil 2 ×) and (*þe*) *man hæt* (CP 3 × and Bo 6 × in prose and 1 × in verse);[143] beside Or (*þe*)

---

[139] Cf. Bede, where the order is *feohtan, winnan*, with *campian* in third place, followed by *gefeohtan* and *gewinnan*; and see, further, Bately, 'The Compilation of the Anglo-Saxon Chronicle', pp. 104, 105, 107, 114 and 122–3.

[140] See, further, Bately, 'King Alfred and the Old English Translation of Orosius', pp. 445, 451, 453, 455 and 456, and 'The Compilation of the Anglo-Saxon Chronicle', p. 119, n. 2. Ps(A) normally uses *gefultumian*, with *fultumian* once. Cf. Or's use of *acwencean* as well as the Alfredian *adwæscan* (Ps(P) *adwæscan* and *gedwæscan*), for which, see *Theodulfi Capitula*, ed. Sauer, pp. 218–19.

[141] Ps(A) differentiates between *mildheortnes* for *misericordia* and *milds* for *miseratio* and *propitiatio*.

[142] See, further, Bately, 'The Compilation of the Anglo-Saxon Chronicle', pp. 104, 107, 113, n. 4, 114 and 123, n. 4. Ps(A) has only *adrifan*.

[143] That Ps(P) shows an apparent preference for *hatte* over *is* (*ge*)*haten*, while the converse is true of CP and Bo, is no argument against common authorship. In both Ps(P) and CP *hatte* is the normal usage with personal names, the only exceptions being one instance of *is gehaten* in Ps(P) (as the variant to the *hatte* immediately preceding in the same verse) and three instances of *is* (*ge*)*haten* in CP (one of

man hæt (115 ×), *is haten* (61 ×) and *hatte* (16 ×) and '890 *Chronicle' is haten*
(1 ×). In addition the accepted works of Alfred frequently use the construction
(*þe*) *we hataþ* (Ps(P) 1 ×), a construction never found in Or or the '890
Chronicle'.[144]

(ii) Ps(P) and the accepted works of Alfred agree in preferring constructions
in *hatan* to those in (*ge*)*nemnan* and *cweþan*:[145] Ps(P) *hatan* (7 ×), *cweþan* (5 ×)[146]
and *nemnan* (1 ×) and Alfredian *hatan* (CP 25 ×, Bo 58 × in prose and 15 ×
in verse and Solil 7 ×), (*ge*)*nemnan* (CP 10 × and Bo 8 × in prose and 4 ×
in verse) and *cweþan* (CP 1 ×);[147] beside '890 *Chronicle*' (as represented by
MS A) (*ge*)*nemnan* (9 ×), *cweþan* (7 ×) and *hatan* (2 ×), Mart (*ge*)*nemnan* (some
140 ×), *hatan* (19 ×), *cweþan* (9 ×) and (*ge*)*ciegan* (5 ×) and Bede *nemnan* and
hatan (each some 75 ×), (*ge*)*ciegan* (some 23 ×) and *cweþan* (some 17 ×), with,
however, numerous variants in the later, 'West Saxonized' manuscripts. Or
here shares the preferences of Ps(P) and the accepted works of Alfred, with
hatan (208 ×), *nemnan* (6 ×) and *cweþan* (1 ×), though it differs from these in
its use of the construction (*þe*) *man nemneþ* and in its avoidance of the
expression 'his/whose name is': Ps(P) *þære nama is* (1 ×) and Alfredian *is
genemned* (CP 8 × and Bo 3 × in prose), *þæs nama is* (Bo 9 × in prose and
1 × in verse) and *þæm is nama* (Bo 1 × in verse, where the demands of
alliteration rule out the use of the normal *þæs* type); beside Or (*þe*) *man nemneþ*
(3 ×) and *is* (*ge*)*nemned* (2 ×). Cf. '890 *Chronicle' is* (*ge*)*nemned* (6 ×) and *þe man
nemneþ* and *þæm is nama* (each 2 ×).[148]

(6) Ps(P) and the accepted works of Alfred agree in that Ps(P) uses the

---

these as a variant to a preceding *hatte*). In Bo the figures for the prose are *hatte* with personal name
eight times and *is* (*ge*)*haten* nine times (once as a variant to a preceding *hatte* and four times in a *duo
nomina* or *tria nomina* construction with several names for the same person, a context not occurring
in Ps(P)). It should be noted that in Ps(P) the longest run of instances of *hatte* uninterrupted by an
alternative construction is two, the norm also in Bo.

[144] *Hatan* is also used frequently in first and second person singular and second and third person plural
constructions in Bo. At first sight the usage of the *Læceboc* seems very similar to that of Ps(P) and
the accepted works of Alfred, with an order of preference *hatte* (22 ×), *we/men hataþ* (5 ×); however,
the majority of instances of *hatte* occur in the paratactic construction 'X hatte wyrt' (e.g., 'nim weax
7 hemlic hatte wyrt' (*Kleinere Denkmäler*, ed. Leonhardi, p. 45, line 31), with 'þa wyrt þe hatte X'
in second place and 'þa wyrt þe X hatte' (the norm in Ps(P) and the accepted works of Alfred) in
third place.

[145] Only instances where these verbs are interchangeable are included in the statistics that follow; the
past participle *gehaten* is taken to be part of the verb *hatan* and *gecweden* of *cweþan*.

[146] In the form *gecweden* and limited to the introductions to pss. II, IV and V.

[147] A second instance of *cweþan* (in the form *gecweden*) is found only in MSS C, Cii and C12, the other
manuscripts reading *genemned* (H) and *gehaten* (R5 and I2).

[148] See, further, Bately, 'The Compilation of the Anglo-Saxon Chronicle', pp. 104, 107, 114 and 123.
The construction *þæs nama is* is also found frequently in Mart (beside *se is on naman*) and Bede, while
GD has a preference for *þæm is nama*. Mart and Bede also share a marked preference for constructions
of the type *is* (*ge*)*nemned* over (*þe*) *man nemneþ*, the latter construction being totally absent from GD.
In the case of Bede the frequency of these constructions is to a large extent determined by the usage
of the Latin source.

Alfredian preferred forms but not the less common ones, whereas Or uses only the less common forms. For example:

(*a*) 'answer': Ps(P) *andswaru* (1 ×) and *andswarian* (6 ×) and Alfredian *andswaru* (CP 3 × and Bo 2 × in prose and 2 × in verse), (*ge*)*andswarian* (CP 4 ×, Bo 34 × in prose and Solil 6 ×), *andwyrd* (Bo 2 × in prose) and (*ge*)*andwyrdan* (CP 7 ×, Bo 17 × in prose and Solil 4 ×); beside Or *andwyrd* (6 ×) and *andwyrdan* (10 ×).[149]

(*b*) 'guilt', 'guilty' etc.: Ps(P) *scyld* (21 ×), *scyldig* (1 ×), *unscyld* (1 ×), *unscyldignes* (2 ×) and *unscyldig* (9 ×) and Alfredian *scyld* (CP 137 × and Bo 5 × in prose and 1 × in verse), *scyldig* (CP 17 ×, Bo 7 × in prose and Solil 1 ×), *unscyldig* (CP 6 × and Bo 8 × in prose and 2 × in verse and *gylt* (CP 4 × and Bo 1 × in prose); beside Or *gylt* (9 ×) and *ungyltig* (1 ×).[150]

(*c*) 'prayer': Ps(P) *gebed* (18 ×) and Alfredian *gebed* (CP 13 ×, Bo prose and Solil each 1 ×) and *ben* (CP 3 × and Solil 1 ×);[151] beside Or *ben* (3 ×). Cf. Bede, which uses both *gebed* and *ben*, with a slight preference for the former.[152]

(*d*) 'proper', 'suitable' (predicative): Ps(P) *cynn* (2 ×) and Alfredian *cynn* (CP 7 × and Bo prose 3 ×) and *gerisenlic* (Bo prose 1 ×); beside Or *gerisenlic* and *gerisne* (each 1 ×).[153]

(7) Ps(P) and the accepted works of Alfred agree against Or in their choice of words for certain concepts. For example, *gigant*, not *ent*;[154] *gimm*, not *gimmstan*; *geþeaht* and *geþeahtere* not *rædþeahtung* and *rædþeahtere*; *eaþmod*, not *eaþmodig*;[155] *mihtig*, nor *cræftig* and *wielde*; *betwuh* etc., not *betweonum*; *geo* and *geogeara*, not *on ærdagum* and *on ealddagum*.[156]

---

[149] See, further, Bately, 'King Alfred and the Old English Translation of Orosius', pp. 444, 451 and 457, and, for the usage in manuscripts of WS, *The West-Saxon Gospels*, ed. Grünberg, p. 321.

[150] One instance of *gylt* in CP occurs in the phrase *ðara scyldegena gyltas*, presumably to avoid repetition of the root *scyld-*. See, further, Bately, 'King Alfred and the Old English Translation of Orosius', pp. 443, 451–3, 455 and 457, and G. Büchner, *Vier altenglische Bezeichnungen für Vergehen und Verbrechen (firen, gylt, man, scyld)* (Berlin, 1968).

[151] Two of the three instances of *ben* in CP occur in the same sentence, with MS H reading *bed* for the second of them (p. 399, line 31). In Ps(A) *gebed* is reserved for *operatio* and *oratio* and *ben* for *deprecatio*, *petitio* and *prex*. Ps(P), however, uses *gebed* indiscriminately. For Ps(P) *healsung*, see above, n. 82.

[152] It frequently renders *prex* and *preces* by the pairs *gebed 7 ben, bena 7 gebeda* etc. GD also has a large number of instances of *ben* beside *gebed* in a ratio of approx. 1:3.

[153] BT also records the construction *hit is cyn þæt* in the Laws of Ine. Ps(P) and the accepted works of Alfred also use *gemetlic*, 'fitting', 'suitable', but never in a construction of this type.

[154] For full details of the distribution of these words in Ps(P), the accepted works of Alfred and Or and for a number of other instances of differences, see Bately, 'King Alfred and the Old English Translation of Orosius', *passim*.

[155] The '890 *Chronicle*' agrees with Ps(P) and the accepted works of Alfred in using *eaþmod*.

[156] Ps(P) and the accepted works of Alfred also show the same preferences in their choice of conjunctions to introduce subordinate clauses; e.g., Ps(P), CP and Bo *ær ær*, a form which I have not noted in Bede, GD or Or, and a marked preference for *for þam* (*þam*) over *for þam þe*, *for þam þæt* etc. and over *forþon*. Indeed given the special relationship between Ps(P) and its Latin source there appears to be no significant difference in usage between Ps(P) and the accepted works of Alfred in respect of the constructions studied by Elizabeth Liggins (see her 'The Authorship of the Old English Orosius', pp. 57–90).

(8) Ps(P) and the accepted works of Alfred agree in their use of a number of phrases and collocations which are more than just reflections of their Latin sources.[157] The existence of these shared mannerisms is, of course, no proof in itself of common authorship; however, their absence from one or other corpus might well have been a strong argument for the contrary. For example:

(*a*) certain word pairs:[158] e.g., *idel 7 unnyt*,[159] *gehydan 7 gehealdan*[160] and *mægen 7 cræft*.[161] See also certain combinations of words, e.g. *swiþe swiþlice*;[162]

(*b*) the rendering of *iudicium* and *iudicia* by *se rihta dom*[163] and *cor* and *anima* by *mod*;[164]

(*c*) fondness for the construction consisting of possessive + demonstrative, which is often taken to be literary Mercian in origin: e.g., Ps(P) *his þone hean naman* and Bo *his þære hean ceastre*.[165]

CONCLUSION

As Bromwich said in his contribution to the question of the authorship of Ps(P), 'to be convinced or to remain unconvinced of the underlying similarity of vocabulary between any pair of works, the reader must really construct his own list'.[166] Having done this for the relevant works, I am convinced that behind the translations, or rather renderings, of CP, Bo, Solil and Ps(P) there was one mind at work (though probably never entirely on

---

[157] For the dangers inherent in ignoring the wording of the underlying Latin sources, see Bately, 'The Compilation of the Anglo-Saxon Chronicle', p. 118 and n. 3, and 'World History in the *Anglo-Saxon Chronicle*: its Sources and its Separateness from the Old English Orosius', *ASE* 8 (1979), 177–94, at 190 and n. 1. In contrast, Bromwich's arguments for Alfred's authorship of Ps(P) would have carried far greater conviction had his lists of correspondences included the Latin equivalents where available.

[158] We may compare word pairs in Bede, such as *mod 7 magen* for *vires*, *geon 7 geomerung* for *gemitus* and *snyttro 7 wisdom* for both *prudentia* and *sapientia*, none of which is found in Ps(P) or the accepted works of Alfred. See, further, Inna Koskenniemi, *Repetitive Word Pairs in Old and Early Middle English Prose*, Annales Universitatis Turkuensis 107 (Turku, 1968).

[159] For Latin *inutiles*: e.g., Ps(P) XIII.4 and XXV.4; beside CP, p. 271, lines 7–8, and Bo, p. 68, line 29. Similar constructions are found in Bede and Ælfric's works.

[160] Ps(P) IX.14 and XXX.21 and 22; beside Bo, p. 131, line 6. CP has *gehydan 7 ophealdan*. See also GD, p. 98, line 20 *geheold 7 gehæl*.

[161] Ps(P) XVII.31 and 37 and XXXVII.10; beside CP, p. 41, line 11, p. 163, line 8, and p. 465, line 5, and Bo, p. 72, line 11, and p. 108, line 28, etc.

[162] Ps(P) XVII.19, XX.1, XXXVII.8 and XLV.1; beside CP, p. 199, lines 15 and 17, Bo, p. 51, line 8, and p. 107, line 31, and Solil, p. 57, line 11, and p. 63, line 15, etc. So also Ælfric, beside Or *swa swiþlice*.

[163] Ps(P) 6 ×; beside CP, p. 43, line 17, and Bo p. 140, line 28, etc.

[164] Ps(P) some 23 ×, occasionally coupled with *heorte*. The normal rendering of *cor* and *anima* is, of course, *heorte* and *sawol*. See, e.g., CP, p. 219, line 2, p. 283, line 11, and p. 306, line 12.

[165] Ps(P) VII.17 and Bo, p. 141, line 7. See also CP, p. 389, line 20 'ðin sio swiðre and *The Life of St Chad*, ed. Vleeskruyer, p. 48.

[166] 'Who was the Translator?', p. 296, n. 2.

its own).[167] Given the claims made by prefaces, scribes, Asser and William of Malmesbury, and given the absence of any evidence to the contrary,[168] it is reasonable to conclude that that mind was King Alfred's.

[167] See Bromwich's comment that 'speculation about the degree of help given to the king by his different assistants cannot be very profitable until there is an absolutely complete Old English Dictionary. Even then the material from the works of King Alfred's reign would have to be transferred to modern card-indexes with electrical sorting machinery before their statistical pattern could be computed. With so many different persons possibly involved, it is doubtful in the extreme if any unanimity in interpreting these statistics could be achieved, so it is likely that the matter must rest where it is' (*ibid.* p. 303, n. 1). I would add that a similar analysis of the usage of, say, the Ælfric canon would be necessary as a control.

[168] I have heard it suggested that King Alfred's involvement in 'his' translations was possibly purely nominal. Lexical studies cannot, of course, either prove or disprove that theory. But, if Alfred's authorship were to be rejected on non-linguistic grounds, the linguistic evidence is still that overall responsibility rested with one man.

Byrhtferth of Ramsey and the early sections of the *Historia Regum* attributed to Symeon of Durham

MICHAEL LAPIDGE

It has long been recognized that the early sections of the so-called *Historia Regum*, a work attributed to Symeon of Durham (*ob. c.* 1130) and preserved uniquely in Cambridge, Corpus Christi College 139 (written *c.* 1164 at Sawley, Lancashire)[1] at 53v–130v, originally constituted a separate work, probably composed in the pre-Conquest period and subsequently incorporated into the *Historia Regum*. Thomas Arnold, who edited the *Historia Regum* for the Rolls Series in 1885,[2] was persuaded 'that the more attentively any experienced person may study the curious document between pages 14 and 94 [of the edition], the more firmly will he be convinced that it is a composition of the tenth...century'.[3] His conclusions were based on the Latin style of the work, which he regarded as 'pretentious and bombastical on the one hand, obscure and ineffectual on the other' and which affiliated the work, in his opinion, with other Anglo-Latin works of the tenth century. Because he believed that

---

[1] The Cistercian abbey of Sawley was formerly in the West Riding of Yorkshire, but (as a result of the county redistribution of 1974) is now in Lancashire. On the date and origin of this manuscript, see the following detailed discussions by D. N. Dumville: 'The Corpus Christi "Nennius"', *BBCS* 25 (1972–4), 369–80; '"Nennius" and the *Historia Brittonum*', *Studia Celtica* 10–11 (1975–6), 78–95; 'Celtic–Latin Texts in Northern England, *c.* 1150 – *c.* 1250', *Celtica* 12 (1977), 19–49; and 'The Sixteenth-Century History of Two Cambridge Books from Sawley', *Trans. of the Cambridge Bibliographical Soc.* 7 (1977–81), 427–44. See also the discussions by D. Baker, 'Scissors and Paste: CCCC 139 Again', *Stud. in Church Hist.* 11 (1975), 83–123, and H. S. Offler, 'Hexham and the *Historia Regum*', *Trans. of the Architectural and Archaeol. Soc. of Durham and Northumberland* n.s. 2 (1970), 51–62, as well as the important article by P. Hunter Blair cited below, n. 6. A facsimile on microfiche of this important manuscript (with printed introduction), edited by D. N. Dumville, is forthcoming as part of a series edited by R. I. Page and published by D. S. Brewer Ltd.

[2] *Symeonis Monachi Opera Omnia*, 2 vols., RS (London, 1885), II, 1–283; there is a translation of the early sections of the *Historia Regum* by J. Stevenson, *The Church Historians of England* III.ii (London, 1855), 425–81 (this translation, however, is based on the earlier edition of the work in H. Petrie and J. Sharpe, *Monumenta Historica Britannica* (London, 1848), at pp. 645–88). My quotations are from Arnold's edition, but I have corrected against the manuscript in all cases, principally because Arnold failed to distinguish marginal and interlinear additions by later hands from the work of the main scribe. A new edition is forthcoming (see below, n. 79).

[3] *Symeonis Opera*, p. xxv.

certain passages in the work betrayed an origin in the congregation of St Cuthbert (then at Chester-le-Street), Arnold referred to the compiler of the early sections of the *Historia Regum* as the 'Cuthbertine'.[4] His conclusions appear to have been accepted by later historians; for example, W. H. Stevenson (who referred to the early sections of the work as SD 1) wrote as follows: 'we may readily grant that SD 1 was an older compilation, but the evidence that it was drawn up in the tenth century is, in the absence of a MS of that period, necessarily hypothetical'.[5] No such manuscript has yet come to light, but in recent times Arnold's postulation of a tenth-century origin for the early sections has been accurately and comprehensively reinvestigated by Peter Hunter Blair.[6] By a series of detailed stylistic arguments Hunter Blair has been able to show that the first five sections of the *Historia Regum* (occupying pp. 3–91 of Arnold's edition) may reasonably be regarded as the work of one author.[7] These five sections are as follows: (1) Kentish legends, particularly pertaining to the Kentish martyrs Æthelberht and Æthelred (pp. 3–13); (2) lists of Northumbrian kings (pp. 13–15); (3) material derived from Bede, particularly the *Historia Abbatum* (pp. 15–30); (4) a chronicle from 732 to 802 (pp. 30–68); (5) a chronicle from 849 to 887, based mainly on Asser (pp. 69–91). Hunter Blair also recognized that two passages had been interpolated at a later date into the material of these first five sections: one concerning the relics of Acca of Hexham (pp. 32–8), the other concerning those of Alchmund, also a bishop of Hexham (pp. 47–50); he reasonably suggested that these interpolations were added at Hexham in the early twelfth century.[8] As to the date of compilation of the five early sections Hunter Blair was able to affirm, albeit cautiously, Arnold's suggestion of a tenth-century date, but he concluded that 'in the end judgement will perhaps rest upon opinions about [their] latinity'.[9]

The present essay is primarily an attempt to offer an opinion about the Latinity of the early sections of the *Historia Regum* and to re-examine the stylistic grounds for regarding them as the work of one author. Hunter Blair pointed to a number of features which, in his view, marked the five sections as the work of one man:[10] the 'florid, bombastic' style which recurs throughout; the device of using three verbs in succession (e.g. *cepit, occidit, subdiditque*); characteristic periphrasis of straightforward statements; the use

---

[4] *Ibid.* p. xvii.

[5] *Asser's Life of King Alfred*, ed. W. H. Stevenson, rev. D. Whitelock (Oxford, 1959), p. lix.

[6] 'Some Observations on the *Historia Regum* attributed to Symeon of Durham', *Celt and Saxon: Studies in the Early British Border*, ed. N. K. Chadwick (Cambridge, 1963), pp. 63–118.

[7] *Ibid.* esp. pp. 114–16.

[8] *Ibid.* pp. 87–90. The Hexham material is not limited solely to these two extensive interpolations, of course; see Offler, 'Hexham and the *Historia Regum*', and D. N. Dumville, 'The Ætheling: a Study in Anglo-Saxon Constitutional History', *ASE* 8 (1979), 1–33, at 26, n. 4.

[9] 'Some Observations on the *Historia Regum*', p. 118.   [10] *Ibid.* pp. 103–4.

of certain formulae (e.g. *Romuleas adire sedes*) and polysyllabic words (e.g. *inedicibilis* and *inedicibiliter*) throughout; and persistent quotation from the *metra* of Boethius's *De consolatione philosophiae*. Recently, while working towards the edition of two tenth-century Anglo-Latin saints' lives which I would attribute to Byrhtferth of Ramsey – namely the *Vita S. Oswaldi* and *Vita S. Ecgwini* – I have been obliged to pay attention to the Latin style of this curious author,[11] and I have been forcibly impressed by the fact that each of the stylistic features identified by Hunter Blair in the five sections of the *Historia Regum* is attested abundantly in Byrhtferth's two saints' lives. At first glance, it would appear, there are grounds for suspecting that Byrhtferth of Ramsey may have been the tenth-century compiler of the early sections of the *Historia Regum*. I shall examine these grounds in some detail, with regard to the Latinity, habits of mind and use of sources, not only in the two saints' lives, but also in the Latin sections of Byrhtferth's *Enchiridion* (as he called it[12]) or *Manual* (as it is more often called) as well as in the Latin *Epilogus* which he prefixed to his commonplace-book of computistical works, a copy of which is preserved in Oxford, St John's College 17.[13] I employ the following abbreviations:

HR   the first five sections of the *Historia Regum* (pp. 3–91 of Arnold's edition, but excluding the two interpolations)

---

[11] See my extensive discussion of the authorship question in 'Byrhtferth and the *Vita S. Ecgwini*', MS 41 (1979), 331–53, as well as my more cursory remarks *ASE* 4 (1975), 91–4, and in 'The Medieval Hagiography of St Ecgwine', *Vale of Evesham Hist. Soc. Research Papers* 6 (1977), 77–93. I do not propose to reinvestigate the question of Byrhtferth's authorship of these two saints' lives here; however, it will emerge from my following discussion that there are too many stylistic oddities and predilections shared by the saints' lives and the *Enchiridion* to be dismissed as coincidence, and that the conclusions I reach concerning the authorship of the *Historia Regum* will in turn corroborate arguments advanced elsewhere concerning Byrhtferth's authorship of the two saints' lives.

[12] Note Byrhtferth's specific statement: 'We gesetton on þissum *enchiridion*, þæt ys *manualis* on Lyden and handboc on Englisc...' (*Byrhtferth's Manual*, ed. S. J. Crawford, EETS o.s. 177 (London, 1929), 132). In other words, the name of the work is *Enchiridion*, and 'manual' and 'handbook' are merely glosses on the Greek word; here, as always, Byrhtferth prefers the obscure word to the commonplace. It is probable that he derived the term from Asser's *Life of King Alfred*: 'quem enchiridion suum, id est manualem librum, nominari uoluit' (ed. Stevenson, p. 75); for Byrhtferth's knowledge of Asser, see below, p. 121.

[13] The manuscript was written at Ramsey during the period 1081 × 1092 and subsequently transferred to Thorney; see C. R. Hart, 'The Ramsey Computus', *EHR* 85 (1970), 29–44, at 31–4, and N. R. Ker, 'Membra Disiecta', *Brit. Museum Quarterly* 12 (1938), 130–5. Evidence that this manuscript is a late-eleventh-century copy of a computistical commonplace-book assembled by Byrhtferth is as follows: (1) it is prefaced by a diagram ascribed to him ('hanc figuram edidit Bryhtferd...', 7v); (2) its computistical contents are prefaced by his signed *Epilogus* (12v); and (3) virtually all the computistical material in the manuscript is drawn on and elucidated by Byrhtferth in his *Enchiridion*; see the important discussion by Peter S. Baker, 'Byrhtferth's *Enchiridion* and the Computus in Oxford, St John's College 17', below, pp. 123–42. Arguments for regarding the manuscript as Byrhtferth's compilation are given by G. F. Forsey, 'Byrhtferth's *Preface*', *Speculum* 3 (1928), 505–22, at 506–7; A. van de Vyver, 'Les Oeuvres inédites d'Abbon de Fleury', *RB* 47 (1935), 125–69, at 144–5; and C. R. Hart, 'The Ramsey Computus', pp. 32–3, and 'Byrhtferth and his *Manual*', *MÆ* 41 (1972), 95–109, esp. 108–9.

VSE   Byrhtferth's *Vita S. Ecgwini*, ed. J. A. Giles, *Vita Quorundum Anglo-Saxonum* (London, 1854), pp. 349–96

VSO   Byrhtferth's *Vita S. Oswaldi*, ed. J. Raine, *The Historians of the Church of York*, 3 vols., RS (London, 1879), I, 399–475

Ench   Byrhtferth's *Enchiridion*, ed. S. J. Crawford, *Byrhtferth's Manual* (see above, n. 12)

Epil   the text ed. G. F. Forsey, 'Byrhtferth's *Preface*' (see above, n. 13)

For convenience, I shall refer to the (allegedly) tenth-century compiler/author of the first five sections of the *Historia Regum* as 'the HR author'.

FEATURES SHARED BY THE EARLY SECTIONS OF THE *HISTORIA REGUM* AND WORKS KNOWN TO BE BY BYRHTFERTH

Words

Like virtually all Anglo-Latin authors of the tenth and eleventh centuries, and like Byrhtferth in particular, the HR author took great pride in embellishing his Latin prose by means of exotic or 'hermeneutic' vocabulary – obscure and rare words, most often grecisms or archaisms, derived from glossaries and difficult authors.[14] It is clear that the HR author went to great pains to collect obscure words, for he is able to employ correctly certain rare technical terms, such as *dotalitium* (p. 4), *suffossorium* (p. 9) and *sumministratio* (p. 4); among these the most unusual is *platoma*, a mutilated spelling by him or a scribe of *platonia* (n. pl., derived probably from Greek πλατύνιον) meaning a 'marble slab' (p. 57). He is at his most characteristic, however, when he is employing pedantic grecisms in lieu of common Latin nouns. Some he employs were common coin in Anglo-Latin sources: *arcisterium* (originally from ἀσκητήριον) for 'monastery' (p. 10), *exenia* (originally for ξείνια, n. pl.) for 'gifts' (p. 8) and *onoma* for 'name' (pp. 4, 75 and 84); these words are frequently employed by Byrhtferth.[15] Less common grecisms used by the HR author are *epinicion* (ἐπινίκιον), a 'triumph' (pp. 19 and 44, where the original scribe has added the gloss *.i. triumphum*), possibly derived from Bede[16] but also employed by Byrhtferth in his *Enchiridion* (*Ench*, p. 230); *pentecontarchus* (from πεντηκοντάρχος) meaning 'captain (of fifty men)' (p. 89, misread by Arnold as *pentecomarchus*) and deriving originally from the

[14] See M. Lapidge, 'The Hermeneutic Style in Tenth-Century Anglo-Latin Literature', *ASE* 4 (1975), 67–111.

[15] *archisterium* (*VSO*, pp. 413, 418, 429 and 431; *VSE*, p. 376); *onoma* (*VSO*, pp. 404 and 410; *VSE*, p. 377; *Ench*, pp. 200 and 202); *exenia* does not occur in Byrhtferth's writings, but is not a rarity.

[16] The following sentence is found in the *Chronica Maiora* which Bede appended to his *De Temporum Ratione*: 'epinicion quippe triumphum, palmam significat' (*Chronica Minora Saec. IV. V. VI. VII*, ed. T. Mommsen, Monumenta Germaniae Historica, Auct. Antiq. 13 (Berlin, 1894–8), 247–327, at 326).

Septuagint but no doubt taken by the *HR* author from Aldhelm.[17] More interesting is the word *hypocrissima* (p. 67). When recounting Asser's story of a wicked princess who was domiciled in a monastery, the *HR* author adds that she adopted the monastic habit *sub specie hypocrissima*, which seems to mean 'under the guise of hypocrisy' or something of the sort. The striking word *hypocrissima* might be explained in one of two ways: either the author intended it as a superlative adjective (hence the phrase would mean 'under the most hypocritical guise'), which would imply that he had in mind an otherwise unattested adjective **hypocrissus*, 'hypocritical'; or else he was attempting to decline the Greek noun *hypocrisis* (ὑπόκρισις) in the genitive but was simply unaware of its correct genitive form (ὑποκρίσεως). Either possibility implies some confidence – albeit unfounded – in dealing with and manipulating Greek vocabulary. A similar confidence is found in Byrhtferth's Latin writings.[18] Grecisms, however, were not the only sort of unusual noun employed by the *HR* author. He sometimes preferred rare abstractions, such as *diuturnitas* (p. 13), possibly derived from Aldhelm,[19] or *tenebrositas* (p. 53), or else diminutives such as *ciuitatula* (p. 88) and *scientiola* (p. 7); Byrhtferth's neologism(?) *urbecula* (*VSO*, p. 419) is exactly parallel in form and meaning to *ciuitatula*. The *HR* author also had a predilection for unusual agentive nouns in *-or*, such as *interemptor* (p. 7), *interfector* (p. 59) and *bellator* (p. 91). Although Byrhtferth employs only one of these three in his saints' lives (*bellator*, *VSE*, p. 352), he displays a great fondness for words of similar form: *habitator* (*VSO*, p. 447), *relator* (*VSO*, p. 409), *somniator* (*VSO*, p. 409), *contionator* (*VSE*, p. 354) and *institutor* (*VSE*, p. 354). In their choice of nouns, Byrhtferth and the *HR* author clearly shared the same taste.

This same taste for the bizarre and unusual is found also in their choice of adjectives. For example, the word *subthronizatus* is not common in Anglo-Latin sources, but it is employed readily by the *HR* author (pp. 52 and 91) and Byrhtferth (*VSO*, pp. 453 and 465; *VSE*, p. 355). Two adjectives used by the *HR* author – *Ambrosianus* (p. 8) and *Gregorianus* (pp. 8 and 52) – have the appearance of being neologisms in context; Byrhtferth uses *Gregorianus* (*VSO*, p. 450) and a very similar-looking form *Ambrosianicus* (*VSE*, p. 389). The *HR* author uses two extremely rare adjectives with the prefix *prae-* that are not attested in classical Latin: *praeamabilis* (p. 66) and *praecordialis* (p. 5); of these, Byrhtferth also employs *praeamabilis* (*VSO*, p.

---

[17] *De Virginitate*, ch. xx (*Aldhelmi Opera*, ed. R. Ehwald, MGH, Auct. 15 (Berlin, 1919), 249, line 17).

[18] E.g. *VSO*, p. 427: 'utendum puto anabibazon uerbo, quod significat sursum scandens'. The word *anabibazo* (ἀναβιβάζω) is not found in glossaries, and whence Byrhtferth learned it is not clear; furthermore, he knew enough about verb conjugation to give (correctly) the masc. nom. form of the present participle (ἀναβιβαζών). One suspects that he learned some smattering of Greek from Abbo.

[19] Ed. Ehwald, p. 75, line 3.

455). A similar situation obtains in *HR* with respect to rare adjectives with the prefix *in-* and the suffix *-bilis*: *inedicibilis* (pp. 13, 46, 52, 54, 84 and 90), *ineuincibilis* (p. 5), *inenarrabilis* (p. 63) and *immarcescibilis* (p. 12); Byrhtferth uses *inenarrabilis* once (*VSO*, p. 414) but uses *inedicibilis* with a frequency equalling that of the *HR* author (*VSO*, pp. 403, 423, 439, 451 and 475; *VSE*, pp. 352 and 376). It should be noted in passing that *inedicibilis* is not attested in classical Latin or in Aldhelm. Perhaps the most striking feature of the *HR* author's use of adjectives is his fondness for polysyllabic superlatives. A number of such superlatives is used to modify the word *rex*: I note *audacissimus* (p. 86), *bellicosissimus* (p. 46), *clementissimus* (p. 72), *famosissimus* (pp. 67 and 86), *inuictissimus* (pp. 45–6) and *praestantissimus* (p. 80). In a similar vein Byrhtferth uses *famosissimus* to modify *rex* twice in *VSE* (pp. 378 and 394) and *praepotentissimus* twice in *VSO* (pp. 420 and 429). Adjectives of this sort (modifying nouns other than *rex*) are found throughout *HR*: *gratiatissimus* (p. 7), *poenitissimus* (p. 62) and *preciosissimus* (p. 9) are three ready examples. The same penchant is shown everywhere by Byrhtferth, who in *Epil* uses *catissimus* (p. 516), *limpidissimus* (p. 517), *luculentissimus* (p. 516) and *opinatissimus* (p. 516) and in *Ench* uses *preciosissimus* (p. 218), the puzzling *sabatissimus* (p. 214; = 'celebrated'?) and *sincerissimus* (p. 228), to name only a few. Such polysyllaby is the hallmark of Byrhtferth's Latin, and one may well think that the superlative effort in this direction is witnessed by two adjectives in *VSO*: *honorificentissimus* (p. 414) and *omnipotentissimus* (p. 429).

Parallel with and complementary to the use of polysyllabic adjectives (especially those terminating in *-ilis*) by the *HR* author and Byrhtferth is their strikingly similar usage of uncommon polysyllabic adverbs terminating in *-iter*. Sometimes the adverbs of this sort which they employ are attested sparsely in classical Latin, but in the majority of cases – particularly those adverbs consisting in five or more syllables – they are extremely rare. In this respect Byrhtferth and the *HR* author are extraordinary in early medieval Latin documents. Some notion of the range and variety of these adverbs in the works under discussion may be gleaned from the following:

In *VSE*: atrociter (p. 391), digniter (p. 358), fiducialiter (p. 362), inedicibiliter (p. 349), ineffabiliter (p. 379), immisericorditer (p. 393), magnanimiter (p. 394), muliebriter (p. 383), nequiter (p. 392), optabiliter (p. 381), pigriter (p. 383), pleniter (p. 393), regaliter (p. 395), unanimiter (p. 377).

In *VSO*: affabiliter (p. 469), agiliter (p. 415), amicabiliter (p. 441), concorditer (p. 414), dapsiliter (p. 464), digniter (p. 405), duriter (p. 450), eneruiter (pp. 405 and 414), fiducialiter (p. 448), honorabiliter (p. 450), indigniter (p. 408), inedicibiliter (pp. 413, 422 and 454), ineffabiliter (p. 453), immarcessibiliter (p. 417), immisericorditer (p. 451), irreprehensibiliter (p. 417), memoriter (p. 423), muliebriter (p. 417), paternaliter (p. 447), praesentialiter (p. 444), regaliter (pp. 425 and 443).

A similar list can be compiled for the *HR* author; in the one which follows I do not include those words which occur in portions of the text of Asser excerpted by the *HR* author (words in italics also occur in either (or both) of *VSE* and *VSO*):

annualiter (p. 91), *atrociter* (p. 70), *digniter* (p. 13), *duriter* (pp. 62 and 71), *eneruiter* (p. 86), hostiliter (p. 75), *immisericorditer* (pp. 51 and 59), *inedicibiliter* (p. 60), inenarrabiliter (p. 60), *memoriter* (p. 74), miserabiliter (p. 53), *nequiter* (p. 41), *pleniter* (p. 91), *regaliter* (pp. 59, 64 and 84), sullimiter (p. 47), uenerabiliter (p. 59).

The number of such words, and particularly the otherwise rare words *inedicibiliter* and *immisericorditer*, common to all three works is particularly significant.

Neither the *HR* author nor Byrhtferth seems to have expended much energy collecting rare and polysyllabic examples of the fourth major class of words, namely verbs. Nevertheless one common peculiarity in the use of verbs may be noted. In all his writings Byrhtferth manifests a marked uncertainty concerning the correct use of the passive infinitive. At one point in *Ench* he writes, 'plurima dici poterant et pluriora referre' (p. 222), where one would have expected *referri*. At another point we read 'eligendo innocenter uiuere cum ipso, et inuidiam de cordis thalamo expellere' (*Ench*, p. 208), where in his uncertainty he has written *uel -li* over *expellere*.[20] A similar error occurs in *Epil*, where he has written 'is [*scil*. Beda], ut delectet... glorificari dindima prisce legis...' (p. 516). Byrhtferth's two saints' lives abound in confusions of this sort. I note two examples: 'quis roboratus ingenio Homeri potest exprimi?' (*VSO*, p. 434), where we would expect *exprimere*, and, on the other hand, 'praecepit rex epistolam ostendere et legere' (*VSE*, p. 379), where we would expect *ostendi* and *legi*. Even when allowances have been made for errors introduced by copyists, it is clear that Byrhtferth did not properly understand the usage of the passive infinitive. The *HR* author displays the identical inability. At one point he writes 'decernens itaque eam honorare' (p. 11), where what is needed is *honorari*, and, on the other hand, he writes 'estuabat sui cordis penetralia suffundi et thalamum pectoris sacris litteris imbui' (p. 74), where active infinitives are clearly intended and needed. In this respect the usage of the *HR* author is indistinguishable from that of Byrhtferth.

[20] That the glosses accompanying the *Enchiridion* in Oxford, Bodleian Library, Ashmole 328 are by Byrhtferth himself has been demonstrated convincingly by Peter S. Baker, 'Studies in the Old English Canon of Byrhtferth of Ramsey' (unpubl. Ph.D. dissertation, Yale Univ., 1978), pp. 51–7, and *idem*, 'The Old English Canon of Byrhtferth of Ramsey', *Speculum* 55 (1980), 22–37.

Phrases

Corresponding to the shared similarities in vocabulary there is a shared similarity in phrasing. There are numerous examples of two- or three-word phrases which are common to HR and the writings of Byrhtferth. I begin by listing some of the more unusual and striking: *cordis penetralia* (HR, p. 74; *VSO*, p. 410), *armipotens rex* (HR, pp. 75 and 78; *VSE*, p. 378, and *VSO*, p. 425), *peramplius et perfectius* (HR, p. 29; *Ench*, p. 50), *aurora illucescente* (HR, p. 9; *VSE*, p. 375), *uice regiminis* (HR, p. 43; *VSO*, p. 450), *infra cordis cubicula* (HR, p. 80; *VSO*, p. 424), *densi uepres* (HR, p. 73; *VSE*, p. 364), *solio subthronizatus* (HR, p. 52; *VSE*, p. 355), *Gregorianus concentus* (HR, p. 52; *VSO*, p. 450) and *sceptro redimitus* (HR, p. 68; *VSE*, p. 379). Alongside these more striking expressions is a host of common expressions which are found throughout the works in question: *celestis regni gaudia* (HR, p. 3; *VSO*, p. 351, etc.), *regali diademate* (HR, p. 57; *VSE*, p. 374, *Ench*, p. 204, etc.), *regnum suscepit gloriose* (HR, p. 58; *VSE*, p. 377, etc.) or *luce clarius* (HR, p. 9; *Ench*, pp. 20, 206 and 244, *VSE*, pp. 350 and 352, *VSO*, pp. 422 and 457, etc.). Similarly, the expression *illud scolastici* is used recurrently by both the HR author and Byrhtferth to introduce quotations (HR, pp. 77 and 90; *VSO*, pp. 400 and 416; *VSE*, p. 355, etc.). Or, again, there is the use of the precious phrases *Romuleae sedes*, *Romulea urbs* and *Romuleae urbis moenia* ('citadels of the Romulean city') for 'Rome', phrases which Hunter Blair noted as characteristic of the HR author.[21] On two occasions the HR author describes Rome in these terms: 'Karolus...Romulee urbis menia ingreditur' (HR, p. 63); 'Romuleas adire sedes cepit' (HR, p. 72). Byrhtferth uses these phrases repeatedly: 'ad urbis Romuleae moenia' (*VSE*, p. 358); 'Romuleae urbis' (*VSE*, pp. 349 and 359 *bis*; *VSO*, p. 433); 'et Romuleae urbis moenia adire' (*VSE*, p. 379); 'reuersus est a Romuleae urbis moeniis' (*VSE*, p. 350); 'uenit...ad locum...Romuleae urbis' (*VSO*, p. 406). Another periphrastic way of describing Rome employed by both the HR author and Byrhtferth is *limina sanctorum apostolorum*. This appears to have been inspired by Bede's *Historia Abbatum*, where the phrases *adoranda apostolorum limina* and *limina beatorum apostolorum* are found.[22] The HR author employs the phrase as follows: 'profectus est dehinc ad limina sanctorum apostolorum' (HR, p. 16); 'ad limina principis apostolorum profectus est' (HR, pp. 71–2); 'ad limina sancti Petri' (HR, p. 72). Byrhtferth makes identical use of it: 'ad limina pretiosorum apostolorum peruenire desiderabat' (*VSO*, p. 405); 'ad limina sanctorum properaret apostolorum' (*VSO*, p. 435 *bis*); 'ad sanctorum limina peruenit gaudens apostolorum' (*VSE*, p. 358); 'ad sancta limina apostolorum

[21] 'Some Observations on the *Historia Regum*', p. 104.
[22] *Venerabilis Baedae Opera Historica*, ed. C. Plummer, 2 vols. (Oxford, 1896) I, 365 and 385.

pretiosorum...uenissemus' (*VSE*, p. 378). Even if the phrase derives ultimately from Bede, it is striking that both authors should have seized upon it and employed it in similar fashion. In any case, expressions such as these are used so frequently by both authors that they take on the appearance of formulae.

It will be seen that the repeated use of such expressions by both the *HR* author and Byrhtferth implies some sort of direct link between them. However, it might be objected that it merely implies a verbal dependence of one author on the other; in other words, that the direct link is one of borrowing, not of common authorship. In order to rebut such an objection it is necessary to demonstrate that the repeated expressions derive from the habitual patterns of one mind expressing itself in characteristic ways and that they are not borrowings made *ad hoc*. I propose therefore to look (at some length) at various shared expressions which might be called formulaic in order to show identical mental habits in their use; as one would expect, these formulaic expressions are used most often at transitional points in the discourse – when the author is embarking on a new discussion, summing up an old, drawing a moral from an event described and so on. In their simplest form these expressions show only minor verbal variation.

When referring back to material discussed at the beginning of his work the *HR* author writes 'in exordio nostre hystorie' (p. 4) or 'in exordio huius operis' (p. 13); Byrhtferth uses an expanded version of this formula in *Ench*: 'in exordio uenerabili huius exigui operis' (p. 198). Or, again, when summing up the achievement of a saint, both authors use a formula with only minor variation: St Edmund: 'sicut finis eius sanctissime uite probauit euentus' (*HR*, pp. 76–7); St Ecgwine: 'sicut finis suae uitae demonstrauit euentus' (*VSE*, p. 354); St Oswald: 'sicut finis suae gloriosae uitae demonstrauit euentus' (*VSO*, p. 418). Or, again, the *HR* author at one point apologizes to those who are familiar with the material of his discussion by saying that it is necessary to instruct those who are not: '...de quorum positione strictim nescientes instruere, obsecro scientibus oneri non sit' (*HR*, p. 23). Byrhtferth in two of his writings makes the identical apology with only slightly varied wording:[23] 'nunc tempus instat ut de millenario strictim loquamur, scientes obsecrans ut oneri non sit' (*Ench*, p. 232); 'seriem...uitae huius...paulatim libet pandere ignotis, ut notis non sit oneri quod ignorantibus manifestari delectat' (*VSE*, p. 353). The *HR* author uses a formula with a similar range of variation – it consists of *placet* or *libet* plus the infinitive *inserere* – when he wishes to say 'it is appropriate to introduce such-and-such into my

---

[23] Byrhtferth uses a similar formula in Old English: 'We byddað þa boceras and þa getydde weras, þe þas þing fulfremedlice cunnon, þæt heom hefelice ne þincen [= *ut oneri non sit*] þas þing þe we medomlice iungum cnihtum gesettað and sendað' (*Ench*, p. 32).

account': 'quorum uitam . . . in exordio nostre hystorie placet inserere' (p. 4); 'libet huic nostro operi inserere quaedam que gesta sunt' (p. 15); 'de cuius passionis honore libet aliqua hystorie nostre inserere' (p. 77). The very same formula is used repeatedly by Byrhtferth: 'que placuit hic inserere' (*VSO*, p. 403); 'in fine huius modici operis placet inserere' (*VSO*, p. 433); 'hic inserere breuiter placet' (*VSO*, p. 422); 'uersus . . . hoc in loco placet inserere' (*VSO*, p. 459); 'abbates . . . quorum nomina hic inserere curauimus' (*VSO*, p. 462); 'nos uero hanc epistolam huic loco inserere nolumus' (*VSE*, p. 360); 'placet huic operi nostro figuram adicere' (*Ench*, p. 206); 'libet hic aliqua curtim inserere' (*Ench*, p. 234). Or, take the example of the phrase 'as the following discussion will demonstrate'. Here the *HR* author and Byrhtferth repeatedly employ the same formula: 'declarat subsequens sermo scriptoris' (*HR*, p. 45); 'ut sequens demonstrabit articulus' (*HR*, p. 47); 'stilus fidelis demonstrabit' (*HR*, p. 56); and 'sequens demonstrabit breuiter sententiola' (*VSO*, p. 420); 'ueluti subsequens declarat topographia' (*VSE*, p. 350); 'sicut inferius stylus demonstrat' (*VSE*, p. 359); 'sicuti formula sequens demonstrabit' (*Ench*, p. 8); 'ueluti luce clara demonstrant margines' (*Ench*, p. 20). Phrases such as these are the building-blocks from which any author constructs his narrative; they are used instinctively, even unconsciously, by an author at points where he is too lazy, or too much in a hurry, to pay close attention to the wording of a merely transitional phrase. As such they are dependable indicators of an author's ingrained mental habits. Of course formulae such as these are employed by all authors of all periods; what is important here is the repeated reliance on the same formula in similar contexts. This may be made clear from the way the *HR* author and Byrhtferth appear to have seized upon a sentence by Bede to express the notion, 'having (briefly) said these things, let us return to the sequence of our narrative'. In his *Historia Abbatum* Bede, after an extensive discussion of Abbot Eosterwine, had returned to his point of departure with the following apology: 'uerum his de uita uenerabilis Eosterwyni breuiter praelibatis, redeamus ad ordinem narrandi'.[24] This sentence was copied by the *HR* author into sect. 3 of his account, and it clearly impressed itself upon him, for there are two adumbrations of it at later points of his narrative: 'his strictim dictis, ad ordinem reuertamur narracionis' (*HR*, p. 55); 'de orthodoxa fide hec pertractantes, ad hystorie nostre narrationem redeamus' (*HR*, p. 61). Throughout the writings of Byrhtferth there are similar reflections of Bede's sentence: 'ad ordinem . . . redeamus proprie relationis' (*VSO*, p. 403); 'ad uiam nostri sermonis redeamus' (*VSO*, p. 429); 'extra uiam paulatim digressimus, sed redeamus ad uiam' (*VSO*, p. 442); 'haec dicta

---

[24] Ed. Plummer I, 373.

sufficiant...nunc ad propria redeamus' (*VSO*, p. 462); 'his peractis, ad ea redeamus quae...gessit' (*VSO*, p. 462); 'nunc igitur redeamus ad ordinem narrationis unde paulatim digressi sumus' (*VSE*, p. 357); 'nunc autem stylus reuertatur scriptoris ad ordinem narrationis' (*VSE*, p. 360); 'his dictis, redeamus uenusto animo unde discesseramus' (*Ench*, p. 40); 'his dictis, redeamus ad nos ipsos' (*Ench*, p. 216). None of these phrases is a *verbatim* repetition of Bede's sentence, yet all are indebted to it.

Each of the above formulas is used at a structural junction in the narrative: after a digression or before a new departure or before the repetition of something well known. It is striking that the *HR* author and Byrhtferth draw upon the identical arsenal of formulas at such points, in ways which (in my opinion) put mere verbal indebtedness out of the question. The point may be made finally by examining the way in which the two authors attempt to emphasize a statement they have made. Almost invariably they both resort to a predictable sort of rhetorical question – 'as to how great/glorious/outstanding he/it was, who can say?'; almost invariably the vocabulary employed is the same: a compound form of *nuntio* (*annuntio, denuntio, enuntio, pronuntio*) or some synonymous verb (*expedio, enarro, edico*). The ancestor of such rhetorical questions appears to have been a sentence from Aldhelm's *De Virginitate*: 'quis urbana uerborum facundia fretus enarrare sufficiat?'[25] However, the many variations wrought upon Aldhelm's sentence betray unmistakably the workings of one mind. Here are four examples from *HR*: 'quot uero...uolumina, quantas...reliquias attulit, quis annunciet?' (p. 16); 'qualiter dilatauit...imperia...quis urbana facundia suffultus possit...edicere?' (p. 89); 'sancta quoque loca qualibus ditauit...quis enunciet?' (p. 89); 'quanta munera suis episcopis...contulit, quis enarret?' (p. 90). These need to be considered in the context of a great many similar ones in the saints' lives of Byrhtferth: 'quam gloriosum habitaculum...praebuit, quis poterit digne perscrutari?' (*VSO*, p. 406); 'quanta summus pater contulit, quis cuncta expediat?' (*VSO*, p. 412); 'quam ardenter alii patres gesserunt...quis roboratus ingenio Homeri potest exprimi?' (*VSO*, p. 434); 'qualiter illud monasterium...ditauit...quis expediet?' (*VSO*, p. 446); 'quis urbanitatis fretus eloquentia potest proferri...?' (*VSO*, p. 447); 'quam gloriose...incitauit principes...quis urbanitatis fretus potest edicere?' (*VSO*, p. 456); 'quam sollemniter suscepti sunt presules...quis digne expediet?' (*VSO*, p. 463); 'quam nobiliter aeditui ornauerunt...quis annuntiet?' (*VSO*, p. 464); 'quot lacrymas...emisit, quis expediet?' (*VSO*, p. 474); 'quis urbana fretus eloquentia potest pleniter inuestigare?' (*VSE*, p. 349); 'quantus...resplenduit fulgor, quis digne centenis linguis redimitus potest

---

[25] Ed. Ehwald, p. 250, line 19.

edicere?' (*VSE*, p. 352); 'quam prudenter columbae simplicitatem retinuit ...qualis stylus pronuntiet?' (*VSE*, p. 354); 'quantum se humiliauerit, quis millenis poterit uerbis explicare?' (*VSE*, p. 355); 'quomodo alter...consolatus est, quis digno fauore pronuntiet?' (*VSE*, p. 359); 'quales grates... retulit, quis in Angligenis denuntiet partibus?' (*VSE*, p. 359); 'quanta laetitia...ardebat...quis explicet? quis adnuntiet? quis rite enarret?' (*VSE*, p. 394). These repeated rhetorical questions betray the habit of one mind relentlessly expressing itself through hackneyed, predictable formulas.

Topics

The interests to which an author repeatedly recurs likewise reveal his mental predilections. I shall argue that many of the recurrent topics handled in *HR* are characteristic of Byrhtferth as we know him from *Ench* and the saints' lives. It should be borne in mind that none of them should properly have any place in a narrative history; for the most part they are digressions, but as such they provide reliable evidence of the author's predilections and interests. One such interest on the part of the *HR* author was in the procedure and ceremony of coronations. Thus of Charlemagne's coronation in Rome it is said 'corona aurea capiti inponitur et regale sceptrum in manibus datur' (p. 64). A similar procedure is remarked in the self-coronation of Cenwulf, king of Mercia: 'imponens sibi coronam in capite, sceptrumque in manu' (p. 59); likewise the coronation of King Egbert: 'diadema totius regni capiti imposuit, maximo sceptro redimitus' (p. 68). These details recall the more famous description of King Edgar's coronation in *VSO*, where the presiding archbishop 'dedit coronam in capite, et benedictionem; contulit ipsi et sceptrum' (p. 438).

A more revealing interest of the *HR* author is in what might be called 'scientific' information. For example, after noting that an eclipse of the moon took place in 752, he goes on to explain at some length what an eclipse is (p. 40; cf. p. 41), a strange intrusion in an historical narrative. His information is taken directly from Bede's *De Natura Rerum*.[26] Now, although Byrhtferth has no occasion to discuss eclipses in *Ench*, he includes a long section on solar and planetary movements (pp. 122–32), and presumably therefore understands what an eclipse is. A direct link between *HR* and *Ench* (via Bede's *De Natura*

---

[26] *Bedae Venerabilis Opera, I: Opera Didascalica*, ed. C. W. Jones *et al.*, Corpus Christianorum Series Latina 123A (Turnhout, 1975), 214. Because the *HR* author prefaced his discussion with 'inquit plinius', Arnold assumed that the source of the discussion was Pliny's *Historia Naturalis* (II.13). However, in spite of what the *HR* author says, his wording agrees with Bede, not with Pliny, and it is apparent that he was copying from a manuscript of the *De Natura Rerum* which was provided with Bede's characteristic source-marks (i.e. *Plinius* must have been written in the margin beside the chapter on eclipses; cf. discussion by Jones, *ibid.* p. 187). This lazy scholarly technique of appearing to quote a primary source by way of a secondary source is not unknown today.

Rerum) is made, however, by the *HR* author's discussion of tides (*à propos* of Lindisfarne). He begins by explaining the terminology for flood-tide (*malina*) and ebb-tide (*ledon*) and then quotes *verbatim* a passage from ch. xxxix of Bede's *De Natura Rerum*.[27] This passage is immediately followed by another *verbatim* quotation from Bede, this time from ch. xxix of the *De Temporum Ratione*.[28] Whoever the *HR* author was, he certainly knew his way around Bede's scientific writings. Now at one point in *Ench* Byrhtferth has occasion to discuss the tides and he too resorts to ch. xxxix of Bede's *De Natura Rerum*: 'Ðonne se mona up arist, ðonne onginð seo sæ to flowanne. Grecas hateð maline sæflod þonne hyt wixst, and ledon þonne hyt wanað; and Beda cwyð...þæt malina onginð fif dagum ær þam niwan monan...' (p. 158).[29] And, just as the *HR* author cobbled ch. xxxix of the *De Natura Rerum* together with ch. xxix of the *De Temporum Ratione*, in particular the latter work's definition that a *punctus* is one fifth of an hour ('punctus autem quinta pars horae est, quinque enim puncti horam faciunt'[30]), so too Byrhtferth in *Ench* stitches on Bede's definition from ch. xxix of the *De Temporum Ratione*: 'we wyllað secgan to soðe fif prican æfter Bedan gesetnysse...forðon fif prican wyrcað ane tid' (p. 162). All this scientific material, particularly the specialist definition of the *punctus* as one fifth of an hour rather than one quarter as is usual elsewhere, is an extraordinary intrusion into an historical narrative and clearly reveals that the *HR* author, like Byrhtferth, had an interest in computus and was well acquainted with Bede's writings on the subject.[31]

Concern with the details of computus engendered in Byrhtferth an exceptional interest in numerology, an interest which is evinced on nearly every page of his writings, ranging from his excessive use of distributive numerals in multiplicative combinations (e.g. *bis bina* for *quatuor*) to the extensive discussion of the symbolical significance of the numbers 1 to 1000 that forms pt IV of *Ench* (pp. 198–234).[32] A similar interest is attested in *HR*, where we find frequent examples of *bis bina* and *bis sena* (pp. 14, 17 etc.) and also protracted numerological circumlocutions, such as the following

---

[27] *Ibid.* pp. 224–5; the passage in question is that in *HR* beginning 'Aestus oceani lunam sequitur' (p. 54) and ending 'transmissa uidetur' (p. 55).

[28] *Bedae Opera de Temporibus*, ed. C. W. Jones, Med. Acad. of America Publ. 41 (Cambridge, Mass., 1943), 233 = *HR*, p. 55: 'sicut enim luna quatuor punctis...quinque enim puncti horam faciunt'. This passage was not identified by Arnold, who consequently ascribed it (erroneously) to the *HR* author.

[29] Note that Byrhtferth's *Beda cwyð* corresponds exactly to the *HR* author's addition *Beda testatur* (p. 55).

[30] *Bedae Opera de Temporibus*, ed. Jones, p. 233.

[31] It is worth noting that these two treatises of Bede were also copied side by side into Byrhtferth's computistical commonplace-book, Oxford, St John's College 17, 62r–5r (the *De Natura Rerum*, acephalous, beginning ch. xvi) and 65v–123r (the *De Temporum Ratione*).

[32] See my remarks, 'Byrhtferth and the *Vita S. Ecgwini*', p. 340.

description of how the two martyred princes Æthelberht and Æthelred received the sevenfold gifts of the Holy Ghost: 'in cuius [*scil.* baptisterii] puri septem gradibus liquoris, septem sunt sortiti dona Spiritus Sancti... uiuere studuerunt uirgines...septenis dierum curriculis, ut septem septies agmentatis et monade supposito...' (p. 5).[33] For elucidation concerning these seven gifts of the Holy Ghost we are obliged to turn to pt IV of *Ench*: 'septem sunt dona Spiritus Sancti, de quibus per Isaiam dicitur...spiritus sapientie, spiritus intellectus, spiritus consilii, spiritus fortitudinis, spiritus scientie, spiritus pietatis, spiritus timoris' (p. 212). As to why the two martyrs should have desired to live pure for fifty days ($7 \times 7 + 1 = 50$) we are again obliged to consult *Ench*; there we learn that the number 50 symbolizes the Day of Judgement (p. 230), which in turn allows us to understand how the *HR* author is able to leap from his mention of the fifty days to the *iubileus*: 'in praesenti uita adquirerent fructum iubelei, hoc est, annum eterne felicitatis' (*HR*, p. 5). But there is a further implication: since each martyr lived pure for fifty days in both body and soul, the number 50 may be doubled, yielding 100, and this of course suggests the hundredth fruit of the biblical parable (Matthew XIII.8): 'hoc...dupplicato, corpore et anima, post peractum uite cursum, fructum caperent centesimum sacratissimis uirginibus consecratum' (*HR*, p. 5). The interpretation of the biblical thirty-, sixty- and hundredfold fruit to mean the three states of marriage, widowhood and virginity was a commonplace in patristic commentary from the time of Jerome and Augustine, but it was an interpretation especially favoured by Byrhtferth, who makes reference to it throughout his writings (*Ench*, pp. 224–6 and 236; *Epil*, p. 516; *VSO*, pp. 406, 408 etc.; *VSE*, p. 355).[34] There is one further example of numerology in *HR* which can best be explained by reference to *Ench*: Archbishop Plegmund was said to be 'praeditus bis binis columpnis, iusticie, prudentie, temperantie, fortitudinis' (*HR*, p. 88). This reference to the four cardinal virtues is explained more fully in *Ench*: 'quaternarius perfectus est numerus et quattuor uirtutibus exornatus – iustitie uidelicet, temperantia, fortitudines, prudentia' (p. 200).[35] Parallels of this sort may be multiplied, but enough has been said to suggest that there is an intimate relationship between the numerological theory in *Ench* and the allusive references to numerology in *HR*.

[33] A similarly verbose way of saying 'fifty' occurs later in *HR*: 'septem uidelicet septimanis dierum et monade, hoc est quinquaginta diebus suppletis' (p. 83).

[34] See, for example, Ambrose, *De Virginibus ad Marcellinam*, I.x (Migne, Patrologia Latina 16, col. 205); Jerome, *Commentarius in euangelium Matthei*, ch. II (PL 26, col. 92); and Augustine, *De Sancta Virginitate*, ch. LXV (PL 40, col. 423). See also my 'Byrhtferth and the *Vita S. Ecgwini*', p. 340.

[35] The grammatical errors (*iustitie* and *fortitudines* for the abl. sg.) presumably originate with the exceedingly careless scribe of Ashmole 328. The four cardinal virtues are listed again at *Ench*, p. 92, and are also found in the Old English homily preserved at the end of Ashmole 328 and printed by Crawford (*Ench*, pp. 247–8). As Baker has shown ('The Old English Canon', pp. 32–4), this homily is almost certainly by Byrhtferth.

Closely related to the tendency towards numerological explanations in both *HR* and Byrhtferth's works is a tendency they share towards figural interpretations of biblical events and persons. On its simplest level this may amount to no more than using Judas Maccabeus as a type of the bellicose warrior: 'quasi Iudas bellicosus processit ad bellum' (*HR*, p. 79); 'uelut alter Iudas prouocatus ad bellum' (*VSO*, p. 445). Elsewhere a more complex mental process is at work. For example, the word *iubeleus* occurs in Leviticus xxv.10 and means simply 'the year of jubilee, the fiftieth year'. However, as I have mentioned, both the *HR* author and Byrhtferth interpreted the number 50 as signifying the Day of Judgement; accordingly *annus iubeleus* comes to mean for them the year, and hence the day, of Judgement. By a further mental leap both authors are able to describe the passage to heaven as 'receiving the remission of the jubilee' (note once again the similar phrasing used by both): 'iubeleique anni remissionem percipere' (*HR*, p. 21); 'sumere ab eo iubelei anni remissionem' (*VSO*, p. 408). In its most extreme and most characteristic form this mental process is able to produce in both authors a striking and singular metaphor, as when, for example, the *HR* author says of someone that he 'passed from the Egypt of this world': *de Egypto huius seculi translatus est* (*HR*, p. 39); the metaphor implies the exodus, the crossing of the Red Sea, the search for the Promised Land, and hence figurally the passage to heaven at death. Once again there is an exact parallel in *VSO*: 'Egyptum pertransiens, factus est conciuis Hierosolymae' (p. 473).

Another form of unpredictable and extraordinary intrusion into the narrative of *HR* may be mentioned: a vigorous outburst against the idle stupidity of clerics. After describing the learning of King Alfred in superlative terms ('O rex prudens!' etc.), the author suddenly, and for no apparent reason, directs the following remarks at clerics who may be among his readership: 'O clerici, attendite et uidete regem in sinu librum deferre die noctuque; uos uero nec legem Dei scitis nec scire uultis' (*HR*, p. 74). There is no context in the work for such an outburst. However, its tenor may be better appreciated by comparing numerous passages in *Ench*, where Byrhtferth – evidently charged with the thankless task of instructing idle clerics – repeatedly upbraids them: 'exterminant huiusmodi mensuras nonnulli clerici imperiti, heu, pro dolor! qui non habere desiderant philacteria sua; uerbi gratia, ordinem quem susceperunt in gremio matris ecclesie non seruant, nec in doctrina sancte meditationis persistunt' (p. 40); 'quoniam sermo iste ad desides congruet clericos…ammonemus…ut discant que ignorant' (p. 58); 'coepi cordetenus ruminare pauca ex plurimis quali medicamine possem clericis proficere, ut alee ludos relaxarent et huius artis notitiam haberent' (p. 58); 'libet hic aliqua curtim inserere, ut habeant minus indocti clerici horum mysteriorum ueritatem quam sequi ualeant absque fuco

mendacii. Hec uero monasterialibus uiris cognita sunt perfecta ratione…'
(p. 234). Byrhtferth's contempt for clerics – derived, apparently, from bitter
daily experience – gives point to his express approbation of King Edgar's
expulsion of clerics from Winchester in *VSO*: 'clericos perosos habuit; nostri
habitus uiros, sicut diximus, honorauit, abiectis ex coenobiis clericorum
neniis' (p. 425). At all events such a disposition would nicely explain the
otherwise unaccountable outburst in *HR*.

Glosses

The *HR* author and Byrhtferth share a delight in glossing and explaining,
even where such explanation is otiose. In *HR* this predilection can take the
form of glosses on Old English names ('cognominabatur ab Anglis Mucel,
eo quod erat corpore magnus et prudentia grandeuus', p. 75) or on scientific
terminology ('ledon…id est minor estus', 'malina…id est maior estus', p.
54). But the most striking and characteristic glosses occur at points where
they are unnecessary: 'Honorius, hoc est honore plenus' (p. 31) or 'egentem
id est miserum' (p. 76). Glossing of this sort reveals both an ingrained
fascination with words and also a mind given over to pedantry, ever
concerned with the ostentatious display of learning. Such glossing is found
on nearly every page of *Ench*, particularly where Byrhtferth employs an
unusual word and wishes to draw attention to it: 'we gesetton on þissum
enchiridion þæt ys manualis on Lyden and handboc on Englisc' (p. 132),
'opipare id est splendide' (p. 222), 'fiat precor Galilea id est transmigratio'
(p. 230), or 'epinicion quod nomen palmam siue triumphum possumus
appellare' (p. 230). Interestingly this last word is also employed in an
ostentatious gloss in *HR*: 'palmam…quod est uerum epinicion' (p. 19; cf.
p. 44, where *epinicion* is glossed by the original scribe *.i. triumphum*). It might
be argued that such glossing is hardly exceptional in a handbook whose main
purpose is didactic. But similar glossing is found also throughout Byrhtferth's
saints' lives ('fallax gloria huius mundi…ideo fallax, quia fallit' (*VSO*, p.
469) or 'topographia id est loci descriptio' (*VSE*, p. 350)) and may be
regarded as a safe index to his mental disposition. In short, this and the other
features I have mentioned indicate that the *HR* author and Byrhtferth shared
identical mental predilections.

Sources

For the most part, inferences drawn from a range of reading common to two
writers – particularly when the texts in question were widely read in
Anglo-Saxon England – can be only corroborative, not decisive. However,
if it can be demonstrated that the *HR* author and Byrhtferth were familiar
with a similar range of texts and hence that their education and learning were

similar, we shall have a wider context in which to view their apparently identical mental predilections. Furthermore, if it can be shown that they knew texts which were otherwise rare or that their quotations from these texts shared readings otherwise unattested, we shall have further grounds for inferring their identity.

First there are the Latin writings of Aldhelm, who was one of the most carefully studied curriculum authors in late Anglo-Saxon England.[36] The *HR* author certainly knew Aldhelm's prose *De Virginitate* well, for many of his sentences are transparent imitations of Aldhelmian models. I have mentioned one example previously: the sentence 'quis urbana facundia suffultus possit...edicere?' (*HR*, p. 89) derives from Aldhelm's 'quis urbana uerborum facundia fretus enarrare sufficiat?'[37] Byrhtferth too, particularly in his saints' lives, was heavily indebted to the prose style of the *De Virginitate*,[38] and G. F. Forsey has compiled a long list of Aldhelmian borrowings in *Epil.*[39] The *HR* author also knew Aldhelm's *Enigmata*; he quotes one of them (no. VI (Luna)) during his discussion of tides (*HR*, p. 55). In a similar manner Byrhtferth quotes two of the *Enigmata* in *VSO* (p. 418; nos. LIX (Penna) and XLVI (Urtica)). It may be worth adding that Byrhtferth knew Aldhelm's *Carmen de Virginitate* as well, for he paraphrases some dozen lines from it[40] in Old English in *Ench* (p. 148).

The *HR* author was evidently familiar with the writings of Bede: large sections of the early part of his chronicle are based on extensive quotations from both the *Historia Ecclesiastica* and the *Historia Abbatum*. Byrhtferth too knew both these works. At one point in *VSO* (p. 439) he quotes a sentence from the *Historia Ecclesiastica* (III.25) not quite *verbatim*, which may suggest that he knew it well enough to quote from memory. There is also sound evidence that he knew the *Historia Abbatum*: the phrase *breuiter praelibauimus* (*VSO*, p. 453) is lifted from ch. IX of that work and the description of St Ecgwine's departure for Rome in the company of Kings Cenred and Offa (*VSE*, p. 378) is based on the account of Benedict Biscop in its ch. II.[41] More striking than his knowledge of Bede's historical works is the *HR* author's

---

[36] See my discussion, *Aldhelm: The Prose Works*, trans. M. Lapidge and M. Herren (Cambridge, 1979), pp. 1–3, and 'The Hermeneutic Style', pp. 73–5.

[37] Ed. Ehwald, p. 250, line 19.

[38] Two examples may be given: the sentence (*VSE*, p. 361) 'sic ex auro hyacincto purpuraque bis tincto cocco siue uermiculo cum bysso retorto' is taken *verbatim* from the prose *De Virginitate*, ch. XV (ed. Ehwald, p. 244, lines 18–19), and the words (*VSO*, p. 413) 'hortante deinde proreta et sonante naucleru' are from ch. II of the same work (Ehwald, p. 230, lines 22–3). Byrhtferth's indebtedness to Aldhelm is immense.

[39] 'Byrhtferth's *Preface*', pp. 514–15.

[40] *Carmen de Virginitate*, lines 23–7 and 74–80. There are also numerous reminiscences of this poem in Byrhtferth's prose – e.g. *tota* [sic] *mentis conamine* (*VSO*, p. 404) is from line 89 – but this is hardly the place to give a list.

[41] Ed. Plummer I, 373 and 365.

knowledge of Bede's hexameter poem *De Die Iudicii* which he quotes entire
for no obvious reason (*HR*, pp. 23–7). It is interesting that Byrhtferth quotes
some twenty lines of this same poem in *VSE* (pp. 356–7), ostensibly as a
sermon delivered by St Ecgwine(!) on the Day of Judgement. The poem was
not unknown in late Anglo-Saxon England,[42] but its extensive citation by
these two authors is a striking coincidence. I have noted above that the *HR*
author was easily familiar with two of Bede's scientific treatises, *De Natura
Rerum* and *De Temporum Ratione*; so too was Byrhtferth, who excerpted both
treatises in his computistical commonplace-book, the 'Ramsey Computus',
and drew on both of them subsequently in *Ench*. One may surmise from *Epil*
that Byrhtferth was also familiar with some of Bede's exegetical writings,
particularly the commentaries on the gospels.[43] It is remarkable that so wide
a knowledge of Bede's writings should be shared by two authors.

Equally remarkable is their shared fondness for, and knowledge of,
Boethius's *De Consolatione Philosophiae*, particularly the *metra*. This work was
known in Anglo-Saxon England from the time of King Alfred onwards,[44]
but the *HR* author and Byrhtferth seem to have absorbed it more enthusias-
tically than anyone else. At almost every turn of his narrative the *HR* author
takes the opportunity to insert a quotation from Boethius: I count twelve
separate quotations from the *metra* and two from the prose of the *De
Consolatione Philosophiae*.[45] Some of the quotations are *verbatim*, some are
paraphrased to suit the context and some are inaccurate, suggesting that the
author was quoting from memory. The *metra* of Boethius do not figure so
prominently in Byrhtferth's writings, but it is significant that in each of them

---

[42] See discussion by L. Whitbread, 'After Bede: the Influence and Dissemination of his Doomsday
Verses', *ASNSL* 204 (1967), 250–66, esp. 252–5 on the *HR* author's knowledge of the poem.
Whitbread assumed that *HR* was compiled at Hexham and hence that its recension of Bede's poem
never left Northumbria; this view will need revision in the light of the arguments presented here.
Also Whitbread was unaware that the poem is extensively quoted in *VSE*.

[43] *Epil*, p. 517: 'edidit idem [*scil.* Beda] quamplurimos sacros apices librorum, elimauitque luce clarius
bis binorum dicta euangelistarum nonnulla'. The works in question must be *In Marcum* and *In Lucam*,
Bede's only known commentaries on the gospels.

[44] See D. K. Bolton, 'The Study of the Consolation of Philosophy in Anglo-Saxon England', *Archives
d'Histoire Doctrinale et Littéraire du Moyen Âge* 44 (1977), 33–78; Miss Bolton studies the commentaries
on Boethius contained in tenth- and eleventh-century English manuscripts. For the literary application
of a knowledge of Boethius by a Winchester poet contemporary with Byrhtferth, see my remarks,
'Three Latin Poems from Æthelwold's School at Winchester', *ASE* 1 (1972), 85–137, at 103–4.

[45] The quotations from the *metra* are as follows: *HR*, p. 14 (I, met. ii, lines 3, 25 and 27), p. 14 (II,
met. vii, lines 12–14), pp. 55–6 (I, met. v, lines 29–36), p. 62 (IV, met. v, lines 21–2), p. 65 (II, met.
i, lines 7–10), p. 66 (II, met. ix, lines 10–12), p. 67 (IV, met. vi, lines 27–9), p. 67 (IV, met. v, lines
21–2, as at *HR*, p. 62, but quoted accurately this time), p. 77 (III, met. iv, lines 1–3), p. 78 (III, met.
v, lines 7–8) and pp. 89–90 (II, met. iv, lines 1–4 and 17–22). A famous sentence from I, pr. iv ('beatas
fore res publicas, si eas uel studiosi sapientiae regerent, uel si earum rectores studere sapientiae
contigisset') is twice quoted in *HR* (pp. 64 and 81) but is not identified by Arnold. Another sentence
from II, pr. v (beginning 'tunc est preciosa pecunia...') quoted on p. 90 of *HR* is erroneously
identified by Arnold.

he finds some occasion to introduce a quotation: in *VSO* one line from II, met. iv (p. 402; the same line is quoted in *HR*, at p. 89); in *VSE* the first three lines of I, met. ii (p. 393; partially quoted in *HR*, at p. 14); and in *Ench* the first line of III, met. ix (see plate facing p. 92; not printed in Crawford's text) slightly remodelled. The way in which these quotations are used suggests that, like the *HR* author, Byrhtferth had an intimate knowledge of Boethius.

Sources of a different sort also imply a link. While describing the campaigns of Alfred against the Danes, the *HR* author mentions the martydom of Edmund, king of East Anglia, in 870, and then digresses somewhat in order to advert to the glory of this event (*HR*, p. 77: 'de cuius passionis honore libet aliqua...inserere'). Although he does not mention any written source, one may suspect from the nature of the discussion that there was one. Now the first written account of the martyrdom is Abbo of Fleury's *Passio S. Eadmundi Regis et Martyris*,[46] which was written at the invitation of Archbishop Dunstan during Abbo's stay at Ramsey, 986–8. It is worth remarking too that the *HR* author inserts a notice concerning the sacking of Fleury by the Vikings and the subsequent dispersal of the monks and that this does not appear to be drawn from any annalistic source; it is possible, as Arnold long ago suggested,[47] that the notice derived directly from Abbo himself. It will be recalled that Byrhtferth had studied with Abbo during his stay at Ramsey – a fact which Byrhtferth frequently acknowledges in his writings[48] – and that Fleury is often mentioned by him.[49] Or, again, sect. 4 of *HR* (pp. 30–68) is basically a chronicle for the years 732–802. Because this chronicle contains much information about York and Northumbria which is not found elsewhere, it has been plausibly suggested that it is based on a set of annals originally compiled at York (or in the vicinity of York) in the early ninth century.[50] It will be convenient to refer to these hypothetical annals as the 'York annals'. What is singularly striking is that many of the entries for the period 732–802 preserved in *HR* but derived from the 'York annals' are found in only one other source: a series of so-called 'Ramsey annals'[51] which are preserved in Oxford, St John's College 17, the manuscript which, as I have noted, is a late-eleventh-century copy of a computistical commonplace-book compiled by Byrhtferth. As Hart, the editor of these 'Ramsey annals' has noted, 'for the whole of the period from 732 to 900, the Ramsey annals

[46] *Three Lives of English Saints*, ed. M. Winterbottom (Toronto, 1971), pp. 67–87.
[47] *HR*, p. 85, n. a.
[48] See especially *Epil*, p. 519: '[Abbo sophista]...per cuius beneuolentiam percepimus huius rei intelligentiam necnon aliarum rerum peritiam'; cf. *Ench*, p. 232 etc.
[49] *VSO*, pp. 413, 417 and 422; *VSE*, p. 391 etc.
[50] Hunter Blair, 'Some Observations on the *Historia Regum*', pp. 86–99.
[51] See Hart, 'The Ramsey Computus'.

and Symeon of Durham [i.e. sect. 4 of *HR*] march hand-in-hand'.[52] The most reasonable explanation of these circumstances is that a copy of the 'York annals' was available at Ramsey in the late tenth century, whence they were used by the compiler of the 'Ramsey annals' and subsequently copied by Byrhtferth into his commonplace-book; it is not impossible that Byrhtferth himself was the compiler of these 'Ramsey annals', though we have no means of proving this. At approximately the same time, and very probably in the same place, the *HR* author drew the material of his sect. 4 from the same 'York annals'. How the 'York annals' came to Ramsey we have no means of knowing, though it is tempting to think of Oswald, the founder of Ramsey who was archbishop of York (972–92), as the agent; but this too is an unprovable conjecture.

There are further links between the *HR* author and Byrhtferth's commonplace-book. While discussing Bede's historical writing (and particularly the *Historia Abbatum*), the *HR* author takes the opportunity of introducing a poem allegedly by Bede on the passage of time and the sequence of the seasons, beginning 'Me legat, annales cupiat qui noscere menses'[53] (*HR*, p. 23). This poem was fairly widely known during the Middle Ages; it occurs in some dozen manuscripts from various parts of Europe. It is not a highly original production, being based on eight lines copied *verbatim* from Dracontius's *Satisfactio*, and it is almost certainly not the production of Bede.[54] However, in one manuscript, and one manuscript only, the poem is followed immediately by a distich which attributes it explicitly to Bede:

> Hos claros uersus uenerabilis edidit auctor
> Beda sacer, multum nitido sermone coruscus.

And the manuscript which preserves this version of the poem uniquely is Oxford, St John's College 17, the copy of Byrhtferth's computistical commonplace-book.[55] Byrhtferth, that is to say, copied the version of the poem attributing it to Bede into his own work-book. It is therefore highly significant that, when for no apparent reason the *HR* author introduces the same poem into his narrative, his version of it should include the above-quoted

[52] *Ibid.* p. 37.
[53] The poem is listed (with bibliography) in D. Schaller and E. Könsgen, *Initia carminum Latinorum saeculo undecimo antiquiorum* (Göttingen, 1977), as no. 9480, and edited in *Anthologia Latina*, ed. A. Riese (Leipzig, 1894), as no. 676, and in *Poetae Latini Minores*, ed. E. Baehrens, 5 vols. (Leipzig, 1879–83) v, at 349–50; for discussion, see L. Bieler, 'Adversaria zu Anthologia 676', *Antidosis: Festschrift für Walther Kraus*, ed. R. Hanslik, A. Lesky and H. Schwabl (Vienna, 1972), pp. 41–8.
[54] See C. W. Jones, *Bedae Pseudepigrapha: Scientific Writings falsely attributed to Bede* (Ithaca, N.Y., 1939), pp. 67 and 77. However, it is well to ask where, if the poem is spurious, Byrhtferth found the distich attributing it to Bede, and to remember that the *HR* author's version of *De Die Iudicii* preserves an eight-line dedication to Acca which marks it as a genuine work of Bede.
[55] The poem is entered on 14r.

distich attributing it to Bede (*HR*, p. 23). This establishes a direct link between the *HR* author and Byrhtferth.

There is another direct link of the same kind. At one point the *HR* author notes that Archbishop Eanbald II of York received the pallium on the feast of the Nativity of the Virgin Mary (8 September) and he thereupon quotes two lines pertaining to this feast:

> Splendet honore dies, est in quo uirgo Maria,
> Stirpe Dauid regis procedens, edita mundo. (*HR*, p. 58)

It is apparent that these lines derive from a metrical martyrology, but they are not found in any such martyrology yet in print. However, Byrhtferth's computistical commonplace-book contains a liturgical calendar (Oxford, St John's College 17, 16v–21v), and into this calendar a metrical martyrology has been interpolated.[56] Significantly the two lines in question are copied against 8 September (20r). By the same token, Byrhtferth twice in *VSO* has occasion to quote from a metrical martyrology: once for the feast of the Four Crowned Martyrs ('Quattuor hi sancti roseis sertis coronati'; *VSO*, p. 463), and again for the feast of St Oswald of York on 29 February:

> Aula Dei patuit Oswaldo pridie Martis
> Pontifici summo alta petendo poli. (*VSO*, p. 472)

As in the case of the lines on the Nativity of the Virgin, these two quotations are not found in any printed metrical martyrology. However, they are both entered in the calendar in Byrhtferth's computistical commonplace-book, against 8 November (21r) and 29 February (17r) respectively. It seems clear, therefore, that Byrhtferth drew the two quotations in *VSO* from the metrical martyrology which he copied into his computistical commonplace-book. It is difficult to avoid the conclusion that the *HR* author did likewise.

I have reserved till the end two similar examples of quotations cited in a singular and characteristic way by both the *HR* author and Byrhtferth. The first is a quotation from the Book of Job, which, in the Vulgate, reads as follows: 'ad nimium calorem transeat ab aquis niuium' (Job XXIV.19) – 'let him pass from the snow waters to excessive heat, and his sin even to hell'. The subject here is singular (*transeat*) and refers to the sinner. At one point the *HR* author, while describing the eternal punishment meted out to a murderer and his evil accomplices, paraphrases this quotation from Job: he makes its subject plural (referring now to the souls of the sinners), puts the corresponding plural verb in the future tense, and then rearranges the

---

[56] I have edited this poem, with commentary and full discussion of the manuscript recensions of the Metrical Calendar of York on which it is ultimately based, as 'A Metrical Calendar from Ramsey', *RB* (forthcoming).

Michael Lapidge

quotation so as to put his new verb and subject at the beginning of the verse: 'transibunt anime de penis niuium'[57] (*HR*, p. 11). Now in each of his saints' lives Byrhtferth finds occasion to paraphrase this same verse from Job, and on each occasion the subject is not the biblical sinner but the souls of sinners; the verse is preceded each time by the words *transibunt animae*, exactly as in *HR*: 'transibunt animae de aquis niuium ad aquas nimium' (*VSE*, p. 357); 'transibunt animae de aquis niuium ad aquas nimium' (*VSO*, p. 451). This highly idiosyncratic use of a biblical quotation could scarcely occur in two authors by coincidence.

I give a final example of idiosyncratic and characteristic use of a quotation. As I have remarked elsewhere,[58] Byrhtferth twice in *Ench* quotes a distich which he has seized upon in Arator's long poem *De Actibus Apostolorum*, a work of some 2300 lines. It is as follows:[59]

> Spiritus alme, ueni! sine te non diceris umquam;
> Munera da linguae qui das in munere linguas. (1.226–7)

Byrhtferth employs these two lines as a sort of personal prayer to ask the Holy Ghost's continuing support of his writing; they are used at points of transition from one part of a work to another. Thus he quotes them to mark the transition from pt II of *Ench* to pt III (p. 134) and a second time as he steels himself to launch into a detailed explanation of paschal reckoning. This time, significantly, they are described explicitly as 'oratio patris Byrhtferði' (p. 150). Similarly, as he prepares to describe the life of St Ecgwine in the prologue to *VSE*, he quotes them again as 'exordium meae orationis' (p. 350). It cannot be a matter of coincidence that the *HR* author, as he finishes his sect. 3 on Bede's writings and prepares to elaborate the material of the 'York annals' in sect. 4, invokes the aid of the Holy Ghost with the same two lines from Arator: 'nos uero ad negotium sollerti cura, Christi clementia succurrente, peragemus, sic orando,

> spiritus alme, ueni, sine te non diceris unquam
> munera da lingue qui das in munere linguas.' (p. 30)

CONCLUSIONS AND FURTHER QUESTIONS

In my opinion the similarities of vocabulary, phrasing, mental predilection and common sources between the works in question are best explained by supposing that the *HR* author was Byrhtferth of Ramsey. A study of the

[57] A later scribe has written *ad calorem nimium* in the margin, thus revealing that *he* recognized the source of the sentence to be the Book of Job; but the main scribe did not (apparently) complete the sentence, or he found it incomplete in his source.
[58] 'Byrhtferth and the *Vita S. Ecgwini*', p. 341.
[59] *Aratoris Subdiaconi De Actibus Apostolorum*, ed. A. P. McKinlay, Corpus Scriptorum Ecclesiasticorum Latinorum 72 (Vienna, 1951), 25.

Latinity of *HR* leads, then, to some appreciable results, as Hunter Blair anticipated. It allows, in particular, the corroboration of his suspicion that these first five sections (pp. 3–91 of Arnold's edition, excluding the two long interpolations)[60] are the work of one author and originally constituted a single work which was subsequently incorporated into the larger structure of the so-called *Historia Regum* attributed (in a manuscript rubric) to Symeon of Durham. We now have serious grounds for regarding these first five sections as an historical compilation made by Byrhtferth of Ramsey, probably in the late tenth century or the early eleventh.[61] It is not possible at the present time to suggest a more accurate dating, since exact dates in Byrhtferth's life are not ascertainable.[62] What Byrhtferth called his historical compilation we have no means of knowing, and perhaps its diverse parts preclude the possibility of arriving at a satisfactory title.[63] For the time being, I suggest a neutral title, such as Byrhtferth's 'Historical Miscellany' or 'Historical Compilation'.

The attribution to Byrhtferth raises several very important questions about his method of work, about the sources on which he drew and about the subsequent transmission of his compilation. These questions can only be mentioned here but are deserving of detailed study. The sources, briefly. Sect. 1 consists in a unique text of the *Passio Sanctorum Ethelberti atque Ethelredi*,[64] as it is called in the manuscript rubric. This work commemorates two Kentish princes who were martyred during the reign of their uncle Egbert, king of Kent (664–73), and who appear to have been venerated principally in Kent. It is not possible to say whether Byrhtferth was the first to commit their *passio* to writing. Some light will no doubt be thrown on this problem when the unprinted *Passio beatorum martyrum Ethelredi atque Ethelbricti*,[65] preserved in

---

60 In addition to the interpolations I have omitted from my discussion sect. 6 (in Hunter Blair's numeration), which carries the history down to 957, because, as far as I am able to judge, its entries have no recognizable Byrhtferthian features. But the question requires further consideration; in any case one must ask why Byrhtferth's historical compilation would have ended at 887, approximately a century before the time he was writing. Furthermore the possibility of alteration and interpolation by the twelfth-century scribes of CCCC 139 must constantly be borne in mind, so that that we remain cautious in regarding every single word in the first five sections as the *ipsissimum uerbum* of Byrhtferth.

61 In the light of my investigations above it is interesting to notice Arnold's inspired insight: 'Let the reader look at pp. 14, 31, 55, 76, 84 and remark the curious way in which illustrative scraps of metre are cited from Boethius...then let him read some pages of the Life of St. Oswald of York, written by a Ramsey monk of the late 10th century; he will feel, I think, that both works belong to nearly the same period, the same grade of culture' (*Symeonis Monachi Opera Omnia* I, xvii).

62 *VSO* mentions Archbishop Ælfric as living and was therefore composed 995 × 1005; *Ench* was being written in 1011; and *VSE* was written probably 1014 × 1020, as I have suggested elsewhere ('Byrhtferth and the *Vita S. Ecgwini*', p. 342).

63 I am reluctant to accept titles used by earlier editors, such as the 'Northumbrian Chronicle' or the *Gesta Veterum Northanhymbrorum*, simply because they apply appropriately only to sect. 4 (incorporating the 'York annals'), whereas sect. 1 is concerned with Kentish history and sect. 5 almost exclusively with West Saxon history. A satisfactory title would have to embrace this regional diversity.

64 The work is listed in the Bollandists' *Bibliotheca Hagiographica Latina*, 2 vols. (Brussels, 1898–9), as no. 2643.   65 *Ibid.* nos. 2641–2.

Oxford, Bodleian Library, Bodley 285 (a Ramsey manuscript of the early thirteenth century), fols. 116–21, has been printed.[66] This text displays many of the stylistic features which I have discussed above and one of its chapters corresponds *verbatim* to a chapter in *HR* (p. 10, §7). There is accordingly an undeniable relationship between the *passio* in Bodley 285 and that in Byrhtferth's historical miscellany. What is interesting is that, according to the twelfth-century *Chronicon Abbatiae Rameseiensis*, the remains of these two Kentish martyrs were acquired by Æthelwine (*ob.* 991), the lay patron of Ramsey, and were translated there at some point in the late tenth century.[67] It is therefore possible that Byrhtferth was asked to celebrate the translation by writing the *passio* and *translatio* of these two martyrs and that he subsequently incorporated part of this *passio* into his historical miscellany; but such conjectures must await the publication of the *passio* in Bodley 285.[68] The source of sect. 2 presents fewer problems. This section consists in a Northumbrian regnal list, which is very closely related to that in the so-called *memoranda* appended 734 × 748 to the 'Moore Bede' (Cambridge, University Library, Kk. 5. 16, 128v)[69] and to that in the genealogical collection in Cambridge, Corpus Christi College 183, a tenth-century manuscript given by King Athelstan to the congregation of St Cuthbert then at Chester-le-Street.[70] Although Byrhtferth's sequence of kings is identical to that of these two regnal lists, there are some minor discrepancies in the years he assigns to various kings, which suggests that he was not using either of these two surviving manuscripts but another now lost that was closely related to them. A similar situation obtains with respect to the sources for sect. 3, namely Bede's *Historia Abbatum* and *Historia Ecclesiastica*. Hunter Blair has observed that Byrhtferth's extensive quotations from the *Historia Abbatum* indicate that he was using a text closely related to that preserved in the tenth-century London, BL Harley 3020, but that at one point his text offered a reading superior to that of any surviving manuscript.[71] Similarly Byrhtferth's quotations from Bede's *Historia Ecclesiastica* contain one reading found only in the eighth-century Southumbrian manuscript, now London BL Cotton Tiberius C. ii.[72] It will be essential to collate this manuscript fully to see

---

[66] See N. R. Ker, *Medieval Libraries of Great Britain*, 2nd ed. (London, 1964), p. 154.

[67] *Chronicon Abbatiae Rameseiensis*, ed. W. D. Macray, RS (London, 1886), p. 55.

[68] An edition of this text has been prepared by Dr David Rollason as an appendix to his forthcoming book, *The Mildrith Legend: a Study in Early Medieval Hagiography in England*. I am grateful to him for supplying me with a transcript of his text.

[69] P. Hunter Blair, 'The *Moore Memoranda* on Northumbrian History', *The Early Cultures of North-West Europe (H. M. Chadwick Memorial Studies)*, ed. C. Fox and B. Dickins (Cambridge, 1950), pp. 245–57, at p. 246.

[70] D. N. Dumville, 'The Anglian Collection of Royal Genealogies and Regnal Lists', *ASE* 5 (1976), 23–50, esp. 25–6 and 32.

[71] 'Some Observations on the *Historia Regum*', pp. 83–4.

[72] *Ibid.* p. 91. On the manuscript, see E. A. Lowe, *Codices Latini Antiquiores* 11, 2nd ed. (Oxford, 1972), no. 191, and N. R. Ker, *Catalogue of Manuscripts containing Anglo-Saxon* (Oxford, 1957), p. 261.

whether it contains any further indication that it may have been Byrhtferth's exemplar or whether he was rather using a now lost manuscript related to it. Byrhtferth's text of Bede's *De Die Iudicii*, also quoted entire in sect. 3, has been collated by the most recent editor of the poem[73] and, as well as preserving the final eight-line dedication to Acca, appears at many points to offer readings superior to any other surviving manuscript. In other words it seems that Byrhtferth had access to some very early and textually sound manuscripts of Bede's writings. Sect. 4 is based on the aforementioned 'York annals'. It will be necessary to compare closely the entries in this section and those for the same period which were included in the 'Ramsey annals' in Byrhtferth's computistical commonplace-book; now that one possible stage in the transmission of these 'York annals' has been suggested (from York to Ramsey in the late tenth century), there is some basis for further study of these important records.[74] Finally sect. 5 is based largely on quotations from Asser's *De Rebus Gestis Ælfredi*. We have knowledge of only one manuscript of this work, which was almost completely destroyed by the Cotton fire in 1731.[75] Nevertheless this manuscript, as it is known from early printed editions of Asser, in many respects agrees closely with the text used by Byrhtferth, and Stevenson thought it probable 'that the compiler [= Byrhtferth] used this very MS'.[76] Hunter Blair has doubted this identification,[77] but at least one of his arguments – the use of *æt* with Old English place-names in *HR* and the absence of such forms in the destroyed manuscript – needs revision, since it is a demonstrable characteristic of Byrhtferth to give place-names with the *æt* formula, regardless of the form given by his source. All these questions need further study. So too it will be necessary to evaluate Byrhtferth's rôle as an historian in the context of other Anglo-Saxon historical writings.[78] Above all a new text of Byrhtferth's historical miscellany is needed to replace the unreliable edition of Arnold.[79]

---

[73] *Bedae Venerabilis Opera IV: Opera Rhythmica*, ed. J. Fraipont, CCSL 122 (Turnhout, 1955), 439–44; cf. also L. Whitbread, 'A Study of Bede's *Versus De Die Iudicii*', *PQ* 23 (1944), 193–221.

[74] It is doubtful whether we shall ever know who compiled the 'York annals'; nevertheless I am forcibly impressed by the conjecture of William Stubbs over a century ago: 'It is not improbable that Alcuin was instrumental in a remote way in the composition of the ['York annals']; the references to events of European rather than domestic interest, and especially to the history of the great emperor, seem to imply it. It ends too about the time of Alcuin's death, as if the writer had not thought it worthwhile to continue it. There is, however, no distinct trace of Alcuin's hand in it...' (*Chronica Magistri Rogeri de Hovedene*, 4 vols., RS (London, 1868–71), I, xi).

[75] On this manuscript, see now H. Gneuss, 'Die Handschrift Cotton Otho A. xii', *Anglia* 94 (1976), 289–318.

[76] *Asser's Life of King Alfred*, p. lix.

[77] 'Some Observations on the *Historia Regum*', p. 101.

[78] There is some exploration of this subject by C. R. Hart, in 'Byrhtferth's Northumbrian Chronicle', *EHR* forthcoming. In many ways Dr Hart's researches on Byrhtferth have run a parallel course to my own and I am grateful to him for showing me his article before publication and for discussing Byrhtferth on many occasions.

[79] An edition of this work is in progress by D. N. Dumville and myself as vol. xvi of *The Anglo-Saxon Chronicle: a Collaborative Edition*, ed. D. N. Dumville and S. D. Keynes.

The later transmission of Byrhtferth's historical miscellany also requires attention. On the evidence of CCCC 139 the work was known in some form at Sawley in the mid-twelfth century. But there is another anonymous (and unprinted) text known generally as the *Historia post Bedam*, which survives in two manuscripts[80] and which appears to derive in part from sects. 2 and 4 of Byrhtferth's work. The *Historia post Bedam* was apparently compiled at Durham sometime near the middle of the twelfth century;[81] it was subsequently incorporated by Roger of Howden almost *verbatim* in his *Chronica* near the end of the twelfth century.[82] Until these and other texts[83] have been carefully studied, it is not possible to form any notion of the circulation of Byrhtferth's historical miscellany in northern England in the twelfth century. These are matters requiring the urgent attention of historians.

For the student of Anglo-Saxon literary culture the emergence of Byrhtferth as a major Anglo-Latin author must have priority. The materials are now available for a detailed study of the education and learning of this curious man. His historical miscellany may now be placed alongside his other four known major works: *Ench*, the computistical commonplace-book (Oxford, St John's College 17, still, unfortunately, unprinted), *VSO* and *VSE*. From the abundant quotations in these works – not all satisfactorily identified by any means – it will be possible to gain an accurate impression of the range of his reading and hence to reconstruct conjecturally the library that was available to him at Ramsey in the early eleventh century. Byrhtferth has inevitably been overshadowed by his mentor, Abbo of Fleury. Rightly so, no doubt: Abbo was one of the two or three most learned men in the Europe of his time. But Byrhtferth's learning was by no means negligible and it seems likely that he will come to be regarded as a major figure in late Anglo-Saxon literary culture.[84]

---

[80] London, BL Royal 13. A. vi (origin unknown, s. xii^med) and Oxford, St John's College 97 (Durham, s. xiii^in).

[81] See *Chronica Magistri Rogeri de Hovedene*, ed. Stubbs I, xxvi–xxviii and xxxi–xxxix; cf. A. Gransden, *Historical Writing in England* c. *550 to* c. *1307* (London, 1974), pp. 225–6.

[82] The passages corresponding to Byrhtferth's sect. 2 and 4 are ptd *Chronica Magistri Rogeri de Hovedene*, ed. Stubbs (with passages from the *Historia post Bedam* in reduced type), I, 3–19.

[83] It has been suggested by A. Gransden (*Historical Writing in England*, p. 31) that some entries from what I call the 'York annals' were incorporated in the so-called *Chronicle of Melrose*; it will be necessary to establish whether Byrhtferth's historical miscellany was the intermediary of these entries in this work. The *Chronicle of Melrose* has been edited in facsimile by A. O. and M. O. Anderson (London, 1936); see their discussion of sources for the early section (p. xi).

[84] I am very grateful to Peter Dronke for commenting on an earlier draft of this article and above all to David Dumville for sharing with me his unrivalled knowledge of CCCC 139 and for advising me on many difficult problems of interpretation.

Byrhtferth's *Enchiridion* and the computus in Oxford, St John's College 17

PETER S. BAKER

More than fifty years after its first appearance in print, Byrhtferth's *Manual*, or *Enchiridion* as he called it himself, is among the most puzzling texts of the Old English prose corpus.[1] Its obscurity is due partly to its unglamorous subject matter – mathematics (computus) and the calendar – but more, perhaps, to its apparently bewildering organization. Humfrey Wanley called it an 'opus miscellaneum', Richard Wülker described it as 'außerordentlich bunter' and Frederick Tupper referred to it as 'that remarkable potpourri'.[2] Indeed the *Enchiridion* seems often enough to wander aimlessly or shift abruptly; it seems to follow no plan and many an intrepid scholar has come away from it with the disquieting feeling that, having read a scientific primer, he has learned shamefully little science. As Heinrich Henel and N. R. Ker pointed out, the text has come down to us disarranged;[3] but the restoration of the misplaced sections to their proper order only partly relieves the confusion. We may as well admit at the outset that Byrhtferth often digressed and often backtracked: as an organizer he was barely tolerable. But if we fail

---

[1] The Old English portions only were printed by Friedrich Kluge ('Angelsächsische Excerpte aus Byrhtferth's Handboc oder Enchiridion', *Anglia* 8 (1885), 298–337). The complete text was first edited by Samuel J. Crawford (*Byrhtferth's Manual*, EETS o.s. 177 (London, 1929; repr. with a table of errata by N. R. Ker, 1966)). That Byrhtferth called his book the *Enchiridion* has most recently been pointed out by Michael Lapidge ('Byrhtferth and the *Vita S. Ecgwini*', *MS* 41 (1979), 331–53, at 337 and n. 31). I cite the text by page and line number. In quotations I have omitted the accents and the italics used by Crawford for editorial expansion of manuscript contractions and for Latin words in Old English passages. I have expanded the ampersand and the abbreviated dates (following Byrhtferth's practice of using the genitive singular of months' names) and altered occasionally Crawford's punctuation. I have, however, retained Crawford's editorial signs: ( ) for words and letters to be omitted, [ ] for words and letters altered and ⟨ ⟩ for words and letters added. I have emended Crawford's text in several places and omitted a few of his emendations.

[2] Humfrey Wanley, *Antiquæ Literaturæ Septentrionalis Liber Alter, seu Humphredi Wanleii Librorum Vett. Septentrionalium...Catalogus* (Oxford, 1705), p. 104; Richard Wülker, *Grundriss zur Geschichte der angelsächsischen Litteratur* (Leipzig, 1885), p. 506; and Frederick Tupper, Jr, 'Anglo-Saxon Dæg-Mæl', *PMLA* 10 (1895), 119. See also Peter Hunter Blair, *An Introduction to Anglo-Saxon England*, 2nd ed. (Cambridge, 1977), pp. 359–60, and Stanley B. Greenfield, *A Critical History of Old English Literature* (New York, 1965), p. 61.

[3] Heinrich Henel, *Studien zum altenglischen Computus*, Beiträge zur englischen Philologie 26 (Leipzig, 1934), pp. 6–7; N. R. Ker, 'Two Notes on MS Ashmole 328 (*Byrhtferth's Manual*)', *MÆ* 4 (1935), 16–19. The text should be read in the following order: 2.1–30.9; 44.28–56.29; 30.9–44.27; and 56.30–end.

to understand the *Enchiridion* the fault is partly our own, for it was not Byrhtferth's intention to write a wholly self-contained book. As Henel ably demonstrated, the *Enchiridion* was designed as a commentary on the computus;[4] this fact is the key we need to unlock the mysteries of Byrhtferth's work. To read it without referring to a computus would be as pointless as to read a biblical commentary without referring to a bible.

In the Middle Ages the word 'computus' could be used of the astronomical science that grew up around the calendar, of books by single authors on this science (e.g. Bede's *De Temporum Ratione* and Helperic's *Liber de Computo*) or of a collection of brief notices, tables and diagrams, usually by various authors, on astronomy and the calendar.[5] When Ælfric included the *gerim* or *compotus* among the books that every priest must have, he was probably taking the word in its third sense.[6] Byrhtferth used *compotus* in its first and third senses;[7] Henel, like most modern commentators, restricted it to its third sense so as to draw a sharp distinction between the computus and more unified works like those of Bede and Helperic.[8] The computus, which usually included a calendar, at first rarely appeared as an independent codex, but rather as the introduction to a psalter or missal. Gradually it became detached from these ecclesiastical books and was transcribed into collective codices containing tracts on natural history, chronology and other practical subjects.

Henel, by citing the numerous computi available to him, demonstrated that Byrhtferth's technique was to quote from the computus and then explicate the quoted passage, drawing on the computistical works of Bede, Helperic and others. Byrhtferth also inserted sections on natural history, grammar and rhetoric and concluded his *Enchiridion* with a treatise on numerology. Unfortunately Henel was unable to identify any one of the computi he studied as the very text that Byrhtferth had explicated.[9] However, as early as 1935, A. Van de Vyver noticed that Byrhtferth often referred to texts written by Abbo of Fleury and preserved in Oxford, St John's College 17, a giant

---

[4] *Studien*, pp. 5–35. Henel's study is still the fundamental guide to the *Enchiridion*; it is supplemented by his 'Notes on Byrhtferth's *Manual*', *JEGP* 41 (1942), 427–43. Throughout this article I am deeply indebted to these studies.

[5] See *Bedae Opera de Temporibus*, ed. Charles W. Jones, Med. Acad. of America Publ. 41 (Cambridge, Mass., 1943), 75–7.

[6] *Die Hirtenbriefe Ælfrics*, ed. Bernhard Fehr, Bibliothek der angelsächsischen Prosa 9 (Hamburg, 1914; repr. with a suppl. intro. by Peter Clemoes, Darmstadt, 1966), 1.52, 2.137 and 11.157 (pp. 13, 51 and 126–7). In the first instance the word *gerim* is glossed *Kalendarium*, which shows that at least one reader understood the word to mean the calendar and (one must assume) the tables needed to make it intelligible.

[7] Byrhtferth translates *compotus* (2.2) as *gerimcræft* (2.9), used of the science; later *compoti* (28.1) is translated *gerimes* (44.33), used of the tables and texts that accompany the calendar.

[8] *Studien*, pp. 1–4. I follow Henel in restricting the sense of 'computus'.

[9] *Ibid.* p. 21: 'das *gerim*, das B. besaß, nicht bekannt und höchstwahrscheinlich auch nicht erhalten ist'.

computistical miscellany; Van de Vyver identified this manuscript as a copy of a collection compiled by Byrhtferth himself.[10] Later Cyril Hart showed the relationship between the *Enchiridion* and St John's 17 (which he abbreviated ' J ') in greater detail. According to him J was written at Ramsey in the late eleventh century and later sent to Thorney; an earlier manuscript of the collection in J must have been the chief source of Byrhtferth's *Enchiridion*.[11] What follows is an abbreviated table of J's contents:[12]

1v–7r	Miscellaneous tables and short texts on medicine, herbs, alphabets, geography, consanguinity etc.[13]
7v	Byrhtferth's diagram of the physical and physiological fours.[14]
8r–12r	Miscellaneous astronomical tables.
12v–13r	Byrhtferth's *Epilogus* or preface to the computistical texts in J.[15]
13v–34v	Computus. It draws heavily on Abbo's works. Its calendar (16r–21v) is an Abbonian calendar and many of its tables also occur in the *Compotus vulgaris qui dicitur ephimerida Abbonis*; this very rubric is found on 25r above the table that begins the *Compotus vulgaris* as printed in Patrologia Latina.[16]
35r–58r	Short texts and extracts from the works of writers on astronomy and arithmetic, with diagrams and tables. These tend to be more theoretical, less like instructions, than the texts in the computus. Several of these tracts are attributed to Abbo: *Ratio Abbonis supra prefatum numerum* (35r),[17] *De*

---

[10] 'Les Oeuvres inédites d'Abbon de Fleury', *RB* 47 (1935), 144–5. Years earlier Charles Singer had written, 'A rather surprising feature of this encyclopædia is the acquaintance with Greek that it betrays especially in the medical sections' ('On a Greek Charm used in England in the Twelfth Century', *Annals of Medical Hist.* 1 (1917), 258–60). Michael Lapidge has pointed out Byrhtferth's great fondness for Greek words ('Byrhtferth and the *Vita S. Ecgwini*', p. 335). Singer's observation provides further evidence that Byrhtferth was the compiler of St John's 17.

[11] See Hart's two articles, 'The Ramsey *Computus*', *EHR* 85 (1970), 29–44, and 'Byrhtferth and his Manual', *MÆ* 41 (1972), 95–109. I am much indebted to the second of these articles.

[12] For a fuller description of the manuscript, see Henry O. Coxe, *Catalogus Codicum MSS. qui in Collegiis, Aulisque Oxoniensibus Hodie Adservantur* (Oxford, 1852) II, 5–8. See also Charles Singer, 'A Review of the Medical Literature of the Dark Ages, with a New Text of about 1110', *Proc. of the R. Soc. of Medicine* 10 (1917), Section of the History of Medicine, 117–27.

[13] The medical texts (J 1v–2v) have been printed by Singer ('A Review', pp. 128–37); the runic alphabet (J 5v) has been printed by René Derolez (*Runica Manuscripta: the English Tradition* (Bruges, 1954), pp. 26–34 and 37–45). Pl. III reproduces J 5v. The Old English glosses on J 6v have been printed by J. V. Gough ('Some Old English Glosses', *Anglia* 92 (1974), 282–3); see also P. Bierbaumer, 'Zu J. V. Goughs Ausgabe einiger altenglischer Glossen', *Anglia* 95 (1977), 119.

[14] The diagram is reproduced as the frontispiece to Crawford's edition of the *Enchiridion* and has been described by Charles and Dorothea Singer ('A Restoration: Byrhtferð of Ramsey's Diagram of the Physical and Physiological Fours', *Bodleian Quarterly Record* 2 (1917–19), 47–51).

[15] George F. Forsey, 'Byrhtferth's Preface', *Speculum* 3 (1928), 505–22. Byrhtferth used the word *epilogus* to mean 'preface'; see Lapidge, 'Byrhtferth and the *Vita S. Ecgwini*', p. 337, n. 32.

[16] Charles W. Jones, *Bedae Pseudepigrapha: Scientific Writings falsely attributed to Bede* (Ithaca, N. Y., 1939), pp. 8 and 60. The *Compotus vulgaris* (with calendar) is badly printed Migne, Patrologia Latina 90, cols. 727–820, and has been discussed by Jones (*Bedae Pseudepigrapha*, pp. 59–79). An Abbonian calendar is also printed in the 'Noviomagus' edition of Bede's scientific works, *Bedae Presbyteri Anglosaxonis...opuscula de temporum ratione* (Cologne, 1537), fols. 1–12. The Old English names of the months from the calendar in J have been printed by Gough ('Some Old English Glosses', p. 283). [17] Cf. *Enchiridion*, 232.9 – 234.13. The attribution to Abbo is Byrhtferth's.

differentia circuli et sperae (37v–8r), *De cursu .vii. planetarum per zodiacum circulum* (38v–9r) and *De quinque zonae caeli* (40r).[18]

58v–61v Bede's *De Temporibus.*

62r–5r A fragment of Bede's *De Natura Rerum*, ch. 16 – end, with marginal and interlinear glosses.

65v–123r Bede's *De Temporum Ratione*, with glosses.[19]

123r–35v Helperic's *Liber de Computo.*[20]

135v–8v Letters from Dionysius Exiguus to Petronius and to Bonifatius and Bonus.[21]

139r–43v Paschal tables, 532–960, with annals. London, British Library, Cotton Nero C. vii, 80r–4v (separated from J by Sir Robert Cotton[22]): Paschal tables, 961–1421, with annals.[23]

[18] Van de Vyver, 'Les Oeuvres', p. 140, attributed *De differentia* and *De cursu .vii. planetarum* to Abbo. For the attribution of *De quinque zonae*, see Harry Bober, 'An Illustrated Medieval School-Book of Bede's *De Natura Rerum*', *Jnl of the Walters Art Gallery* 19–20 (1956–7), 78 and 93.

[19] The three works of Bede have most recently been edited by Charles W. Jones (*Bedae Venerabilis Opera, VI: Opera Didascalica 2*, Corpus Christianorum Series Latina 123B (Turnhout, 1977)). John Leland (*c.* 1503–52), in his *De Rebus Britannicis Collectanea* (ed. Thomas Hearne, 2nd ed., 6 vols. (London, 1770–4) IV, 97), speculated, with little or no evidence, that Byrhtferth wrote the glosses in J; see Peter S. Baker, 'Byrhtferth of Ramsey and the Renaissance Scholars', *Anglo-Saxon Scholarship: the First Three Centuries*, ed. Milton McC. Gatch and Carl T. Berkhout (forthcoming, Boston, Mass., 1982). In fact there is evidence to suggest that Leland was right. For example, a gloss on 15r–v that summarizes parts of Hrabanus Maurus's *Liber de Computo* (quoted below, pp. 136–7) uses the polysyllabic adverb *indiuisibiliter* (see Lapidge, 'Byrhtferth and the *Vita S. Ecgwini*', p. 336) and uses *binos*, a word of which Byrhtferth was fond, instead of Hrabanus's *duo* (cf. *Enchiridion* 10.6, 200.12–14 and 204.5). Michael Lapidge has pointed out to me that a gloss to *De Temporum Ratione*, ch. 36 (J 89v), 'Annus iubeleus est annus remissionis', recalls wording both in the *Vita S. Oswaldi* and in Byrhtferth's portion of the *Historia Regum*; see Lapidge, 'Byrhtferth of Ramsey and the Early Sections of the *Historia Regum* attributed to Symeon of Durham', above, pp. 97–122, at 111. A gloss to *De Temporum Ratione*, ch. 8 (J 71v) is similar: 'Iubeleus annus remissionis'. Byrhtferth's obsession with numerology is also represented in these glosses; for example, a gloss to *De Temporum Ratione*, ch. 35 (J 88v–9r), which lays out in tabular form the concordance of the seasons, the qualities and the elements, resembles other diagrams and discussions by Byrhtferth (see below, p. 133 and n. 40). A gloss to *De Temporum Ratione*, ch. 1 (J 66v) closely resembles the *Enchiridion*, 224.25 – 226.8: 'Sexagenarius numerus ad uiduas et continentes pertinet, quod etiam in ipsa digitorum computatione ostenditur: digitus a digito premitur, sicut praesens lectio pandet Beda docente. Centesimus fructus ad perfectionem pertinet, dum carnis incorruptionem domino promittunt, tanto magis praemium percepturi, quanto uberiorem et grauiorem deo fructum proferunt; cuius perfectio in ipsa digitorum computatione demonstratur quemadmodum centenarius numerus de leua transit in dextram.' The gloss is, as Crawford's note to 224.26 shows, largely quoted from Haymo, but several words and phrases (e.g. *Sexagenarius* and *Centesimus fructus*) are shared by the gloss and the *Enchiridion* but not by Haymo's text. This gloss, I should note, cannot be the source of the passage in the *Enchiridion*. A thorough study of the glosses in J might reveal further signs of Byrhtferth's authorship. Some Old English glosses on 74r have been printed by A. S. Napier ('Contributions to Old English Lexicography', *TPS* 1903–6, 278–9) and glosses on 71v and 76r–v by Gough ('Some Old English Glosses', pp. 283–4).

[20] On the connection of the version of Helperic in J with Abbo, see Van de Vyver, 'Les Oeuvres', pp. 147–9, and P. McGurk, 'Computus Helperici: its Transmission in England in the Eleventh and Twelfth Centuries', *MÆ* 43 (1974), 1–5. McGurk is preparing a new edition of the *Liber de Computo*.

[21] Edited from other manuscripts by Bruno Krusch (*Studien zur christlich-mittelalterlichen Chronologie*, Abhandlungen der Preußischen Akademie der Wissenschaften 8 (Berlin, 1938), 63–8 and 82–6).

[22] N. R. Ker, 'Membra Disiecta', *Brit. Museum Quarterly* 12 (1937–8), 131–2.

[23] The annals down to the year 1111 have been edited by Hart ('The Ramsey Computus', pp. 38–44).

144r–55v   Paschal tables, 1422–2612, with annals as far as 1536.
156r–77v   Miscellaneous short tracts on the computus, grammar, prosody, medicine
                etc.[24]

Henel knew of the existence of J but did not have the opportunity to examine it first hand.[25] Had he done so, he would no doubt have seen that its computus was a copy of the very one that Byrhtferth had explicated. The J computus (13v–34v) is a long series of tables and short texts, preceded directly by Byrhtferth's *Epilogus*, which ends as follows:

Post huius denique epilogii descriptionem libet articulum flectere ad totius libri recapitulationem, quia post huius terminationem constant Abbonis sophiste dicta, alumpni Benedicti patris, per cuius beneuolentiam percepimus huius rei intelligentiam nec non aliarum rerum peritiam. Dissertissimi uiri itaque Heririci expositiones ultima pars huius codicis concludit honestissime.[26]

A computus was generally a concise presentation of essential material; thus the one in J could, despite its length, be considered a *recapitulatio*, or summary, of longer scientific works. If so, Byrhtferth's statement that 'Abbonis sophiste dicta' are to follow the *recapitulatio* makes sense, for Abbonian texts do indeed follow the J computus. Helperic's (Herici, Heririci) *Liber de Computo* is not found at the very end of J, as promised in the *Epilogus*, but it is the last major text in J, being followed by the Paschal tables and a highly miscellaneous group of texts that have the look of afterthoughts. So much in Byrhtferth's work appears to be afterthought[27] that I cannot doubt that the *Epilogus* describes an early stage in the compilation of a codex that later grew by accretion.

It has long been established that the *Enchiridion* was originally divided into four books (only the rubric for bk III remains).[28] In another article I have tried to show that the two short Old English texts that follow bk IV in the

---

[24] The medical texts (J 175r–7v) have been printed by Singer ('A Review', pp. 137–49).

[25] 'Byrhtferth's *Preface*: the Epilogue of his *Manual*?', *Speculum* 18 (1943), 297: 'I am greatly hampered... by not having a first-hand knowledge of J since, due to the war, it is impossible to obtain photostats.'

[26] Forsey, 'Byrhtferth's *Preface*', p. 519, corrected from J. In quoting the texts in J I have printed the hooked *e* without the hook, modernized capitalization and punctuation and expanded all abbreviations, including those for dates.

[27] E.g., the postscript to the *Enchiridion* (pp. 247–50), the long digressions on grammar, prosody and rhetoric in the same work (94.12 – 100.20 and 170.17 – 180.14) and the long glosses to the *Vita S. Ecgwini*, which expand the narrative as well as explain it; see Lapidge, 'Byrhtferth and the *Vita S. Ecgwini*', pp. 351–2.

[28] Wanley (*Catalogus*, pp. 103–4) listed thirteen sections in the *Enchiridion*. Karl M. Classen (*Über das Leben und die Schriften Byrhtferðs, eines angelsächsischen Gelehrten und Schriftstellers um das Jahr 1000* (Dresden, 1896)) thought that it was to be divided into three books. Crawford thought that it was to be divided into four, but at the time of publication of his edition he did not know where to begin bk II. He later decided to begin it at 58.10 (Henel, *Studien*, p. 8, n. 25). I follow Henel's view that bk II should begin at 62.8.

only reasonably complete manuscript, Oxford, Bodleian Library, Ashmole 328, and which generally have not been allowed to be Byrhtferth's, are in fact parts of the *Enchiridion*. The first (pp. 240–2) concludes bk IV, and the second (pp. 247–50) is a postscript to the entire work.[29] Bk I (2.1 – 62.7) introduces the reader to the basic concepts (e.g. the year, the months, the concurrents) necessary to the use of the calendar. Bk II (62.8 – 134.5) concerns time and its divisions. Bk III (134.6 – 197) deals specifically with the reckoning of the date of Easter. Bk IV (198.1 – 242.30), a treatise on number symbolism and the ages of the world, has little to do with the computus and so does not concern us here. The whole work is interlarded with digressions and long rhetorical flourishes, which sometimes obscure its organization. As Henel clearly saw, each of the books of the *Enchiridion* falls naturally into sections; although there is no evidence that Byrhtferth intended formal chapter divisions, I shall refer to these sections as chapters. I divide the *Enchiridion* into books and chapters as follows:[30]

I   Basic concepts in the computus
    1   The year and its parts (2.1 – 22.4)
    2   Basic computistica (22.5 – 38.19)
    3   Bede's verses (40.1 – 58.9)
    4   Review (58.10 – 62.7)
II   Time and its divisions
    1   The twelve months (62.8 – 100.20)
    2   The seven embolisms (100.21 – 112.5)
    3   Divisions of time (112.6 – 134.5)
III   The reckoning of Easter
    1   General introduction (134.6 – 148.27)
    2   The reckoning of Easter (150.1 – 170.16)
    3   Miscellanea (170.17 – 197)
IV   Numbers and the ages of the world
    1   Number symbolism (198.1 – 234.13)
    2   The ages of the world (234.14 – 242.30)
V   Postscript: Ammonitio amici (247–50)

In the following pages I shall attempt to show that each of the first three books of the *Enchiridion* is keyed to a specific section of the J computus, which it summarizes or explicates. The whole of the computistical section of Byrhtferth's work draws its source material freely from the various texts in J but depends on the computus alone for its coherence.

---

[29] 'The Old English Canon of Byrhtferth of Ramsey', *Speculum* 55 (1980), 32–4.

[30] My chapter divisions differ somewhat from Henel's: he ended I.1 at p. 26 and I end it at p. 22, my II.1 combines two of his chapters, my III.1 and 2 divide a single chapter of his and my III.3 combines five of his under the heading 'Miscellanea'. Differences are otherwise minor.

SURVEY BOOK BY BOOK

Book I

The J computus (13v) begins with the words 'Incipit compotus tam Grecorum quam Latinorum et Egyptiorum ceterorumque', similar to several of the incipits of computi listed by Henel,[31] but even more similar to the incipit quoted in the beginning of bk 1, ch. 1 of the *Enchiridion*: 'Incipit compotus Latinorum ac Grecorum Hebreorumque et Egiptiorum, nec non et Anglorum' (2.2–3). In J we find, as a gloss to the incipit, 'Compotus Latine, Grece dicitur cyclus uel rithmus, secundum Egyptios latercus, secundum Macedones calculus', while in the *Enchiridion* we find, 'Compotus, Grece ciclus aut rithmus, secundum Egiptios latercus, iuxta Macedones dicitur calculus' (2.4–6). After a few words on the number of months in the year, Byrhtferth translates the incipit: 'Her onginð gerimcræft æfter Ledenwarum and æfter Grecum and Iudeiscum and Egiptiscum and Engliscum þeodum and ma oðra' (2.9–11). Here, in the first few lines, he sets the pattern that he will follow for most of bk 1, namely to alternate Latin and Old English passages.

Before moving further into the J computus, Byrhtferth supplies his readers with some of the information necessary to an understanding of it. In the next several pages he discusses the year and its divisions, the origin of the leap-year, the solstices and equinoxes, the physical and physiological fours and other matters (2.12 – 22.4), drawing mainly from Bede and Helperic and not from the computus itself. The text of Helperic that he used was closely allied with that in J; for example, one can see from a later passage in bk 1 that an error already in the precursor of J that Byrhtferth used was taken into the *Enchiridion*. Crawford emends the passage to make it conform to the text in the Patrologia Latina:[32] 'Quid ergo (totiens) necesse est et totiens addere .xxx. et retrahere cum lunaris etas ⟨illo anno per singulas kalendas numero regularium constet? Ob hoc⟩ illo anno pronuntiande nulle epacte' (34.24–7). The error, however, probably did not arise during the copying of the *Enchiridion*, for Byrhtferth translates the corrupt text: 'Hwylc neod ys hyt þæt man swa oft do ⟨.xxx.⟩ to and eft wiðteo, þonne þæs geares ne beoð nane epactas?' (38.14–15). A comparison with J (127r) dramatically explains the source of the error: 'Quid ergo necesse est totiens et totiens addere triginta et retrahere, cum lunaris aetas illo anno nulle pronuntiande sunt epactae?'

---

[31] Henel, *Studien*, pp. 10–11.

[32] PL 137, col. 30: 'Quid ergo necesse est toties addere xxx et retrahere cum lunaris ætas illo anno per singulas Kalendas numero regularium constet? Ob hoc eo anno nullæ pronuntiantur epactæ.' In quoting the following passage I correct Crawford's text from Ker's table of errata (see above, n. 1).

Byrhtferth quoted the Latin text of Bede less extensively than he did that of Helperic, so it is difficult to demonstrate his dependence on the text of Bede in J.[33] However, he did quote the marginalia that accompany the works of Bede in J. A good example is his discussion of the zodiac in Latin and Old English; the passages are found in bk 1, ch. 1:

Est unus circulus qui zodiacus uel horoscopus siue Mazaroth appellatur, nec non sideralis, per quem sol et luna et stella Saturni, Iouis et Martis, Veneris et Mercurii decurrunt (4.2–5).

An circul ys þe uðwitan hataŏ zodiacus oŏŏe horoscopus oŏŏe Mazaroth oŏŏe sideralis. Þurh þæne yrnŏ seo sunne and se mona and þas steorran Saturnus and Iouis, Martis and Veneris and Mercurius (4.22–5).

There is nothing to correspond to these passages in the computus itself and Crawford could cite only rough analogues for them. However, in the margin of J 88r we find the following gloss to *De Temporum Ratione*, ch. 34: 'Hec zona que uocatur zodiacus, et sideralis dicitur, et mazaroht [*sic*] et horoscopus uocatur cingit celum .xii. sideribus distincta per que sol et luna decurrunt, sed et stella Saturni, Iouis, Martis, Ueneris, Mercurii per eam decurrunt.' The closeness of the texts quoted in the *Enchiridion* and those in J will demonstrate itself as our discussion continues.

Byrhtferth opens ch. 2 with these words: 'Tempus est reuelare mysteria que a senpectis nobis demonstrata sunt, id est concordia mensium duodenorum, de quibus sic sumit textus libri: Ianuarius, Augustus et December .iiii. nonas habent, nona .x. kalendas post idus et dies .xxx. unum' (22.5–12). The *textus libri* that Byrhtferth quotes is the very text that is found directly beneath the incipit of the J computus (13v). In fact, all of the Latin material in the *Enchiridion* from here to 26.3 is quoted directly from the *prologus* (26.5) or first paragraph of the computus. The quotation is so exact that there is no need to give the passage from J here.[34] Now Byrhtferth temporarily gives up quoting the Latin source and provides only an Old English translation.

---

[33] In fact, Byrhtferth's quotations from Bede differ widely from the copy in J, but most of the differences may be due to the corrupt state of our manuscript of the *Enchiridion*. Two points bear mentioning, however. At 74.26 Crawford emends *hos* to *h*[*a*]*s*; but while the latter is the reading of J, the former is the reading of Jones's edited text (*Bedae Venerabilis...Opera Didascalica* 2, p. 408). Here the *Enchiridion* contains a well-attested reading that disagrees with another well-attested reading in J. At 76.1 Crawford emends *quinque* (clearly an error) to *quattuor*; but the mistake is repeated twice: once in a later quotation of the passage from Bede and once in Byrhtferth's Old English explanation of the passage (76.20). Since it is unlikely that a copyist made the same error three times independently, the reading probably originated either with Byrhtferth himself or with his source manuscript. The error is not in J (91v). These circumstances suggest that Byrhtferth may have used a text of *De Temporum Ratione* somewhat different from that in J.

[34] Note, however, that following the words 'et dies .xxviii.' in the *Enchiridion* (24.9) J has 'et in bissexto .xxix.', which Byrhtferth omits.

His source is the second half of the *prologus*, in the right-hand column at the top of 13v. Altering somewhat the order of the Latin text, Byrhtferth first translates as follows:

Enchiridion	J
Þæt ys to witanne þæt þa monðas þe habbað .iiii. nonas æfter kalendas, þæt hig habbað to idus .xiii. dagas and to .ii. kalendas eahtatyne. Gif hig beoð gesamnode, þonne beoð þær .xxxi. And þa monðas þe habbað .vi. nonas æfter kalendas, hig habbað .xv. dagas to idus and to pridie kalendas ⟨.xvi. Gif hig beoð gesamnode, þonne beoð þær⟩ .xxxi. (26.7–14).	Menses qui habent .iiii. nonas in idus habent .xiii. et in .ii. kalendas .xviii., qui simul conexi fiunt .xxxi. Menses qui habent .vi. nonas faciunt in idus .xv. dies et in .ii. kalendas .xvi., qui coniuncti fiunt .xxxi.

In J the above passage occurs beneath the following, which Byrhtferth translates next:

Enchiridion	J
Ianuarius, Augustus and December kalendas, þæt ys se forma dæg, and .vi. idus and .xviii. and .xi. and .iiii. kalendas beoð anes dæges. Martius, Maius, Iulius and October kalendas and .viii. idus and .xi. and .iiii. kalendas beoð anes dæges. Aprilis, Iunius, September and Nouember kalendas and .vi. idus and .xvii. kalendas and .x. kalendas and .iii. kalendas beoð anes dæges. Februarius kalendas, ⟨.vi.⟩ idus and .xv. kalendas and .viii. beoð anes dæges (26.15–22).	Ianuarius, Augustus et December kalendas et .vi. idus et .xviii. kalendas et .xi. kalendas et .iiii. kalendas una die sunt. Martius, Maius, Iulius et October kalendas et .viii. idus et idus et .xi. kalendas et .iiii. kalendas una die sunt. Aprilis, Iunius, September et Nouember kalendas et .vi. idus et .xvii. kalendas et .x. kalendas et .iii. kalendas una die sunt. Februarius uero kalendas et .vi. idus et .xv. kalendas et .viii. kalendas una die sunt.

The long section that follows discusses the concurrents, ferial regulars, lunar regulars and epacts (28.1 – 30.9, 44.28 – 56.29 and 30.9 – 38.19). The discussion is drawn from various sources but is all directed towards the explanation of the tables in the J computus. Each of the three tables that belong with this section (pp. 26 and 38) is taken from J 13v.

Ch. 3 covers much the same territory as ch. 2, namely the months, ferial regulars and lunar regulars; however, it draws not on the tables of J 13v, but on the 'Versus Bedae' (not really by Bede)[35] on 14r. Byrhtferth quotes the verses and supplies an Old English translation. Hart has noted that the

[35] The attribution of mnemonic verses on the computus to Bede was common in the Middle Ages, but these verses were not actually written by him; see Jones, *Bedae Pseudepigrapha*, p. 2. For bibliography on the verses that Byrhtferth quotes, see Dieter Schaller and Ewald Könsgen, *Initia Carminum Latinorum Saeculo Undecimo Antiquorum* (Göttingen, 1977), nos. 1716, 7613 and 14907.

version in the *Enchiridion* shares certain peculiarities of spelling with that in J;[36] the two versions also share variant readings, e.g. *pariterque* (42.3) for *pariter*, *semper* (42.5) for *tantum*, *Iulius* (42.8) for *Iunius* and *retinet* (*retenet* 44.14) for *retentat*.[37] The copy in the *Enchiridion* also contains errors not found in J; these must be blamed either on Byrhtferth's own carelessness or – perhaps more probably – on the carelessness of the scribe of Ashmole 328 and his predecessors. In ch. 4 Byrhtferth admonishes his pupils to leave their dice-playing and study the computus; then he briefly reviews the concurrents, ferial and lunar regulars and epacts (58.10 – 62.7). He ends bk I having painstakingly covered just the first two pages of the J computus (13v–14r).

Book II

Bk II, if it were supplied with a title, might well be called *De Temporibus*. Throughout, Byrhtferth draws often on Ælfric's *De Temporibus Anni*[38] and Bede's *De Temporum Ratione*, but each of the three chapters of the book (62.8 – 100.20, 100.21 – 112.5 and 112.6 – 134.5) has as its primary source a section of the J computus. Ch. 1 is drawn mainly from the calendar on 16r–21v. This calendar is Abbonian, but it includes matter not found in the Abbonian calendars printed in the *Patrologia Latina* and in *Noviomagus*. We should expect information such as the etymologies of the Latin names of the months to have particularly interested Byrhtferth. At the very beginning of bk II Byrhtferth etymologizes *Ianuarius*: 'Ianuarius dictus est eo quod sit limes et ianu⟨a⟩ anni' (62.13–14). Crawford, in his note to this passage, identifies the source as Isidore's *Etymologiae*, but it comes from Isidore through the calendar in the J computus: 'Ianuarius dictus est...quia limes et ianua sit anni' (16r).

A few more examples of Byrhtferth's reliance on this calendar must suffice, for almost all the information on the months in ch. 1 (including the recapitulation near the end, 88.28 – 90.23) comes from the calendar. The long section on March (78.23 – 84.6) provides an excellent example of how Byrhtferth handles his sources. After giving some technical information on the month (78.24 – 80.12), Byrhtferth turns to a discussion of the creation, which was believed to have taken place on .*xv*. *kalendas Apriles* (18 March). His major source is Ælfric's *De Temporibus Anni*, ch. 1, which describes the six days of creation one by one, but Byrhtferth adds the date of each day of creation. He could easily have deduced this information either from *De Temporibus Anni*, ch. 2, or from *De Temporum Ratione*, ch. 6, both of which

---

[36] 'Byrhtferth and his Manual', p. 107, n. 36.

[37] This partial collation is based on Crawford's emendations and notes to the *Enchiridion*. I have noted where the versions in J and the *Enchiridion* differ from the sources printed by Crawford or where Crawford found it necessary to emend his text and the error is found also in J.

[38] This work is not in J. It has been edited by Heinrich Henel (*Aelfric's De Temporibus Anni*, EETS o.s. 213 (London, 1942)).

give the dates of the first and fourth days of creation, but he found more immediate sources in J. In the calendar for March (17r) each day of creation is marked:

xv	kl.	i	Fecit deus lucem. Primus dies saeculi.
xiiii		ii	Firmamentum celi.
xiii		iii	Aridam.
xii	kl.	iiii	Solem et lunam.
xi		v	Natatilia et uolatilia.
x		vi	Quadrupedia et hominem.
ix	kl.	vii	Requieuit.
viii			Octauis merito gaudet conceptio Christi.[39]

Further along in J, in the margin of *De Temporum Ratione*, ch. 5, the same material is expounded between decorative columns (69v):

Figura cunctis hec pandet quo sit primus dies saeculi et quid supernus opifex gessit octo diebus. .xv. kalendas Apriles dixit deus, fiat lux, et facta est lux. Inde est primus saeculi dies eo in loco constitutus. .ii. dies, .xiiii. ⟨kalendas Apriles⟩ fecit deus firmamentum. .iii. dies, .xiii., herbas et ligna pomifera. .iiii. dies, .xii., solem et lunam et stellas et omnia sidera. .v. dies, .xi., reptilia et uolatilia et cete grandia et aues celi et pisces maris et omnia uiuentia que de aquis facta sunt. .vi. dies, .x., iumenta et reptilia et bestias terre et hominem, id est masculum et feminam, creauit deus. .vii. dies, .ix., requieuit deus ab omni opere suo et benedixit diei septimo. .viii. kalendas...

The fragmentary text is followed by nine blank lines within the columns. Perhaps the scribe intended to write '.viii. dies, .viii. kalendas Apriles' and, seeing that he had erred (through homoeoteleuton), left off intending to come back and correct his work later. Probably the original gloss went on to discuss the eighth day, as Byrhtferth does in the *Enchiridion* (82.25 – 84.3).

For Byrhtferth it was of great significance that the eighth day of the world was a Sunday, the day of the Resurrection, and that 25 March was the date of the Annunciation. That such coincidences as this could invest a number or date with special spiritual significance demonstrates the strong numerological bias that gave rise to bk IV of the *Enchiridion* and to the many numerological digressions found throughout Byrhtferth's works.[40] In bk IV

---

[39] This entry for .*viii*. *kalendas Apriles* is a hexameter from a metrical calendar from York, preserved in the calendar of the J computus; see Michael Lapidge, 'A Metrical Calendar from Ramsey', *RB*, forthcoming.

[40] Byrhtferth's diagram of the physical and physiological fours (see above, n. 14) is yet another example of his fascination with numerology. The significance of the number four comes up repeatedly in his work; see the *Enchiridion*, 10.4 – 14.4, 90.24 – 92.27 and 200.10 – 204.18. A gloss by Byrhtferth to the *Vita S. Ecgwini* briefly explicates the number four (Lapidge, 'Byrhtferth and the *Vita S. Ecgwini*', p. 352); another explication of the number four in the margin of *De Temporum Ratione*, ch. 35 (see above, n. 19) is perhaps also Byrhtferth's work. For further examples of Byrhtferth's numerology, see Lapidge, 'Byrhtferth and the *Vita S. Ecgwini*', pp. 339-40.

he says of the number eight, 'peracto iudicio, cum fuerit celum nouum et terra noua, ipse erit, ut prephati sumus, sempiternus' (214.20–2). Byrhtferth sees the six ages of the world as parallel to the six days of creation; the seventh 'day' will be the day of judgement and the eighth 'day' the eternal day that is to follow the judgement. He expounds this point at length in the Old English conclusion of bk IV (240.11 – 242.12). Because the eighth day of the world was a Sunday Byrhtferth calls it *halig sinnadæg* (82.30 – 84.1; cf. 240.26–7); because the eighth day foreshadows the eternal day he says, 'þonne ealle dagas ateoriað, þonne þurhwunað he aa on his symbelnysse' (84.1–2). Byrhtferth probably based his discussion of the eighth day on *De Temporum Ratione*, ch. 71.[41]

Byrhtferth interrupts his discussion of February with a long passage on the leap-year and the *saltus lunae* (64.3 – 78.12). As Hart has pointed out, the major sources for this section are Ælfric and Bede; but Byrhtferth does not lose sight of the fact that he is in the midst of a discussion of the calendar. He speaks of the leap-year because it occurs in February and of the *saltus lunae* because the leap-year has reminded him of it. In the middle of this digression he writes, 'Ac seo ræding pingð þæne scoliere mid scearpum pricele, þe þus ys awriten on þam bocfelle: "Gemun ðu, la rædere, þæt þu gedo þy feorðan geare þæt Februarius monð hæbbe þrittig nihta ealdne monan, and gedo þæt Martius hæbbe eallswa, þy læs þe þæt Easterlice gescead ahwar tealtrige"' (72.6–11). What is *seo ræding* (the lesson) that Byrhtferth refers to and where is this *bocfell*? It is, in fact, near the bottom of the calendar for February in the J computus (16v); though Byrhtferth has digressed, his pupil still has the computus open in front of him: 'Memento quod anno bissextili lunam Februarii mensis .xxx. dies computes, et tamen lunam Martii mensis .xxx. dies habeat sicut semper, ne paschalis lune ratio uacillet.'[42] Ch. 1 closes with a digression on synaloepha, 'þæra bocera saltus', inspired by the discussion of the *saltus lunae*.

Ch. 2, a discussion of the seven embolisms in the decennovennal cycle, is taken from the *Lectiones de .vii. embolismis* in the J computus (14v–15r). The correspondence between the translation in the *Enchiridion* and the Latin text in J is extraordinarily close. For example, when Byrhtferth quotes the beginning of the first *lectio* (100.25–6) the quotation is identical to the version in J except for a numerical error (in the *Enchiridion*, .xii. for .xxii.). Indeed, whenever Byrhtferth quotes the Latin text of the *Lectiones* the quotation is

---

[41] The idea of the eighth day of the world as a foreshadowing of the eternal day apparently comes from Augustine's *De Civitate Dei*, XXII.30. I have not found it in Ælfric's works, though his Letter to Sigeweard identifies the eternal day as the eighth age of the world (*The Old English Version of the Heptateuch*, ed. S. J. Crawford, EETS o.s. 160 (London, 1922), 70).
[42] See also Henel, *Studien*, p. 19.

identical, or very nearly so, to the corresponding passage in J. In one instance Byrhtferth takes a Latin gloss from J into his text: where J reads 'cetere [*gloss*: scilicet lunationes] in ordine exeunt', the *Enchiridion* reads 'Ceterae, scilicet lunationes mensium, in ordine exeunt, id est currunt' (102.17–18). Here 'scilicet lunationes mensium' is apparently inspired by the Latin gloss in J, while 'id est currunt' is Byrhtferth's own addition. This is not the only place in the *Lectiones* where Byrhtferth adds to his source; we find other additions at 102.15–17 and 20–2, 104.23–5 and 106.5–13, 20–1 and 22–3.

At 106.20 Crawford notes that Byrhtferth's Old English translation does not agree with the Latin source as printed in the footnotes. However, a look at the fourth *lectio* in J (corresponding to the *Enchiridion*, 106.11 – 108.3) shows that, though Byrhtferth has added somewhat to his source, no doubt for the sake of clarity, no serious discrepancy exists:

Enchiridion	J
Soðlice on þam endl[yftan] geare þæs circules, þonne se forma embolismus byð on þam endecad[e], þæt ys on þam endlufon gear[um], þonne beoð . xx. ^{tig} epacte, and forþan byð se mona on kalendas Septembris and Octobris . xxv . , and on kalendas Nouembris and Decembris . xxvii. ; on kalendas Ianuarii . xxviii⟨i⟩. ; on quarta nonas Ianuarii . xxx. ^{tig} nihta eald, and he byþ þær geendod, and se mona byð embolismus. . . . on kalendas Februarii . sxx.: þesmona gebyrað Ianuario. . . . on kalendas Martii . xxviii . ; on . vi. nonas Martii . xxix . : þes byð Februarius mona. Witodlice se mona þe onginð on . v. nonas Martii niwe and byð adwæsced oððe geendod þrittig nihta eald on kalendas Aprelis, he byð Martius mona. And se mona þe byð anre nihte eald on . iiii . nonas Aprelis, he byð Aprilis, and he byð adwæsced nigon and twentig nihta on pridie kalendas Mai. And se ðe onginð prima on kalendas Mai, he byð his; and he sceal geendian þrittig nihta eald. Þa oðre fyliað heora gewunan.	DE PRIMO ANNO EMBOLISMI IN ENDECADEM. In primo anno igitur embolismi in endecada sunt epacte . xx . , et iccirco est luna in kalendas Septembres et Octobres . xxv. , in kalendas Nouembres et Decembres . xxvii. , in kalendas Ianuarias . xxviiii . , in . iiii . nonas Ianuarias . xxx . , et terminatur illic; luna embolismi est. In kalendas Februarias . xxx . ; ipsa est luna Ianuarii. In kalendas Martias . xxviii . , . vi. nonas Martias . xxix . ; luna Februarii est. Illa autem luna que . v. nonas Martias incipit e extinguitur . xxx . in kalendas Apriles luna Martii est. Et illa que . iiii . nonas Apriles initiatur prima luna ipsius est, et extinguitur . xxix . in . ii. kalendas Maias. Et illa que initiatur prima in kalendas Maias ipsius est [*gloss*: luna]. Cetere [*gloss*: lunationes] ordinem suum sequuntur.

Another passage where Crawford notes a serious disagreement with the Latin source he prints occurs in the seventh *lectio*. Once again, however, the text of J agrees entirely with Byrhtferth's translation:

Enchiridion	J
And se mona þe byð ⟨prima⟩ on kalendas Iulii and byð adwæsced oððe ateorod . iii . kalendas Augusti þrittig nihta eald, he byð Iulius mona. Se soðlice þe on pridie kalendas Augusti byð niwe, he witodlice healt his endebyrdnysse and geendað . xxix . on . v . kalendas Septembris: forþon byð niwe mona on . iiii . kalendas September, and on . iii . kalendas luna secunda, and on pridie kalendas luna . iii . On kalendas Septembris, na quarta æfter þam gerime, ac quinta, for þæs monan oferhlype, id est propter saltum (110.26 – 112.5).	Illa uero que initiatur prima in kalendas Iulias et extinguitur . iii . kalendas Augustas . xxx . luna Iulii est. Illa autem luna que . ii . kalendas Augustas prima est, iam ordinem suum tenet, terminatur enim . xxix., . v . kalendas Septembres. Ideo namque euenit luna prima quarto kalendas Septembres, et . iii . kalendas Septembres secunda, pridie kalendas tertia. In kalendas Septembres non . iiii . secundum compotum, sed . v . propter saltum.

Ch. 3 is headed *De anno et die et nocte et horis et eius partibus* (112.6–7). As Crawford's notes show, most of the material from here to 120.7 is derived ultimately from various parts of Hrabanus Maurus's *Liber de Computo* (not in J).[43] However, this material is gathered in a long gloss that occupies the margins of J 15r–v; this gloss, which announces its source as 'Rabbanus', is surely the immediate source of most of the material in this section of the *Enchiridion*. For example, the following passages on the 'atom' are remarkably similar:

Enchiridion	J
Ic wene, la uplendisca preost, þæt þu nyte hwæt beo [atomos], ac ic wylle þe þises wordes gescead gecyðan. Tomos on Grecisc on Lyden ys gereht diuisio and on Englisc todælednyss, and atomos on Grecisc on ⟨Lyden⟩ indiuisio, þæt ys untodælednyss. Fif ⟨un⟩todælednyssa hiw synt: an bið on lichaman, oðer on þære sunnan, þridde on þam gebede, þæt ys on boclicum cræfte. Se læsta dæl on þam stæfgefege ys littera.... Eac þes atomos byð on þam getele, swylce ic cweðe þam preoste þas þing to bysne... Todæl þa eahta; þonne beoð þær feower to	Quid sit atomus dicamus. Sunt enim quinque species. Tomos Grece diuisio dicitur Latine. Atomos indiuisio. Est atomos in corpore...Atomos est in sole tenuissimus puluis. Atomos est in oratione littera. Atomos est in numero unum. Verbi gratia, Octo diuide in quattuor, quattuor in binos, binos in singulos; sola unitas indiuisi-biliter permanet. Est ergo atomus

---

[43] Recently edited by Wesley M. Stevens, 'Rabani Mogontiacensis Episcopi De Computo', in *Rabani Mauri, Martyrologium, De Computo*, Corpus Christianorum, Continuatio Mediaevalis 44 (Turnhout, 1979), at 163–323.

Enchiridion	**J**
lafe. Todæl þa feower, þonne beoð þær twa to lafe. Todæl þa twa; þonne byð an to lafe; þæt ys untodallic.... Feowertyne todælednyssa synd on þam dæge, þa synd þus genemde: Atom[o]s ys þæt læste getæl... Oðer todælednyss hatte momentum, þridde minutum, feorðe punctus, fifte hora, syxte quadrans, seofoðe dies, eahtoðe ebdomada, nigoða mens[i]s, teoða triformis uicissitudo, endlyfta annus, twelfta etas, þrytteoða seculum, feowerteoða mundus (116.28 – 120.7).	trecentesima et septuagesima .vi. pars unius ostenti. Sunt enim quattuordecim diuisiones temporum, id est atomos, ostentum, momentum, partes, minutum, punctos, hora, quadrantes, mensis, uicissitudo, annus, saeculum, aetas.

With the addition of several examples Byrhtferth's text is considerably longer than the gloss in J, which nevertheless follows the order of the *Enchiridion* more closely than do the sources that Crawford cites. The next passage in the *Enchiridion* (120.8 – 122.6) is translated closely from a marginal gloss to *De Temporum Ratione*, ch. 3 (J 67v). The first sentence of this gloss resembles the last sentence quoted above; the remainder is much closer to Byrhtferth's text than are Crawford's sources:

Diuisiones temporis .xiiii. sunt, id est atomos, momentum, minutum, punctum, hora, quadrans, dies, ebdomada, mensis, uicissitudo triformis, annus, etas, saeculum, mundus. .dlxiiii. atomi unum momentum efficiunt. Quattuor momenta minutum complent. Duo minuta dimidium punctum faciunt. Quattuor puncti unam horam in sole efficiunt. Sex hore quadrantem complent. Quattuor quadrantes unum diem. .vii. dies ebdomadam faciunt. Quattuor ebdomade mensem complent. Tres menses uicissitudinem triformem quattuor temporum, id est ueris, estatis, autumni, hiemis. Hec .iiii. tempora que habent .xii. menses annum efficiunt. Quattuor anni cyclum bissextilem faciunt. .xv. anni cyclum indictionalem efficiunt. .xix. anni cyclum decennouenalem perficiunt. Sic .xix. anni cyclum lunarem explent. .xxviii. anni cyclum solarem complent percurrentes, donec in se reuertantur. .dxxxii. anni cyclum magnum faciunt, quando secundum solem et lunam et bissextum et saltum, in unum diem mensis et in unum diem ebdomade in eadem luna omnes cycli in unum conueniunt. Etas, sicut dicuntur sex etates saeculi. Saeculum autem est totum spatium ab initio mundi usque ad finem. Mundus uero est uniuersitas que constat celum, terram, mare.

Characteristically Byrhtferth fills out his source with definitions and other material, for example, 'Ebdomada Grece, septimana dicitur Latine' (120.14–15) and 'þ[æt] iunge preostas ne mihton næfre aredian, forþam þe ⟨hyt⟩ ys uneaðe cuð þam ealdum witum' (120.25–6).

The remainder of bk II is drawn from various sources, as Hart has shown.

The discussion of the planets (128.12 – 130.4) comes from J 37v[44] and the section on the hours of the month and year (126.7–27) could easily have been calculated from the calendar. Except for the last pages of ch. 3 the material in bk II of the *Enchiridion* is drawn almost entirely from the J computus (14v–21v).

Book III

Following the calendar in the J computus are twenty-five dense pages (22r–34v) of tables and instructions, only a few of which could have interested a priest concerned mainly with calculating the dates of the moveable feasts and only a few of which Byrhtferth used in bk III of the *Enchiridion*. This book is more self-contained than the preceding two; it draws on and explicates, but can be read without referring to, the computus. Only ch. 2, which presents the tables essential to the Easter reckoning, is closely tied to the computus, but we may consider the first chapter as prolegomena, building up to the second.

The history of trial and error and controversy leading to the establishment of the method of calculating the date of Easter is complex and fascinating,[45] but the method itself, as Byrhtferth taught it, was very simple. All that the priest needed was a calendar and knowledge of the position of the year in the paschal (decennovennal) and solar cycles. For example, 1011, the year in which Byrhtferth wrote,[46] was the fifth year in the paschal cycle and the twelfth year in the solar cycle, or cycle of concurrents. Turning to the mnemonic for the paschal cycle ('Nonae Aprilis') in J (28r) or in the *Enchiridion* (facing p. 150) the priest would find that the 'Easter terminus', the date of the full moon in the lunar month that began on or after *.viii. idus Martias* (8 March), was *.xi. kalendas Apriles* (22 March) and that the regular that year was five. Next he would look at the table of concurrents in J (13v) or in the *Enchiridion* (facing p. 150) and find that the concurrent that year was seven. He would add the regular of five to the concurrent of seven and, because the sum was greater than seven, subtract seven to find that the terminus would fall on the fifth day of the week, Thursday. Then it would be a simple matter to count forward to the first Sunday after the terminus, *.viii. kalendas Apriles* (25 March). That day would be Easter. In this way the priest could calculate the date of Easter years in advance.

Bk III, ch. 1 (134.6 – 148.27) is a general account of Easter, beginning with an account of Passover drawn from Exodus (134.6 – 136.3), a discussion of

[44] Abbo's *De cursu .vii. planetarum* (see above, p. 126 and n. 18).

[45] Jones, *Bedae Opera de Temporibus*, pp. 6–122, is an excellent introduction to the subject, which is, however, seemingly inexhaustible. Recent studies include August Strobel's massive *Ursprung und Geschichte des frühchristlichen Osterkalenders* (Berlin, 1977) and Kenneth Harrison, 'Easter Cycles and the Equinox in the British Isles', *ASE* 7 (1978), 1–8.

[46] Classen (*Über das Leben und die Schriften Byrhtferðs*, p. 19) dated the *Enchiridion* from internal evidence.

the date of Easter (i.e. the first Sunday after the fourteenth day of the lunar month that begins on or after 8 March, 136.4 – 138.20) and an interpretation of the passage from Exodus, concluded with a rhetorical flourish (138.20 – 144.3). Next come Byrhtferth's *feower gesceadwisnyssa* for reckoning the date of Easter (144.4–21, from the J computus, 34r) and then the outside limits in the solar and lunar calendars for the various moveable feasts and the *claves terminorum* (144.22 – 146.36). This material is commonplace; some of it can be found in J (13v).[47] Finally Byrhtferth etymologizes *Paschalis* and ends the chapter with a rhetorical flourish (146.37 – 148.27).

Ch. 2 (150.1 – 170.16), which contains instructions for reckoning the date of Easter, is organized around three tables from the section of the J computus that follows the calendar. Two leaves have been lost from this chapter (between 154.5 and 154.6 and between 164.8 and 164.9); the lost material can be supplied in part from J. The first lost leaf very probably contained a diagram similar to the one on J 28r, showing how to calculate the Easter terminus by counting on the joints of the fingers (cf. 154.6–13).[48] The second leaf contained, on one side, the end of Byrhtferth's explanation of the ages and phases of the moon. N. R. Ker noticed that the sentence left incomplete at 164.8 could be reconstructed from Abbo's *De cursu .vii. planetarum per zodiacum circulum* (J 38v):[49]

Enchiridion	J
Þonne þu, arwurða broðor, gehyrst þæt se mona beo fram þære sunnan twelf fæca, þonne undergyt þu, swylce ic þus cweðe, 'Byrhtferð mæssepreost stent on þam twelftan stede æfter þam biscope Eadnoðe, oððe he sitt...' (164.4–8).	Ergo dum primam lunam .xii. partibus semper a sole distare audis, ita intellige, ac si .xii. fratibus distet ABBO a suo abbate. Et ita .xiii. aliquo loco resideat in ordine.

Ker also observed that tables of the termini of Lent and Easter probably occupied the verso of this lost leaf, completing a five-part table of the termini of moveable feasts.[50] Indeed the text of the *Enchiridion* (164.12–17) indicates that tables of the termini for the beginning of Lent and for Easter preceded the surviving tables for the Rogation days, Pentecost and Septuagesima. A similar set of five tables on J 28v follows the same order: Lent, Easter, Rogation, Pentecost and Septuagesima.

The first table that Byrhtferth explicates in ch. 2 (150.7 – 156.30) is the paschal cycle (facing p. 150; J 28r). This first section of the chapter contains, among other things, an account of how the cycle was revealed to St

---

[47] See also Henel, *Studien*, pp. 30–1 and 45–6.
[48] See Henel, 'Notes', pp. 436–8.
[49] 'Two Notes on MS Ashmole 328', p. 18.
[50] *Ibid*, pp. 18–19.

Pachomius (150.17–29), drawn from the J computus (28r); instructions for counting on the fingers, mentioned above; and an account of how often the terminus falls in March (154.29 – 156.10), translated directly from a gloss to *De Temporum Ratione*, ch. 59, in J (100r). The first section is followed by a brief digression on the tides (156.31 – 158.16). The second section of the chapter (158.17 – 164.8) explicates a table for determining the moon's age (facing p. 160; J 24v).[51] After introducing this table (158.17 – 160.24) Byrhtferth explains how to calculate how long the moon will shine each night of its age (160.25 – 162.24). His account is drawn from Bede's *De Temporum Ratione*, ch. 24. In Bede's work, as in Byrhtferth's, it follows an explanation of a table of lunar letters; it is also excerpted on J 36r. Next Byrhtferth gives the Greek names for the phases of the moon in a paragraph based on a passage from Abbo's *De cursu .vii. planetarum* (J 38v):

Enchiridion	J
Monoides he byð geciged prima, diatomos tyn nihta eald oððe fif and twentig, amphicirtos twelf nihta eald oððe feower and twentig, panselenos fiftyne (162.29 – 164.1).	Siquidem prima monoides, id est singularis, et .xii. partibus ab eo distat semper oriens, et ita singulis diebus .xii. partibus ab eo recedens. Dum ad .lxx. partes celi peruenerit fit diatomos, id est sectilis quasi clara usque ad centrum. Et cum praedictis partibus .xlv. adiecerit, amphicirtos, id est maior media minor plena. Cum uero .clxx. panselenos dicitur, id est omni parte plena.

Byrhtferth has simplified Abbo's explanation in a highly unByrhtferth-like manner; note, however, that both J and the *Enchiridion* use the corrupt spelling monoides (for $\mu\eta\nu\text{o}\epsilon\iota\delta\acute{\eta}s$).[52] The diagram that illustrates this passage (facing p. 164) is also taken from Abbo's *De cursu .vii. planetarum* (J 38v). The Abbonian passage, and with it Byrhtferth's account of the age of the moon, ends in the lacuna at 164.8, mentioned above. The third and last section of ch. 2 (164.9 – 170.16) explicates the tables of the termini of moveable feasts, incomplete in the *Enchiridion*, as I have said, but found on J 28v. The table of epacts on p. 170, from J 13v, illustrates the last paragraph of this section (170.10–16).

Ch. 3 (170.17 – 197) is a highly miscellaneous and digressive compilation that draws little from the computus. It opens with an account of rhetorical figures taken mainly from Bede's *De Schematibus et Tropis Sacrae Scripturae*

---

[51] Not, as Crawford writes, 'de regularibus terminis paschae'; see Henel, 'Notes', pp. 439–41.

[52] I think the Abbonian text a far more likely source than Martianus Capella (cited in Crawford's notes), whom Byrhtferth apparently did not use again in the *Enchiridion*. Martianus was only beginning to be widely read in Anglo-Saxon England according to J. D. A. Ogilvy (*Books known to the English, 597–1066*, Med. Acad. of America Publ. 76 (Cambridge, Mass., 1967), 199).

Liber[53] and, after a rhetorical flourish, discusses briefly the table of lunar letters, which a priest could use to find the age of the moon (180.26 – 182.21). Such tables, exceedingly common in medieval computi, could be divided into two parts, like the one that accompanies *De Temporum Ratione* on J 81r,[54] or presented whole, like the one in the J computus (22v). The version in the *Enchiridion* was to have been in two parts (see 182.5–6 and plate), but the scribe of our manuscript, finding that he had not lined up his columns correctly, abandoned it after having filled only six columns of the first part. Having finished with the lunar letters, Byrhtferth has finished with the computus. He lists the signs used by the grammarians and then the signs for weights (182.22 – 192.35) and closes with tables of the Roman, Hebrew and Greek alphabets (194.1 – 197).

CONCLUSIONS

I have not attempted to catalogue the full extent of Byrhtferth's indebtedness to J, but only to present enough evidence to show that the organizational principle of the *Enchiridion* is simply to follow the order of the J computus. It does so, it is true, by fits and starts, for Byrhtferth was all too easily distracted by matters not related to the computus, but the pattern is plain enough: bk I covers J 13v–14r, bk II covers 14v–21v and bk III covers 22r–34v. This computus and the other works in the same manuscript provided most of Byrhtferth's sources; and even where Crawford's notes show that Byrhtferth used works not in the manuscript (e.g. Hrabanus Maurus's *Liber de Computo* and Isidore's *Etymologiae*) we sometimes find the same material copied into the margins of J. Byrhtferth doubtless drew liberally from the books in the library at Ramsey, but he had already collected the works he considered most important into his own anthology. These findings should be set beside the growing evidence of the importance of anthologies and commonplace books to medieval authors. The Old English scholar will think particularly of Wulfstan's commonplace book, London, British Library, Cotton Nero A. i,[55] and of Ælfric's commonplace book in Boulogne-sur-Mer, Bibliothèque Municipale 63.[56] The J corpus is important to the student of Byrhtferth in

---

[53] This has been discussed by James J. Murphy ('The Rhetorical Lore of the *Boceras* in Byrhtferth's *Manual*', *Philological Essays: Studies in Old and Middle English Language and Literature in honour of Herbert Dean Meritt*, Janua Linguarum Series Maior 37 (The Hague, 1970), 111–24). See also Milton McC. Gatch, 'Beginnings Continued: a Decade of Studies of Old English Prose', *ASE* 5 (1976), 236 and n. 4.

[54] Jones has printed a one-part version of the table (*Bedae Opera de Temporibus*, p. 225). The table as printed by Jones can be used with the calendar in J.

[55] See Henry R. Loyn, *A Wulfstan Manuscript*, EEMF 17 (Copenhagen, 1971), 49.

[56] See Enid M. Raynes, 'MS Boulogne-sur-Mer 63 and Ælfric', *MÆ* 26 (1957), 65–73, and Milton McC. Gatch, *Preaching and Theology in Anglo-Saxon England* (Toronto, 1977), pp. 129–33.

Princeps Merciorum gentis: the family, career and connections of Ælfhere, ealdorman of Mercia, 956—83

A. WILLIAMS

Ælfhere, ealdorman of Mercia from 956 to 983, is not an immediately familiar figure. Yet he was one of the most powerful men in the political life of his day. The author of the *Vita Oswaldi* was in no doubt of his importance in the disturbances which followed the death of Edgar:

Thus also the earldorman of the Mercian people, Ælfhere by name, appropriating enormous revenues, which blind the eyes of many, ejected...with the advice of the people and the outcry of the crowd, not only the sheep, but the shepherds also. Those who before were wont to ride on caparisoned horses, and to join with their fellows in singing the mellifluous song of King David, you could then see bearing their burden, not borne, as the patriarch of old, by a chariot into Egypt; or else walking with companions or friends, without a scrip, without shoes, and thus involuntarily fulfilling the words of the holy gospel.[1]

Ælfhere's present obscurity is a result of the tendency of historians to concentrate upon the development of royal and 'central' government and correspondingly to neglect the underlying political tensions of pre-Conquest England, at least before 975. The impression gained by reading many otherwise excellent studies is of the king as an isolated figure, accompanied perhaps by one or two churchmen, poised above an undifferentiated mass of subjects, described only in terms of their social divisions into noblemen and commoners and never as individuals with a rôle to play in political life. Perhaps it is this which gives that curiously impersonal quality to much of the writing on pre-Conquest England; 'the administration' and 'the economy' proceed on their way unencumbered by personal ambitions, struggles and achievements. Attempts have been made to remedy this situation and to replace the great secular nobles in their rightful place as advisers, helpers and sometimes opponents of the English kings. For, just as it is impossible to understand the reign of Edward the Confessor without

---

[1] *StO*, pp. 443–4, trans. *EHD*, pp. 912–13. (For abbreviations, see below, n. 3.)

TABLE I THE FAMILY OF ÆLFHERE

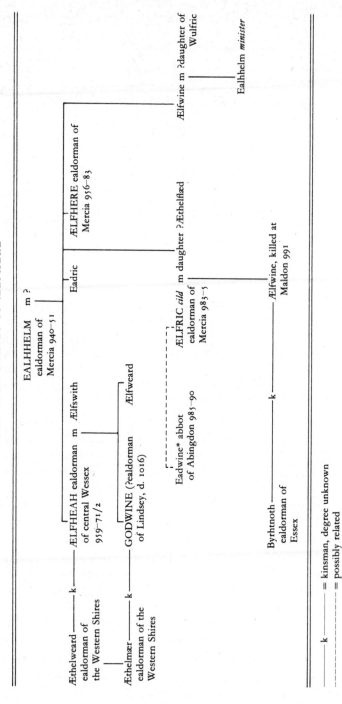

* For the question of Eadwine's relationship to Ælfric *cild*, see below, n. 138.

144

reference to Godwine of Wessex and Leofric of Mercia, it is impossible to study the reigns of Edgar and Æthelred II without a knowledge of the rival families of Ælfhere of Mercia and Æthelwine of East Anglia. Æthelwine's family has been the subject of an article by Dr Hart,[2] and this study is an attempt to present Ælfhere and his kin in their proper light.[3]

The family to which Ælfhere belonged and of which he was the most distinguished member first acquired power in the reign of Edmund. Although several of its members were described as kinsmen by successive kings,[4] its origins are strangely obscure. The father of Ælfhere can be identified as Ealhhelm, who was made ealdorman by Edmund in 940 (see table I).[5] His sphere of authority seems to have lain in central Mercia; it probably centred upon the diocese of Worcester, itself roughly co-terminous with the ancient kingdom of the Hwicce.[6] It seems that on, or soon after, his appointment Ealhhelm was given the lands of the defunct abbey of Evesham. In the thirteenth-century Evesham Chronicle the secularization of the abbey's lands (and indeed the expulsion of the monks) is attributed to 'quidam nefandissimus princeps huius patriae, Alchelmus nomine', further described as 'quasi lupus rapax, primus raptor huius ecclesie'. The spoliation is dated to the time of Edmund, *non illo sancto*, which would seem to indicate the identity of *Alchelmus princeps* and ealdorman Ealhhelm.[7] There is no need to believe that Ealhhelm actually expelled the monks from Evesham. Monastic

---

[2] C. Hart, 'Athelstan "Half King" and his Family', *ASE* 2 (1973), 115–44. Dr Hart has commented elsewhere that 'a full-scale investigation of Ælfhere's career is badly needed' (*ECNENM* (see below, n. 3), p. 261).

[3] The following abbreviations have been used: Chadwick, *Institutions*, = H. Munro Chadwick, *Studies in Anglo-Saxon Institutions* (Cambridge, 1905); *Chron Abingd* = *Chronicon Monasterii de Abingdon*, ed. J. Stevenson, Rolls Ser. (London, 1858); *Chron Evesh* = *Chronicon Abbatiae de Evesham*, ed. W. Dunn Macray, RS (London, 1863); *ECEE* = C. Hart, *The Early Charters of Eastern England* (Leicester, 1966); *ECNENM* = C. Hart, *The Early Charters of Northern England and the North Midlands* (Leicester, 1975); *ECTV* = M. Gelling, *The Early Charters of the Thames Valley* (Leicester, 1979); *ECW* = H. P. R. Finberg, *The Early Charters of Wessex* (Leicester, 1964); *ECWM* = H. P. R. Finberg, *The Early Charters of the West Midlands* (Leicester, 1961); *EHD* = *English Historical Documents* I, ed. D. Whitelock, 2nd ed. (London, 1979); Robertson, *Charters* = *Anglo-Saxon Charters*, ed. A. J. Robertson, 2nd ed. (Cambridge, 1956); S = P. H. Sawyer, *Anglo-Saxon Charters: an Annotated List and Bibliography*, R. Hist. Soc. Guides and Handbooks (London, 1968); *StO* = 'The Anonymous Life of St Oswald', *The Historians of the Church of York and its Archbishops*, ed. J. Raine, RS (London, 1879–94), I, 377–475; *VCH* = *The Victoria History of the Counties of England*; Whitelock, *Wills* = *Anglo-Saxon Wills*, ed. D. Whitelock (Cambridge, 1930). I am most grateful to Dr Simon Keynes for reading and commenting upon this article and for saving me from numerous errors; those which remain are mine.

[4] Ælfhere is called *propinquus* by Eadred (S 555) and described as *ex parentela regis* in the witness-list to a charter of Eadwig (S 582). His brother Ælfheah is called kinsman by Eadred (S 564), Eadwig (S 585–6) and Edgar (S 702) and Edgar also addresses their brother Ælfwine as *propinquus* (S 802).

[5] Chadwick, *Institutions*, pp. 182 and 187–8. The identification of Ealhhelm as Ælfhere's father rests on the appearance of his name in the poem on the Battle of Maldon (*The Battle of Maldon*, ed. E. V. Gordon (London, 1937; repr. Manchester, 1976), p. 83).

[6] For the divisions of Mercia at this time, see Chadwick, *Institutions*, pp. 196–7.

[7] *Chron Evesh*, p. 77.

life had doubtless ceased at some earlier date,[8] and the abbey's estates were used by the king to endow Ealhhelm so that he might fulfil his duties as ealdorman. The Evesham account goes on to describe how, on the death of Ealhhelm, the abbey's lands were appropriated by the thegn Wulfric, also described as *sancte ecclesie raptor*, and Bishop Oswulf. Oswulf was bishop of Ramsbury from 950 to 970. His connection with the lands of Evesham seems perfectly respectable. He was given land at Dumbleton, Gloucestershire, and Aston Somerville, Worcestershire by Abbot Cynath,[9] who, as Armitage Robinson showed, was abbot of Evesham in the time of Athelstan.[10] If Oswulf was a friend of one of Evesham's last pre-reform abbots, it seems entirely reasonable that he should have been entrusted with the direction of some of its estates. Wulfric too seems to have a respectable background. He is presumably the Wulfric *miles* to whom in 949 Eadred gave twelve *cassati* at Bourton-on-the-Water, Gloucestershire, with land at Maugersbury and Daylesford, since this land was later claimed by Evesham.[11] If Eadred's charter is genuine, Wulfric received some of the abbey's land before Ealhhelm's death, since Ealhhelm continues to sign Eadred's charters until 951. Wulfric may be identical with a man of the same name who had some connection with Ealhhelm's son Ælfwine;[12] he has also been identified with St Dunstan's brother Wulfric, to whom Dunstan entrusted the management of Glastonbury's lands.[13] If this is so, it is a further indication of a connection between Ealhhelm's family and Wulfric, since Ealhhelm's sons were benefactors of Glastonbury, and Ælfwine, already mentioned, became a monk there. The dealings of Ealhhelm's family with Evesham have a long and by no means uncomplicated history, which will be recounted in what follows.[14]

Ealhhelm's last signature as ealdorman occurs in 951. Among the six or seven ealdormen who regularly witness between 940 and 951 his name usually appears in fourth or fifth place.[15] He was not the only ealdorman in Mercia at the time. Æthelmund, who was appointed at the same time as Ealhhelm, must also have exercised authority in Mercia,[16] and so must Athelstan, who was appointed later in the same year. Dr Hart has suggested that, as

[8] D. Knowles, *The Monastic Order in England* (Cambridge, 1963), p. 34; J. Armitage Robinson, *The Times of St Dunstan* (Oxford, 1923), p. 40.
[9] S 404.
[10] Robinson, *Times of St Dunstan*, pp. 36–40. It is likely that Oswulf received the actual conventual buildings.
[11] S 550. Bourton-on-the-Water and Maugersbury are listed among the possessions of Evesham in the statement attributed to St Ecgwine, dated 714 (S 1250) and Æthelred II restored one *mansa* at Maugersbury to the abbey (S 935).
[12] See below, pp. 154 and 155.
[13] *ECNENM*, pp. 371–2. But see also below, p. 154.
[14] See below, pp. 168–70.
[15] *ECNENM*, p. 328.
[16] Chadwick, *Institutions*, p. 196.

Athelstan's signature as ealdorman always appears just below that of his namesake, Athelstan 'Half King', ealdorman of East Anglia, his ealdordom may have lain in south-eastern Mercia. In 955 a third Athelstan, distinguished on one occasion as Athelstan *Rota*, became an ealdorman. His sphere of office was certainly Mercia, since after 957 he witnessed charters issued by Edgar as king of the Mercians. That it lay in south-eastern Mercia is suggested by his marriage with Æthelflæd of Damerham, whose lands lay in Essex and the south-east, Suffolk and Berkshire.[17] It seems reasonable to conclude that the two Athelstans in turn held south-eastern Mercia as their ealdordom, and that Æthelmund, who continues to sign until 965, held the north-western provinces of the old Mercian kingdom.[18]

The main political events of Ealhhelm's term of office were the loss and recovery of the Five Boroughs and the struggle for the Norse kingdom of York. What part, if any, he played in these happenings is unknown. Æthelweard, writing towards the end of the tenth century, says that it was Wulfstan, bishop of York, and the ealdorman of the Mercians who expelled Rægnald and Anlaf from the city of York and restored it to obedience to Edmund.[19] This is presumably a reference to Edmund's conquest of Viking Northumbria in 944 and the expulsion of Olaf Sihtricson and Rægnald Guthfrithson. What part was played by the Mercians is unclear, but in any case the unnamed *dux Merciorum* mentioned by Æthelweard is more likely to have been Æthelmund, who presumably held Chester as part of his ealdordom, than Ealhhelm.

Much more can be discovered about Ealhhelm's children than about Ealhhelm himself.[20] He left four sons, Ælfheah, Eadric, Ælfwine and Ælfhere, and at least one daughter.[21] The most eminent was Ælfhere of Mercia, but before his career is discussed it will be convenient to identify and describe his siblings. The brother who approached him most closely in importance was Ælfheah, ealdorman of central Wessex under Eadwig and

---

[17] Hart, 'Athelstan "Half King"', p. 126, n. 6; *ECNENM*, pp. 299–300.

[18] *ECNENM*, pp. 287–8.

[19] *The Chronicle of Æthelweard*, ed. A. Campbell (London, 1962), p. 54.

[20] The name of Ealhhelm's wife is unknown. Bridgeman suggested that she was Ælfwyn, daughter of Ealdorman Æthelred and Æthelflæd, Lady of the Mercians (C. G. O. Bridgeman, 'Wulfric Spot's Will', *Collections for a History of Staffordshire*, William Salt Archaeol. Soc. (1916), pp. 53–4). It would be nice to believe it, but there is nothing to suggest such a relationship and the arguments which Bridgeman adduced in favour of the theory have been superseded. Ealhhelm may have had some connection with Æthelflæd, if he is identical with the thegn to whom she gave land in Derbyshire, probably in 914 (*Charters of Burton Abbey*, ed. P. H. Sawyer, Anglo-Saxon Charters 2 (London, 1979), 1–2). His name is not common.

[21] His daughter married Ælfric (probably Ælfric *cild*), father of the Ælfwine killed at Maldon in 991. Gordon suggested that she was Æthelflæd Ealhhelm's daughter, who received a bequest from Wynflæd about 950 (Gordon, *Battle of Maldon*, p. 83; Whitelock, *Wills*, p. 14). For a possible fifth son, called Ælfweard, see below, pp. 169–70.

Edgar.[22] Ælfheah may in fact have been the eldest brother, since it seems he was married by 940 to a lady named Ælfswith, who seems to have been a person of some importance in her own right, to judge by the charters addressed to her, or to her and her husband jointly. Nothing of her origin is known, however. She first appears in 940, when a charter of Edmund conveys twenty *mansae* at Batcombe, Somerset, to 'meo propinquo et fideli ministro vocitato Elswythe'.[23] Since Ælfheah left this estate to his wife, it seems likely that the grant was in fact made to Ælfheah and Ælfswith jointly and that Ælfheah's name has been accidentally omitted by the copyist.

Ælfheah himself received a grant of eight *cassati* at Compton Beauchamp from Eadred in 954. Since this charter describes him as *minister*,[24] he presumably witnessed charters of Eadred, but his name is a common one; several thegns called Ælfheah witness charters in this period and it is not possible to identify Ealhhelm's son among them. His first certain appearance as a witness is in 955, when he attests a charter of Eadwig in company with his brother Ælfhere.[25] He is probably to be identified with the thegn who regularly witnesses Eadwig's charters in 956 and 957.[26] Eadwig is well known for his extensive grants to laymen, and both Ælfheah and his wife were recipients of the royal generosity.[27] In his case Eadwig's munificence was not misplaced, for when the kingdom was divided in 957 Ælfheah remained with the king in Wessex, whereas Ælfhere supported Edgar in Mercia. Though Ælfhere was made ealdorman in 956, Ælfheah's appointment as ealdorman of central Wessex did not take place till 959, and before this date[28] he was probably a royal seneschal.[29] His tenure of this office might help to explain why it was his younger brother who received their father's ealdordom; the

---

[22] Ælfheah is usually described as ealdorman of Hampshire, but his authority probably extended over Berkshire, Wiltshire and Dorset as well (*ECNENM*, p. 257; Chadwick, *Institutions*, pp. 195–6).

[23] S 462. Ælfheah left a life-interest in this estate to his wife. For another grant to Ælfheah and Ælfswith jointly, see S 747.

[24] S 564. It is possible that Ælfheah is also to be identified with the recipient of ten *manentes* at Farnborough, Berkshire, given by Athelstan in 937 (S 411). Both Compton Beauchamp and Farnborough were given to Abingdon by Ælfheah, and in the former case the donor is certainly the ealdorman (*Chron Abingd* 1, 78–9 and 157–8).

[25] S 582.

[26] Robertson, *Charters*, pp. 338–9.

[27] S 585–6, 639 and 662. The endorsement of the last charter describes Ælfswith as Eadwig's kinswoman.

[28] Robertson, *Charters*, pp. 338–9. Dr Hart identified his predecessor in the ealdordom as Æthelsige, who signs from 951 to 958 ('Athelstan "Half King"', pp. 120 and 128).

[29] S 597 and 1292. Professor Whitelock argued that Ælfheah became ealdorman in 956 and must be distinguished from Ælfheah the seneschal (*discifer, cyninges discðegn*) who signs S 597 (956) and S 1292 (956 × 957) (Whitelock, *Wills*, pp. 121–2). It is true that the signature Ælfheah *dux* appears on charters dated before 959, but in all cases his title is clearly an error (Robertson, *Charters*, pp. 338–9). One version of Eadwig's charter concerning Buckland (S 639) addresses Ælfheah as *dux*, but it is too corrupt for reliance to be placed upon it. Eadwig's grant of land on the Nadder to Ælfheah *minister* (S 586) is dated 956, but it must belong to 959, and Ælfheah witnesses S 658 and 660 (both dated 959) as *dux*.

position of seneschal would enable him to exercise patronage on behalf of his kinsmen and was presumably valuable in its own right.

One of Ælfheah's closest associates was Ælfsige, bishop of Winchester, and briefly archbishop-elect of Canterbury. Ælfheah's appointment as ealdorman would have thrown them into contact, since Winchester must have been the centre of his authority, but their friendship was of longer standing than that. In his will, which must have been drawn up in the late 950s, Ælfsige speaks of Ælfheah as *minnan leofan freond*, and he not only left him an estate at Crondall, Hampshire, but also made him protector of his will and guardian of his kinsmen.[30] Since Ælfsige was not a monk, but a 'married' clerk, his reputation has suffered somewhat. Armitage Robinson writes reprovingly that 'of... Ælfsige, no good is recorded', and goes on to remark that 'the irregularities of the clerks (of Winchester) are the less surprising if the bishop's seat had been unworthily filled for more than ten years'.[31] William of Malmesbury accused him of having bought the see of Canterbury and of insulting the tomb of his saintly predecessor, Archbishop Oda.[32] Both Oda and Bishop Ælfheah, Ælfsige's predecessor at Winchester, were men of exceptional piety, with whom he could not compete. Ælfheah's friendship with Ælfsige cannot have done him much good with the 'reform party' with whom his brother Ælfhere was later embroiled. Ælfsige was made archbishop on the death of Oda, which took place on 2 June, probably in 958.[33] He did not hold the archbishopric long, for he was frozen to death in the Alps as he journeyed south to Rome to be invested with his pallium, probably in the winter of 958–9. In his will he mentions an unnamed sister, his 'kinswoman' and his 'young kinsman'; these are presumably the relatives whom he commends to the protection of his friend Ælfheah. The 'young kinsman' is presumably Godwine of Worthy, Bishop Ælfsige's son, who, since he died in battle against the Danes in 1001, must have been still a child in 959.[34] Ælfsige's 'kinswoman' is presumably his wife, to whom he left the bulk of his patrimony, with reversion to his sister and his 'young kinsman'.

Ælfheah's own will, preserved in the *Codex Wintoniensis*, reveals a little

---

[30] Whitelock, *Wills*, pp. 16–17. For the position of protector (*mund*) of the testator's will, see M. Sheehan, *The Will in Medieval England* (Toronto, 1963), pp. 43–4. People of Ælfsige's rank normally appointed the king as protector, which makes the bishop's choice of Ælfheah more significant.

[31] Robinson, *Times of St Dunstan*, p. 113.

[32] *Willelmi Malmesbiriensis Monachi De Gestis Pontificum Anglorum*, ed. N.E.S.A. Hamilton, RS (London, 1870), pp. 25–6 and 165.

[33] *Memorials of St Dunstan*, ed. William Stubbs, RS (London, 1874), pp. xciv–xcv. There is some doubt about the year of Oda's death (E. John, *Orbis Britanniae and Other Studies* (Leicester, 1966), p. 192).

[34] *Anglo-Saxon Chronicles* 1001 A: *Two of the Saxon Chronicles Parallel*, ed. Charles Plummer (Oxford, 1892–9) I, 132. The engagement took place during the harrying of Hampshire in that year and the name immediately preceding that of Godwine in the list of slain is that of Wulfhere, *bisceopes ðegn*, which suggests that Godwine still had connections with the Old Minster.

more about his associates.[35] He died in 971 or 972 and his will was probably drawn up in the late 960s. He bequeathed an estate at Wycombe, Buckinghamshire, to his kinsman Æthelweard, and, although this is a very common name in the tenth century, it seems likely that this was Æthelweard the Chronicler, later ealdorman of the Western Shires, who claimed descent from Æthelred I and was therefore, like Ælfheah, a kinsman of the West Saxon kings.[36] Another close friend of Ælfheah's was the lady Ælfthryth, daughter of Ordgar, ealdorman of Devon, and second wife of Edgar.[37] To her, Ælfheah bequeathed an estate at *Scyræburnan* (unidentified). He also made bequests to her sons by Edgar: thirty mancuses and a sword to the elder ætheling (Edmund, who predeceased his father) and an estate at Walkhampstead (now Godstone), Surrey, to the younger ætheling (the future Æthelred II). In his will Ælfheah calls Ælfthryth his *gefæðeran*, a word denoting 'the relationship between godparents and parents, or between godparents of the same child'.[38] Perhaps Ælfheah was godparent to one or other of the æthelings. Ælfthryth was one of the witnesses to his will, in company with Bishop Æthelwold, Æthelwine of East Anglia, Ælfhere, Ælfwine (Ælfheah's brother) and Æscwig, abbot of Bath.

Æfheah's will not only reveals to us something of his personal friendships but also allows us to reconstruct his landed wealth in more detail than is possible for other members of his family, whose wills, if they made any, do not survive. Table 2 (below, pp. 152–3) lists the estates which he held at some time: seven in Wiltshire, seven in Berkshire, four in Surrey, three in Buckinghamshire, two in Somerset, two in Hampshire, one or possibly two in Middlesex and one unidentifed. This is not an exhaustive list of the estates held by Ælfheah, since he bequeathed to his wife Ælfswith 'all the other estates which I leave'. The hidages for the seven estates for which assessments are given or can be supplied from other evidence amount to 270 hides.[39] Four of the estates mentioned in Ælfheah's will were claimed by Malmesbury

---

[35] Whitelock, *Wills*, pp. 22–5.

[36] Campbell, *Chronicle of Æthelweard*, p. 39.

[37] Ordgar became ealdorman of the Western Shires soon after his daughter's marriage to Edgar (*ECNENM*, p. 272). His son Ordwulf founded Tavistock Abbey (H. P. R. Finberg, *Lucerna* (London, 1964), pp. 189–95).

[38] Whitelock, *Wills*, p. 123.

[39] The hidages of *Suðtune*, Littleworth and Charlton are given in the will itself. Batcombe must be the estate of twenty *mansae* given by Edmund in 940 (S 462), Wroughton the estate of thirty *mansae* given by Eadwig in 956 (S 585) and Crondall the estate left to Ælfheah by Ælfsige of Winchester with reversion to the Old Minster; its hidage was forty-five *cassati* when Edgar restored it to the abbey (S 820). Faringdon, Berkshire, must have included the twenty hides at Kingston which Ælfhere later sold to Osgar of Abingdon, since he had received the estate from Ælfheah, and the only estates bequeathed to Ælfhere under his brother's will were Faringdon, Aldbourne and the reversion of Batcombe (S 1216). Other charters in favour of Ælfheah, who may or may not be identical with the ealdorman, are S 440, 475, 1736 and 1746. Charters in favour of Ælfswith, which again may or may not relate to the ealdorman's wife, are S 593, 1720 and 1748.

Abbey as part of its original endowment: Wroughton, Charlton, Chelworth and Purton.[40] Two of the charters by which Malmesbury sought to authenticate its ownership gave hidages for Purton (thirty-five *manentes*) and Chelworth (four *cassati*). None of the charters has been found satisfactory, but taken together they suggest that Malmesbury had, or could fabricate, a claim to some of Ælfheah's estates. All four lie in Wiltshire, and Chelworth at least was associated with a former ealdorman of the area (S 1205). It is possible that some of the estates of Malmesbury were used to endow the ealdorman of Wessex, as those of Evesham were used to endow the ealdormen of central Mercia. Malmesbury was reformed, at the earliest, in the late 960s, which may explain why Ælfheah left the abbey the estate at Charlton. This does not of course prove that the estates at Chelworth and Purton claimed by Malmesbury were identical to those held by Ælfheah, but it is a possibility, and so we may tentatively add another thirty-nine hides to the total hidage of Ælfheah's estates. But this still leaves the hidage of eleven out of the twenty estates listed in the will unaccounted for. If the nine estates for which hidages can be supplied amount to 309 hides, it seems reasonable to assume that the hidages of the remaining eleven would yield a similar total. On top of this there are the unnamed estates bequeathed by Ælfheah to his wife. Presumably the estates known to have been granted to Ælfheah by successive kings but not mentioned in his will are among these, including four *mansae* on the River Nadder, Wiltshire, given by Eadwig (S 586), ten *mansae* at Buckland, Berkshire, given by the same king (S 639), twenty *cassati* at Merton and five at Dulwich, given by Edgar to Ælfheah and Ælfswith jointly (S 747). Ælfheah sold ten hides at Sunbury and twenty hides at Send to Dunstan (S 1447). A figure in the region of seven hundred hides in all for Ælfheah's landed endowment does not seem unreasonable, a very respectable total. Moreover his wife Ælfswith was herself possessed of at least fifty hides. William de Eu, one of the foremost barons of the post-Conquest period, held something in excess of 336 hides in eight counties.[41]

Ælfheah's will refers to his brothers in the plural but only Ælfhere is named as a legatee. Ælfwine, who witnessed the will, is probably the man named elsewhere as the brother of Ælfhere, but before discussing him, reference must be made to Eadric, named as the brother of Ælfheah the seneschal in the witness-list to an exchange of lands dated 956–7.[42] Little else is known of him. He is possibly the recipient of a grant of fifty *mansae* at Meon, Hampshire,

---

[40] For the charters assigning these four estates to Malmesbury, see S 305 and 322 (Wroughton, Charlton and Purton), S 149 (Purton only), S 356 (Chelworth only) and S 1038 (all four).

[41] *VCH Dorset* III, 47.

[42] S 1292.

TABLE 2 THE LANDS OF ÆLFHEAH

Name of estate	Shire	Hidage	Source of information
Wroughton	Wiltshire	30 *mansae*	Will; S 585
Chelworth	Wiltshire	4 *cassati*	Will; S 356 and 1205*
Charlton.	Wiltshire	20 hides	Will
Inglesham	Wiltshire	Not known	Will
Aldbourne	Wiltshire	Not known	Will
Wyritun (?Purton)†	Wiltshire	35 *manentes*	Will; S 149*
'On the Nadder'	Wiltshire	4 *mansae*	S 586
Batcombe	Somerset	20 *mansae*	Will; S 462
Sudtune‡	Somerset	15 hides	Will
Littleworth§	Berkshire	120 hides	Will
Cookham	Berkshire	Not known	Will
Thatcham	Berkshire	Not known	Will
Faringdon	Berkshire	Not known	Will
Kingston‖	Berkshire	20 hides	S 1216
Compton Beauchamp	Berkshire	8 *cassati*	S 564
Buckland	Berkshire	10 *mansae*	S 639

Aylesbury	Buckinghamshire	Not known	Will
Wendover	Buckinghamshire	Not known	Will
Wycombe	Buckinghamshire	Not known	Will
Walkhampstead (Godstone)	Surrey	Not known	Will
Merton	Surrey	20 cassati	S 747
Dulwich	Surrey	5 cassati	S 747
Send	Surrey	20 hides	S 1447
Sunbury	Middlesex	10 hides	S 1447 and 702
Tudingatuna (?Teddington,)	Middlesex)	Not known	Will
Froxfield	Hampshire	Not known	Will
Crondall	Hampshire	45 cassati	Will, S 820
Scyreburna	?	Not known	Will

TOTAL: 386 hides
+ 300 (estimated)

686 hides

In addition it is possible that Ealdorman Ælfheah is to be identified with the grantee of 10 *manentes* at Farnborough, Berkshire (S 411), given by Athelstan (see above, n. 24). His wife Ælfswith held estates of 10 *cassati* at Kemsing, Kent (S 662), and 40 *mansae* at Kington, Wiltshire (S 866).

* For the reasons for believing these estates to be those named in Ælfheah's will, see above, pp. 150–1.
† For this identification, see *ECW* p. 72.
‡ For the suggestion that *Suðtune* lay in Somerset, see Whitelock, *Wills*, p. 122.
§ For this identification, see *ECTV*, p. 56.
‖ Either Kingston Bagpuize or Kingston Lisle; see *ECTV*, pp. 58–9.

given by Eadwig in 956, since land at Froxfield was included within the boundaries and Ælfheah disposed of an estate at Froxfield in his will. The land at Meon seems to have belonged to Queen Eadgifu, whose lands were confiscated by Eadwig and restored by Edgar.[43] A thegn called Eadric is said to have bestowed land at Leckhampstead, Berkshire, on Abingdon, and, since both Ælfhere and Ælfheah gave land to this house, he may perhaps be their brother. Edmund gave ten *mansae* at Leckhampstead to his *minister* Eadric in 943.[44] Eadwig gave three estates in Berkshire and one in Surrey to a thegn called Eadric, all of which passed to Abingdon.[45] Since he is not mentioned in Ælfheah's will, he probably predeceased him.

Rather more can be discovered about Ælfwine. He is identified as Ælfhere's brother in an endorsement of Edgar's time to an earlier charter.[46] Ælfwine seems to have been the heir of one Wulfric, described as a thegn of both Edmund and Eadred and probably identical with the despoiler of Evesham already mentioned in connection with Ælfwine's father. This Wulfric has been identified by Dr Hart with the brother of St Dunstan, and, since the lands of Wulfric were bequeathed to Glastonbury, this seems not unlikely. Professor Sawyer, however, identifies with him Wulfric *pedisequus* and suggests a relationship with the Mercian noblemen Wulfric Spot.[47] The Wulfric with whom Ælfwine was connected had twenty-five *manentes* at Grittleton and twenty hides at Nettleton, both in Wiltshire, which he bequeathed to his wife with reversion to Glastonbury. The bequest was fulfilled by Ælfwine, Wulfric's heir, when he became a monk of that house. Wulfric also left Horton, Dorset, to Glastonbury and this bequest was also fulfilled by Ælfwine.[48] The identity of Wulfric's heir and Ælfhere's brother can be established by a charter of Edgar, dated 975, granting three *mansiunculae* at Aston, Shropshire, to Ealhhelm *minister*, at the request of the king's 'venerable kinsman' the monk Ælfwine.[49] His monastery is not named, but the charter is dated from Glastonbury, and it is reasonable to assume that he was a monk of this house.[50] Ealhhelm was, of course, the name of Ælfwine's father and it is probable that the recipient was Ælfwine's son, since the name is an uncommon one, but he is otherwise unknown. However

---

[43] S 619 and 811.

[44] *Chron Abingd* I, 103–5 and 476–7; S 491. S 665 is a forgery, based on S 491, attributing the grant to Eadwig (*ECTV*, p. 51).

[45] S 620–2 and 654. The estates concerned lay at Padworth, Welford and Longworth in Berkshire and Pyrford in Surrey. For other possible references to Eadric, see *ECNENM*, p. 318.

[46] S 1276.

[47] *ECNENM*, pp. 371–2; Sawyer, *Charters of Burton*, p. xlviii. If Ælfwine was connected (? by marriage) with an important Mercian family, his adherence to Edgar after 957 is explained.

[48] S 472, 504 and 1743.

[49] S 802.

[50] *ECWM*, p. 149.

it seems reasonable to conclude that the king's kinsman, the heir of Wulfric and Ælfhere's brother were one and the same man. The nature of Ælfwine's relationship with Wulfric is unknown, but, since Wulfric cannot have been his father, it is perhaps possible to suggest that he was his father-in-law.[51] Like his brothers Ælfwine bore a very common name and any attempts to identify him further must be conjectural. Both Eadred and Eadwig made grants to *ministri* called Ælfwine; either or both may relate to our Ælfwine.[52] A thegn of this name also witnesses a number of Eadwig's charters in 956 and 957. Only two charters of Eadwig after the division of the kingdom are witnessed by Ælfwine, but from 957 to 959 this name figures prominently among the thegns who attest Edgar's charters as king of the Mercians and in 959 Edgar gave ten *cassati* at Highclere, Hampshire, to the *minister* Ælfwine. After Edgar's succession to the kingdom reunited on his brother's death, the name of Ælfwine continues to appear in a prominent place among the thegns who witness Edgar's charters until 970.[53] It is possible that these attestations belong to Ælfhere's brother and that Ælfwine, like Ælfhere, supported Edgar in the division of 959. If this was so, his profession as a monk took place presumably in or after 970. His brother Ælfheah left the reversion of his estate at Batcombe to his brothers, which must mean Ælfwine as well as Ælfhere, and Ælfwine appears as a witness to his brother's will. As we have seen, he was still alive in 975. It is not known when he died.

The most illustrious of the sons of Ealhhelm was Ælfhere, who was appointed ealdorman by his kinsman Eadwig in 956.[54] He had received an estate in Somerset from Eadred in 951[55] but is otherwise unknown before 955, when he witnessed a charter of Eadwig as Ælfhere *ex parentela regis, minister*.[56] It is because of his late appearance in comparison with Ælfheah (who as we have seen was already married in 940) that I have suggested that possibly Ælfhere was the younger of the two. Nevertheless he was the first to obtain the office of ealdorman, possibly because Ælfheah already held the office of king's seneschal. Ælfhere's ealdordom was probably that held by

---

[51] Wulfric, described as a thegn of King Edmund, left Grittleton and Nettlecombe (also called Nettleton) to the abbey after the death of his wife. Ælfwine his *successor* fulfilled the bequest when he became a monk of that house, apparently in Edgar's reign. Wulfric also left Horton to the abbey with his body; this bequest also was fulfilled by his *successor in hereditate* Ælfwine (William of Malmesbury, *De Antiquitate Glastoniensis Ecclesiae, Adami de Domerham Historia de Rebus Gestis Glastoniensis*, ed. Thomas Hearne (Oxford, 1727) 1, 72–3, 76, 85 and 101).

[52] S 559 and 594, relating to three hides at Barkham and fifteen hides at Milton, both in Berkshire.

[53] For the attestations of Ælfwine and other estates which may have belonged to him, see *ECNENM*, pp. 277–8. Edgar's charter granting Highclere is S 680.

[54] He signs charters of Eadwig in this year as *dux*.

[55] S 555. The estate consisted of twenty *mansiunculae* at Buckland Denham, Somerset. Ælfhere's identity can be established by the fact that the king addresses him as *propinquus*.

[56] S 582. Ælfhere's name also appears among the *ministri* in the witness-list to S 567, an alleged charter of Eadred dated 955.

his father between 940 and 951, since Æthelmund, who was appointed at the same time as Ælfhere's father, was still in office, probably in the north-west of Mercia, and Athelstan *Rota*, whom Eadwig appointed in 955, probably held the south-eastern shires of Mercia.[57] He signs charters of Eadwig in 956 and 957, though he was outranked by Athelstan 'Half King', ealdorman of East Anglia, and Edmund, ealdorman of the Western Shires. Eadwig gave him twenty *mansae* at Cuddeson, Oxfordshire, and twenty more at Wormleighton, Warwickshire, in 956, and by 957 had added forty hides at Westbury-on-Severn, Gloucestershire.[58] Apart from these three Mercian estates, totalling eighty hides, and his twenty hides in Somerset, it is likely that he held at least some of the lands of Evesham Abbey, formerly held by his father. The account of Ælfhere's relationship with Evesham, as told in the Evesham Chronicle, is by no means easily unravelled,[59] but he had control of the abbey lands at some point and 956 seems the likeliest date for him to have acquired an interest in them. According to the Evesham Chronicle he held Evesham and Offenham, with other estates which he used to endow priests (presumably the secular canons who inhabited the abbey), thegns (*milites*) and other associates (*amici*). Since another estate said to have been in the possession of Ælfhere's family was Lenchwick, it seems likely that what Ælfhere held was the hundred of *Fisseberg*, which consisted of a core of estates valued at fifty hides and two outliers separately assessed.[60] Possession of the Evesham estates would add fifty or so hides to Ælfhere's known lands. From Edgar he received five hides at Orchardleigh, Somerset, and from Æthelred II, ten *mansae* at Olney, Buckinghamshire.[61] Under his brother's will he received Aldbourne, Wiltshire, the hidage of which is unknown, Faringdon, Berkshire, which presumably included the twenty hides at Kingston which he sold to Osgar of Abingdon, and the reversion of twenty hides at Batcombe, Somerset.[62] He can therefore be shown to have disposed of upwards of two hundred hides of land, and, if we had his will, as we have his brother's, it may be suspected that we should find that this does not represent anything like the sum total of his wealth. The *Vita Oswaldi*'s description of him 'prospering according to this world's grandeur' and 'appropriating enormous

57 See above, pp. 146–7.
58 S 587–8 and 1747. The grant of Westbury was confirmed by Edgar (S 1760) and Ælfhere later gave the estate to Glastonbury 'for my own soul and King Edgar's' (*De Antiquitate, Adam de Domerham*, ed. Hearne I, 85).
59 See below, pp. 168–70.
60 D. C. Cox, 'The Vale Estates of the Church of Evesham, *c.* 700–1086', *Vale of Evesham Hist. Soc. Research Papers* 5 (1975), 26–33. One of the outliers was Ombersley, but, for the question of whether Ælfhere held this estate, see below, p. 169. I am very grateful to Mr Cox for drawing my attention to this paper and for his helpful comments on the history of the Evesham estates.
61 S 1759 and 834.
62 S 1216.

revenues' suggests that he was a rich man. It is interesting that one of these phrases used by the *Vita Oswaldi*, 'florens secundum saeculi dignitatem' is almost an exact translation of the adjective *woruldgesælig* used in the poem on the Battle of Maldon to describe his father Ealhhelm.[63] It seems the family had a reputation for riches.

But in 956 Ælfhere's career was only just beginning. He owed his position to his royal kinsman Eadwig, and Eadwig's appointments were not regarded with universal favour by early commentators. The *Vita Dunstani auctore B* accused him of 'ruining with vain hatred the shrewd and wise and admitting with loving zeal the ignorant and those like himself'.[64] This may be mere spite, occasioned by Eadwig's alienation and subsequent expulsion of Dunstan, and Æthelweard described the king as one who 'deserved to be loved'.[65] But he made enemies, and in 957 the northern peoples threw off his rule and made his brother Edgar their king. Edgar took the title 'king of the Mercians'. The northern bishops and ealdormen supported him, while those south of the Thames remained loyal to Eadwig. Despite the language used by the *Vita Dunstani*, the division had little to do with ecclesiastical reform and took shape on political, rather than religious, lines.

After the division of the kingdom Ælfhere attained the pre-eminent position among Edgar's lay supporters previously enjoyed by Athelstan 'Half King', ealdorman of East Anglia, who retired about this time. Ælfhere's name appears first among those of the ealdormen who witness Edgar's charters from 958 to 959, outranking all the rest.[66] This pre-eminence is perhaps not so surprising. Ælfhere controlled the heartlands of English Mercia (including the episcopal see of Worcester), and, if Edgar wished to rule with any credibility as 'king of the Mercians', he needed Ælfhere's willing support. It is likely that it was at this time that he became ealdorman of the whole of Mercia, the other ealdormen in the area being his subordinates – a position he certainly held in the early 960s. The *Vita Oswaldi* calls him *princeps Merciorum gentis*,[67] a title applicable to no one since the death of Æthelflæd in 918 and the forcible removal of her daughter Ælfwyn in the following year. The *Vita Oswaldi* was of course describing the events of 975–8, and after 970 Ælfhere was the only ealdorman in Mercia, but even before this he appears in the leases issued by Oswald, bishop of Worcester, with the title 'ealdorman of the Mercians' and his permission to the grants is recorded along with that of the king.[68] If the thegn who signs at the head of the *ministri* in Edgar's

---

[63] *StO*, p. 444; Gordon, *Battle of Maldon*, p. 82.
[64] *St Dunstant*, ed. Stubbs, p. 35, trans. *EHD*, p. 901.
[65] Campbell, *Chronicle of Æthelweard*, p. 55.
[66] Hart, 'Athelstan "Half King"', p. 127, n. 1.
[67] *StO*, p. 443.
[68] S 1299, 1300–2 (962), 1297 and 1303–6 (963). Examples could be multiplied.

charters of these years is rightly identified as Ælfhere's brother Ælfwine, as suggested above, his rise to power affected his family as well as himself. Nor did his position deteriorate after the succession of Edgar to the whole kingdom in 959. Ælfhere witnessed most of Edgar's charters as premier ealdorman, often with his brother Ælfheah, now ealdorman of central Wessex by Eadwig's grant, in second place.[69] Although Ælfheah and Eadric had supported Eadwig, while Ælfhere and possibly Ælfwine followed Edgar, no break in family solidarity seems to have occurred. The kinsmen seem simply to have been hedging their bets. Edgar gave land to Ælfheah, and perhaps Eadric also, as well as to Ælfhere and Ælfwine. The whole kin, it seems, shared in the fortune of their illustrious brother.

The political history of Edgar's reign is notoriously obscure and it is difficult to trace Ælfhere's career between 959 and 975. Presumably he took direct control of north-western Mercia after 965, in which year Æthelmund signs for the last time, since no successor is recorded.[70] Presumably he also administered the ealdordom of south-eastern Mercia after 970 in succession to Athelstan *Rota*; at all events he had some sort of jurisdiction over Hertfordshire in the late 970s.[71] Moreover it seems that after the death of his brother Ælfheah in 971 or 972 Ælfhere was administering the ealdordom of central Wessex, since no successor is found to Ælfheah until the appointment of Æthelmær in 977.[72] The earldordom of eastern Wessex seems to have been untenanted between 957 (when a certain Ælfric was made ealdorman by Eadwig, only to vanish almost immediately) and the appointment of Edwin, probably by Edward the Martyr.[73] Who administered the south-eastern provinces during those years is not clear, but Ælfhere attended a council in London in the later years of Edgar's reign, with the leading men of west Kent, to hear a suit concerning land in that county claimed by the bishop of Rochester.[74] The remaining ealdorman in Wessex, Ordgar, ealdorman of the Western Shires from 964 to 970, seems to have been a friend of the family; at all events Ælfhere is described by the *Liber de Hyde* (admittedly a late source) as a particular favourite of Ordgar's daughter, Queen Ælfthryth, whose connection with his brother Ælfheah has already been remarked.[75]

Some set-backs must also be mentioned. The creation of the ship-soke of Oswaldslow in the mid-960s cannot have been a welcome development,

[69] S 680 (959), 683, 685 and 687 (960). Other examples could be given.
[70] For Æthelmund's last appearance, see *ECNENM*, pp. 287–8.
[71] *Ibid.* p. 300, and see below, p. 165.
[72] Hart, 'Athelstan "Half King"', p. 134; *ECNENM*, pp. 285–6.
[73] *ECNENM*, p. 267; Robertson, *Charters*, p. 366; S 828–9.
[74] *Charters of Rochester*, ed. A. Campbell, Anglo-Saxon Charters 1 (London, 1973), 53–4.
[75] *Liber Monasterii de Hyda*, ed. Edward Edwards, RS (London, 1866), p. 206.

creating as it did an area of independent jurisdiction in the very heartland of Ælfhere's authority.[76] It is true that most of Oswald's leases acknowledge the consent of Ælfhere as ealdorman of the Mercians as well as that of the king; but, once created, the leaseholds of Worcester were subject, under the king, to the bishop or his *archductor*, not to the ealdorman.[77] The reform of Evesham about 970 also meant a diminution in Ælfhere's landed estates, for it seems that he was required to restore the lands which he and his father had held and which had previously belonged to the abbey.[78] Moreover Evesham itself may have been the centre of another liberty of the same kind as Oswaldslow, comprising the hundred of *Fisseberg* – the very land, in fact, which Ælfhere had himself controlled.[79] It has been suggested too that Pershore Abbey also held a similar ship-soke; its original endowment was a triple hundred.[80] It is perhaps significant that Pershore, like Evesham, preserved a tradition of hostility to Ælfhere, coupled with a belief that he had deprived the abbey of its lands. Pershore, like Worcester, was a house associated with Oswald, and, though Ælfhere and his family were generous to Glastonbury and Abingdon, none of Oswald's foundations got so much as a penny-piece from any member of the kin.

But, whatever the limits of Ælfhere's authority, it is clear that in the latter part of Edgar's reign he was at the height of his power. It has long been recognized that Edgar's Fourth Code implies a fourfold division of England into the kingdom of Wessex, the ealdordoms of Mercia and East Anglia and the earldom of Northumbria.[81] The last three were ruled by Ælfhere, Æthelwine and Oslac respectively.[82] These three men represent an élite among the nobles of their day, set apart from the other ealdormen by the wide-ranging nature of their power.[83] It was perhaps inevitable that conflicts

---

[76] For Oswaldslow, see John, *Orbis Britanniae*, pp. 178–9; Eric John, *Land Tenure in Early England* (Leicester, 1964), pp. 89–90. For ship-sokes generally, see F. E. Harmer, *Anglo-Saxon Writs* (Manchester, 1952), pp. 266–7.

[77] This is clear from the *Indiculum* of Oswaldslow (*Hemingi Chartularium Ecclesiae Wigorniensis*, ed. Thomas Hearne (Oxford, 1723) I, 294: trans. R. Allen Brown, *Origins of English Feudalism* (London, 1973), pp. 133–4: 'whether to fulfill the service due to him [Oswald] or that due to the king they [the Worcester tenants] shall always with all humility and submissiveness be subject to the authority and will of that *archductor* who presides over the bishopric').

[78] See below, pp. 169–70.

[79] Cox, 'Vale Estates of Evesham', pp. 36–40.

[80] *Ibid.* p. 39; Eric John, 'War and Society in the Tenth Century: the Maldon Campaign', *TRHS* 5th ser. 27 (1977), 180–1. The entry for the manor of Pershore in Domesday mentions 'the land of Turchil, King Edward's steersman' (*VCH Worcestershire* I, 300).

[81] Chadwick, *Institutions*, p. 178, n. 1, where the parallel with Cnut's arrangements is pointed out.

[82] Æthelwine succeeded his brother Æthelwold, who died in 962. For Oslac, see D. Whitelock, 'The Dealings of the English Kings with Northumbria in the Tenth and Eleventh Centuries', *The Anglo-Saxons: Studies in some Aspects of their History and Culture presented to Bruce Dickins*, ed. Peter Clemoes (London, 1959), pp. 77–9.

[83] Fisher listed the various references to the terms *princeps*, *regnum* etc. used in connection with the East Anglian ealdordom and its holders (D. J. V. Fisher, 'The Anti-Monastic Reaction in the Reign of

should arise between such men, evidently possessed both of ability and of ambition. The death of Edgar was the occasion for a head-on collision between Ælfhere of Mercia and Æthelwine of East Anglia.

The outbreak of hostilities must have been long brewing. The disturbances which arose after the death of Edgar centred upon two problems, the disputed succession and the monastic reform movement, in relation to both of which Ælfhere and Æthelwine held opposing views. That Ælfhere had some reason to support Ælfthryth's surviving son has already been demonstrated and it has been suggested that there was some connection between the family of Æthelwine and that of Æthelflæd Eneda, mother of Edward the Martyr.[84] Similarly, in relation to the monastic reform movement, Æthelwine appears as *dei amicus* and Ælfhere as 'the blast of the mad wind which came from the western territories'.[85] But this is from a source close to Oswald; and it is Oswald himself who seems to be the key in this rivalry. He was of course a close friend of Æthelwine, but as has been suggested, the creation of the liberty of Oswaldslow cannot have been welcome to Ælfhere. The fact that Æthelwine was a friend to a man whom Ælfhere must have regarded as a political rival cannot have helped their relationship. But something more basic may be suspected as the root cause of their hostility. It may have originated, as Mr Fisher suggested, in 'some purely personal enmity',[86] in which case it is irrecoverable. But two possibilities may be considered. Firstly, the rise of Ælfhere and his kin coincided with, if it did not cause, a diminution in the power of Athelstan 'Half King' and his family. Before the appointment of Ælfhere and Athelstan *Rota*, Athelstan 'Half King' is likely to have been in charge of central and southern Mercia. Indeed as regards the south-eastern provinces of Mercia it has been suggested that this ealdordom had been held by the father of Athelstan 'Half King' and possibly by his brother also.[87] Athelstan *Rota*'s allegiance is not known; it is perhaps significant that he was brother-in-law to Byrhtnoth of Essex, who became one of Æthelwine's staunchest supporters.[88] But, even if he is regarded as a member of Æthelwine's faction, the fact remains that after 970 it was

---

Edward the Martyr', *Cambridge Hist. Jnl* 10 (1952), 265; see also Hart, 'Athelstan "Half King"', p. 138). For Ælfhere, see the remarks of Plummer (*Two Chronicles* II, 164): '(his) position stands out strongly in the charters and he seems to have retained something of that semi-royal position which Æthelred enjoyed'.

[84] Æthelflæd was the daughter of Ordmær, possibly the same who exchanged Hatfield, Hertfordshire, with Athelstan 'Half King' for land in Devon (*Liber Eliensis*, ed. E. O. Blake, Camden 3rd ser. 92 (London, 1962), 79, n. 6; Hart, 'Athelstan "Half King"', pp. 129–30.

[85] *StO*, p. 444.

[86] Fisher, 'The Anti-Monastic Reaction', p. 269.

[87] It is also possible that Æthelwold, the son of the 'Half King', had hoped to receive the ealdordom of central Wessex, which Eadwig bestowed upon Ælfheah. It had at one time been held by Eadric the brother of the 'Half King' (Hart, 'Athelstan "Half King"', pp. 116, 118, 120 and 126–8).

[88] *Ibid.* p. 126, n. 6.

Ælfhere who seems to have exercised control in this area. Secondly there is the more general question of the precise spheres of influence of Ælfhere and Æthelwine. Æthelwine, in succession to his father and brother, was ealdorman of East Anglia. Naturally this meant East Anglia proper as well as Essex; but it has been shown by Dr Hart that the ealdordom also included the shires which had once been the eastern part of the old kingdom of Mercia and which were still called 'Mercian' in the late tenth century.[89] It was in this area that the reformed Benedictine houses – Ramsey, Peterborough, Thorney and Ely – were established, and it is in this area that the opponents of the movement are found. The *Vita Oswaldi* attributes the disturbances in the eastern districts to the influence of the 'mad wind' from the west, which can scarcely be other than a veiled reference to Ælfhere. He had connections there, for his sister had at some time married Ælfric *cild*, Ælfhere's successor to the ealdordom of Mercia, who held land in Huntingdonshire and bought estates in Northamptonshire for the endowment of Peterborough Abbey.[90] Is there any evidence to suggest that Ælfhere was attempting to encroach upon Æthelwine's sphere of authority? The answer to this question, I suggest, lies in the history of Mercia in the course of the tenth century and it is to this that I wish for a moment to turn.

The separation of 'East' and 'West' Mercians goes back to the division of the old Mercian kingdom, in 877, between the area of Danish settlements in the east, on the one hand, and the West Midlands, on the other; King Ceolwulf, the 'foolish king's thegn' (the description is from the *Anglo-Saxon Chronicle*, a West Saxon source) to whom the Danes had entrusted the whole kingdom in 874, presided over the western portion from 877 until his death in about 879. This arrangement persisted after the Mercians' recognition of King Alfred as their lord. But the history of the former Mercian kingdom under the West Saxon kings was not entirely happy.[91] It might have been expected, for example, that, as Edward and Æthelflæd overran the Danish settlements in the early tenth century, the eastern provinces would revert to the lords of Mercia. But in fact the eastern Mercian provinces (apart from the territory of the Five Boroughs) eventually became part of the ealdordom of East Anglia. Moreover, still more originally Mercian territory was taken over by Wessex. Æthelred, as Lord of Mercia, held the Midlands south and

---

[89] *Ibid.* p. 121; Chadwick, *Institutions*, pp. 198–9.

[90] Robertson, *Charters*, pp. 76–7; *ECEE*, pp. 169 and 178–9. He was the father of Ælfwine, killed at Maldon, to whom Ælfheah bequeathed an estate at Froxfield, Hampshire (Whitelock, *Wills*, p. 22). In *The Battle of Maldon* Ælfwine boasts of his descent from the kin of Ealhhelm, but he also claims kinship with Byrhtnoth, ealdorman of Essex (Gordon, *Battle of Maldon*, p. 56).

[91] One of the supporters of Æthelwold in his rebellion against his cousin Edward the Elder was Byrhtsige, son of the ætheling Berhtnoth, who may have been a scion of the Mercian royal house (*ASC* 904 A, 905 CD (= 903): *Two Chronicles*, ed. Plummer I, 92–5).

west of Watling Street, including Oxford, London and the districts dependent upon them. In 911, on Æthelred's death, Edward took these towns and their dependent regions, which probably included Buckinghamshire, into his own hands.[92] It was in fact probably this area, excluding London, which constituted the later ealdordom of south-eastern Mercia.[93] In 919, Ælfwyn, daughter and heir of Æthelred and Æthelflæd, was carried off into Wessex, never to be heard of again, and the Mercian ealdordom was abolished. It was in the years 919–24 in all probability that the West Midlands were shired without regard to the previous regional and tribal groupings into which the kingdom had been divided. Attributing this act to Edward the Elder, Sir Frank Stenton remarked that 'it was certainly the work of a king who had no respect for the ancient divisions of Mercia'. That his rearrangement aroused opposition in Mercia is clear; Edward's last act was to lead an expedition against Chester and replace the garrison there because it had rebelled against him in alliance with the Welsh.[94] In fact Edward's policy in general meant a diminishing of Mercian autonomy. The burh began to replace the shire as the important unit of organization, and in Wessex itself the number of ealdormen was decreased, each now being responsible for a group of shires, rather than, as before, a single county. Chadwick, who first drew attention to these developments, made some observations on the significance of such changes for the kingdom of Mercia:

...these changes...synchronised apparently with the disappearance of the Mercian national council. One of the king's main objects probably was to prevent the possibility of Mercia again becoming a separate kingdom – an object which would certainly be furthered both by dividing Mercia, as was done in 911, and by combining the southern counties in such a way as to increase the powers of their earls.[95]

Who administered the western shires of Mercia between 919 and 940 we do not know. It is extremely hard to link the ealdormen whose names are

---

[92] *ASC* 912 ACD (= 912): *Two Chronicles*, ed. Plummer I, 96–7; Chadwick, *Institutions*, pp. 206–7; Robertson, *Charters*, pp. 247 and 494.

[93] Hart ('Athelstan "Half King"', p. 116) suggests that Æthelfrith, father of Athelstan 'Half King', held south-eastern Mercia under Ealdorman Æthelred and that Buckinghamshire was included in his *scir*.

[94] F. M. Stenton, *Anglo-Saxon England*, 3rd ed. (London, 1971), p. 337. Professor Sawyer has suggested that the shiring of the West Midlands took place under Æthelred and Æthelflæd, when the borough of Worcester was constructed (P. H. Sawyer, *From Roman Britain to Norman England* (London, 1978), p. 197). But, in view of the connection of the burh of Worcester with the bishop and the fact that the diocese coincided roughly with the *provincia* of the *Hwicce*, it seems unlikely that the *provincia* was divided as a result of the construction of the burh. Moreover the burh of Warwick was not built until 914 (*ASC* 917 A, 915 CD (= 914): *Two Chronicles*, ed. Plummer I, 98–9) and it is highly unlikely that the shire of Warwick predates the burh. For a discussion of the shiring of the West Midlands in general, see D. C. Cox, *VCH Shropshire* III, 3–4.

[95] Chadwick, *Institutions*, p. 225.

recorded in these years with any specific areas.[96] In 940, as we have seen, three ealdormen were appointed to the region which had been the ealdordom of Æthelred: Æthelmund to the north-western provinces, Ealhhelm to central Mercia and Æthelstan to the south-east. The eastern Midlands (apart from the Five Boroughs) were part of the ealdordom of East Anglia of Athelstan 'Half King'.[97] This arrangement still persisted in 957, when 'the northern peoples' withdrew their allegiance from Eadwig and chose Edgar as their king. It is at this moment that the Mercian council, last heard of 'electing' Athelstan as king in 924, makes its reappearance. In the account of a lawsuit concerning Sunbury in Middlesex, which began in Eadwig's reign and continued after the division of 957, it is stated that 'in the meantime it happened that the Mercians chose Edgar as king and gave him control of all the royal prerogatives (7 *him anweald gesealdan ealra cynerihta*)'. The suit was then referred to Edgar for judgement, and the Mercian council (*Myrcna witan*) upheld Eadwig's decision.[98] At the same time references to the pre-Edwardian divisions of Mercia begin to appear again; a charter of Edgar as king of the Mercians, dated 958, refers to the province of the *Magonsæte*, and a little later, in 963, we hear of the province of the *Wreocensætan* (*Wrocensetna*) once more.[99]

This re-emergence (if that is not too strong a word) of the Mercian council and the pre-Edwardian local groupings may have been accompanied by a degree of legal autonomy. In the eleventh century three major divisions of English law were recognized: West Saxon law, Mercian law and the Danelaw. To quote Sir Frank Stenton, 'the recorded points of difference between Mercian and West Saxon law are few and technical'.[100] But, if Mercian law was not obviously different from West Saxon legal custom in content, its geographical limits were quite precise: it operated in Cheshire, Shropshire, Herefordshire, Staffordshire, Worcestershire, Warwickshire, Gloucestershire and Oxfordshire.[101] The question which concerns us here is: at what date was Mercian law recognized as something different from West Saxon law? Alfred used Offa's code in drawing up his own, which rather suggests an attempt to amalgamate the two customs.[102] In view of Edward the Elder's

---

[96] It has been suggested that Uhtred, who signs 930 × 934, held the north-western provinces of Mercia (*ECNENM*, p. 362). See also the following note.

[97] Hart, 'Athelstan "Half King"', p. 121. The three divisions of Mercia may be ancient. Æthelred, Lord of Mercia, probably held the territory of the *Hwicce* himself, to judge from his connection with the burh of Worcester (S 223), and it is possible that Æthelfrith and his eldest son Ælfstan in succession held the south-eastern provinces (see above, p. 160).

[98] Robertson, *Charters*, p. 90.

[99] S 677 and 723; Stenton, *Anglo-Saxon England*, p. 337.   [100] *Anglo-Saxon England*, p. 506.

[101] Chadwick, *Institutions*, p. 198; Stenton, *Anglo-Saxon England*, p. 505.

[102] The fact that this seems to be the last appearance of Offa's code may be significant; however, it is possible that it may survive after all (P. Wormald, '*Lex Scripta* and *Verbum Regis*: Legislation and Germanic Kingship from Euric to Cnut', *Early Germanic Kingship*, ed. P. H. Sawyer and I. N. Wood (Leeds, 1977), p. 112, n. 40).

attitude towards Mercia it is unlikely that he would have accorded it any status, and what little we know of Athelstan suggests that he followed his father's policy. It is true that he was accepted as king by the Mercian council, but that is its last meeting until after 957. Edmund, who appointed three ealdormen to the area, with no one (apparently) to exercise overall authority, is an unlikely candidate to have admitted any corporate identity to the Mercians. The most probable circumstances for any such recognition are those pertaining in 957. The Danelaw, as a recognized legal entity, owed its existence to Edgar, and something of the same kind may have been granted to the Mercians also. The acceptance of Edgar as king by the Mercians in 957 has been seen as the final step in the identification of Mercian and West Saxon interests[103] and this may be true in the sense that there was no question of total Mercian hegemony. But what was the price? In his study of Edgar's relations with the Danelaw Niels Lund suggested that the accession of Edgar to northern England had its background at least partly in the particularism of the Danelaw and Mercia and that he was set up by the magnates of these provinces who wanted to preserve their customary law.[104] In the case of the Danes it is easy to see why they wanted this, since Danish legal custom differed considerably from that of the English. But, as we have seen, the differences between Mercian and West Saxon legal custom were minimal. It is possible that the distinction was made on grounds not so much of legal practice as of political self-consciousness. It is no doubt true that the Mercians were not trying to assert their independence of Wessex, but some form of 'renegotiation of the terms of entry', to use modern parlance, may have been underway. Some indication that Edgar and his supporters may have been receptive to Mercian self-consciousness is provided by the recent work of Dr Nelson, who attributes to Edgar 'an idea of empire smacking more of confederation than autocracy, and harking back, therefore, to an earlier Anglo-Saxon tradition of *ducatus* – leadership of allied peoples, based on consent and common defence interests, as distinct from *regnum* based on conquest and military domination'.[105]

If this analysis is correct, it is interesting that this re-emergence of Mercian self-consciousness coincides almost exactly with the rise of Ælfhere to power. It seems that, though himself a West Saxon, not a Mercian, he became identified to some extent with the aspirations of the people among whom the basis of his power lay. In the years following 957 all the areas formerly held by Ealdorman Æthelred came into his hands. He already held the

[103] D. J. V. Fisher, *The Anglo-Saxon Age* (London, 1973), p. 272; cf. Stenton, *Anglo-Saxon England*, p. 366: 'there is no trace of any particularist feeling behind this revolution'.

[104] Niels Lund, 'King Edgar and the Danelaw', *MScand* 9 (1976), 182.

[105] J. Nelson, 'Inauguration Rituals', *Early Germanic Kingship*, ed. Sawyer and Hill, p. 69.

shires of central Mercia; with the death of Æthelmund in 965 he held direct responsibility for Cheshire, Shropshire, Staffordshire, Herefordshire, Worcestershire, Warwickshire and Gloucestershire. Oxfordshire and Buckinghamshire constituted the ealdordom of Athelstan *Rota* and after his death or retirement in 970 passed into Ælfhere's sole control also. By 970 therefore Ælfhere held the lands of the former Lords of Mercia. What light does this throw on his relations with Æthelwine? The answer, I believe, is that the reconstruction of the Mercian ealdordom under Ælfhere involved the transfer to his control of areas which had once been the preserve of Æthelwine's family, specifically the south-eastern ealdordom comprising Oxfordshire and Buckinghamshire. It is odd that in the eleventh century Oxfordshire was in the region where Mercian law operated, while Buckinghamshire was part of the Danelaw, though it had never been conquered or settled by Danes. The explanation may lie in the struggle between Ælfhere and Æthelwine for the control of this area in the 970s. Ælfhere already held an estate in Oxfordshire, given him by Eadwig.[106] In the late 970s he heard a lawsuit concerning land in Hertfordshire which touched Æthelwine himself. After the death of Edgar the monks of Ely sued Æthelwine and his brothers for possession of Hatfield, which Æthelwine had seized from the abbey, claiming that it was his patrimony.[107] He seems to have had a reasonable case, and, in the event, the monks bought back Hatfield from the brothers in exchange for land in Huntingdonshire.[108] The agreement was made at Slaughter, Gloucestershire, before Ælfhere, Æthelwine (perhaps the son of Æthelmær, ealdorman of Hampshire),[109] Ælfric *cild* (a Huntingdonshire landowner, as we have seen) and 'tota gente que cum eis erat'. The account not only presents an interesting reversal of rôles but also points to Ælfhere's control over south-eastern Mercia in this period. Another indication pointing in the same direction is Æthelred II's grant to him of an estate in Buckinghamshire in 979. But in the later years of Æthelred's reign, after the fall of Ælfric *cild* in 985, Oxfordshire and Buckinghamshire formed part of the ealdordom of Essex.[110] Oxfordshire's position remained ambiguous in

---

[106] S 587.   [107] *Liber Eliensis*, ed. Blake, pp. 79–80.

[108] Æthelwine claimed that the land at Hatfield had been given to his father in exchange for the family patrimony in Devon but that it had been taken from him by Edgar *per violentiam* and given to Ely.

[109] The identification is suggested by Blake (*Liber Eliensis*, p. 80, n. 5). Hart identified the Æthelwine who heard the case as the great ealdorman (*ECEE*, p. 234), but, since he was one of the parties, this seems unlikely. The whole point of hearing the case in Gloucestershire seems to have been to remove the decision from too close proximity to the very powerful defendant. It is perhaps significant that in the same period, between the death of Edgar and the accession of Æthelred II, Æthelwold entertained Ælfric *cild* at Ely, in the company of the ætheling and his mother Queen Ælfthryth (*Liber Eliensis*, ed. Blake, p. 86).

[110] S 883. Leofsige, ealdorman of Essex, appealed unsuccessfully against the actions of Æthelwig, the king's reeve in Buckinghamshire, and Wynsige, the reeve of Oxford. For Æthelred's grant of Olney, Buckinghamshire, to Ælfhere, see below, p. 170.

the eleventh century, for, though it was under Mercian law, it seems to have been in the administrative control of the East Anglian earls; Buckinghamshire definitely became part of the Danelaw.[111] It may well have been the quarrel between Ælfhere and Æthelwine over this area, and its repercussions, which ultimately decided the boundary between *Myrcna laga* and *Dena laga*. Whether the south-eastern ealdordom was the limit of Ælfhere's ambition we cannot tell; his sister's marriage to a man whose interests lay in eastern Mercia is suggestive, especially since Ælfric *cild* was closely associated with Ælfhere and eventually succeeded him. Clearly the quarrel which started over the south-eastern ealdordom quickly spilt over into the eastern Midlands generally. This area, though part of the East Anglian ealdordom, was, as we have seen, inhabited by people described as 'the eastern Mercians'. The *Vita Oswaldi* describes Ælfwold, Æthelwine's brother, standing at their head against the insidious influence of Ælfhere; Byrhtnoth of Essex is also named as one of Æthelwine's supporters. His opponents are not named, but they must have included Ælfric *cild*. The situation was serious, for Æthelwine assembled an army as well as a council and Ælfwold killed one of his opponents, who had seized the land of Peterborough.[112] It is quite understandable that Æthelwine should resent the emergence of a rival who, not content with stepping into the pre-eminent position formerly enjoyed by Æthelwine's father, proceeded to encroach on territory at one time the preserve of his family. But it is also clear that Ælfhere's hostility was the more dangerous because it played upon the suppressed aspirations of the Mercian people.

Ælfhere's activities within his own ealdordom in the same period were inspired by similar motives. There is no reason to regard him as particularly 'anti-monastic'. The attitudes of all parties towards the reform movement were as much political as religious. Æthelwine was no 'friend of God' so far as Ely was concerned, and it has been suggested that only his friendship with Oswald prevented him from being accused of 'anti-monastic' activities himself.[113] All the lay noblemen of the time had cause for alarm at the great increase in wealth and power enjoyed by the reformed monasteries in the 960s and 970s and the sometimes dubious means they employed to acquire land. Ælfhere in most respects displayed the piety normal to a man of his time. He was a benefactor of Abingdon,[114] but his main devotion was to

---

[111] Chadwick (*Institutions*, pp. 198–210) discusses the enlargement of the Danelaw from the Five Boroughs and the kingdom of York to the fifteen counties of the eleventh century, dating the extension to the time of Cnut.

[112] *Liber Eliensis*, ed. Blake, pp. 84–6; *StO*, p. 446. Ælfric *cild* was in dispute with Æthelwold over the endowment of Thorney (*ECEE*, pp. 169 and 178–9).

[113] Fisher, 'The Anti-Monastic Reaction', p. 267.

[114] S 1216.

Glastonbury, to which he gave the estates of Buckland Denham, Orchardleigh and Westbury-on-Severn and the relics of nine 'holy virgins' as well as fulfilling his brother's bequest of Batcombe.[115] He signed an alleged charter of Edgar to Glastonbury as 'ego Elphere dux domine mee sancte Marie Glastoniensis ecclesie libertatem omni devocione cum sigillo sancte crucis confirmavi'.[116] The charter is forged, but it at least preserves the tradition that Ælfhere had some particular fondness for the monastery. It was here that he was buried and his name is listed with those of Athelstan 'Half King' and others 'quorum quilibet centum libratas terre cum multis aliis bonis contulit Glastionie'.[117] His brothers Ælfheah and Ælfwine were also generous with donations and Ælfwine, as we have seen, became a monk there.

It was not therefore hostility to the church or to the reform movement that motivated Ælfhere but political considerations. It has already been suggested that the creation of Oswaldslow was the root cause of Ælfhere's quarrel with the reform movement and lies behind his encouragement of the 'anti-monastic' movement after 975, and the creation of Oswaldslow was itself as much a political as a religious act. The close friendship between Oswald himself and Æthelwine cannot but have exacerbated the tensions already created by the removal of a great part of the ealdorman's territory from his direct power. Worcester itself was too powerful to be directly threatened and most of the leases issued by Oswald in the period 975 to 978 acknowledge the consent of Ælfhere as before.[118] But the other Mercian monasteries, most of them Oswald's foundations,[119] did not fare so well. Winchcombe was disbanded and its abbot Germanus expelled, never to return. This is the only abbey specifically mentioned by the *Vita Oswaldi*, which, like the Ramsey Chronicle, is fairly vague in its accusations.[120] However, Deerhurst, Pershore and Evesham are all known to have been affected, and Pershore and Evesham both preserved traditions about their spoliation which implicate Ælfhere. Ælfhere had particular reasons to be displeased with the reform of Evesham, and, if Pershore possessed a liberty similar to that of Oswaldslow, his motives for attacking that house can readily be understood. But both accounts are late and garbled in transmission. In

[115] *De Antiquitate, Adam de Domerham*, ed. Hearne I, 85 and 100; S 1737, 1747 and 1759–60; Whitelock, *Wills*, p. 125; *John of Glastonbury Cronica*, ed. James P. Carley, BAR Brit. Ser. 47 (1978), I, 22–3; A. Watkin, 'The Great Chartulary of Glastonbury', *Somerset Record Soc.* 64 (1956), 610. Ælfheah also gave land at Cranmore, Somerset (*De Antiquitate, Adam de Domerham*, ed. Hearne I, 86).
[116] S 783.
[117] *John of Glastonbury Cronica*, ed. Carley I, 36.
[118] No leases are extant for 975–6. Those issued in 977 (S 1330–6) and 978 (S 1337–9) all acknowledge the consent both of the king and Ælfhere. It is perhaps significant that the two leases issued by Oswald in the early 970s (S 1328 dated 973 and 1329 dated 974) do not acknowledge Ælfhere's permission.
[119] Knowles, *Monastic Order*, pp. 51–2.
[120] *StO*, pp. 443–5; *Chronicon Abbatiae Rameseiensis*, ed. W. Dunn Macray, RS (London, 1886), pp. 71–3.

particular little can now be gleaned from the Pershore tradition. The house was apparently reformed about 970 and its first abbot was Foldbriht, one of the monks who had followed Æthelwold from Glastonbury to Abingdon.[121] The date of his death is unknown[122] and the history of the abbey in the later tenth century is obscure. The Annals of Pershore are now known only from extracts made by Leland, which record that the wicked earl 'Delfer', presumably Ælfhere, despoiled the abbey of its land but that his heir, Odda, restored to the house all that had been taken from it. The Odda of this story must be Odda of Deerhurst, a kinsman of Edward the Confessor. Leland concluded that he was Ælfhere's son, but this is not possible; Odda does not begin to witness until 1014 and Ælfhere died in 983.[123] However, he was at one time earl of the *Hwicce*, which had formed the heartland of Ælfhere's ealdordom, and could in this sense be described as his heir.[124] He refounded Deerhurst and was buried at Pershore, where his stone coffin was found in 1259.[125] Odda may therefore be regarded as Pershore's benefactor, but whether Ælfhere was really responsible for its decline is less certain. He may have had a motive for attacking it, but the Pershore account is too garbled for any definite conclusion to be drawn.

Deerhurst and Pershore were both Oswald's foundations, though Pershore's abbot had been one of Æthelwold's followers. At Evesham, however, Æthelwold himself was regarded as the founder.[126] On the whole Ælfhere and his kin appear to have been on good terms with Æthelwold and benefactors of Abingdon. But the *Anglo-Saxon Chronicle* speaks of Ælfhere attacking monasteries established by Æthelwold[127] and the Evesham Chronicle specifically accuses him of expelling its monks and seizing its estates. The account may be summarized as follows. The lands which Ealhhelm had seized from the abbey were restored by Edgar, but in the reign of Edward the Martyr 'dux quidam sceleratissimus, Alferus nomine, potentissimus huius patriae dominator' expelled the monks from Evesham (among many other abbeys) and seized Evesham itself and other estates, of which he gave one to his brother Ælfweard, another to his thegns and some to secular clerks. However on his deathbed (i.e., in 983) he repented of his crimes and gave

---

[121] John, *Orbis Britanniae*, pp. 200–3.

[122] Foldbriht witnesses as abbot in 970. He is named as Pershore's first abbot in S 786, the alleged confirmation charter, dated 972. The *Vita Oswaldi* mentions his death and his confession to Abbot Germanus (*StO*, pp. 439–40). Whether this took place before or after Germanus's expulsion from Winchcombe is not entirely clear; John (*Orbis Britanniae*, p. 203, n. 1) dates it before his expulsion, Hart (*ECNENM*, p. 256) afterwards (when St Ælfheah was at Bath, after the suppression of Deerhurst).

[123] Robertson, *Charters*, p. 456; *ECNENM*, p. 350.

[124] E. A. Freeman, *The History of the Norman Conquest of England* (Cambridge, 1867–79) II, 339 and 565.

[125] H. M. and Joan Taylor, *Anglo-Saxon Architecture* (Cambridge, 1965–78) I, 209.

[126] Knowles, *Monastic Order*, p. 52.

[127] *ASC* 975 E: *Two Chronicles*, ed. Plummer I, 121–2.

to the monk Freodegar Evesham itself and Offenham, together with forty hides of his own to replace the land he had shared out among the secular clerks and *aliis amicis suis*. Freodegar, however, was unable to expel the secular clerks and a short while afterwards gave Evesham to a certain powerful man, Godwine *princeps*, in exchange for Towcester, Northamptonshire. Godwine bribed the king to allow this transaction, and the estates passed through various vicissitudes until Abbot Ælfweard, who became abbot of Evesham in 1014, finally regained them. But only on the death of Godwine in the battle of Ashingdon in 1016 did Evesham finally feel secure. Meanwhile the conventual buildings, with the lands held by the secular clerks, passed through a variety of ecclesiastical hands beginning with those of Æthelsige, bishop of Sherborne, who signs for the last time in 990.[128]

Given that Æthelwold was regarded as Evesham's founder, Freodegar is probably to be identified as Frithugar, another of the monks who followed him from Glastonbury to Abingdon. But Evesham's first abbot was Osweard, who signs as abbot between 970 and 974. Frithugar must have been one of his successors. Dr Hart identified him with the Freothegar who, as abbot, signed a charter of Edgar which is wrongly dated 967, but the correct date for it seems to be 972 not 974 as Dr Hart argued, so that the Freothegar who signs it cannot have been abbot of Evesham.[129] Edgar is said to have restored to the abbey the lands held by Ealhhelm, which after Ealhhelm's death (according to the Evesham account) were held by Wulfric and Bishop Oswulf. Oswulf died in 970 and his death may well have been the event which enabled Æthelwold and Edgar to reform the house. But Wulfric is not heard of after 956, and given that Ælfhere from that year was holding the same ealdordom as his father had held, it seems reasonable to assume that he was already holding Evesham's estates as part of his ealdordom. Presumably pressure was brought upon him to restore them to the church. After the death of Edgar he may well have taken the lands back again, but a close look at the Evesham account suggests that there was only one expropriation, that of Godwine. Ælfhere is said to have taken Evesham itself, Offenham, Ombersley, which he gave to his brother Ælfweard, Bevington, which he gave to his thegns (*militibus suis*), and other lands, which he gave to secular clerks. But the restoration attributed to him covered only Evesham and Offenham, with forty hides of his own to replace land once held by the abbey but now granted by him to his 'friends' and to secular clerks. Ombersley cannot therefore have been held by the abbey after the restoration. But it is listed as one of the estates given by Frithugar to Godwine. Now, Ombersley is said to have been given by Ælfhere to his brother Ælfweard. This is the

128 *ECNENM*, p. 290.
129 *Ibid.* pp. 335–6; Sawyer, *Charters of Burton*, p. 36.

only mention of a brother of Ælfhere called Ælfweard, and, while it is not impossible that he had an otherwise unknown brother of this name, it is worth pointing out that the two sons of Ælfheah were called respectively Godwine and Ælfweard. Bevington was not obtained by the church until the eleventh century and may therefore be discounted from the argument.[130] The Evesham account has two spoliations and two restorations in the years following the death of Edgar; I suggest that we have only one of each. Ælfhere, around 970, or perhaps 974 if this is when Frithugar became abbot, restores Evesham and Offenham, with other lands, in such a way as to safeguard the position of the secular clerks of Evesham. This makes it impossible for Frithugar to complete the reform of Evesham, since he cannot get rid of the secular clerks, who no doubt received aid and encouragement from Ælfhere, especially after 975. Finally, after Ælfhere's death, Frithugar gives up the struggle and comes to an arrangement with Godwine, whose interest would arise from the fact that he was Ælfhere's nephew.

The political dispute between Ælfhere and Æthelwine was resolved, if that is the word, by the murder of Edward in 978. What part Ælfhere played in this assassination is unknown. Edward was stabbed to death at Corfe, while visiting his stepmother and half-brother, at the instigation of the 'nobles and chief men' who surrounded Ælfthryth.[131] The *Vita Oswaldi*, which devotes some space to the crime, assigns responsibility to no specific person or persons, but Ælfhere would certainly fall into this general category. It was Ælfhere who superintended the removal of Edward's body from Wareham to Shaftesbury, where it was reinterred with great ceremony in 979.[132] Whether one regards this as 'an attempt at expiation by the guilty party'[133] or not, the murder was followed by the coronation of Ælfhere's young protégé as king and one of Æthelred II's earliest actions was to grant to Ælfhere ten *mansae* at Olney, Buckinghamshire, in the area over which Æthelwine and he had been in dispute.[134]

If the *Liber de Hyde* is right in its estimation of Ælfthryth's favour to Ælfhere we should expect to find him playing an important part during the minority of the young king, and indeed he retained his position as premier ealdorman until his death in 983. He was buried at Glastonbury, and his brother-in-law, Ælfric *cild*, succeeded him as ealdorman of Mercia.[135] But the

[130] Cox, 'Vale Estates of Evesham', p. 32.   [131] *StO*, p. 449.

[132] *ASC* 980 DE (= 979): *Two Chronicles*, ed. Plummer I, 123; *StO*, p. 450.

[133] Fisher, 'The Anti-Monastic Reaction', p. 269. Far from implicating Ælfhere in the murder the *Passio* of Edward represents him as indignant at the king's miserable burial and zealous in the move to translate the body (Christine Fell, *Edward King and Martyr* (Leeds, 1971), pp. 8–9).

[134] S 834.

[135] *ASC* 983 CDE: *Two Chronicles*, ed. Plummer I, 124–5. For Ælfhere's burial at Glastonbury, see *John of Glastonbury Cronica*, ed. Carley I, 36. His brother Ælfheah was buried there also (Whitelock, *Wills*, p. 121).

family did not retain its position long. Ælfric *cild* was exiled for treason of an unspecified kind in 985 and the ealdordom of Mercia was left vacant until 1007.[136] It is not certain whether Ælfhere was ever married[137] and no children are recorded.[138] Nor did his brothers' children ever acquire the rank or influence he and Ælfheah had enjoyed. Godwine, Ælfheah's son, is the only one of whom we can say anything positive, if he is indeed the Godwine *princeps* mentioned in the Evesham Chronicle, as suggested above. The Evesham account says that Godwine *princeps*, holder of Towcester, North-amptonshire, was killed at the Battle of Ashingdon in 1016. He can perhaps be identified with Godwine, ealdorman of Lindsey, whose death in that battle is recorded in the *Anglo-Saxon Chronicle*.[139] He in turn is probably the Godwine who led an English force against a host of Danes who had ravaged Northumbria and Lindsey in 993; the English defeat was attributed by the *Chronicle* to the flight of Godwine and the two other English leaders, Fræna and Frithugist. Fræna, like Godwine, was a Northamptonshire thegn, if he is to be identified with Frane *æt Rogingeham* (Rockingham, Northamptonshire), who was a benefactor of Peterborough.[140] Whether Godwine Ælfheah's son is Godwine of Lindsey is not certain, but, given the connection of both with Ælfhere, the balance of probability is in favour of the identification. All the same, even if Godwine Ælfheah's son did obtain a military command in

---

[136] *ASC* 985 CDE: *Two Chronicles*, ed. Plummer I, 124–5; S 896 and 937. The charge, as recorded in S 937, recalls the accusation of the *Chronicle* against Eadric Streona in 1016: 'he betrayed his royal lord and all the nation of the English' (*ASC* 1016 CDE: *Two Chronicles*, ed. Plummer I, 152). Leofwine, who begins to witness as *dux* in 994, may have been ealdorman of Mercia, but more probably he held only the province of the *Hwicce*. This was certainly his position after Eadric Streona became ealdorman of the whole of Mercia in 1007 (*ASC* 1007 CDE: *Two Chronicles*, ed. Plummer I, 138; *ECNENM*, p. 344; Pauline Stafford, 'The Reign of Æthelred II, a Study in the Limitations on Royal Policy and Action', *Ethelred the Unready: Papers from the Millenary Conference*, ed. David Hill, BAR Brit. Ser. 59 (1978), 29, n. 69).

[137] A widow called Eadflæd held land at Wormleighton, where Ælfhere had possessed an estate. This manor and two others belonging to the same woman were seized by Ælfric *cild* but subsequently forfeited to the king, who gave them to Abingdon (S 896 and 937). It is possible that she was Ælfhere's widow.

[138] Florence of Worcester describes Ælfric *cild* as Ælfhere's son (*Florentii Wigornensis Monachi Chronicon ex Chronicis*, ed. B. Thorpe (London, 1848–9) I, 147 and 148). This is probably an inference from the fact that Ælfric succeeded him as ealdorman of Mercia. An Abingdon source gives Ælfhere two sons, Eadric *major domus regiae* and Eadwine, abbot of Abingdon (*Chron Abingd* I, 357), but comparison with Florence shows that this Eadric is to be identified either with Ælfric *cild* or with Ælfric ealdorman of Hampshire (*FW Chron*, ed. Thorpe I, 147, n. 5; Simon Keynes, *The Diplomas of King Æthelred 'the Unready' 978–1016* (Cambridge, 1980), p. 177, n. 91). The suggestion that Odda of Deerhurst was the son of Ælfhere has already been discussed (see above, p. 168). Dr Hart calls Godwine a son of Ælfhere rather than Ælfheah (*ECNENM*, p. 336; cf. Robertson, *Charters*, p. 458). It is true that only Ælfweard is definitely said to be the son of both Ælfheah and Ælfswith his wife, but this need not mean he was not Ælfheah's son (Whitelock, *Wills*, pp. 22 and 24).

[139] *ASC* 1016: *Two Chronicles*, ed. Plummer II, 198.

[140] *ASC* 993 DEF: *Two Chronicles*, ed. Plummer I, 126–7; *ECEE*, p. 244.

The laws of Cnut and the history of Anglo-Saxon royal promises

PAULINE STAFFORD

The 'first' and 'second' law codes of Cnut are the last surviving codes issued in the name of an Anglo-Saxon king.[1] They are the final fruit of the interest in kingship and law and in the inter-relationship of the two which characterized the period following the monastic revival in England and which is especially associated with the name of Wulfstan, archbishop of York. Although they are far from being complete codifications of Anglo-Saxon law, they draw extensively on earlier legislation. They are different in kind from much tenth-century law, which is usually more limited and administrative in content and character, and their nature and purpose invite further consideration.

Cnut's laws, like the later laws of Æthelred, have been convincingly attributed by Professor Whitelock to the hand of Archbishop Wulfstan.[2] His characteristic style is clear through to the concluding homiletic clause of II Cnut, and there can be little doubt that he was responsible for the entire final form of both codes. A shorter piece of legislation from Cnut's reign, preserved in Cambridge, Corpus Christi College 201 (designated D), is also attributed to Wulfstan's hand, and Professor Whitelock has demonstrated its priority in time to the two full codes. She sees the D code as the product of the meeting of king and witan at Oxford in 1018. The preamble speaks of a meeting of the witan at which *frið* and *freondscip* were established between the Danes and the English, and its first clause refers to a general undertaking to observe the laws of King Edgar. The *Anglo-Saxon Chronicle* for 1018

---

[1] My thanks are due to Patrick Wormald, who read an earlier draft of this paper, to Dr Janet Nelson for comment and criticism and for her generous help on the dating of the Anglo-Saxon coronation *ordines*, and especially to Dr Simon Keynes for detailed criticism from which this paper benefited enormously.

[2] See Dorothy Whitelock, 'Wulfstan and the Laws of Cnut', *EHR* 63 (1948), 433–52, and 'Wulfstan's Authorship of Cnut's Laws', *EHR* 69 (1955), 72–85. See also now the important article by Patrick Wormald, 'Æthelred the Lawmaker', *Ethelred the Unready: Papers from the Millenary Conference*, ed. D. Hill, BAR, Br. Ser. 59 (Oxford, 1978), 47–80, and my own forthcoming 'Laws of Æthelred and Anglo-Saxon Lawmaking'. On Wulfstan generally, see D. Bethurum, 'Wulfstan', *Continuations and Beginnings*, ed. E. G. Stanley (London, 1966), pp. 210–46. References to the laws throughout are to the edition of F. Liebermann, *Die Gesetze der Angelsachsen* (Halle, 1903–16) I.

mentions a meeting convened in Oxford (following the paying off of Cnut's Danish fleet), at which the Danes and the English reached an agreement, and one manuscript adds that this was done 'according to Edgar's law'.[3] This must be the meeting which issued the D code. The preamble to D also states that the witan 'agreed that they would, with God's help, investigate further at leisure what was necessary for the nation'.[4] Professor Whitelock argues that this further thought resulted in the codes now known as I and II Cnut, which incorporate material from D. In other words D should be regarded as a separate piece of legislation, inspired and written by Wulfstan in 1018,[5] which then formed one of the several codes used by him in drawing up I and II Cnut.

Closer examination of the structure and content of I and II Cnut not only confirms the use of D in their compilation but reveals more of the methods and intentions of their compiler. I Cnut is the religious code, so distinguished by its content although its preamble does not refer to it specifically in this way.[6] It is essentially a development of certain parts of the D code, but substantial sections have been added. Two sections have been lifted from VIII Æthelred, that on Church *grið*[7] and that on sanctuary and the behaviour of priests.[8] Elsewhere the compiler has combined various earlier laws to provide a complete statement on a particular theme, as for example when he treats ecclesiastical dues[9] and feasts and fasts.[10] Much of the material is taken from Wulfstan's own work and from earlier legislation associated with the archbishop. Thus, whenever it draws upon D it is drawing largely from V and VI Æthelred, which themselves provide the bulk of D's content, whilst much of the extra material is from VIII Æthelred. The code ends with

---

[3] *Anglo-Saxon Chronicle* 1018 D: *Two of the Saxon Chronicles Parallel*, ed. C. Plummer (Oxford 1892–9) I, 154.

[4] 'and hig gecwædan þæt hi furðor on æmtan smeagan woldan þeode þearfe mid Godes filste': Whitelock, 'Wulfstan and the Laws of Cnut', p. 440.

[5] It may well not represent word for word the enactments of Oxford 1018. Cf. Wormald on the relationship of V and VI Æthelred and related texts to the meeting at King's Enham, 'Æthelred the Lawmaker', pp. 49–58.

[6] In this it is similar to II Edgar which begins simply 'Ðis is seo gerædnys þe Eadgar cyng mid his witena geðeahte gerædde, Gode to lofe 7 him sylfum to cynescipe 7 eallum his leodscipe to þearfe' (MS G), whereas the secular ordinance III Edgar begins 'Þis is ðonne seo worldcunde gerædnes, þe ic wille þæt man healde' (MS D). I Cnut begins 'Ðis is seo gerædnes, þe Cnut ciningc mid his witena geþeahte geredde, Gode to lofe 7 hym sylfum to þearfe; 7 þæt wæs...' (MS A). II Cnut begins 'Þis is seo woruldcund gerædnes, þe ic wylle mid minan witenan ræde, þæt man healde ofer eall Englaland' (MS G). The links and similarities between I and II Cnut and Edgar's laws demonstrate the desire to observe earlier legislation and perhaps suggest that Wulfstan was in some way responsible for the preservation of texts of Edgar's codes.

[7] I Cnut 2.3 – 3.1 (cf. VIII Æthelred 1–5).

[8] I Cnut 4–5.4 (cf. VIII Æthelred 18–27.1, omitting 26).

[9] I Cnut 8–14 combines material from D with VIII Æthelred 7, 8, 10, 11 and 11.1 and II Edgar 2, 2.1 and 2.2.

[10] I Cnut 14.1 – 17.3 is largely made up of material from D plus II Edgar 5.

sections from a Wulfstan homily,[11] quotations from Wulfstan's *Canons of Edgar*,[12] and a section on bishops, the tenor of which, if not its precise wording, links it with *Polity*.[13] There are novel chapters. Most are of an exhortatory type and can be matched elsewhere in Wulfstan's work;[14] only one contains significant new ideas on lordship.[15] I Cnut is a systematic and very complete statement on the questions of church peace and sanctuary, priestly purgation and status, and ecclesiastical dues and feast days, and less so on sexual sins. All are concerns which were close to Wulfstan's heart.

Cnut's 'second' or secular code draws far less on D and on the 'Wulfstan' laws of Æthelred. A preliminary glance might suggest that it is the addition of Edgar's laws to D, as agreed at Oxford in 1018. Its opening section and several other chapters derive from Edgar's 'third' code.[16] But II Cnut does far more than merely incorporate III Edgar into D. Like I Cnut it deals fully and systematically with a number of topics: royal rights, court procedures, surety and so on. It utilizes earlier law in exactly the same way as I Cnut. Wherever a full statement on a topic is available in earlier legislation it is lifted into II Cnut, just as the section on *grið* is taken from VIII Æthelred into I Cnut. Elsewhere a codification of statements on a given topic is compiled from several sources. Thus II Cnut on surety is taken from I Æthelred, which contains a full and sophisticated statement on this subject.[17] Similarly II Cnut on breach of *borh* derives from Alfred's law on this topic.[18] Where no full statement exists in prior legislation II Cnut compiles one. The section on courts and their meetings and the procedures of hundred and tithing, II Cnut 17–22.3, is taken largely from III Edgar but with amplifications from elsewhere[19] and some novel additions.[20] The section on procedures is drawn from many sources.[21] In the case of marital offences, a few statements from earlier legislation are amplified with many *apparently* novel decrees.[22] II Cnut

[11] I Cnut 22–22.4 (cf. *Wulfstan. Sammlungen der ihm zugeschriebenen Homilien nebst Untersuchungen über ihre Echtheit*, ed. A. Napier (Berlin, 1883), pp. 20–1).

[12] I Cnut 22.5 and 22.6 (cf. *Wulfstan's Canons of Edgar*, ed. Roger Fowler, EETS o.s. 266 (London, 1972), ch. 22).

[13] I Cnut 26 (cf. *Die 'Institutes of Polity, Civil and Ecclesiastical'*, ed. K. Jost, Swiss Stud. in Eng. 47 (Bern, 1959), ch. 5, p. 62).

[14] E.g., I Cnut 4.1 and 4.2, 18, 23, 24 and 25.

[15] I Cnut 20–20.2; see below, n. 25.

[16] II Cnut 15.1 – 18.1 (cf. III Edgar 2–5.2, with some additions); II Cnut 20a (cf. III Edgar 6); II Cnut 25–6 (cf. III Edgar 7–7.3).

[17] II Cnut 30–33.2 (cf. I Æthelred 1.1–4.3, omitting 3 and adding I Cnut 31a).

[18] II Cnut 57–9 (cf. Alfred 3, 4.2 and 7).

[19] II Cnut 22 (cf. Æthelred 1.1); II Cnut 19 (cf. Ine 9).

[20] These are sometimes (but not invariably) given in the first person plural, indicating that this is what *we* add (e.g., II Cnut 20 and 20.1).

[21] II Cnut 22.3 (cf. II Athelstan 23.2); II Cnut 23 (cf. II Æthelred 8); II Cnut 23.1 (cf. *Swerian* 8); II Cnut 24 (cf. IV Edgar 6.2).

[22] There are parallels between II Cnut 50–54.1 and Edward and Guthrum 4 and the Penitential of Pseudo-Theodore ch. 19.8 (ptd *Ancient Laws and Institutes of England*, ed. B. Thorpe (London, 1840)).

thus follows the same principle of compilation as I Cnut's. Both seek to provide extensive statements on a variety of topics drawing on earlier legislation with a limited amount of emendation and addition.

Three sections do not at first sight accord with this principle: chs. 12, 14 and 15, chs. 61–66.1 and chs. 69–83. There are virtually no precedents in earlier legislation for the content of any of these. However, the first two groups fit into the logic and general intentions of I and II Cnut. Chs. 12, 14 and 15 are the famous statements of the king's pleas in Wessex and the Danelaw. They are part of an extensive section, II Cnut 8–15.3, dealing with the king's rights, covering such areas as the coinage, weights and measures, the *trimoda necessitas*, forfeiture by holders of bookland and so on. Chs. 61–66.1 deal with major and often bootless crimes such as *griðbryce*, *hamsocne*, *reaflac* and harbouring outlaws. As elsewhere in I and II Cnut these crimes are drawn together. They are the great crimes which the king and his agents will suppress, using the mechanisms and procedures dealt with in earlier parts of II Cnut. They are followed in chs. 67–68.3 by admonitions on the making of just judgements, and on the need to take such factors as age, status and compulsion into account. These could be read as a rounding off of the extensive treatment of crimes and procedures for bringing criminals to justice which constitute chs. 16–66.1, though they also link these with the following sections on abuses and royal oppressions. Up to ch. 68.3 II Cnut shows a unity of purpose and treatment. Most of it is traceable to earlier law or presents a systematic statement on some new topic. There are interesting additions. Some merely amplify earlier law or make it more precise.[23] Others reflect a desire to specify the situation in the Danelaw[24] or to deal with problems of lordship,[25] two matters which may have been of particular concern to Cnut's advisers.

I and II Cnut are excellent examples of skilled legal drafting, sophisticated and knowledgeable codifications comparable to, for example, I Æthelred. Their association with Wulfstan requires emphasis. Other laws associated with the archbishop, such as V, VI, VII and VIII Æthelred, have earned an evil reputation among legal historians.[26] Yet when his purpose required it Wulfstan could clearly produce detailed, precise and codified legal statement. Further enquiry into Cnut's laws may reveal the nature of that purpose. Chs.

For earlier though not identical legislation on rape, adultery and concubinage, see Æthelberht 10, 11, 14, 16, 31 and 35; Wihtred 3, 4 and 5; Alfred 8, 11, 25 and 29; and the decrees of the papal legates, *Councils and Ecclesiastical Documents*, ed. A. Haddan and W. Stubbs (Oxford, 1869–71) III, 453 and 455–6.

[23] See, e.g., II Cnut 19.1, 19.2, 20, 22.1, 22.1a, 24.1, 24.2, 24.3, 29.1 and 30.3a.

[24] E.g., II Cnut 15.1a, 15.3 and 15.

[25] I Cnut 20.1 and 20.2 and II Cnut 20.1, 22.2 and 27.

[26] H. G. Richardson and G. O. Sayles, *Law and Legislation from Æthelberht to Magna Carta* (Edinburgh, 1966), p. 27.

69–83 of II Cnut, which remain to be considered, may hold the key. They were certainly included in the code by Wulfstan, since the only two chapters which can be paralleled are linked to his work.[27] In certain respects their content associates them with that concern for the Danelaw which has been seen as a theme in Cnut's laws, and they must therefore be connected in some way with its general purposes; but in others they stand apart from the rest of I and II Cnut. They do not codify any topic or topics and their content is almost entirely novel. They have an internal coherence, however, deriving from a distinct subject matter. Ch. 69 opens with the words 'Now this is the mitigation (*lihtingc*) by which I wish to protect all the people from what they were hitherto oppressed with all too greatly.' The theme which binds chs. 69–83 together and separates them from the rest of the code is 'mitigation'. The use of the first person singular in ch. 69 is of some interest. Elsewhere in II Cnut it appears only in the prologue and in ch. 1. The use of the king's personal statement in this way as a sort of authentication occurs at the beginning of other codes.[28] Its occurrence at the beginning of ch. 69 raises the possibility that these thematically unified chapters once existed as a separate piece of legislation.

Chs. 69–83 deal with abuses of lordship, to some extent those of all lordship but specifically those of the lordship of the king. Ch. 69 itself deals with extortion by royal officials. The king promises that from now on they will provide for him from his own property. Chs. 70 and 70.1 concern the devolution of the property of the intestate, protecting them against arbitrary forfeiture. The payment of heriot provides a guarantee against such arbitrary action. Ch. 71 therefore defines the level of heriots to be paid. Chs. 72, 73 and 74 protect the rights of widows and children, including provisions for their peaceful enjoyment of property and the protection of widows and maidens from forced marriage. The same ideas of limiting liability and responsibility, and therefore the opportunities for unjust forfeiture and exaction, emerge in chs. 75 and 76, which deal with crimes committed with stolen weapons and the limited liability of wives and children for crimes of theirs husbands and fathers. Ch. 77 considers desertion of the lord on the battlefield, but specifically the fate of the property of the deserter – the lord may take it but the bookland goes to the king. Ch. 78 remits the heriot of a man who dies before his lord in battle, by implication defending the rights of his heirs without such a payment. Ch. 79 defends the right of any man who has fulfilled the obligations arising from his land during his lifetime to

---

[27] II Cnut 73, on the remarriage of widows (cf. VI Æthelred 26.1); II Cnut 76.2, limiting the liability of a wife and child (cf. *Wulfstan*, ed. Napier, p. 158).

[28] See III Edgar 1 and 1.1 and the fragment of X Æthelred Prologue and Prologue 2. Wormald ('Æthelred the Lawmaker', p. 53) suggested that X Æthelred might be the official version of the Enham decrees.

pass it on uncontested. Ch. 80 protects the rights of all men from the king downwards over their hunting, and ch. 81 guarantees the peaceful possession of gifts from the lord. Ch. 82 is a general guarantee of all men's peace, and the whole section closes with a general warning in ch. 83 to all who might violate it. The final chapter of II Cnut is 84, a lengthy, homiletic warning in Wulfstan's style of the need to love God and obey the law. It is significant that chs. 69–83 had not only a distinctive beginning but also a separate ending. Their overall object is thus the eradication of abuses. Although other lords are sometimes specified, it is clear that most of these are abuses of royal power. The chapters deal with heriots, widows, heirs, forfeitures, orphans and the passing on of land, and they are designed to protect a man's landholding and inheritance from rapacious and arbitrary action. They guarantee the rights of all men to their land, hunting and so on, and they guarantee the peaceful enjoyment of land so long as the obligations from it are fulfilled. Those obligations in terms of heriot and the circumstances of its rightful remission are specified.

No historian of Norman or Angevin England could fail to see parallels in conception and content between these last chapters of the laws of Cnut and the coronation charter of Henry I or even to see presages of the Great Charter itself. At the opening of ch. 69 Cnut offered a mitigation and protection from those things by which the English were formerly oppressed. In the first chapter of his coronation charter[29] Henry I promised to take away all those evil customs by which the kingdom was unjustly oppressed. The specified nature of these evil customs and their proposed remedies offer some remarkable parallels with Cnut's law: the need of widows and wards to be protected (chs. 3 and 4), the just level of reliefs by which land shall be redeemed (ch. 2), the rights to devise money and make a will (ch. 7), rights over royal forests (ch. 10) and the nature of landholding by military service (ch. 11). These are again potentially the abuses of all lordship, but specifically those of the king's lordship as practised, or malpractised, by Henry's brother William Rufus.[30] Some specific exactions, such as *monetagium* referred to in ch. 5, are Norman innovations and we should expect no parallel in Cnut's laws, just as the consequences of death on the battlefield in Cnut's law could be a problem particular to the early eleventh century and the fight against the Vikings. In chs. 9 and 13 of his charter Henry I harks back to the good old law of King Edward's days. Cnut's references to the laws of Edgar do not occur in I and II Cnut but they have a similar significance. In its offers to eschew the unjust actions of the king as overlord, the coronation charter

---

[29] The coronation charter of Henry I is ptd Liebermann, *Gesetze* I, 521–3, and *The Laws of the Kings of England from Edmund to Henry I*, ed. A. J. Robertson (Cambridge, 1925), pp. 276–83.

[30] See Henry I's coronation charter, ch. 6. A revised translation of ch. 6 is offered by S. E. Thorne, 'Henry I's Coronation Charter, c. 6', *EHR* 93 (1978), 794.

of Henry I provides general and detailed comparisons with chs. 69–83 of II Cnut.

Could these chapters of II Cnut be the equivalent of a coronation charter issued by Cnut at the beginning of his reign and perhaps originally codified in a separate document? The great political importance of such a document could easily have led to its incorporation into I and II Cnut. It would simply have been one of the many pieces of existing legislation on which the compiler of I and II Cnut drew, copied out in its entirety precisely because of its significance. There is even an attested meeting of the witan at which this charter could have been promulgated. II Cnut 30.1 refers to a *gemot* at Winchester as a limit of legal memory:[31] this was presumably a meeting early in Cnut's reign which made legal pronouncements, to be dated before I and II Cnut (which were issued at Christmas at Winchester, 1020 × 1023). But to date this Winchester meeting to 1016 × 1017 and to assign to it the issue of a coronation charter is to pile speculation upon speculation. The plausibility and possibility of Cnut's having issued a coronation charter and the general significance of his great legal statement in I and II Cnut require further investigation.

The coronation charter of Henry I has been interpreted as a specific application of the general terms of his coronation oath.[32] That same coronation oath was taken not only by Henry but also by Anglo-Saxon kings from the late tenth century onwards.[33] By it the king promised to defend and keep in peace the church and the Christian people, to forbid and extirpate robbery and wicked deeds and to ensure that all judgements were made with justice and mercy. The oath was normally accompanied by a sermon on the duties of Christian kingship. The admonition as delivered by Dunstan in the late tenth century stressed the need to protect widows, stepchildren and foreigners, to deliver no wrong judgement, to forbid theft, adultery and incest, to destroy witches and wizards, to drive out kinslayers and perjurers, to give alms to the old and needy and to have wise and chaste counsellors and stewards.[34] Both the oath and the sermon are glossed extensively by the laws of Cnut. I Cnut defines the rights and freedoms of the church which

---

[31] Those who have not failed in oath or ordeal since this *gemot* are to be treated leniently. This chapter re-enacts the similar limit of legal memory in I Æthelred 1.2, which refers back to the prior *gemot* at *Bromdun*. Wormald ('Æthelred the Lawmaker', p. 63) dated *Bromdun* to Æthelred's coming of age in 984–5. It might date closer to his accession. III Athelstan 3 demonstrates that such limits of legal memory are not always coronations, comings of age etc.

[32] R. Foreville, 'Le Sacre des rois anglo-normands et angevins et le serment du sacre (XI–XIIe siècles)', *Proceedings of the Battle Conference on Anglo-Norman Studies, 1978*, ed. R. Allen Brown (Ipswich), 1979, p. 57; *Select Charters*, ed. W. Stubbs, 9th ed. (Oxford, 1913), p. 116.

[33] This oath is ptd *Memorials of St Dunstan*, ed. W. Stubbs, Rolls Ser. (London, 1874), pp. 355–7. For its date, see below, p. 185.

[34] See *Memorials*, ed. Stubbs, pp. 356–7. This consecration address follows the oath in London, British Library, Cotton Cleopatra B. xiii (56r) and Oxford, Bodleian Library, Junius 60 (2r), the latter being a copy made from BL Cotton Vitellius A. vii before the fire of 1731.

the king is to uphold. II Cnut deals with great crimes and the necessary procedures for bringing men to justice, the making of just judgements and all the categories of wicked evil-doers of whom Dunstan spoke. Cnut's laws thus make more explicit the ideas expressed in the king's coronation oath, constituting, as they do, an extensive statement of the duties of Christian kingship. They also contain a section on royal rights. This is the counterpart of the stress on the king's duties in his oath, and it is conceivable that the king's own 'further thought' after Oxford 1018 led to the inclusion of such definition. If royal rights are not to be abused they should be clearly known. Again Cnut's laws fit into the idea of 'just kingship'. Finally, I and II Cnut represent the adoption and restatement of much tenth-century legislation in the name of an incoming conqueror. 'The laws of Edgar', so often referred to early in Cnut's reign,[35] should be understood, following Professor Whitelock's suggestion, as 'the laws of the English', 'customary law', 'the good old law', rather than simply as II–IV Edgar.[36] They are the equivalent of references to the laws of Edward the Confessor in the reigns of William I and Henry. A conquering king is being asked to subscribe to the laws of the conquered people. He is also guaranteeing the good law of the past, with the imputation, as we shall see, that it had recently been abused. Cnut's laws thus gloss his coronation oath, define and express the rights and duties of a Christian king and respect the laws of the conquered. If Cnut issued a coronation charter it would find an obvious place in those laws as a specific development of the coronation oath and as another expression of the relationship between conquered people and conqueror. A coronation charter would have a logical home in II Cnut, but did it ever have a separate existence?

II Cnut 69–83 show signs of having been a separate piece of legislation, but that need not necessarily mean that they represent a distinct coronation charter. In his recent study of the laws of Æthelred, Patrick Wormald dealt with the legislation issued by that king in 1014 on the occasion of his return from exile. He suggested that VIII Æthelred, a purely ecclesiastical code, represents only half the legislation of that year. The secular counterpart has 'sunk without trace' into the laws of Cnut.[37] I Cnut has been seen to draw heavily on VIII Æthelred. It is likely that II Cnut would have drawn on some lost secular legislation of that year, especially since, like VIII Æthelred, it would presumably have been the work of Wulfstan. The relationship between this lost legislation and the surviving II Cnut must be hypothetical. Some of the codified sections of II Cnut may have first appeared in the 1014 secular

---

[35] See, e.g., *ASC* 1018 D, in *Two Chronicles*, ed. Plummer I, 154; the preamble to the D code of Cnut's laws; Cnut's letter of 1020. Other laudatory references to Edgar are associated with Wulfstan, e.g. *ASC* 963 D (*ibid.* pp. 114–15).

[36] Cf. M. Clanchy, 'Remembering the Past, and the Good Old Law', *History* 55 (1970), 165–76.

[37] Wormald, 'Æthelred the Lawmaker', p. 59.

code, just as the laws on church *grið* were first brought together in VIII
Æthelred and then lifted into I Cnut. But it is unlikely that *all* the codified
sections of II Cnut are to be so explained. Comparison between I Cnut, VIII
Æthelred and D shows that, although I Cnut utilized both the others, it drew
on other legislation to achieve its purpose. Some of the systematic statements
in II Cnut were probably gathered there for the first time. But it is conceivable
that the totally 'novel' sections of II Cnut represent Æthelred's legislation
of 1014. Although that law itself is lost, we know enough of the circumstances
of its issue to guess at its content.

After Swein's death the witan decided to send to Æthelred, 'and they said
that no lord was dearer to them than their natural lord, if he would govern
them more justly than he did before'. Æthelred responded by sending his
son Edward, who conveyed a message from the king 'and said that he would
be a gracious lord to them, and reform all the things which they all hated;
and all the things that had been said and done against him should be
forgiven... And complete friendship was then established with oath and
pledge (*mid worde and mid wedde*) on both sides.'[38] Æthelred was received back
on condition that he would rule better, remedy hated abuses, forgive injuries
and be a true lord. His commitment to these conditions was sealed by an oath.
This suggests that the lost legislation would have been concerned with
precisely the sort of abuses of royal power contained in II Cnut 69–83, abuses
of royal lordship which the king eschews in his promise to be *hold hlaford*.
The form of VIII Æthelred shows that the legislation which issued from such
commitments was fuller than a simple list of royal abuses. Inevitably Wulfstan
would have desired to define 'true lordship' in broader terms and to stress
that such lordship was concerned with the establishment of right law. VIII
Æthelred thus provides a detailed definition of certain church rights which
were probably guaranteed in some more general commitment to ecclesiastical
liberties in 1014. The final form of the lost secular legislation might thus have
been similar to II Cnut. Wulfstan would have had the same end in view in
both cases, a legal commentary on 'just kingship'. II Cnut 69–83 may thus
represent the original specific commitments which Æthelred made in 1014.
They would have been incorporated in the final legislation of that year in
the same way and for the same reasons as a coronation charter of Cnut would
have been included in his full code. Whether they preserve the specific form
of the 1014 commitments[39] or merely their content, an ultimate origin here
for these chapters of Cnut's laws is a distinct possibility.

The inclusion of these chapters in the laws of Cnut shows that Cnut also

---

[38] *ASC* 1014 C: *Two Chronicles*, ed. Plummer I, 145 (text); *The Anglo-Saxon Chronicle: a Revised Translation*,
ed. Dorothy Whitelock *et al.* (London, 1961; rev. 1965), p. 93 (translation).

[39] There are difficulties in seeing them as such since no ecclesiastical rights or abuses are mentioned.
The same problem arises in accepting them simply as a coronation charter, since again reference to
the liberties of the church would be expected.

committed himself to eradicate these abuses. That commitment may date from no earlier than I and II Cnut themselves, i.e. 1020 × 1023. But such commitments are often undertaken very early in a reign. Promises of good government and respect for English law were required of William I at his coronation, as we shall see. Henry I's coronation charter shows a king securing his position early in a new reign with promises of good government and vilification of his predecessor. If I and II Cnut represent a general adherence to Anglo-Saxon law, consolidating a series of promises from the coronation oath through the undertakings at Oxford in 1018 to this final definition of 'just kingship', do chs. 69–83 record an earlier and specific set of commitments? Did Cnut issue a coronation charter to secure support and to cast aspersions on the reputation, and thus the heirs, of his predecessor? There can be no certain answer to this question, but its probability is linked to the political circumstances early in Cnut's reign.

The years from 1014 to 1020 were a time of turmoil. Æthelred had returned from exile and had made undertakings to reform abuses which would have been fresh in the minds of many. The months following his death on 23 April 1016 saw a hard fight for the throne between Cnut and Edmund Ironside. This culminated in a division of the kingdom which was reversed only by Edmund's untimely death on 30 November 1016. The first statement in the *Anglo-Saxon Chronicle* for 1017 is that in this year Cnut 'feng to eall Angelcynnes rice' (MS E), 'feng to eall Engla landes rice' (MS D). *Feng to rice* is the phrase normally used to describe royal accessions and their attendant ceremonies in the tenth and eleventh centuries and it seems most probable that Cnut was consecrated in the winter of 1016–17, with the haste later exhibited by William I and Henry. His position at this date was not entirely secure. Edmund Ironside had sons, admittedly young; but he also had younger brothers. One of these, Eadwig, was in England in 1017 almost certainly trying to make good his claims. Edmund's two half-brothers, Emma's sons Edward and Alfred, were in Normandy with their mother and her powerful family. The enigmatic reference later in 1017 to the expulsion of an Eadwig king of the peasants (*ceorla kyning*) argues for other disturbances and difficulties in these early months of Cnut's reign.[40] The king's insecurity in the winter of 1016–17 is perhaps reflected by his appointment of the Englishman Eadric to the important ealdormanry of Mercia and by his own decision not to trust Wessex to any subordinate but to keep it in his own hands. Before the end of 1017 he was feeling sufficiently assured to act in a more arbitrary fashion. Several prominent Englishmen, including Eadric, were slain; Eadwig the ætheling and Eadwig, king of the ceorls, were driven

---

[40] The possibility of peasant risings as early as this should not be ruled out: see R. H. Hilton, *Bond Men Made Free* (London, 1973), ch. 2, esp. pp. 64–71.

out and by August Cnut had brought Emma back from Normandy and had married her. The successful negotation of this marriage, which neutralized potential Norman and possible English support for Emma's disinherited sons, may have formed the basis for this new confidence. But the political situation of the winter of 1016–17 could have led to a conciliatory gesture on Cnut's part, especially one which stressed the abuses of the rule of a predecessor whose sons were still active contenders for the throne. Cnut made other moves to vilify Æthelred's memory early in his reign.[41] His subsequent activity shows him capable of conciliation when the situation required it. The acceptance of Edgar's law at Oxford in 1018 may have been prompted as much by trouble in Scandinavia as by a desire for legitimation. Cnut spent part of 1019 in Denmark sorting out his difficulties, and his triumphant return in 1020 shows him as a conqueror, though as one anxious to be accepted as a legitimate Christian king. At Cirencester he outlawed yet another prominent English noble, Ealdorman Æthelweard, and in the same year gave thanks for his victory by the consecration of the minster at Ashingdon, an action directly comparable to William's later foundation of Battle. Yet this consecration also demonstrates his total acceptance of a Christian framework for his actions, and this is underlined by the letter which he wrote to the English people in this year[42] stating the programme of action of a Christian king. This letter, like I and II Cnut, interprets Cnut's intentions in a broad Christian context, arguably reflecting the mood of 1020. The promises on specific abuses perhaps belong to the immediate circumstances of his accession, perhaps to the conciliatory mood of 1018.

Political circumstances, particularly those surrounding accession, were always important in producing royal promises and concessions. Western Frankia in the second half of the ninth century had seen rapid and related developments in coronation/consecration rituals, coronation oaths and specific commitments on the parts of kings.[43] The development of royal unction provided ideal opportunities for persuading kings to make promises

---

[41] Wormald ('Æthelred the Lawmaker', p. 54) plausibly attributes the order to celebrate St Edward's mass-day to Cnut, not Æthelred. The same law called for the celebration of Dunstan's feast, and it should be recalled that Dunstan was not only a great religious leader but a supporter of Edward and an opponent of Æthelred in 975. Cnut may have underlined his point by encouraging the cult of other murdered princes: note the reference to his interest in Wigstan and in his translation to Evesham in the Life of St Wigstan, *Chronicon Abbatiae de Evesham*, ed. W. D. Macray, RS (London, 1863), pp. 324–32.

[42] Liebermann, *Gesetze* I, 273–5; *English Historical Documents c. 500–1042*, ed. Dorothy Whitelock, 2nd ed. (London, 1979), no. 48.

[43] These developments are discussed by M. David in 'Le Serment du sacre du IXe au XVe siècle', *Revue du Moyen Age Latin* 6 (1950), 5–272, esp. at 47–121, and by W. Ullmann in *The Carolingian Renaissance and the Idea of Kingship* (London, 1969), esp. at pp. 80–110. J. Nelson ('Inauguration Rituals', *Early Medieval Kingship*, ed. P. H. Sawyer and I. Wood (Leeds, 1977), pp. 59–62) has stressed how closely they are in bound in time and development with the episcopal initiatives in anointing and coronation.

and statements of intent, although there was no united ecclesiastical order with a master-plan to shackle kings.[44] These attempts to bind the king and all other ranks of society to their duties were articulated most clearly in the work of Hincmar and in such ceremonies as the consecration at Metz in 869. They herald the separation of kingship and king, office and man, and in the hands of Hincmar were developed into important theoretical curbs on the king.[45] But by stressing the importance of kingship, its duties and its central function in Christian society such statements on 'just kingship' strengthened, as much as they bound, kings. Wulfstan was no Hincmar and his later articulation of similar ideas carried no threat of deposition.[46]

These oaths and promises, and the consecration rituals to which they were often attached, evolved from the interaction of ecclesiastical ideas and political circumstances. To stress either one at the expense of the other is to create a false dichotomy. Hincmar with the theoretical apparatus of a Carolingian churchman moulds the ideas which surface from the political situation of mid- and late-ninth-century Frankia. Internal problems caused by the Carolingian inheritance and the power of the nobility were exacerbated to a dangerous degree by external attack. At Strasbourg in 842 Charles and his brother Louis undertook to work for 'peace', 'justice' and 'the good of all'. At Coulaines in 843 Charles the Bald promised to honour his *fideles* and treat them with justice and equity, just as his *fideles* were to promise to honour and serve him. The context for these promises was the struggle between Charles and his brothers over the inheritance. The feelings of collapse engendered by this struggle and the Viking invasions led certain churchmen to call for social and moral regeneration through the adherence of all men, including the king, to their duties. Political pressure could force the king to make even more specific commitments and concessions to win support. In 858 Charles the Bald took an oath to his people in exchange for a reciprocal undertaking from them prompted by massive rebellion and defection among his nobility to his brother Louis the German. Charles's consecration promise as king of Lotharingia in 869 was due to Hincmar's influence plus the knowledge of a need to secure that kingdom against the counter-claims of brothers and nephews. When his own son Louis the Stammerer made undertakings to his nobility in 877 they grew directly out of the problems which faced him as he tried to establish himself on the throne. Ninth-century

---

[44] J. M. Wallace-Hadrill, *Early Germanic Kingship* (Oxford, 1971), p. 135, and see below, n. 46.

[45] See J. Nelson, 'Kingship, Law and Liturgy in the Political Thought of Hincmar of Rheims', *EHR* 92 (1977), 241–79.

[46] I cannot agree with D. Bethurum's contention that Wulfstan extolled the position of bishops over that of kings and anticipated Gregorian ideas; see her '*Regnum* and *Sacerdotium* in the Early Eleventh Century', *England before the Conquest: Studies in Primary Sources presented to Dorothy Whitelock*, ed. P. Clemoes and K. Hughes (Cambridge, 1971), pp. 129–45.

Frankia and early-eleventh-century England faced similar problems – external attack which was interpreted as moral punishment and internal defections which were only partly related to those attacks but which were often seen as both their cause and their effect. It would hardly be surprising if Wulfstan and Hincmar sought similar remedies – penance and, when political circumstances allowed it, promises of just rule. The events of 1014–20 provided those circumstances, and Cnut's consecration was the ideal opportunity and probably the only royal anointing at which Wulfstan officiated.[47]

The idea of a coronation promise, which developed in Western Frankia in the later ninth century, arose in England in the later tenth. Recent redating of the Old English coronation *ordines* has shown that there was an English coronation *ordo* in use before 900, the so-called First *Ordo*, and that the Second *Ordo* belongs to the tenth century, being in its earliest forms pre-973.[48] It is now possible to assess some of the true novelty of the Dunstan *Ordo* which was probably used for the first time at the second, imperial consecration of Edgar in 973. In the so-called First *Ordo* and in the Second *Ordo* in its pre-973 forms the newly crowned and anointed king addressed three *orders* to his people at the end of the ceremony.[49] They are a statement of intent, an order to the people to which the assembled respond with *amen*. In 973 this threefold *order* was transformed into a threefold *promise*. The content remained the same, but the promise was now made by the king *before* the anointing, after his procession into the church, his prostration, the *Te Deum* and his election.[50]

---

[47] If there was a consecration in the brief reign of Edmund Ironside it is possible that Wulfstan was present.

[48] On the dating of the First *Ordo*, see J. Nelson, 'The Earliest Royal *Ordo*: some Liturgical and Historical Aspects', *Festschrift for W. Ullmann*, ed. M. Wilks and B. Tierney (forthcoming). On the dating of the Second *Ordo*, see P. L. Ward, 'An Early Version of the Anglo-Saxon Coronation Ceremony', *EHR* 57 (1942), 345–61, and C. Hohler, 'Some Service Books of the Later Saxon Church', *Tenth-Century Studies, Essays in Commemoration of the Millennium of the Council of Winchester and 'Regularis Concordia'*, ed. D. Parsons (London and Chichester, 1975), pp. 67–9. In *The Claudius Pontificals*, ed. D. Turner, Henry Bradshaw Soc. 97 (1971), at xxx–xxxiii, Turner ascribes the earliest version of the Second *Ordo* to the coronation of Athelstan. The version which he edits, *ibid.* pp. 89–95, is from an early-eleventh-century Canterbury pontifical (BL Cotton Claudius A. iii). This is the version with the *promissio* at the beginning, and it appears also in the so-called Pontifical of Dunstan (Paris, Bibliothèque Nationale, Lat. 943; late-tenth-century, from Sherborne) and in the Pontifical of Bishop Sampson (Cambridge, Corpus Christi College 146; first half of the eleventh century, from the Old Minster, Winchester). I am very grateful to Janet Nelson for information on the dating of these *ordines*.

[49] The version of the First *Ordo* in the Leofric Missal (Oxford, Bodleian Library, Bodley 579) states 'Rectitudo regis est noviter ordinati et in solium sublimati populo tria precepta sibi subdito praecipere.' The version in the Egbert Pontifical (BN Lat. 10575) prefaces this with the rubric 'Primum mandatum regis ad populum'.

[50] Both the *ordo* in the Dunstan Pontifical and the description in the 'Vita Oswaldi', *Historians of the Church of York and its Archbishops*, ed. J. Raine, RS (London, 1879–94) I, 436–8, agree on these details of Edgar's consecration. The 'Vita Oswaldi' was written during the 990s, by which time an *ordo* with the *promissio* at the beginning was in use. The change to a *promissio* before consecration probably dates to 973. In a personal communication Janet Nelson associates the version of the Second *Ordo* in the Dunstan Pontifical with 973.

The Old English version of this coronation promise, as used for Edward the Martyr or Æthelred (or both) in the 970s, has survived.[51] In 975 or 979 (or both) it was a written vernacular promise delivered to the king by Dunstan and then laid upon the altar. In both surviving manuscripts it is accompanied by a short homily on the duties of kingship delivered by the officiating archbishop.[52] This consecration homily is again reminiscent of ninth-century Frankia and should probably be associated with Dunstan.[53] The importance of the homily and the promise is underlined by the fact that both are in the vernacular, whereas almost every other part of the consecration ritual would have been in Latin. In 975 or 979 the king had made a promise of just kingship as a condition of consecration and that kingship had been defined in a vernacular homily. In 973 just kingship may have expressed itself immediately in legislation.[54] These ideas may have come to full fruition in 1014.

The history of English royal accessions over the next half-century shows the line of development these ideas could take. It must be assumed that Edward the Confessor was required to make a coronation promise in 1043. Archbishop Eadsige certainly reminded him of his duties as king.[55] But it is in the accession of the conquering William that the closest parallels to Cnut lie and that some idea of what may have happened on Cnut's accession may be found. In 1066 the officiating archbishop, Ealdred, demanded a coronation promise from William the Conqueror identical to the one taken by Anglo-Saxon kings in the 970s and later by Henry I.[56] It is perhaps this promise which is meant when the D manuscript of the *Anglo-Saxon Chronicle* states that Ealdred had William swear that he would rule as well as any king before him. But Ealdred asked for more in 1066 than the coronation oath. William had to promise to treat all his subjects equally, both English and French,[57] an additional guarantee necessary from a foreign conqueror. What we know

---

[51] See above, n. 33.

[52] See above, n. 34.

[53] This was known to Wulfstan and inspired sections of *Wulfstan*, ed. Napier, no. L, and *Polity*. But the sermon is not in Wulfstan's distinct style and its manuscript traditions do not suggest connection with him. BL Cotton Cleopatra B. xiii was an Exeter book and the mutilated BL Vitellius A. vii from which Junius made his transcript was a Ramsey manuscript.

[54] C. Hart, 'Athelstan Half-King and his Family', *ASE* 2 (1973), 133, n. 6, associates IV Edgar with 973 on the grounds that ch. 15 entrusts the law's distribution to Ealdormen Ælfhere and Æthelwine, who were dominant 970 × 975. Ch. 15 also mentions Earl Oslac. It should be noted that these three may be singled out solely because they had Danes under their jurisdiction. Any date between 963 and 975 is possible, though 973 must remain a strong candidate.

[55] *ASC* 1042 E, 1043 C: *Two Chronicles*, ed. Plummer I, 162–3; *Willemi Malmesbiriensis Monachi De Gestis Regum Anglorum Libri Quinque*, ed. W. Stubbs, RS (London, 1887–9), I, 239.

[56] The identity is demonstrated by Florence of Worcester, *Chronicon ex Chronicis*, ed. B. Thorpe (London 1848–9) I, 228–9. Foreville's recent remarks on the subject, 'Le Sacre des rois', p. 56, are vitiated by a failure to recognize that such a promise was already part of the Anglo-Saxon coronation ceremony.

[57] William of Malmesbury, *De Gestis Regum*, ed. Stubbs II, 307. Foreville sees this as the origin of the two oaths of the Angevin coronation ('Le Sacre des rois', pp. 56–7).

of the early years of Cnut's reign suggests a similar range of undertakings and reminders of duty. In view of the history of the Anglo-Saxon coronation it seems certain that he took the coronation oath. He had certainly subscribed to the good laws of the English by 1018 and his letter of 1020 stressed the application of his laws to Dane and English alike.[58] The consecration address which Wulfstan made to him may even be preserved in the homily *Larspell*.[59]

Consecration and its attendant oaths and admonitions are only the final act which closes the process of political manoeuvring by which a king gained the throne. Negotiations with the nobility in advance of consecration fostered the idea of 'reform' or 'commitment' in exchange for support. In 957, 975 and 1035 rival candidates sought support in struggles for the English throne. Unfortunately the details of the negotiations of these years have not survived. More is known of the circumstances of Edward the Confessor's accession and coronation in 1042–3. Edward became king in London on 8 June 1042, largely with the help of Earl Godwine and Bishop Lyfing.[60] William of Malmesbury details Edward's prior negotiations with Godwine and the debate over his acceptance by the nobility at Gillingham.[61] Even if William is not entirely trustworthy, Edward seems to have made promises at least to Godwine. Support was necessary because such meetings as that at Gillingham were not mere rubber-stamps. Between 957 and 1100 a series of disputed successions, royal exiles and foreign conquests may have fostered ideas of royal commitments and definitions of good kingship. The making of coronation oaths which dates from these years may have gone hand in hand with oral, if not written, promises on specific issues which must have accompanied many of these negotiations.

The first certainly attested written coronation charter to issue from such circumstances and negotiations in England is that of Henry I. Henry's insecurity at the beginning of his reign prompted his dash to London for consecration via the treasury at Winchester.[62] He had been building up support for a bid for the throne before 1100[63] and would have been well aware of the capital to be made out of a charter which both vilified his brother's

---

[58] The letter of 1020, ch. 9, refers to any who contravene God's law or secular law, *Denisc oððe Englisc*. II Cnut Prologue stresses that this law is to be held *ofer eall Englalande*.

[59] This homily (*Wulfstan*, ed. Napier, no. L) deals with the duties of kings and other rulers in society. Plummer (*Two Chronicles* II, 222) suggested that it was the sermon preached by Eadsige to Edward the Confessor in 1043. In spite of Karl Jost's doubts (*Wulfstanstudien*, Swiss Stud. in Eng. 23 (Bern, 1950), 249–61), D. Bethurum (*Homilies of Wulfstan* (Oxford, 1957), pp. 39–41) attributes its authorship to Wulfstan. She feels that it may never have been preached as a sermon but that it presents a collection of notes for a sermon later to be addressed to a meeting of the witan.

[60] Florence of Worcester, *Chronicon*, ed. Thorpe I, 196–7.

[61] William of Malmesbury, *De Gestis Regum*, ed. Stubbs I, 237–9.

[62] On the circumstances of Henry's accession, see C. Warren-Hollister, 'The Strange Death of William Rufus', *Speculum* 48 (1973), 637–53.

[63] See J. Le Patourel, *The Norman Empire* (Oxford, 1976), pp. 342 ff.

rule[64] and showed himself as a 'good lord' prepared to do away with evil customs.[65] The charter which details these abuses is an amplification of the coronation oath[66] which was already in use by 1016. In diplomatic form Henry's charter is related to the notificatory writ. Æthelred II used a similar, probably oral, form of address to notify his concessions to the witan in 1014.[67] Again there are possible parallels in the early years of Cnut. In the years 1016–17 Cnut's political position and his desire to cast aspersions on Æthelred could easily have led him to subscribe to a series of reforms already current in the 1014 legislation. The ideas, the diplomatic forms and the political situation which brought Henry I's coronation charter into being in 1100 were all present at the beginning of Cnut's reign. The making of a coronation charter in 1016–17 is plausible even though it can never be entirely proven.

The archbishops who performed the ceremonies of consecration and played their part as ecclesiastical leaders in the negotiations surrounding successions were ideally placed to articulate and mould wider discontent. A succession of Norman and Angevin archbishops from Anselm to Stephen Langton influenced the development of royal commitments by acting as a voice for grievance.[68] Their Anglo-Saxon predecessors (Dunstan in the 970s, Eadsige in 1042–3, Wulfstan and perhaps Lyfing in 1014–20) played a similar rôle. Like his contemporary Ælfric, Wulfstan believed in the ecclesiastical duty to admonish and guide kings.[69] In his late work, the *Institutes of Polity*, he laid as strong an emphasis on royal duties as he did on those of all other ranks of society. The events of 1014–20 provided him with opportunities, such as those which had earlier been open to Hincmar, to define 'good kingship' and to give it practical legal expression. It is almost certainly to Wulfstan that we owe the shift from specific grievances to the wider statements of VIII Æthelred and especially I and II Cnut.

The ideas of 'good lordship' articulated in these years are constant themes of medieval political theory. Their content is often vague and is rarely defined except at times of political crisis. Their statement, especially in the early Middle Ages, was normally in the hands of ecclesiastics who possessed a theoretical framework for determining royal action and binding kings to their

---

[64] E. Mason, 'William Rufus, Myth and Reality', *JMH* 3 (1977), 1–20.

[65] The fact that he did not do so is irrelevant; cf., e.g., H. B. Teunis, 'The Coronation Charter of 1100: a Postponement of Decision. What did not Happen in Henry I's Reign', *JMH* 4 (1978), 135–44. Cnut, whilst apparently eschewing malpractices, is emphatic in his laws on the detailing of royal rights.

[66] See above, n. 33.

[67] Æthelred *het gretan* his witan. F. Harmer (*Anglo-Saxon Writs* (Manchester, 1952), p. 16, and App. 4, no. 3) pointed out that this communication was apparently in writ form.

[68] See Foreville, 'Le Sacre des rois', pp. 61–2, on Anselm, Henry of Winchester, Theobald of Bec, Thomas Becket and Stephen Langton.

[69] See Ælfric's sermon for the Sunday after Ascension, *Homilies of Ælfric. A Supplementary Collection*, ed. J. C. Pope, EETS 259–60 (London, 1967–8), 372–92, and Wulfstan's *Polity*, chs. 5 and 6, on bishops.

duties. Political opportunity allowed translation from general idea into specific undertaking. The marriage of ecclesiastical theory and political realities produced the coronation oath, itself no mere empty form in these centuries, and in certain circumstances coronation charters and other royal commitments.

Coronation charters must be read carefully for insight into royal government. They usually express dislike of strong, arbitrary or active monarchy. Henry I's charter reflects the strong rule of Rufus[70] and Magna Carta itself has been seen as at least in part a commentary on Angevin despotism. A time of weakness and insecurity often allows the articulation of long-standing as much as novel grievances. Definitions of 'misrule' usually indicate a dislike of arbitrariness, a failure to satisfy conflicting ambitions, and/or a too rapid growth of royal power. The royal commitments in the last chapters of Cnut's laws, whether they belong to Æthelred in 1014 or Cnut in 1016–17 or both, should throw light on late-tenth- and early-eleventh-century England.

The strength of the late Old English monarchy, as demonstrated in such areas as the coinage,[71] is becoming a generally accepted fact. A measure of royal rights can be gained from II Cnut 8–15.3. The reign of Æthelred had seen evidence of the continued growth of royal power. Patrick Wormald has denoted a 'deepening sensitivity [in Æthelred's laws] to the legal, and thus fiscal, rights of the crown', a sensitivity which inevitably expressed itself in financial exaction.[72] It appears that Æthelred was also responsible for raising the level of heriots.[73] The pegging of heriots was one of the reforms offered in II Cnut 69–83. The other 'abuses' mentioned there must also have been current grievances. A picture begins to emerge of Æthelred and perhaps also of Edgar as kings who exploited their rights of lordship to the full: who married widows and heiresses to gain allies; who took lands rightly belonging to other lords in the forfeitures of their thegns; who extended such forfeiture to the property of wives; who took unfair advantage of intestacy and did not always accept the due heriot as a guarantee of peaceful landholding; and whose activities in these areas were so assiduous that they appeared to be depriving many heirs of their rights. Æthelred's insistence on rights of trial, lordship and thus forfeiture of all men who held bookland[74] takes on extra significance against such a background. The constant desires of kings to fill their coffers, punish their enemies and reward their friends lie behind all such

[70] See above, n. 64.
[71] I have discussed this, its unpopularity and its enforcement in 'Historical Implications of the Regional Production of Dies under Æthelred II', *BNJ* 48 (1978), 35–51.
[72] Wormald, 'Æthelred the Lawmaker', p. 65.
[73] On this see N. Brooks, 'Arms, Status and Warfare in Late-Saxon England', *Ethelred the Unready*, ed. Hill, pp. 89–90.
[74] I Æthelred 1.14 and III Æthelred 11.

'abuses'. Resentment at the growth of such royal rights and interference would have been intensified by the additional exaction which the Viking attacks necessarily occasioned, especially by failure in the face of such attack and perhaps by the character of Æthelred himself. It must have played a part in the history of his unhappy reign. Æthelred's exile and return provided an opportunity for the statement of these grievances, and the continuing turmoil in the early years of Cnut allowed their reiteration and a general stress on the duties of Christian kings. The events of 1014–20 must taken their place in the history of 'feudal monarchy'. The political circumstances within which late-tenth- and eleventh-century kings operated were not fundamentally different from those of the late eleventh and twelfth centuries. Foreville saw the first steps towards Magna Carta in the undertakings made by William I and Henry I. The journey towards Runnymede may have begun earlier.

Sprouston, Roxburghshire: an Anglo-Saxon settlement discovered by air reconnaissance

J. K. S. ST JOSEPH

Crop-marks revealing an archaeological site at Sprouston (NT 758362), Roxburghshire, the subject of this paper, were observed and photographed from the air on 22 July 1964, but the character of the site did not become evident until further observations were made in August 1970. In the flying programmes of the Committee for Aerial Photography of the University of Cambridge Sprouston has been photographed from the air on fourteen subsequent occasions. The vertical and oblique photographs, 111 in all, in the University Collection, together with oblique photographs taken during the last few years by staff of the Royal Commission on Historical Monuments for Scotland, are the sole source of information about the site. No trace of any of the features to be described is ordinarily visible on the surface, as is only too apparent from walking over the ground.[1]

The site lies 2¼ miles north-east of Kelso, on the farm of Whitmuirhaugh, in Sprouston parish, on the south-east bank of the Tweed near the point where it swings northwards and then eastwards in its generally east-north-easterly course to Berwick. The crop-marks extend over some 20 acres, comprising a gently undulating spread of gravel, between about 75 ft and 100 ft above Ordnance Datum. The area is bounded on the south-west by a scarp eroded by the Tweed, there flowing in a short south–north reach: northwards the ground slopes down to the present alluvial plain, the lower part of which is liable to flood. The site itself is on a rapidly draining gravel soil, well above flood level. The crop-marks, best seen in barley or oats, fall within three fields, which are in a normal agricultural rotation. This means that only a part of the site is visible in any year, since but one field, or two

---

[1] The discovery was briefly described in the Twentieth Report (for 1969–70) of the University Committee for Aerial Photography, *Cambridge University Reporter* 101, Special no. 16 (1971), p. 116. A short account of the site with sketch-plan based upon air photographs held by the Royal Commission on Historical Monuments for Scotland has recently been published by N. Reynolds, 'Dark Age Timber Halls and the Background to Excavation at Balbridie', *Scottish Archaeol. Forum* 10 (1980), 50–2 and fig. 7.

Mr B. McCririck, of Whitmuirhaugh, kindly allowed me to walk over his fields.

at most, is under cereal crop at a given time. The crop-marks (see pls. I, IIa, IIb and IV and figs. 1 and 2) indicate features of several periods. A broad ditch curves in an arc across the high ground immediately above the river scarp at the south-west end of the site. This ditch, which is interrupted by several causeways, probably defines a small promontory fort, some two acres in area. A small ring ditch, seen in some photographs immediately north of the outbuildings of Whitmuirhaugh, seems unrelated to the principal site. Particular interest is focused upon the remaining assemblage of crop-marks, which are quite unusual by reason of their detail and variety, comprising boundary ditches, an oval enclosure defined by double ditches, timber buildings of various kinds and apparently graves, carefully grouped in rows as in a planned cemetery.

The moment in July 1970 when these features were observed in all their detail was reminiscent of the occasion just twenty-one years previously when the remains at Old Yeavering (see pl. IIIa), and at Milfield (see pl. IIIb) were first seen and photographed in a similar reconnaissance. At that time the significance of Old Yeavering was not fully appreciated; indeed to guess what wealth of information was to be revealed by Dr Hope-Taylor's meticulous excavations,[2] continued over many seasons, would hardly have been possible.

The general geographical setting of Sprouston has already been mentioned, but its relation to the two other settlements just named must be described. Sprouston lies 11 miles west-north-west of Old Yeavering measured in a straight line, but some 12 miles should be reckoned as the distance by any reasonable route, which would follow initially the valley of the Bowmont Water upstream from Yeavering. A distance of $11\frac{1}{2}$ miles separates Milfield and Sprouston, but the effective distance should be reckoned a little more, depending on precisely what route is chosen. The settlement at Old Yeavering lies on the floor of a narrow valley overlooked by Yeavering Bell, while that at Milfield, $2\frac{1}{4}$ miles to the north, is in the broader valley of the Till near the point at which it contracts after its widening north of Wooler to form a low-lying basin some 3 miles across, surrounded by hills. The eastern half of that basin is marshy and under natural conditions would be very liable to flood. The Bowmont Water,[3] curving in a broad sweep from Kirk Yetholm nearly to Wooler, embraces the northern element of the Cheviot Hills. By contrast the direct route westwards from the Bowmont Water to Sprouston crosses more gentle, undulating country, hardly rising above 500 ft, as may be seen from the modern road B6396. Dr Hope-Taylor has emphasized the evidence for a considerable density of occupation

---

[2] B. Hope-Taylor, *Yeavering. An Anglo-British Centre of Early Northumbria*, Dept of the Environment Archaeol. Reports 7 (London, 1977).

[3] Below Westnewton, where the Bowmont Water is joined by the College Burn, the stream is known as the River Glen.

I Sprouston, Roxburghshire, a general view, looking north-north-east (20 July 1964)

II Sprouston, Roxburghshire, the crop-marks
a An oblique view (2 August 1970)
b A vertical view (2 August 1970), scale *c.* 1:3450.
North is the direction of the diagonal through the top left corner

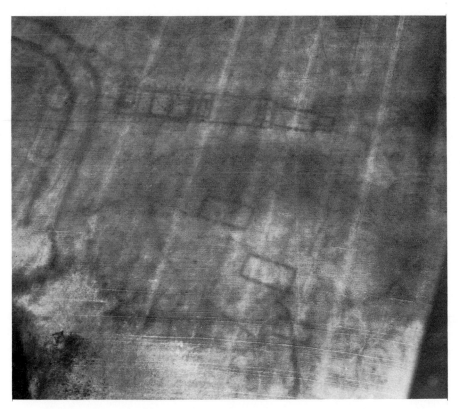

IIIa Old Yeavering, Northumberland, an oblique view of the crop-marks, looking south
(9 July 1949)

IIIb Milfield, Northumberland, an oblique view of the crop-marks at the north-west part of the site,
looking south-south-west (20 July 1972)

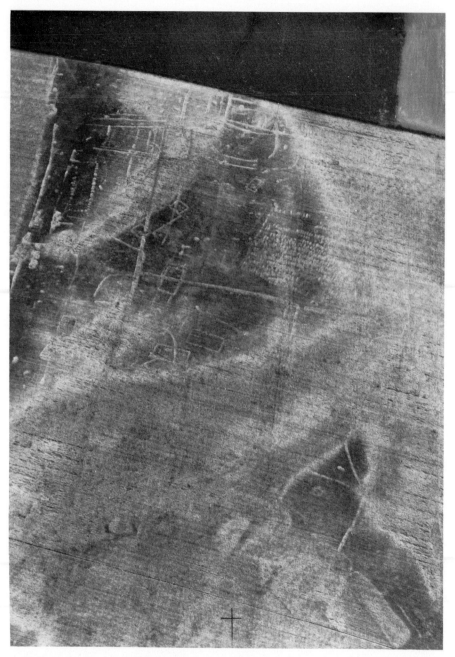

IV Sprouston, Roxburghshire, an oblique view of the principal crop-marks, looking north-east
(2 August 1970)

continuing over a long period in this part of Northumberland.[4] The valley of the middle Tweed, comprising extensive tracts of land on light alluvial soils, was a comparable area of dense settlement. Around Old Yeavering much of the evidence may still be seen as earthworks; by the Tweed earthworks for the most part have long been levelled by agriculture and the evidence is coming to light only slowly through continuing air reconnaissance.

Sprouston affords extensive views up and down the Tweed, as well as across the river to the north-west. The situation is strikingly different from, for example, that of the early ecclesiastical site at Ninekirks, Brougham, in Westmorland, hidden away in a bend of the Eamont valley in a secluded position.[5] The plan of Sprouston (fig. 1) has been drawn after consideration of all the photographs in the Cambridge collection, those of 1970 being particularly useful. When small features within relatively large fields are being plotted, accuracy is not easy. To plan individual buildings within limits of error of a few feet has been the aim. Discrepancies of 5–10 ft may well arise between elements in different parts of the site. The plan (fig. 1) represents an interesting exercise in interpretation, rendered incomparably easier than it might have been by photographs of analogous features at Old Yeavering and at Milfield (see pls. IIIa and IIIb) and, above all, by the results of excavation at Yeavering now available in Dr Hope-Taylor's report.

The buried features seen in pls. I–IV appear as marks in the crops lighter or darker than the normal growth, the differences in tone depending principally on the nature of the vegetation, the weather during the whole growing season and the date of photography in relation to the time of ripening of the crop. Natural differences in the soil have also caused responses in the vegetation. The growth of the crops has varied with the depth of humus and with the free-draining quality of the soil: the better-drained soils yield crop-marks of buried features with greatest clarity. Thus pl. I gives an impression of the undulations by which the gravel terrace gives way to the flood-plain, represented by the triangular area of dark growth to the left of the further field by the river bend. The photography, though spread over a good many years, was obtained mostly in the second half of July, when buried features usually appear as dark lines. However, the ripening of a crop may mean that photographs taken at the very end of July or in August exhibit a reversal of the usual tones, so that disturbances in the ground are seen, sometimes with remarkable clarity, as areas of lighter growth of a crop (photographs of 1970 (pls. IIa, IIb and IV) and of 1978).

Excavation at Old Yeavering has shown that many of the features there

---

[4] *Yeavering*, pp. 17–20.
[5] J. K. S. St Joseph, 'Air Reconnaissance: Recent Results, 46', *Antiquity* 52 (1978), 236–8 and pl. xxxiib.

had a complicated history. Timber structures were altered and rebuilt; parts of the cemetery became a confusion of overlapping graves. By no means all these changes could be discerned on aerial photographs and the same may well be true of Sprouston, so that the comparative simplicity of the building-plans may be misleading. Experience shows that on many soils only disturbances larger than a certain minimum size promote crop-marks, while smaller features may not be seen at all save under very favourable conditions. Construction-trenches packed with firm gravel offer almost the same resistance to root penetration as undisturbed subsoil, while the effect of modern ploughing must be considered: shallow disturbances may have been obliterated.

At Sprouston, two closely set and almost parallel ditches limit the site to the north-west and north-east (see fig. 1). Whether there was a similar boundary along part of the south-east side is not apparent: the crops there do not show clear growth-differences. To the north-east two segments of ditch and a linear ditch appear beyond the bounds just indicated. These may not be contemporary with the parallel ditches. At the north angle of the whole site three straight lines of narrow ditch define an area shaped roughly as a parallelogram with fragmentary crop-marks inside. Further south-east two widely spaced, curving ditches enclose a roughly oval area, nearly an acre in extent. Both ditches are interrupted on the south as for an entrance. Does this enclosure correspond in some fashion to the 'Great Enclosure' at Old Yeavering?[6] Long lines of ditch delimit or subdivide parts of the central area of the site. Not all are contemporary. Fig. 1 gives an impression of a gradually developing and changing plan: some ditches cut the oval enclosure, others cross ground occupied at some time by timber buildings. To establish an order of succession is impossible from the photographs alone.

Special interest attaches to the buildings which are of several distinct types. The largest (*a*), aligned north-east–south-west, having its principal uprights set a few feet apart, measures about 90 × 28 ft.[7] The individual post-pits are clearly visible on photographs. The next largest building (*b*), aligned east–west, stood a little to the south. The outline is marked by a continuous construction-trench. It comprises a 'hall' of about 47 × 29 ft, with a narrower extension some 15 ft in length at either end. To the south-west is a smaller building (*c*), almost rectangular, but the sides appear to be slightly bowed. The length is about 34 ft, the width 20 ft at the widest part. The crop-marks suggest that there is a line of post-pits just outside the construction-trench round the north-eastern half of the building, as if two building periods may be

---

[6] Hope-Taylor, *Yeavering*, pp. 78–87.

[7] All dimensions are given in imperial units to facilitate comparison with the Yeavering report, where, in the text, imperial units only are used.

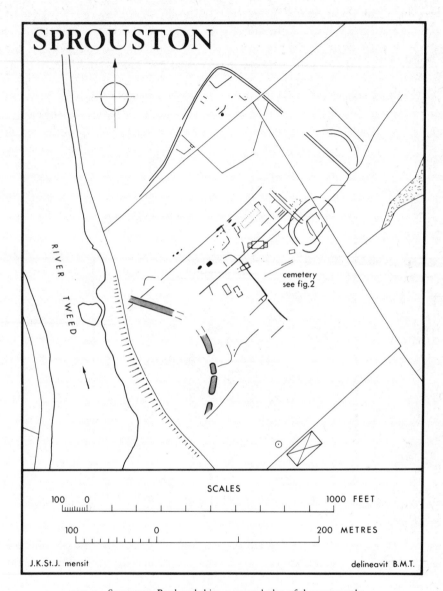

SPROUSTON

RIVER TWEED

cemetery
see fig.2

SCALES

100   0   1000 FEET

100   0   200 METRES

J.K.St.J. mensit   delineavit B.M.T.

FIG. 1   Sprouston, Roxburghshire, a general plan of the crop-marks

represented. There is a hint of an extension at the west end: the crop-marks are not clear enough for certainty. South-west again are two matching buildings (*d* and *e*) each approximately 38 × 20 ft. The eastern of the two has a gap, as for a door, at the centre of each long side. Lastly, somewhat to the east, and not far from the entrance to the oval enclosure, are indications of a small rectangular structure (*f*) about 21 × 15 ft.

At several places there are disturbances (shown in solid black on the plan) considerably larger than ordinary post-pits. Some may be refuse pits; some delves for gravel; the largest, shaped as a rectangle 22 × 18 ft, might be the sunken floor of a rectangular building. South of the oval enclosure the photographs show over an area approximately 145 × 100 ft what are almost certainly graves. This area is represented at a larger scale in fig. 2, which is

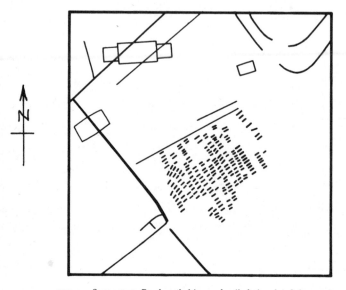

FIG. 2 Sprouston, Roxburghshire, a detailed sketch of the cemetery

an interpretative sketch, representing an attempt to distinguish individual graves. The actual pattern is almost certainly more complicated, but the arrangement of the graves in rows comes out clearly enough. The general orientation is east-north-east–west-south-west.

Care is necessary in comparing the structures revealed by air photography at Sprouston with the results of excavation at Old Yeavering. Just as at Yeavering the complexity of the timber structures could not have been appreciated from study of air photographs, so also in all probability at Sprouston. Though the photographs (pls. I–IV) almost certainly present

simplified pictures, certain comparisons may be made, having regard to the
different settings of the two places. Old Yeavering lies in a narrow valley
that had long been an important route in the general network of communications. Sprouston is set in the Tweed basin beside the river, possibly near
a convenient fording-place; otherwise there is no apparent good reason why
communications should be focused just there. Whether or not the oval
enclosure at Sprouston corresponds in some measure to the 'Great Enclosure'
at Yeavering can be settled only by excavation. The comparison should not
be pressed: the oval enclosure might be of a period different from the rest
of the site.

As to the timber buildings, correspondences are more securely based. At
Sprouston, the large structure with uprights founded in post-pits (a)[8] is, in
point of technique, represented by Yeavering A6 and A7, small houses or
huts that Hope-Taylor places in his Phase I of 'post-Roman' development
there. However, the size, 90 × 28 ft, is closest to that of Yeavering A4, about
85 × 38 ft.[9] The simplicity of the structure seems unmatched at Yeavering,
but this simplicity may be more apparent than real: a building of a 28-ft span
would seem to call for centre-posts and perhaps buttresses, but no such
features appear on the photographs. Building (b) at Sprouston closely
matches A1(b) at Old Yeavering (see pl. IIIa).[10] Approximate dimensions of
49 × 29 ft, with a narrower extension of 15 ft at either end, compare with
47 × 25 ft, with narrower extensions of $16\frac{1}{2}$ ft; an analogous building may be
discerned at Milfield (see pl. IIIb). The lines of post-pits visible just outside
the foundation-trenches of building (c) at Sprouston suggest reconstruction,
as occurred so often at Yeavering. The two buildings (d) and (e), arranged
en echelon, both 38 × 20 ft, correspond closely with building C2,[11] while their
relative positions recall the whole C group of buildings at Old Yeavering.

At both places there were cemeteries, but the graves at Yeavering do not
ordinarily promote any marks on air photographs. The strings of graves and
overlapping interments at Old Yeavering are not apparent at Sprouston,
where the photographs suggest neatly arranged rows of graves. Only
excavation can reveal whether this represents the actual state of affairs.

Air photographs of Sprouston have revealed nothing to match the most
distinctive building of all at Old Yeavering, namely the structure with tiered
staging arranged as in a *cuneus* of a Roman amphitheatre. Again, there is no
evidence for the elaborate and careful setting out of the different elements
of the plan: of its nature, this would have to be sought by digging, which

---

[8] For the reference letters, see above.
[9] Hope-Taylor, *Yeavering*, pp. 58–62 and fig. 24.
[10] *Ibid.* pp. 49–50 and fig. 13.
[11] *Ibid.* p. 91 and fig. 38.

might also reveal whether the buildings were laid out in 'Yeavering units'.[12] Nevertheless the resemblances between the two sites undoubtedly show that they are closely comparable. The buildings at Sprouston would seem to be of the same generation as some of those at Old Yeavering: the correspondence is perhaps closest to Hope-Taylor's post-Roman Phase IV, which he assigns to the years 547–616.[13]

While there is evidence both from place-names and from archaeology for Anglian settlement in the vicinity of Sprouston, there is very little early evidence for this particular site, with nothing specifically pre-Conquest.[14] Nevertheless there is enough to indicate the general importance of Sprouston and to indicate that it was an Anglo-Saxon settlement. The name appears to be derived from an Old English personal name *Sprow* + OE *tun*, thus meaning 'Sprow's settlement'. Nicolaisen[15] regards the place-name as indicative of relatively early settlement on three grounds. It is first mentioned in the early twelfth century, which is early for Scotland; the settlement is in a good situation in the Tweed basin, not far from Kelso; and OE *tun* is compounded with an Old English monothematic personal name, held to be early. As to later history, the place is mentioned in the foundation charter of David, prince of Cumberland, to the monks of Selkirk in 1114; it remained in Crown hands until the end of the twelfth century and then passed to the de Vesey family for the duration of the thirteenth; it had various distinguished (including some royal) owners thereafter. In 1256 'the king and queen of England, accompanied by a numerous retinue of knights, earls and barons, took up their residence for some days at Sprouston'. The place was ravaged or burnt on various occasions in the fifteenth and sixteenth centuries.[16]

The settlements at Old Yeavering (*Ad Gefrin*) and at Milfield (*Maelmin*) are mentioned by Bede: they were judged by him of significance for the theme of his history. Sprouston is not established as another *villa regia*; the evidence points to a settlement of a more modest kind. That yet a third settlement should come to light close at hand need occasion no surprise. But the number of such settlements in Northumbria with buildings exhibiting the remarkably sophisticated techniques of timber construction which are such a feature of Old Yeavering must surely be limited. All three sites lie in arable land that has long been cultivated; indeed these were the very circumstances that led to the discoveries. Only when such a settlement is found on land unploughed in modern times, so that stratified levels remain intact, will the full

---

[12] *Ibid.* pp. 125 and 129.
[13] *Ibid.* p. 319 and fig. 78.
[14] In this paragraph I have drawn very largely on information that Dr Simon Keynes has kindly supplied.
[15] W. F. H. Nicolaisen, *Scottish Place-Names: their Study and Significance* (London, 1976), pp. 36 and 38.
[16] A Jeffrey, *The History and Antiquities of Roxburghshire and Adjacent Districts*, 4 vols. (London, 1857–64) III, 192–9.

archaeological potential of these sites be realized. Meanwhile the photographs (pls. I–IV) provide yet further proof of the value of air reconnaissance as an instrument of discovery and of its power to illuminate what is vague or uncertain in the written record.

Histories and surveys of Old English literature: a chronological review

DANIEL G. CALDER

Literary history emerges when critical readers in sufficient number move beyond primary recognition of individual texts into a secondary awareness of a scheme, a sense of the connections that exist between these texts.[1] Literary history considers the development of a whole body of literature, tracing multifarious influences and innovations through time. In the course of Anglo-Saxon studies the slow and sporadic reappearance of the literary remains resulted in the late flourishing of a schematic or historical overview. As Wellek reminds us, 'the antiquarian study of Anglo-Saxon remained... outside the main tendency towards literary history'[2] that occurred in late-seventeenth- and early-eighteenth-century England. So, too, the special quality of Old English poetry itself contributed to the laggard creation of a history. It is difficult to map the path of a literature in which all dating is only good guessing and in which a tenaciously conservative oral–formulaic style makes attempts at suggesting influence hazardous.

Circumstance explains the late publication of many Old English texts, for the early Renaissance interest in matters Anglo-Saxon was in part antiquarian, but mainly politico-religious. The sermons of Ælfric and the *Anglo-Saxon Chronicle* became weapons in the successive battles fought during the century of Protestant reformation. They represented the 'purity' of the native church uncontaminated by the theological and ceremonial accretions of the High Catholic Middle Ages. Remote, obscure, and unreadable by all but a few, these ancient documents were hardly taken as 'literature', and indeed what may reasonably be called the 'corpus' did not even reach print until well past the middle of the nineteenth century. Even now some prose texts are still not edited, existing only in manuscript. Thus the notion of constructing a literary history to explain this body required several centuries to form; it was not until Henry Morley's *English Writers* (vol. I, 1864; vol. II, 1888) that a book devoted solely to the history of Old English literature appeared.

---

[1] Or, as René Wellek puts it: 'Genuine literary history became possible only when two main concepts began to be elaborated: *individuality* and *development*' (*The Rise of English Literary History* (Chapel Hill, N.C., 1941), p. 25).

[2] *Ibid.* p. 22.

Daniel G. Calder

In reviewing most of the histories and surveys, both those that treat Anglo-Saxon literature separately and those that place it in a larger framework, we come to appreciate the many and changing conceptions of this literature which scholars and critics (not always identical) have had over the past four hundred years. The outlines are not sharp and clear – more than one fundamental misconception has survived for generations and persists in a few dark corners even today. But the greater movements reveal themselves and follow, not surprisingly, the philosophical and literary prejudices of their own times. The purpose of this essay, then, is threefold: (1) to sketch these larger shifts in taste and attitude towards Old English literature, (2) to state briefly the emphases of each history and to reach a quick evaluation of it and (3) to deal with the goodly number of items that crop up again and again from work to work and which, together, comprise the major issues of scholarship and interpretation. These issues include Christian/pagan preconceptions; establishment of dates and chronology, poem boundaries and the Cædmonian and Cynewulfian canons; metrical, stylistic and aesthetic appreciation, leading to attempts to define the nature of the verse; assessment of foreign influences – the Latin, Celtic and Germanic strands; persistent belief in the 'realism' of Old English poetry; growing perception of the formulaic style; and belief in the development (or usually in the 'degeneration') of that style. All these points of discussion have produced quite contradictory resolutions, and no author attacks them all. They do not in themselves constitute a common grid which we could handily impose on every history. But they are the recurring motifs of the whole enterprise. By documenting the various answers given to these perplexities we can begin to perceive the significant alterations in critical posture that have come with successive cultural generations.

Early efforts to detail the course of English literature as a whole share a common structure and approach. The catalogues of John Leland and John Bale in the second half of the sixteenth century, for example, are biographical lists of British writers. In their treatment of Anglo-Saxon literature they lean heavily towards the Anglo-Latin authors from the seventh century to the eleventh. Of men whose work remains important because it is in the vernacular they count Alfred and *Cedmonus Simplex* as the chief exemplars, while the record of Cædmon and his works they predictably condense from Bede.[3] This tradition held well through the seventeenth century and recurs in the *Compendiosa Enumeratio Poetarum* (1670) of Milton's nephew, Edward Phillips, who touches on Anglo-Saxon and in fact all medieval English writing before the fourteenth century only long enough to echo Bale and

---

[3] See John Bale, *Illustrium majoris Britanniae scriptorum...Summarium* (Ipswich, 1548), and John Leland, *Commentarii de Scriptoribus Brittanicis*, ed. Antonius Hall (Oxford, 1709).

move on: 'Let us pass over the artless Cædmon, Odo "the strict," Henry of Huntingdon, Geoffrey Arthur of Monmouth...'[4]

George Hickes was the first scholar to sketch a comprehensive view of all old Germanic literature, including Old English. His approach was essentially grammatical and metrical, not literary or historical, though the addition of Humphrey Wanley's catalogue of Anglo-Saxon manuscripts gives his work roughly the form of a survey. Hickes's *Thesaurus*, published in 1705, was long in preparation and massive in its final form, but it contains so many odd opinions that most of his ideas were abandoned when a more rigorous scholarship after the German model took hold: for instance, a century or so later John Kemble, himself trained in Germany, was to refer to the *Thesaurus* as 'that miracle of ill directed industry and mistaken learning'.[5] The marvel is that the early investigations of the old 'northern' languages were undertaken at all, given current attitudes. Hickes was typical of his time in having less than high admiration for the texts he spent much of his life arranging and decoding. With his classical biases in language and poetry and his consequent attempt to base the rules of Anglo-Saxon metrics on a prosody appropriate only to Greek and Latin, he caused frustration for himself and for his followers who pursued this chimera during the next hundred years or so; it was not until the nineteenth century that a more accurate picture of the Old English metrical system prevailed. Hickes's strictures on the poetic style mirror his failure to understand the poetic metre. While he found the study of Anglo-Saxon poetry pleasant and useful (p. 203), the poetry itself is *spinosa* ('thorny', p. 177). He objects, as do many who come after him, to the poetry's essential qualities: its obscure transpositions of words, its tendency towards periphrases and cryptic utterance, its syntactic violations, its frequent synonymic appositions and its delight in ellipsis (pp. 190–203). For Hickes Old English poetry is a deformed variant of Old English prose.

Wanley's catalogue, listing all the Anglo-Saxon manuscripts then known, is likewise a monumental, yet flawed, achievement. We need look no farther than his description of the Exeter Book to see clearly its deficiencies, for he divides the poems, unmarked in the manuscript, in the most haphazard way. The three parts of *Christ* and the two of *Guthlac* he strangely cuts and recombines. He notices a poem on Juliana and another on the phoenix, but the many lyrics, riddles and other short poems which comprise more than half the codex he dismisses almost without comment (pp. 280–1). Though the numerous errors and faulty perceptions do not lessen the value and

---

[4] *Edward Phillips's 'History of the Literature of England and Scotland'* (a translation from the *Compendiosa Enumeratio Poetarum*), ed. Daniel G. Calder and Charles R. Forker, Salzburg Stud. in Eng. Lit. (Salzburg, 1973), p. 42.

[5] John M. Kemble, 'Letter to M. Francisque Michel', Francisque Michel, *Bibliothèque Anglo-Saxonne* (Paris and London, 1837), pp. 12–13.

importance of Hickes's and Wanley's contributions to Anglo-Saxon studies at their beginning, they account for the retarded development of a history of the Anglo-Saxon literary achievement.

This delay persists through the eighteenth century, manifesting itself most obviously in the one work which must be considered the foundation of modern English literary history. Thomas Warton's *The History of English Poetry*, in three volumes (1774–81), begins at the 'close of the eleventh century'. His rationale, stated in his Preface, is especially interesting. He adumbrates a strong progressive view of history and culture, one which sees contemporary society as a kind of apex of civilization:

In an age advanced in the highest degree of refinement, that species of curiosity commences, which is busied in contemplating the progress of social life, in displaying the gradations of science, and in tracing the transitions from barbarism to civility.

That these speculations should become the favourite pursuits, and the fashionable topics, of such a period, is extremely natural. We look back on the savage condition of our ancestors with the triumph of superiority; we are pleased to mark the steps by which we have been raised from rudeness to elegance: and our reflections on this subject are accompanied with a conscious pride, arising in great measure from a tacit comparison of the infinite disproportion between the feeble efforts of remote ages, and our present improvements in knowledge (1, i).

But he believes the Anglo-Saxons to be even pre-barbaric. This is his explanation:

Some perhaps will be of opinion, that these annals ought to have commenced with a view of the Saxon poetry. But besides that a legitimate illustration of that jejune and intricate subject would have almost doubled my labour, that the Saxon language is familiar only to a few learned antiquaries, that our Saxon poems are for the most part little more than religious rhapsodies, and that scarce any compositions remain marked with the native images of that people in their pagan state, every reader that reflects but for a moment on our political establishment must perceive, that the Saxon poetry has no connection with the nature and purpose of my present undertaking ...The beginning of these annals seems therefore to be most properly dated from that era, when our national character began to dawn (*ibid.* p. vi).

I have quoted Warton at length because his opinions, so strongly expressed, sum up several issues in Anglo-Saxon studies, issues which can be traced in the literary histories down through the nineteenth century to the present day. They are the questions of race and national character, infancy, progress, the barbaric and the civilized, and the connection, if any, that the Anglo-Saxon and his art had with the post-Norman world. The history of Old English literary history is characterized by the slow, still incomplete, retrieval of sympathy for these old creations.

The isolation which historical events and the judgements of classically trained scholars forced upon Old English literature shows itself in the first great endeavour to redirect attention towards Anglo-Saxon culture. Sharon Turner's *The History of the Anglo-Saxons* ignited both scholarly and public interest in England's Germanic origins and also contained the first genuine literary survey. Its effect must not be underestimated. John Petheram (*An Historical Sketch of the Progress and Present State of Anglo-Saxon Literature in England* (1840)) provides this report on the publication of Turner's first edition in successive volumes between 1799 and 1805; the work, he says,

appears to have excited an attention not only towards [the Anglo-Saxons'] history, but by the addition to it of an account of their language and literature, a slow but gradually increasing attention has been awakened; a deep, and, from time to time, a still deeper interest has been created amongst us, as one after another of the literary productions of our simple and unpretending ancestors have been brought into view from their sleep of ages (p. 118).

A paradox confronts us here, for, without question, we should trust Petheram's commentary, but, when we examine Turner's own nearly derisive attitudes, we wonder how his history could ever have provoked the general enthusiasm Petheram describes. Turner begins with what was to become a favourite metaphor, that of the Anglo-Saxon period as the childhood of the English race, and he claims that Anglo-Saxon consisted mainly of nouns and pronouns, like the speech of a child (5th ed., 1828 II, 343). Since 'true poetry is the offspring of cultivated mind' (p. 345), he finds Anglo-Saxon poetry extremely rude, with its subjects of war and religion and its absence of love and of rules of conduct (pp. 338–9). He hesitates even to grant it the name of poetry, believing it to be such only because it is different from prose (p. 343). Nonetheless he divides this poetry into three categories: (1) songs or ballads, (2) lengthened narrative poems or romances and (3) poems which can loosely be called lyric (p. 346). In his opinion Anglo-Saxon scops did not yet understand the art of narration and the genuine ballad (of which he warmly approves) originated when the old Saxon poetry began to decline (pp. 350–1). Like Hickes, he inveighs against 'the laboured metaphor, the endless periphrasis, the violent inversion, and the abrupt transition' (p. 351).

Much of Turner's chapter on literature is devoted to a long summary of *Beowulf* with specimen translations, but he cuts short his illustration of the encounter with the dragon because he finds it lacks the interest of the first half of the poem (p. 351). He opines, too, in a strange dislocation of chronology, that *Judith* was written when Anglo-Saxon poetry began to improve (pp. 365–6). In addition to vernacular literature he touches upon the development of the Latin post-classical epic, the works of Aldhelm and

Bede. Yet so much remains uncovered that this foray into historical survey can hardly be called complete. Turner himself puts it succinctly: 'In thus considering our ancient poetry as an artificial and mechanical thing, cultivated by men chiefly as a trade, we must not be considered as confounding it with those delightful beauties which we now call poetry' (p. 341). No one reading his chapter could find him guilty of this mistake. His characterization is more severe than Warton's. The latter excluded the literature because it was beyond his scheme; Turner, having included it as a necessary adjunct to his political history, seems bent on whipping it soundly.

In 1809 John Josias Conybeare, having been appointed to the professorship of Anglo-Saxon in the University of Oxford, intended to rescue Old English literature from both oblivion and detraction. The published result of his efforts is a mélange: a long essay on poetic metre (made up of several lectures), an 'Arranged Catalogue of All the Extant Remains of Anglo-Saxon Poetry' and substantial specimens (*Illustrations of Anglo-Saxon Poetry* (1826)). Although he died before he saw the project through the press, his brother William, also an Anglo-Saxon scholar, edited, enlarged and oversaw the final version. The lectures on metre are chiefly important for their recognition of alliteration as the structural principle of the Old English verse line (Rask in Denmark was writing on the same subject at the same time) and for their identification of 'parallelism' as an aspect of the poetry's verbal design. The commentary on the poems also reveals much good common sense, correcting more than one error that had previously gone unchallenged. Conybeare speculates that the early conquerors of Britain undoubtedly brought traditional songs with them from Germany, but that the first poetry of which we have any certain record is Cædmon's (p. 3). He assigns *Widsith* to the fifth century, because of its historical allusions, though he thinks it may be 'a translation or *rifaccimento* of an earlier work' (p. 29), he brings *Bede's Death Song* to public attention for the first time (p. 7), and he corrects Turner's misrepresentation of Beowulf as Hrothgar's enemy (p. 31). His detailed examination of the 'Cædmon' poems leads him to the important conclusion that their stylistic idiosyncracies can be explained only by assuming that each poem had a different author (pp. 183–90). He criticizes Wanley's inaccurate division of the poems in the Exeter Book, especially the vagueness about the poems in its latter half (p. 198), but more or less accepts Wanley's treatment of the first half, including the eccentric splitting of the *Christ* poems. His illustrations from the Exeter Book take in only seven short poems and *The Phoenix*.

Several attitudes expressed by Conybeare and his brother need special scrutiny, for they have significant consequences for the Anglo-Saxon scholarship which came after. The first is implicit in this proposition by William: 'If the editor is not deceived, the fragment in the Exeter MS.

describing a ruined city once the abode of the Eotens, entirely desolated by war and fire, probably relates to the same destruction of Finsburh' (p. 174). This specific notion did not take hold, but the pervasive tendency to explain one detail in extant Old English literature by reference to another certainly did. The idea of a combined narrative behind *The Wife's Lament* and *The Husband's Message* still has adherents. This propensity was natural and inevitable, given the paucity of the surviving materials and the seemingly forever clouded significance of many items. A final extension of this habit of explaining within a literary closed circuit comes when scholar-critics, subtly or overtly, favourably or unfavourably, compare Old English literature to later works. Such comparison – *x* in Old English is like *y* in later English literature – is not a simple procedure but an elusive and distorting one that assumes, at least for the moment of comparison, the existence of something without a history called 'English literature'. This corpus has no chronology, only rank and value; hence, for example, the infinitely many times that *Genesis B* has been praised because it seems Miltonic.

Very closely related to this is the mimetic, particularly dramatic, bias in English belletristic criticism (Shakespeare's achievement strikes far and deep). William Conybeare's own adoption of this perspective is shown in his discussion of the *Passus* section of *Christ I*; quoting from his brother John, he says,

It is...a *dialogue* between the Virgin Mary and Joseph, imitated probably from some of those apocryphal writings current in the middle ages under the titles of the Life, or the Gospel, of the Virgin...It will be readily agreed that this subject, from its sacred and mysterious nature, is ill adapted to the purposes of poetry. The general absence of taste and refinement which characterized the age in which the poem was originally written, may fairly be pleaded in defence of its author; but in the present day no such excuse could well be discovered for a translator. Indeed, I should have felt disposed to have passed over the poem without notice, had not the dramatic form in which it is written rendered it an object of some curiosity. Dialogues of this kind were probably in our own country, as in Greece, the earliest and rudest species of the drama; and that here preserved is unquestionably by many years the most ancient specimen of this kind of poetry existing in our native language (p. 201).

To which William adds as a footnote: 'The reader, however, is desired to remember the remarks of the editor on the dramatic form of parts of the Junian Cædmon.' Here are laid bare two great principles of judgement which scholar-critics have used in their literary histories of Old English: what is dramatic and tasteful (a rather variable tenet, to be sure) is good. Unfortunately for Old English literature little was found dramatic and much untasteful.

These critical yardsticks remained in use throughout the nineteenth century and still find employment occasionally today. Yet a reversal of some of the earlier denigrations was not long in coming, the second edition of Warton's *History* (1824) signalling the change. In this version, in four volumes, the editor, Richard Price, refers his readers to Turner if they wish to pursue what Warton had omitted, and he then adds this personal comment: 'Indeed there is nothing more striking, or more interesting to the ardent philologer, than the order and regularity preserved in Anglo-Saxon composition, the variety of expression, the innate richness, and plastic power with which the language is endowed' (1, 112). Price's was one of the lone voices that struggled in counterpoint against the persistent general cries of barbarism. Another was Thomas Wright's, in an essay on Anglo-Saxon poetry in *Fraser's Magazine* (12 (1835), 76–88). Prompted to take up his pen in defence of Anglo-Saxon literature because of recent ignorant remarks, Wright shows his generous sympathy towards the artistic products of the Anglo-Saxon era. He passes by the prose writings with a brief apology – 'they are numerous, frequently not very interesting, yet often filled with noble sentiments and acute observations' (p. 81) – though Alfred's translations merit his special praise. As for the poetry, he turns the wheel of accepted judgement nearly full circle:

The characteristics of Anglo-Saxon poetry may be described in a few words, – they are loftiness of expression, exuberance of metaphor, intricacy of construction, and a diction differing entirely from that of prose – precisely the characteristics of the poetry of a people whose mind is naturally poetical, but which has not yet arrived at a state of cultivation and refinement (p. 81).

Only in the last statement is there an echo of the familiar 'childhood of the race' point of view. The history of Old English poetry he divides into two stages, 'a period when it was full of freedom, and originality, and genius, and a later time, when the poets were imitators, who made their verse by freely using the thoughts and expressions of those who had gone before them' (p. 82). By the time of this essay the question of alliteration had been settled, but other fundamental issues had not. Correcting another link in the chain of errors concerning the mere narrative of *Beowulf*, Wright sets Conybeare straight on the interpretation of Unferth's speech. He prints Unferth's entire attack to rectify Conybeare's mistaken reading that Unferth rails at Beowulf's 'piratical exploits' (p. 84). Wright also possessed an intuitive sense for Old English poetic style, for, like Conybeare, he insists that the 'Cædmon' poems have no single author; and he notices, perceptively, the formulaic correspondences between Old English and Old Norse poetry (pp. 87–8).

This natural affinity for the aesthetic values of Old English poetry was partially shared by Henry Wadsworth Longfellow, as he demonstrated in a review essay published three years later (*North Amer. Rev.* 47 (1838), 90–134).

Longfellow encourages his readers to study the Anglo-Saxon language (p. 91), and he paints this picture for those who would take up the challenge: 'Through such gate-ways will they pass, it is true, into no gay palace of song; but among the dark chambers and mouldering walls of an old national literature, all weather-stained and in ruins. They will find, however, venerable names recorded on those walls; and inscriptions, worth the trouble of decyphering' (p. 91). The American poet and translator possessed a reasonable knowledge of both Anglo-Saxon history and the history of Anglo-Saxon studies, though it is difficult to discern whether his jaunty humour is intentional: he writes, 'Thus did mankind go reeling through the Dark Ages; quarrelling, drinking, hunting, hawking, singing psalms, wearing breeches, grinding in mills, eating hot bread, rocked in cradles, buried in coffins, – weak, suffering, sublime' (pp. 98–9). Despite such rhetoric, Long-fellow attempts to provide a comprehensive survey of the literature as it was known in his day. He explains the rudiments of Anglo-Saxon poetic style and includes a long summary of *Beowulf*, though in a manner better suited to children's fantasy. The miracle of Cædmon wins extensive coverage, as does the Cædmonian corpus. *Judith* receives high praise and *The Battle of Brunanburh*, *The Menologium* and *The Rhyming Poem* are accorded full quotation. But, although Longfellow is aware of the Exeter Book through Conybeare's *Illustrations* (one of the volumes he is reviewing), his treatment of that codex is necessarily as inadequate as his model's. The Vercelli Book, of course, had not yet been printed.

Anglo-Saxon prose Longfellow deals with cursorily. The *Saxon Laws* and the *Chronicle* are for him the two great landmarks (p. 125). He greatly admires Alfred and quotes at length from the translation of Boethius, concluding with passages from the prose dialogue of *Solomon and Saturn* and Ælfric's *Colloquy*. He apparently had no great knowledge of nor any interest in the homiletic literature. Conceived as a 'sketch', his essay was the first American work on Anglo-Saxon literature and, whatever its idiosyncracies, it is one of the most satisfactory of the early surveys. Its lapses were not his fault. His attitude may be described as a kind of cheery Gothicism mixed with a curiosity about the domestic realities of Anglo-Saxon life. But his stated intent is to convey a sympathy for this literature, however 'rough-hewn' it may be (p. 134).

John Petheram, in 1840, likewise called his volume a 'sketch'. Since it owed its inception to his plan to produce a bibliography, the work remains utilitarian, historical and unliterary. He may indeed have had a great attachment to the period; he comments that libraries are full of Anglo-Saxon 'materials sufficient to convince the most sceptical that they had made great progress in civilization – we have considered them a race of piratical barbarians, whose history and whose institutions were unworthy of our study' (p. 2). Nonetheless, apart from Ælfric and Alfred – the latter called 'the principal creator of English literature' – he finds little of worth in the many Anglo-Saxon religious texts (p. 13).

Ludwig Etmüller's historical survey occupies only one section of his *Handbuch der deutschen Literaturgeschichte* (1847), for the whole volume covers the literary endeavours of Germania – Old English, Old Scandinavian, Middle Dutch and German. Nevertheless the portion devoted to Anglo-Saxon is not scanty and there is an attempt to understand various aspects of the literature – folk traditions, the influences of foreign invaders and the impact of the church. In some respects Ettmüller's is the first real literary history of these literatures, and it is interesting to note how many of the topics and controversies of modern criticism seem to originate with him. He finds two major strands in these early medieval works – the native folk and the ecclesiastical traditions. He subdivides his subject according to generic categories – epic, lyric, wisdom poetry, riddles and charms. If only briefly, he lists nearly all the Anglo-Saxon texts then available to scholars and many of his comments reveal a good intuitional appreciation of them as literature. While he maintains that *Beowulf*, as we have it, is a reworking of many older epic odes repeatedly changed by later authors (p. 130), he also disputes, on grounds of subject, style and idiom, a single Cædmonian authorship for the Junius poems (pp. 135–9). The space he gives to Anglo-Saxon prose is less satisfactory; he furnishes mainly a list of the major types and titles. Most appealing is his honest esteem for the literature, particularly its lyrics (pp. 139–41). Important, too, is his concern for the sources of the poems, especially the Christian Latin sources of the Cynewulfian school; and he posits that *Guthlac* depends on Felix's life of that saint (p. 134).

The greater portion of another early German survey, Ottomar Behnsch's *Geschichte der englischen Sprache und Literatur im ältesten Zeiten bis zur Einführung der Buchdruckerkunst* (1853), focuses on historical and anthropological questions. The literary treatment is neither lengthy nor comprehensive. But even at this early date certain tendencies which were to become typical of the German school appear. Behnsch concentrates on the development of the Anglo-Saxon literary genres (pp. 31–44), although he discusses them mainly with reference to Anglo-Latin literature. However, in regarding the vernacular lyric, and indeed the epic, as religious rather than 'folk' in origin (pp. 65–6), he stands far apart from later German speculators, who ordinarily set the folk above the cleric.

Two French studies come next chronologically, very different from each other in quality and impact. The first, Frédéric Eichoff's *Tableau de la littérature du nord au moyen âge*, like Ettmüller's survey, treats of more than Anglo-Saxon matters. Although it reflects a certain naive enthusiasm for Anglo-Saxon art, a French reader in the 1850s would have been hard pressed to glean from it much systematic information about Old English literature, and its influence was negligible. It concludes with a few quick sentences on Gildas, Aldhelm and Boniface. By contrast, Hippolyte Taine's famous *Histoire de la littérature anglaise* (1863) (translated into English by H. Van Laun as *History of English Literature* (2 vols., 1871), from which I quote) was certainly one of the most influential documents in literary and social criticism during the nineteenth century. Applying theories of scientific determinism to literature, Taine held that anything in literature can be explained by one of three external circumstances: race (nationality), surroundings or milieu, and epoch (1, 23 ff.). For him literature proceeds from man's animal nature; man creates literature as a silk-worm produces silk. Yet, in spite of Taine's desire to have a scientific, mechanical and value-free criticism, he lapses into subjective judgement frequently enough, and his opening section on Anglo-Saxon literature has all the characteristics of a highly personal reaction. Not surprisingly a good portion of his chapter on 'The Saxons' is in terms of his three categories. The surroundings were foggy and dank; the race he pictures as follows: 'Huge white bodies, cool-blooded, with fierce blue eyes, reddish flaxen hair, ravenous stomachs, filled with meat and cheese, heated by strong drinks; of a cold temperament, slow to love, home-stayers, prone to brutal drunkenness: these are to this day the features which descent and climate preserve in the race' (*ibid.* p. 26). Inside the brute, however, lives a man of truly free and heroic spirit. A German hero is truly heroic (*ibid.* p. 38). *Beowulf* Taine finds especially heroic, rude as he finds its poetry to be (*ibid.* p. 41). Such a race possesses a 'natural' poetry: 'They do not speak, they sing, or rather cry out. Each little verse is an acclamation, which breaks forth like a growl; their strong breasts heave with a groan of anger or enthusiasm, and a vehement phrase or indistinct expression rises suddenly, almost in spite of them, to their lips' (*ibid.* pp. 41–2). This portrait of the Saxons (and by implication all the German races) as a wildly passionate breed remained basic to ideology and criticism for nearly a century. These gloomy people were predisposed to accept Christianity and their capitulatory conversion to this new religion shows up in the poetry with their enthusiasm, 'their natural condition', unchecked (*ibid.* p. 45). Taine mentions Cædmon, but he is more interested in those religious poems that corroborate his notion of the Germans as a morbid people. And it is the savageness of selected Old Testament pieces that greatly impresses him, the hatred of Judith, the terror of the drowning in the Red Sea (*ibid.* p. 48). But beyond the adoption of Christianity, the Anglo-Saxons made no progress in the assimilation of the superior Graeco-Roman civilization (*ibid.* pp. 50 ff.). Their prose works are meagre, for they lacked the art of thinking and reasoning and the uncultivated mind has force only in 'the oneness of its sensations' (*ibid.* p. 53). Taine was not the first to express such opinions; however, he was the most powerful and the most ideological proponent of these racial perspectives. His successors were legion.

The first volume of Henry Morley's *English Writers*, published in 1864, was popular, though not perhaps as influential as Taine's *Histoire*, because its philosophical positions were less boldly announced. In fact, Morley's basic ideas are quite similar to Taine's. He insists that there are no breaks in English national life and that underneath surface disparities lies the one, unchanging English mind (p. 4). His treatment is highly unsystematic: much of the old literature of the Teutons is randomly thrown together, though *Beowulf* has a chapter of its own. Morley embroils himself in the scholarly disputes about myth and history in *Beowulf* and any literary appreciation is kept at a respectable distance. Vol. II (1888), however, presents a more focused and comprehensive view of Old English literature. Morley here finds his nationalistic views both contained in and validated by Old English texts: 'The power of the English character, and therefore of the literature that expresses it, lies in [the] energetic sense of truth and [the] firm habit of looking to the end' (p. 44). In part the renown of Morley's second volume rests more on Henry Bradley's famous review than on the intrinsic worth of the book itself. In this review (in *The Academy* of 24 March 1888) Bradley proposed that the 'First Riddle' had nothing to do with Cynewulf or the ensuing riddles but was instead a dramatic soliloquy spoken by a woman whose lover is an outlaw (p. 198). His remarks on Morley *per se*, however, have their own value: he wishes vol. I had never been published, since it is so filled with errors; he chastises Morley for still believing that Cædmon was the author of the Junian poems; he remarks on Morley's 'favourite contention that the imaginative elements in English literature are due to the admixture of Celtic blood in the English people' (p. 197); but he congratulates him on propounding that Cynewulf wrote only the three poems which were then known to include the runic 'signature'.

The 1870s saw the publication of two extremely important contributions: Henry Sweet's 'Sketch of the History of Anglo-Saxon Poetry', which he contributed to the second volume of the fourth edition of Warton's *History* (1871), and Bernhard ten Brink's *Geschichte der englischen Literatur* (1877) (translated into English by Horace M. Kennedy as *History of English Literature* (1883), from which I quote).

Sweet obviously saw himself as a defender of Old English poetry, and his sane principles of a critical relativism are a new voice in the halls of Anglo-Saxon scholarship. His remarks have a refreshing, combative tone:

This simplicity and freedom of form, which is characteristic of the earliest poetry of all the Teutonic nations, has led narrow-minded and superficial writers to describe Anglo-Saxon poetry as lines of bad prose, joined together by alliteration; forgetting that the highest artistic excellence is attainable in many ways, and that the metrical laws which suit one language, are totally out of place in another of different structure...The leading principle in Anglo-Saxon poetry is to subordinate form to matter (p. 5).

To be sure, he is not without his own personal and nationalistic preconceptions; he adheres to sides in many a scholarly debate which now seem unproven or absurd. He jumps into the fray over the comparative merits of Old English and Old Norse literature and he asserts that Old English comes off the better. Old Norse, he believes, was too technical and undeveloped and finally degenerated 'into a purely mechanical art, valued only in proportion to the difficulty of its execution. The Anglo-Saxons, on the other hand, whilst preserving the utmost technical simplicity, developed not only an elaborate epic style, but what is more remarkable, produced lyric and didactic poetry of high merit' (p. 6). To those who complain of the 'deep gloom' of Anglo-Saxon literature Sweet responds by counterposing its 'high moral idealism' and its descriptions of nature which, in their vividness and individuality, 'make them not inferior to the most perfect examples of descriptive poetry in modern English literature' (pp. 6–7). Traceable back to the early nineteenth century, such Romantic insights here come to dominate the critical field of vision. That Old English was a 'nature' poetry is an idea which has never really disappeared, even under recent concerted attacks.[6]

Sweet acknowledges that the poems we possess may consist of palimpsests that preserve original strophic odes under successive additions and transformations. He is, nevertheless, wary of wielding the editor's emending pen to pare away the layers. Of *Beowulf* he notes, 'the poem as we have it, has undergone considerable alterations. In the first place there is a distinctly Christian element, contrasting strongly with the general heathen colouring of the whole. Many of these passages are so incorporated into the poem, that it is impossible to remove them without violent alterations of the text; others again are palpable interpolations' (p. 10). *Beowulf*, *Widsith* and *The Battle of Finnsburh* are the main examples of 'national epics'. Apart from these the other major category in Old English poetry is religious narrative, though Sweet insists that the poems of this sort 'are entirely national in treatment: the language, costume and habits are purely English; there is no attempt at local or antiquarian colouring' (p. 14). The implicit lament over an absence of local colour betrays his late-nineteenth-century leanings towards a realistic bias in literature derived from an essentially Romantic sensibility. With neither of the two religious 'authors' does Sweet manage well. He admits

---

[6] See E. G. Stanley, *The Search for Anglo-Saxon Paganism* (Cambridge, 1975; repr. of articles originally published in *N&Q* 209–10 (1964–5)).

that Cædmonian poetry has considerable metrical power, but finds it wanting in structure and often mere paraphrase (p. 15). And he accepts credulously the entire Romantic biography of Cynewulf and the swollen canon that accompanied it. This biography posited the existence of a wayward, wandering minstrel who was converted to Christianity in his old age. The conclusion to Sweet's essay declines rapidly into a series of almost disconnected points. He leaves us with the pronouncement that *The Dream of the Rood*, which Cynewulf composed as an introduction to *Elene*, is the 'most valuable of the religious lyrics' (p. 18). Errors of fact and theory, most of which he shared with his contemporaries, do not vitiate, however, his effective defence of Old English poetry, a defence he based on the rational assumption that this literature should be examined and judged on its own terms.

The *Geschichte* of ten Brink stood for several generations as the authoritative literary history. This authority stemmed not so much from a surpassing originality as from a compelling ability to assimilate the major forces in the critical milieu and express them well. These forces or concerns were, as we have seen, race, myth (pagan and Christian) and the historical development of poetical styles and types. But ten Brink mirrors in his attitudes the dominant strain of nineteenth-century myth criticism. For example, he attributes the origin of the Beowulf myth to northern climate and geography:

In such a land developed the myth of Beowa, the divine hero who overcame the sea-giant, Grendel, and fighting the fire-spitting dragon, – also a personification of the raging sea – slew and was slain. But Beowa did not remain forever dead. He is essentially Frea in a new form, the bright god of warmth and fruitfulness, whose gold-bristled boar decked the helmets of the English warriors (1, 2).

These warriors, members of a melancholy and emotional race (*ibid.* p. 7), inherited from their ancestors a strophic and hymnic poetry. The style of this poetry gained stability at the time strophic form disappeared and was replaced by extended narrative. However, the full blossoming of an English epos was arrested. It withered from within and collapsed under pressures from without, for the introduction of Christianity 'destroyed the productive power of epic poetry. The vital continuity of the mythical tradition was interrupted' (*ibid.* p. 28). Ten Brink identifies himself with the neo-paganism and vitalism that inevitably accompany late-nineteenth-century myth criticism. And present too is the dangerous idea that the strength and value of a literature depend on its authenticity, its power to embody the purity of 'the folk', and its 'manly' commitment to heroic risk.

As a consequence of his recognition of the distance between Anglo-Saxon poetry and its primitive origins ten Brink provides the first full commentary on the influence of Latin syntax and rhetoric on these Germanic pieces, though the marriage, he feels, is not always blessed. Cynewulf is a case in point:

His taste is not so cultivated as his faculty of imagination and his power of language. Sometimes his subject-matter is obnoxious to our sense; at other times our ardour is dampened by the ever-crowding outbreaks of the poet's enthusiasm. In the last instance the discord between the old form and the new matter prevents a quite complete enjoyment (*ibid.* p. 59).

Of course, we are not to trust his remarks with respect to Cynewulf, since he also thinks Cynewulf to have been the author of vastly more poems than he actually was, and he subscribes as well to the fictional biography then current.

Ten Brink deserves praise for the space he allots to Anglo-Saxon achievements in prose. He reveals his usual sensitivity to style in his dicta on various authors. Ælfric's style, he says, 'is conspicuous for clearness and graceful finish. His language has a more modern garb as to form and phrase than the Ælfredian, and adapts itself more easily to the sequence of thought' (*ibid.* 106). The popularity of ten Brink's work derives not only from its impressive command of all English literature, but also from the clear ring of authority his voice still carries.

Throughout the history of Anglo-Saxon scholarship, and especially in the nineteenth century, critics made a general assumption that any monument from Germania could be used to explain any phenomenon from a Germanic culture. The most persistent manifestation of this idea was the equation of Norse mythology, written down in late medieval times, with the occasional allusion or curious practice recorded in Old English literature. Br. Azarias, for example, made this his guiding principle in *The Development of English Literature: the Old English Period* (1879). Anglo-Saxon 'philosophy', so called, he derives entirely from late Scandinavian sources. But the most extreme case of this dubious procedure shows itself in *The Englishman and the Scandinavian: a Comparison of Anglo-Saxon and Old Norse Literature* by Frederick Metcalfe (1880). One chapter is even entitled 'The Mythology of Germany, Scandinavia, and England Alike'. Connected to such an assumption is a series of related positions, all of them elevating the values of a pagan culture scholars deem to be present in the virile literature of the north. Thus for Metcalfe the poetry of war is the northern scop's highest achievement; and of the battle in *Judith* he says, 'Never was war painted more to the life' (p. 130). His complete distrust for all Mediterranean culture is patent: 'Nowhere is the stubborn nationality of our forefathers more thoroughly shown than in the way these epic poems continued to assert themselves in spite of the so much over-prized book-learning and the ultramontane feelings which mastered their prose' (p. 139). Such an attitude finds its natural parallel in a rejection of the Christianity associated with 'book-learning' and 'ultramontane' sympathies: 'Next this old poetic literature yielded to another influence. It was kidnapped, and its features so altered and disguised as not to be recognisable. It was supplanted by Christian poetical legends and Bible lays, produced in rivalry of the popular lays of their heathen predecessors' (p. 155). As literary history Metcalfe's comparative study is not of enduring value, but as a symbol of a whole way of seeing Old English literature it is a treasure.

The fact that John Earle's small book, *Anglo-Saxon Literature* (1884), was published by the Society for Promoting Christian Knowledge is obviously revealing, for, so far as possible, the book emphasizes the development of the Christian strand in Anglo-Saxon life and letters. Earle begins with a history of Anglo-Saxon scholarship and includes sections on ancillary subjects – art, archaeology, palaeography and the like. His major division is between primary and secondary poetry, the former being 'rooted in the native genius of the race' as opposed to the latter 'manifestly of Latin material' (p. 119). He does not imply, however, that the two remained utterly distinct. But his critical methods seem somewhat curious, and he concludes a long summary of *Beowulf* by noting that it closes, like the *Iliad*, 'with a great bale-fire' (p. 133). He has no doubt that *Beowulf* is a Christian poem written in the tenth century. Proof of both religious affiliation and date he derives from internal evidence:

A pardonable fancy might see the date conveyed in the poem itself. The dragon watches over an old hoard of gold, and it is distinctly a heathen hoard (hæðnum horde, 2,217) of heathen gold (hæðen gold, 2,277). In the same context we find that the monster had watched over this earth-hidden treasure for 300 years; and if this may be something more than a poetical number, it may possibly indicate the time elapsed since the heathen age. Three hundred years would bring us to the close of the ninth or the beginning of the tenth century (pp. 136–7).

The logic here is demonstrably circular. Earle's interests are cultural and partisan, not literary. He seems more taken with Anglo-Saxon cattle than with the poetry (*vide* his long excursus on the West Saxon laws, pp. 160 ff.), and we are not surprised to find him more at home among the Old English homilies than among less spiritual texts.

Earle later composed a history of English prose which deserves brief mention (*English Prose: its Elements, History, and Usage* (1890)). Here he contends that English prose began in the Old English period and that England thus has 'a longer pedigree of prose literature than any other country in Europe' (p. 369). Passing over Ine's laws, he begins in the eighth century, where he finds 'the first continuous narrative in prose' (p. 370). Such prose, however, was greatly inferior to the mature poetry of the time. Earle offers an Old English translation of a charter issued by Æthelbald, king of Mercia, in 744 and part of the Cynewulf and Cyneheard episode in the *Chronicle* as examples. Only a severely limited portion of the book is devoted to Old English prose. Earle praises Alfred's prose for its 'unconscious strength and dignity', but he chooses little of it to print (p. 375). He notes that in the tenth century a standard in prose was achieved for the first time, and he includes some charters, translations of the bible and the prose dialogue of *Solomon and Saturn* (p. 377). Wulfstan is present, though Ælfric is barely mentioned. Earle comments thus on the last flowering of Anglo-Saxon prose: 'The language of the Eleventh century presents, in its best specimens, little to distinguish it from that of the Tenth, and this is but the natural result of the fact that a standard or norm had now been attained. The prose diction had entered into a condition of stability and permanency' (p. 383). The full history of Anglo-Saxon prose literature was yet to be written.

As Richard Wülker emphasizes, his *Grundriss zur Geschichte der angelsächsischen Literatur* (1885) is a descriptive outline of the research in the area and not really a literary history (p. vi). The first section comprises a historical review of work in philology and the second a compendium of various dictionaries, readers, collections, histories and specialized studies available for the study of Old English language and literature. But the third section, which represents the bulk of the work, provides a survey of the literary monuments, divided into sixteen sub-sections with much bibliographical information. The topics cover the standard repertoire of mid-nineteenth-century German scholarship, especially full being the treatment of questions of dating and authorship, both determined by stylistic analysis. The importance of the work lies in its dissection of the main scholarly controversies; the essay on *Beowulf*, for example, concentrates on the pagan/Christian dispute, the battle over Müllenhoff's *Liedertheorie* and dating (pp. 292–307). Wülker decides in favour of a Christian redactor who worked over old lays, probably shortly after 650. He concentrates on examining the evidence on the vexed questions in Anglo-Saxon scholarship. Often his analysis succeeds – he cuts off many a spurious branch from the growing Cynewulfian tree and he discounts the existence of any specifically dramatic forms among the Anglo-Saxons – though he allows some egregious errors to remain (pp. 385–6).

Gustav Körting used a title similar to Wülker's for a volume spanning the whole of English literature, *Grundriss der Geschichte der englischen Literatur* (1887). For the Anglo-Saxon period, however, his effort cannot match Wülker's. He is unabashed in his pan-Germanic outlook and insists that the

English are Germanic, not a 'mixed people' (*Mischvolk*), despite the addition of Norman and other races (p. 1). These assertive racial biases are closely related to his belief in the gender identifications of nations. He believes that the Anglo-Saxons developed away from their (good) masculine, Germanic heritage towards a (bad) feminine, Christian state of weakness. This peculiar mixture of the coarse and the effeminate manifests itself in the poetry, especially in the lyrics (p. 29). Such literary dicta are not very noteworthy, though his Germanic racial ideas are (and are disturbing). Still he is not without a certain sense on some matters: he goes one step beyond Wülker and assigns only the 'signed' poems to Cynewulf (p. 50). However, he dismisses Ælfric's works as insignificant for literary study and would have us accept that none of the religious prose has any value (p. 74).

Karl W. A. Ebert's survey of Old English literature in the third volume of his *Allgemeine Geschichte der Literatur des Mittelalters im Abendlande* (1887) places strong emphasis on Latin literature as both a precedent and an accompaniment to the emerging national literatures. His treatment of the Latin backgrounds to Old English poetry and prose is excellent, especially when compared with contemporary surveys. His remarks on individual texts are not remarkable, but his general concern for defining the essence of Anglo-Saxon political, religious and literary culture is. He considers that the Anglo-Saxons represent a highly developed, individual branch of the Germanic family tree and that their swift reception of Christianity must be taken as a sign of their national maturity. In addition, Anglo-Saxon paganism had taken on a more monotheistic cast before the conversion than had its German counterparts, probably as a result of its separation from its continental roots (p. 4). Old English poetry, however, he claims, still retains its ur-Germanic spiritual idealism, contrasting sharply with the Celto-Romanic tendency towards a sensual realism (p. 8). Ebert also deserves praise for the full consideration he gives to Old English prose.

The title of J. J. Jusserand's volume, *Histoire littéraire du peuple anglais* (1894) (which he translated into English as *A Literary History of the English People* (3 vols., 1895–1909); I quote from the first volume), states his own emphasis succinctly enough. His is not a '"History of English Literature", but rather a "Literary History of the English People"' (p. ix). But, if Jusserand has a special fondness for the English, it is for the 'people' who emerged in the centuries after the Norman Conquest, as his assessment of late-eleventh-century England makes plain: 'Out of this chaos how can a nation arise? a nation that may give birth to Shakespeare, crush the Armada, people the American continent? No less than a miracle is needed. The miracle took place: it was the battle of Hastings' (p. 93). Surely even the most partisan observer would see some exaggeration in this. But for anyone who believes, as Jusserand did, that the English love death, whereas the French love life (p. 57), such exultation at the Saxon defeat would be hard to suppress.

Jusserand holds that Old English literature is not *English* literature. After examining *The Phoenix* he states, 'There are, doubtless, rays of light in Anglo-Saxon literature, which appear all the more brilliant for being surrounded by shadow; but this example of a poem sunny throughout is unique. To find others, we must wait till Anglo-Saxon has become English literature' (p. 78). One suspects he means 'until it has become French literature'. He is full of the old platitudes concerning the lack of refinement in the products of those passionate, emotional scops. Paradoxically, though, his section dealing with Old English literature confuses it completely with Old Norse poetry. Without a moment's hesitation he equates the works in Grein's *Bibliothek der angelsächsischen Poesie* with Vigfusson and Powell's *Corpus Poeticum Boreale*: 'The resemblances between the two collections are striking, the differences are few. In both series it seems as if the same people were revealing its origins, and leading its heroes to Walhalla' (pp. 40–1). Granting that Old English poetry has 'a force, a passion, a grandeur, unexampled at that day' (p. 40), Jusserand remains so naturally out of sympathy with the literature that his chapter on Old English has value only as a curio, for placing an English national treasure in a decidedly foreign perspective.

W. J. Courthope's chapter on 'The Poetry of the Anglo-Saxons' in his widely read *History of English Poetry* (1895) is predictably unhelpful, for he begins with the assumption that the poetry of Chaucer, 'the fitting starting-point of the History', bears no relation to the Anglo-Saxon (p. xxvii). Not expecting to find poetry of merit from this era, Courthope succeeds in not finding it. He rests content in dividing Old English poetry into three classes, making some casual remarks about race, language and prosody before moving on to more serious art. His three classes are: (1) poems revealing an unmixed cast of Teutonic thought (but liable to alteration by monks); (2) poems composed after the conversion, mainly on scriptural materials and (3) poems in which a Latin ecclesiastical education prevails over the Teutonic spirit (pp. 82–3).

One of the most important critics of medieval literature, W. P. Ker, wrote no history of Anglo-Saxon literature as such. His remarks, often eccentric, are scattered through three books, *The Dark Ages* (1897), *Epic and Romance* (1897) and *English Literature: Medieval* (1922). But taken as a whole they comprise an overview. His depreciation of *Beowulf* has been made available to those who have never read him by Tolkien, but even his inability to come to terms with the narrative mode of *Beowulf* does not prevent him from bearing witness to its artistic stature: '*Beowulf* is unmistakably heroic and weighty. The thing itself is cheap; the moral and the spirit of it can only be matched among the noblest authors' (*The Dark Ages*, p. 253). Actually *Beowulf* only suffers from a common plague, as we see in his comments on *Exodus*: 'few mediæval poems are more effectively concentrated on the right points in the story' (*ibid.* p. 260). Ker's work has such simple hard-headedness that one readily excuses him on those occasions when he goes wrong. He captures nearly half a century of academic folly in this pronouncement: 'Much has been written about the conjectural biography of Cynewulf, and some of the worst logic in the world has been applied to the subject' (*ibid.* p. 261). About Cynewulf's style he speaks with great precision. It is, he says, 'distinguished by a sensitive use of language, a rhetorical grace, not unconscious: he is a correct poet' (*ibid.* p. 262). And even though he joins company with those who perceive a deep cleavage between Anglo-Saxon literature and the main stream of English poetry – 'Dr Johnson is hardly farther from *Beowulf* than Chaucer is' (*ibid.* p. 17) – he ends by according it high value. He insists on the 'literate' quality of Old English poems and disbelieves that they are orally composed. The poetry has the 'characteristics of an accomplished literary school, with a fully developed language and a regular traditional method of expression' (*ibid.* p. 247). If Ker finds the literature of historical adventure, clearly told, superior to the dense and ornamented style of many Old English religious works, he expresses thereby a taste widely shared.

Stopford A. Brooke wrote two histories of Old English literature – the first, published in 1892, *The History of Early English Literature, being the History of English Poetry from its Beginnings to the Accession of King Ælfred*, the second, *English Literature from the Beginning to the Norman Conquest*, appearing in 1898. The former, as its subtitle indicates, deals almost exclusively with the poetry, while the second deals also with prose, in two long chapters. Brooke's preoccupations and predelictions do not change from one volume to the next, however. Of all those who have reacted to Old English literature with irritating cultural narcissism, he is the epitome. His late-nineteenth-century sensibilities – a racial pride, a Romantic exuberance to the point of overbearing enthusiasm, and a sentimental Christianity – vitiate his broad knowledge and committed scholarship. He himself puts it bluntly: 'Questions of race are often questions of literature' (*English Literature from the Beginning to the Norman Conquest*, p. 8). And the genius of Old English literature derives at base from the mixture of the Germanic and Celtic imaginations. The Germans created a 'whole world of fearful imagination...which has never left our literature' (*ibid.* p. 12), while the Celts had a 'more imaginative way of looking at man and nature...a more intense sense of life in all things' (*ibid.* p. 22). His critical discussions of individual poems are effusive, smug and insular. *Beowulf* is described as having 'the gentleness of Nelson, and his firmness in battle...Fear, as also in Nelson, is wholly unknown to him...It is a trait worthy of the captains at Trafalgar' (*ibid.* p. 63). Believing the entire Romantic biography of Cynewulf and accepting the riddles as his work, Brooke writes of Riddle VIII: 'This is of a quality almost unimaginable in poetry of the eighth century. It is like poetry of our own time. The "power of clouds" is a phrase Wordsworth might have used' (*ibid.* p. 93). The Storm Riddle prompts this comparison: 'The first two lines describe the old moon with the young moon in her arms long before Sir Patrick Spence saw it. The rising of the sun over the roof of the world, his setting, the dust and dew and the advent of night are done with the conciseness and force of Tennyson' (*ibid.* p. 95). He praises the gentleness of Christianity and speaks of Bede's *Ecclesiastical History* as 'full of lovely and tender stories' (*ibid.* p. 100).

If Stopford Brooke endows Old English literature with Romantic effulgence, George Saintsbury, in *A Short History of English Literature* (1898), dismisses it with witty condescension. In the slightly pretentious tone of the gentleman-scholar, Saintsbury makes light of the efforts of the scops for thirty-seven pages before passing on, in the next 770, to the real English literature. Like Jusserand, though not perhaps for like reasons, he believes that the Conquest was a good thing for English literary history (pp. 29–31). He is genuinely bored by pre-Conquest poetry and finds the prose even 'of less literary interest than the verse' (p. 19). Given this attitude, we should not expect, nor indeed do we find, much of lasting value on Old English in his very popular history; only because of its influence and widespread use does it warrant inclusion. The aesthetic of Old English poems is so far removed from his idea of poetry that any appreciation on his part is impossible; he believes in the superiority of Latin culture and its poetic modes and thus can praise the *Deor* poet for his 'advance' in inventing the stanza: 'He had grasped the *stanza*, the great machine for impressing form upon the almost formless void; and he had grasped the *refrain*, which is not only a mighty set-off to poetry in itself, but has the inestimable property of naturally suggesting rhyme, the greatest and most precious of all poetical accidents' (p. 7). To those well acquainted with Old English literature Saintsbury's errors are apparent; his general audience, however, were no doubt as unaware of the mistakes as they were attuned to his patronizing wit.

Saintsbury's work was published in 1898 and by 1900 his opinions had already made their way to Japan through the lectures of the Irish-American journalist and writer, Lafcadio Hearn. Saintsbury had determined that the secular poems were better than the religious because they were 'original' and not translated. For the less than thirty pages occupied by the elegies in the Grein–Wülcker edition he would gladly abandon most of the religious verse (p. 15). And this is how Hearn reshapes that idea for his students at the

Imperial University of Tokyo: 'The bulk of old English literature, being religious, need not greatly interest us at present: we can dismiss it with a few paragraphs. But there was some profane literature – which would make...about 30 pages in print. And these 30 pages are, from the literary point of view, worth more than all the religious literature of the time.'[7] His lectures are valuable for their misconceptions. If he rejects Christian poetry, it is because it is Christian. The vestigial pagan elements in it he finds good. But one who can believe that 'it was the old pagan poetry in the heart of Cædmon that may have inspired Milton'[8] can believe anything, and Hearn's chapters are error-ridden.

In 1901 Charlton Lewis, decrying the state of the art, complained that all the existing histories 'are either very elementary in treatment or so crowded with barren statements of unimportant facts' that they never give the student a proper sense of the literature. He wanted his own endeavour, *The Beginnings of English Literature*, to be an introduction to the study of Elizabethan and later English literature rather than a history of Anglo-Saxon literature as such (p. iii). His book is simple and old-fashioned even for that time. We need not detail his particular version of the uncouth poetry, its lack of form, the Viking spirit of the warlike bards and the denigration of the monastic system and of its Christian literary models. That story is by now too familiar.

It is with a sense of relief and renewal, then, that we turn to one of the great monuments in Old English literary history, Alois Brandl's 'Die angelsächsische Literatur' (1901).[9] After noting that English literature begins as a purely Germanic phenomenon, Brandl states that it displayed an independence which cannot be observed in any other Germanic people toward the spiritual hegemony of Rome (p. 941). The next five hundred years, however, brought a Romanization in themes, thoughts and forms which is also unparalleled in England's Germanic relatives. Brandl assumes that there existed a period rich in heathen poetry prior to the completion of the conversion in the seventh and eighth centuries. Excepting a few fragments, however, there are no literary remains of a purely heathen character, a fact explained by the monopoly which clerics held over literacy. Thus the division of works into Christian and pagan categories for the period before Alfred can be only tentative and relative, and Brandl rejects the old dogma of chronology which automatically assigned works of a pagan nature to a date earlier than works of obvious Christian piety (p. 945).

Because of the difficulty attending any attempt to divide the various Anglo-Saxon literary epochs in a usual way, Brandl chooses to organize his

---

[7] *A History of English Literature in a Series of Lectures by Lafcadio Hearn [1900–3]* (Tokyo, 1927) I, 20–1.
[8] *Ibid.* p. 35.
[9] Hermann Paul, *Grundriss der germanischen Philologie*, 2nd ed., 3 vols. (Strassburg, 1901–9) II, 941–1134.

history by genre, a method which also has the advantage of revealing the influence of Old Germanic traditions on later works (p. 946). What he calls 'Old Country' poetry (*Altheimische Dichtung*) comes in two forms, which are socially distinct: (1) the magical formulae of the heathen priests and (2) the courtly poetry of the scop and gleeman. Priestly poetry tended to be very conservative, preserving the names of the old gods and retaining the abnormally short verses which are also characteristics of Old Norse ritual poetry; the courtly poetry rarely reveals such conservative traits (pp. 954–5). After fully discussing strophic form and the various kinds of lament, Brandl turns to the didactic poetry which he divides into 'spells' and 'lar' (teachings): 'spells' were used by heathen priests to impress the stories of the gods on the people; the 'lar' were more pedagogical and less emotional in tone (p. 960). Of all the extant didactic poems, only the Cotton Gnomes approach the genre of the 'spell'. In another major category, 'Old World Genres' (*Altweltliche Gattungen*), are to be found most of the types ordinarily recognized as belonging to Anglo-Saxon literature: the *Merkverse* (mnemonic verses), *Sprichwörter* (adages, of which only a few isolated examples survive), riddles, lyrics and epics. Brandl remarks on the strong epic tendencies that occur in both the riddles and the elegies, and he posits the existence of tavern songs (*Gesellschaftslieder*), although none has survived (p. 973). *The Battle of Finnsburh* is the closest to the original genre of the gleeman's lay (p. 983). Brandl compares *Beowulf* with these lays and rejects the theory that the poem represents a mere expansion on a series of such songs (p. 1004).

In his treatment of the Christian poetry Brandl devotes much space to dating, sources and the relations of the poems to older genres. Cædmon is obviously the father of Anglo-Saxon religious poetry (p. 1028), but Cynewulf and his school mark off the major division in Old English Christian poetry and Brandl uses this fact to date the poems. In sum, he describes the development of Christian poetry in the two centuries from Cædmon to the disaster of 866–70 as the enrichment of the old Germanic genres by the new Christian spirit. This led to numerous experimental creations and to a literate tradition. The narrator's sense of detail was sharpened and Nature was seen in a more benign perspective. The sense of reason became more reflective and perception more intimate, even mystical. New genres appeared (such as the saint's legend); end-rhyme was introduced and metaphor developed. On the other hand, traditional myths and legends lost their transmitters among the aristocratic scops and the comitatus system became only a thin veneer when applied to Christian heroes. Much of the power and feeling in the poetry was lost with the transition from an oral to a written medium as the centre of gravity shifted out of the material world into the moral sphere (p. 1051).

Unlike most of his predecessors and many of his successors, Brandl provides a detailed history of Anglo-Saxon prose. He treats the legal documents and the religious writings before Alfred (pp. 1051–62). The single most important and original piece of prose before Alfred himself is, of course, the *Anglo-Saxon Chronicle* (Brandl does not allow *Chronicle* and uses *Annals* instead). To try to cover in detail his handling of Alfred's translations would be inappropriate; he continues to demonstrate a superb command of the scholarship and shows his usual sensitivity to stylistic nuances and variation among the works ascribed to the king.

Next follows an examination of the secular poetry from the tenth century to the early twelfth. In comparison to the long works of the preceding period those of this era are of only modest proportions and, unfortunately, it is the last works that seem to contain the most innovative motifs (p. 1075). Alliterative verse was still employed, but mechanically. End-rhyme was also used, but rarely with consistency. Pure alliteration probably dominated until about 1000, that is until the codification of the old Anglo-Saxon poetry in the form of *Beowulf, Judith* and the Exeter and Vercelli Books. After this point end-rhyme became dominant, though consistent use of this technique did not establish itself until about 1200 (p. 1076). Brandl treats the second great period of Anglo-Saxon prose as spaciously as he does the first, finally dividing its homiletic writings into two types: (1) the story-telling homily of Ælfric and (2) the moralizing sermon of Wulfstan (p. 1112). Homilies of the story-telling type used themes from both gospel and apocryphal sources and, despite their low literary value, for the first time presented biblical narratives and saints' lives not in a Germanic guise meant to appeal to the nobility but in their unaltered Hebraic or Italian garb. Brandl's thoroughness permits him to include the many minor texts from the end of the Anglo-Saxon period. At the time of the Norman Conquest the basis for a new poetry had been created with the introduction of end-rhyme; homiletic prose had developed a style capable of powerful expression; in the area of education there was a tight network spread over the entire land. The Norman conquerors, however, overturned the social order and, occupying all the important positions and appropriating the lands of the Anglo-Saxon nobility, took patronage away from both the Anglo-Saxon schools and the Anglo-Saxon poets (p. 1133). Brandl's history is unquestionably one of the finest achievements in Old English scholarship. It is mature, reasonably objective and unbiased, systematic, detailed, based on an extraordinarily broad and accurate scholarship and sensitive to the aesthetic values inherent in the literature.

None of the contemporary work can match Brandl's history and none of it is remembered now as especially important except for the collaborative volume in *The Cambridge History of English Literature*. F. St John Corbett's chapters on Old English poetry in his *A History of British Poetry* (1904) are a good example of this period, though they are deficient in themselves. Unable to get his facts straight, even such facts as were established at that time, Corbett hardly represents the high point of early-twentieth-century scholarship or critical perception. He still maintains the ancient fantasy that Cædmon wrote *The Dream of the Rood* (p. 46) and a single quotation on *Beowulf* will suffice to show both his inaccuracies and his defective critical attitude:

[*Beowulf*] is a Norse saga, and illustrates, in a highly romantic and picturesque manner, some of the early Gothic customs and superstitions. The use of metaphors is common in the poem, but it contains only five similes – a lack of the latter being a characteristic of Anglo-Saxon poetry.... It is thought that it was written in the fifth century. It was edited, in the form in which we now have it, in the eighth century (p. 7).

Cynewulf's single redeeming feature is his ability to compose sea poetry (p. 48).

Corbett, of course, was certainly neither the first nor the last to see the Anglo-Saxon scops as budding John Masefields. An American history published a year later harps on precisely the same theme. William Vaughn Moody's *A History of English Literature* (1905) finds this spark in Old English poems: 'this sea-faring life, full of danger and change, was the fruitful source of early poetry. Whenever an Anglo-Saxon poet mentions the sea his lines kindle' (p. 2). The Anglo-Saxons were, though, pagan savages, and 'in studying the early poetry, we must put out of our minds...all those ideals of life and conduct which come from Christianity, and remember that we have to do with men whose gods were only magnified images of their own wild natures' (pp. 2–3). Consequently, Moody sees the Christian passages in a good many poems as 'Christian coloring' (he is, of course, not alone here). The 'Cædmon' poems make good battle-hymns (pp. 12–14). Moody discusses no saints' lives, no religious poems. Cynewulf is mentioned, but not the title of any poem, though the riddles and *The Phoenix* are dubbed 'Cynewulfian' (pp. 14–16).

A most curious item lodged among the surveys is Edmund Dale's *National Life and Character in the Mirror of Early English Literature* (1907). Dale does not focus on Anglo-Saxon literature but on 'the ever-developing character of the Englishman in the successive ages of his early career' (p. 1). We find nothing new in his analysis. By permitting 'the Englishman to speak for himself' (p. 1) through his own writings, Dale manages to paint a violent, passionate creature, totally given over to 'the full realisation of personality' and tenaciously devoted to individual liberty (pp. 32–3). But Dale's methods are so bizarre that his conclusions are immediately suspect. When he speaks of Cynewulf's Juliana and her father as representative of an English family (p. 50), we realize that he has no sound sense of the sources and no notion of the complex way in which Anglo-Saxon literature fuses its diverse traditions.

The search for the English national character was also the self-imposed task of M. M. Arnold Schröer, who begins his *Grundzüge und Haupttypen der englischen Literaturgeschichte* (1906) by criticizing existing histories for pretending to objectivity and lack of national bias (p. 5). Bias is what the proper literary history *should* offer. Although he gives a survey of the literature, Schröer is mainly concerned that his German view of the English should tint the way in which Germans read English literature, starting with Anglo-Saxon. The main characteristics of English culture are (1) a slow but steady development, (2) conservatism and (3) easy acceptance of what is foreign and new (pp. 14–15). These characteristics have their origin in the insular isolation and in the constant racial mixture which led to the peculiar vitality of the English. This *Lebenskraft* balances the common English tendency towards *Verrücktheit* ('craziness', 'spleen'). The eccentrics, cranks and oddballs are basically melancholics because of the foggy climate; their strange upbringing permits a certain freedom of self-determination denied to the Germans. This leads to 'stubbornness' (*Dickköpfigkeit*), 'foolishness' (*Torheit*) and 'oddity' (*Absonderlichkeit*). Another aspect of this freedom is English egotism, often manifested in an 'insulting ruthlessness' (*verletzende Rücksichtslosigkeit*) (pp. 18–19). Schröer may be less Romantic in his portrayal of the English national character than Dale, but he is no less sure that such concerns are the stuff of literary history and the foundation of critical procedure.

In sharp contrast to the amusing and eccentric studies of Dale and Schröer stands the imposing *Cambridge History* (1907). But, as the product of many hands, it is difficult to characterize precisely. Composition by committee has always resulted in the loss of a striking personal idiom. The work is conservative, straightforward, comprehensive and sensible. The chapter on 'Runes and Manuscripts' (pp. 7–18) must have been welcome to its early readers, for such material did not often find its way into the conventional history. None of the several authors attempts any detailed criticism; the approach is descriptive and historical. Occasionally we get a whiff of snobbery: '[Ælfric] refused to be led astray by the example of Latin syntax and preferred simple constructions. Unfortunately, as time went on, he deferred more and more to the preferences of his audience, and debased his prose by throwing it into the rhythmical alliterative form popular with the vulgar' (p. 141). Still the clarity of the style and organization of the separate essays reasonably made this history a major resource for students and scholars for over half a century.

In spite of its misleading title, F. J. Snell's *The Age of Alfred* (1912) covers all Anglo-Saxon literature. The work is marked by an insistence that all good literature is 'realistic'. Needless to say, this slant falls awkwardly on much Old English poetry. Snell is neither the only critic nor even the most important or representative to hold this attitude, but it biases all his judgements so clearly that its application to Old English literature can be profitably identified here. The resulting dislocation is quite extreme. According to Snell, for example, Cynewulf's 'dithyrambic strains exhibit more passion than imagination. Intent on self-expression rather than self-discipline, he will not accept the common limitations of art, which is concerned as much with little as with great things, with picturesque detail no less than sweeping generalisations, with the concrete no less than the abstract' (p. 5). Furthermore the 'absurdities' of Widsith's far-flung travels must be explained away 'as a burlesque dating from a period when the minstrel's art had fallen into some disrepute, as a satire on the boastful propensities of the vagabond, illiterate, gain-seeking race of gleeman' (p. 26). Finally, Snell indicts the aesthetic of all Old English narrative poetry:

we come to the *scóp's* style of narration with respect to the marshalling of his facts. Here we light upon an undoubted weakness of Anglo-Saxon poetry, in which there is seldom any regard for the gradual development of a plot, the character of the actors being always thought of as vastly more important than the circumstances leading up to the critical points of a relation (p. 54).

This is only a later version of the old neo-classical complaints about lack of form. Now the dissatisfaction stems from the poet's inability to narrate his 'picturesque details' or 'facts'.

Von Kaedmon bis Kynewulf: eine literarhistorische Studie (1913) by Gregor Sarrazin requires some special attention because of its ample follies and idiosyncracies. Sarrazin set himself the task of tracing the outlines of a more reliable chronology of Anglo-Saxon literature than had previously been realized (p. 2). He has sharp words for the recent scholarly work, but he praises in contrast the older scholars for their great sensitivity to style (p. 1). Although deploring the pedantic rule-consciousness of modern scholars, he adopts five 'objective' criteria, which, used together, can help him in approximating the actual sequence of the Old English texts: (1) metrical–grammatical, (2) syntactic, (3) lexical, (4) stylistic and (5) literary historical (pp. 2–7). Sarrazin remarks that a synthesis of all these permits the chronology of the early Anglo-Saxon poems to be determined with a high degree of probability. Still, he regards the sense for style, for what he calls the 'literary physiognomy', as the scholar's most valuable tool (p. 9).

It is unnecessary to review each of Sarrazin's uncommon conclusions. Some of them include the assertion that the Scandinavian tradition was the major contributor to the supernatural elements in *Beowulf*. Indeed, for him,

Scandinavian romanticism and mysticism affect the spiritual poetry, in that simple Old Testament stories give place to ecstatic legends full of wonders and visions (p. 61). For complicated reasons he believes that *Beowulf* must have been composed between 730 and 740 (p. 74); the poem's affinities with contemporary Scandinavian epic poetry are striking (pp. 86–9); and it shares so many features with the riddles that identity of authorship is proposed (p. 112). In fine, *Beowulf*, the riddles, *The Dream of the Rood* and the works of 'Kynewulf' should all be ascribed to one author; whether or not one wants to call this poet 'Kynewulf' is of little importance (p. 125). Sarrazin's history is an astonishing document, for, unlike so many of its nineteenth-century predecessors, it does not derive from the author's unacknowledged personal bias. In a dogged and pseudo-scientific way he subjects the literature to a painstaking analysis, only to reach a series of conclusions that border on the ludicrous. His is an archetypal example of reliance on intuition gone astray.

Charles S. Baldwin's *An Introduction to English Medieval Literature* (1914) need detain us only briefly. Placing more emphasis on the history and backgrounds than on the poems, Baldwin reveals an interesting fusion of two well-established perspectives. When discussing the poetry he harks back to the notion that Anglo-Saxon civilization was England in its infancy. But he goes on to compare *Beowulf* with Roman and Greek epics, demonstrating that the Anglo-Saxon poem and the classical models work in much the same way. By implication, therefore, *Beowulf* is nearly as good as Homer or Vergil. Still, all Anglo-Saxon literature is defective in form, and for all his insistence on the literary achievement of the early English, Baldwin does not abandon the old characterization of their art as loose and clumsy (pp. 51–3).

Whereas Baldwin attempts to give *Beowulf* its due by comparing it to the *Iliad* and the *Aeneid*, Hubert Pierquin devalues it by allotting it one paragraph in his entire volume, *Les Lettres, les sciences, les arts, la philosophie et la religion des Anglo-Saxons* (1914). *Judith* he finds more to his taste, because the poet has added to the scriptural narrative the colours and customs of his own time (p. 39). Very wrong in fact and very French in attitude, Pierquin's opinions come straight out of the eighteenth century, and one wonders why he even bothered to write a description of a literature he disliked so intensely and found so unsuited to his aesthetic ideals. Another work which should be noted in passing is Allen R. Benham's *English Literature from Widsith to the Death of Chaucer* (1916), imitating the writing of political history. It is a source book and not in any strict sense of the word a literary survey, Benham acknowledging that 'most of the space...is given to the backgrounds, – political, social, industrial, and cultural – which largely determine the literary output' (p. xi). Strong ideas on the genesis of art are certainly implicit in the original design and in this statement, but Benham does not make the connections between the backgrounds and the art.

Andreas Heusler, in *Altgermanische Dichtung* (1923), concerns himself with three broad and related topics: the origin of the poems, the merging of separate traditions, and the implications of generic and thematic history for form and style. First Heusler accounts for the early and widespread literary use of the vernacular in England in contrast to Germany and the Frankish empire. He believes that the explanation lies in the strength of local traditions in relation to foreign ecclesiastical influence, as evidenced in the use of Anglo-Saxon for writing laws and keeping annals (p. 3). But for him the greatest difference between England and Germany was that many Anglo-Saxon clerics learned the art of the secular poet in order to employ it on ecclesiastical themes (pp. 3–4). Wanting to search out the pure Germanic core of Anglo-Saxon poetic art, Heusler establishes these criteria: 'Germanic' poems must be (1) secular, (2) not imitations of any Roman genres, (3) not derived from books nor intended for transmission in books and (4) alliterative in form (including all the rhythmic and stylistic elements which accompany alliteration) (p. 6). He divides the genres of Germanic poetry into two main classes, the 'lower' and the 'higher'. The 'lower' genres comprise rituals, charms, gnomes, catalogue poems and brief lyrics. He cautions that these kinds are not peculiar to any one people but are characteristic of a particular cultural stage. The advantage of the Germanic texts lies in the relatively ample testimony they give us of this stage, a representation either lacking or very sparse in classical literatures (p. 105). Heusler sees the special Germanic contribution to these genres as coming from the metrical style, the alliterative verse with its implications for rhetorical development. And since in England the poetry was mostly written by clerics, he finds this body of poetry an important exception, 'composed', as it was, by the common people. This is true folk poetry. The court singer is responsible for the introduction of the 'higher' genres; he first appears in the eighth and ninth centuries (pp. 108–9) and is demonstrable in *Beowulf, Widsith* and *Deor*. A part of the king's retinue, though not a warrior, he has a fairly evident official position. His repertoire consists of heroic lays and encomia and, probably, catalogue poems. The first two of these were sung to the harp and the scop performed both his own and others' work. The scop did not, however, represent a separate caste (p. 112). While much of Heusler's work has been replaced by a more sophisticated criticism derived from oral–formulaic studies, his organization of basic concepts produces a plan far superior to the usual haphazard approach, which imposes too many rigid notions of aesthetic value based on untenable prejudice.

In 1924 another French examination of Old English turned the tables on many an outworn dogma. Emile Legouis's chapter on Anglo-Saxon literature in his *Histoire de la littérature anglaise* (translated by Helen D. Irvine as *A History of English Literature: the Middle Ages and the Renascence* (1926), from which I quote), is more a prologue to his history than a detailed survey in itself. But his perspective is sharp and strongly stated: 'Anglo-Saxon literature is not a direct expression of the pagan age' declares a heading (p. 3). 'Nothing', he says, 'is...more illusory than to take the extant Anglo-Saxon literature for a primitive product, and to seek in it the reflection of Germanic barbarism' (pp. 3–4). The *Germania* of Tacitus has nothing to do with England, and by the time we reach the world portrayed in the texts 'everything derived from the barbaric past had been purified and ennobled, and also enervated, in an atmosphere of Christianity which already was almost one of chivalry' (p. 4). Legouis also jettisons the hallowed practice of interpreting Old English through Old Norse literature: 'It is no less dangerous to merge in a single whole Anglo-Saxon poetry and the poetry of the Scandinavians, or continental Germanic poetry where it was still pagan' (*ibid.*). In purely artistic matters he still harbours some of the received notions. Old English cannot measure up to French literature: *Beowulf* is flawed and childish, though 'the work...of an artist' (p. 14); Cynewulf had a 'befogged intelligence, led away by words rather than guided by ideas' (p. 26); 'the metrical life of Saint Guthlac makes a painful impression of emptiness' (p. 28). Prose Legouis treats most summarily. His focus is squarely on the poetry, which, 'taken as a whole, is a continuous piece of edification, elegiac in its dominant tone. It is a long Christian lamentation breathed by ingenuous and fervent men' (p. 5). The pronouncement itself, however effusive, is a fresh wind in the musty caverns of Anglo-Saxon literary history.

Precisely because Ernest A. Baker's larger topic is the English novel, his short chapter on 'Anglo-Saxon Fiction' in the first volume of *The History of the English Novel* (1924) has great interest. He opens a special window on the literature and his characterization of Old English narrative art is appealing:

Anglo-Saxon fiction is rather a postscript to ancient literary history than the true beginning of English fiction. There was no prose fiction of native origin in Old English, the stray scraps of prose romance that are extant being translations from Latin writings, which themselves appear to be derived entirely from narratives in Greek...There is plenty of good narrative in Anglo-Saxon literature, but little of that kind which is story-telling for the sake mainly of a good story (p. 50).

Baker sees Old English fiction as lofty, epical, dramatic and pictorial, but not intimate, humorous or unheroic (p. 50). He articulates perspectives not often encountered in the usual history. Cynewulf, for example, is 'degenerate' but 'from the historical point of view may be regarded as marking the transition to romance' with his 'stories of incident rather than of deeds' (p. 52). Since Baker's survey is of fiction he deals with *Apollonius of Tyre* at some length, which is a rarity in the ordinary histories. He asserts that the history of the English novel does not begin with Anglo-Saxon narrative but that some Anglo-Saxon fiction shows 'qualities of mental habitude and temper that have persisted right to this day and have helped to shape the novel' (p. 61). These qualities are 'far less of definite narration and far more of sensuous evocation of the whole scene' and 'the didactive and moralising propensity' (pp. 61–2). Even if one cannot support all Baker's generalizations, the criticism of Old English 'fiction' gains from being viewed within an extended context and from not being the single subject under discussion.

Percy G. Thomas in *English Literature before Chaucer* (1924) offers a straightforward and uninteresting survey. We should note only that he picks up an idea that has clearly taken hold by his time: along with a growing number of critics he believes that Old English literature 'is a product of an advanced civilisation' (p. 3). 'Barbaric' has begun to recede as an appropriate adjective for Anglo-Saxon.

Accompanied by excellent illustrations of Anglo-Saxon manuscripts, Levin Schücking's portion of *Die englische Literatur im Mittelalter* (1927) gives adequate coverage to the field. Maintaining that poetry was the greatest literary contribution of Anglo-Saxon culture from the sixth century to the ninth (pp. 1–2), Schücking understandably places more emphasis on this than on prose. Like Sarrazin, though certainly not with Sarrazin's peculiar results, he outlines the historical development of Anglo-Saxon poetry (pp. 2–3). He calls attention to the major shifts which occurred in the Anglo-Saxon period: the shift from a poetry about heroic sentiments and deeds to a later poetry dedicated to women or to the honour of an individual, and a corresponding thematic change from a poetry of war to a courtly poetry. He sees the 'sublime' as the central theme in Anglo-Saxon poetry, but while the early culture emulated ideal forms, it never developed into one which prized realism because of an interest in social activity or beauty because of a new-found desire for pleasure (pp. 7–8). He describes the interplay between secular and ecclesiastical life in the Old English 'lyric hymns'. The court and the monastery were the two centres of this culture and they gave birth to a lyric poetry which sang of saving the kingdom and the soul. In each case the hymns are of danger and conquest, and each ultimately affected the other (pp. 13–14). Schücking's history follows the common German pattern of generic and cultural explanations for the historical data.

A brief essay by Aldo Ricci, 'The Anglo-Saxon Eleventh-Century Crisis' (*RES* 5 (1929), 1–11), becomes perforce a survey of Anglo-Saxon literature. Ricci seeks to identify the cause of this crisis not in external circumstances (i.e., the attacks of the Danes) but in a spiritual crisis of the people themselves, first noticeable in the ninth century (p. 2). He would have us see a progression in Old English literature from the 'most primitive' Christianity of Cædmon to the true Christianity of Cynewulf (pp. 5–6). Then, after 820, came the Anglo-Saxon 'Dark Ages' from which the civilization never quite recovered (p. 8). Poetry goes into a great decline and learning, even when revived, is more humble: 'Attractive as the figure of Ælfric is, what a world of difference between him and Bede.' Ælfric is significant only in the history of English prose and not as a culturally important figure (p. 8). In the Norman Conquest lies an English parallel to the fall of Rome, for Anglo-Saxon culture never succeeded in reconciling the conflict between its two forms of spiritualism – pessimism and optimism – and its codes of ethics – revenge and love (p. 11). Ricci's explanations are, finally, too simplistic.

In 1932 R. W. Chambers composed a classic essay, *The Continuity of English Prose from Alfred to More and his School*. First he dismantles the assumption, most recently and most forcefully enunciated by Ricci, that Anglo-Saxon culture and letters were decadent long before the Conquest. He insists that responsible scholarship should recall the superior craftsmanship in metal-work and manuscript illumination that persisted long after the invasion (p. lxix). Whether these achievements also indicate continued literary excellence is a separate issue. The variety of Anglo-Saxon prose especially impresses him. He writes:

To the translations made in Alfred's day, and to the Laws, Charters and Wills, we have to add Gospel Translations, Monastic Rules, Saints' Lives, Oriental legends both religious and secular, Dialogues, rudimentary Scientific, Medical and Astronomical works, Herbals, Lapidaries, even the Novel, in the story of *Apollonius of Tyre*. The fact that England was placed on the line of so many trade routes must have had something to do with this variety (pp. lxxvi–lxxvii).

His flaw is an excessive nationalism and at times an exaggerated elevation of Anglo-Saxon prose. Yet, in the context of the state of neglect into which the study and appreciation of this prose had fallen, his remarks seem less a partisan bias than a justified rectification. There was a continuous historical line of English prose reaching from Alfred and Ælfric through to the Renaissance, he claims, in the sermon and in devotional treatises (p. lxxxix). These explain the resurgence of prose writing after a break of nearly three centuries, for, even though the tradition of Old English prose was strangled only gradually and did not die a sudden death, as the poetic tradition did (p. lxxxi), the Norman Conquest eventually stopped the flow. Chambers's long essay is, of course, not a survey of Anglo-Saxon prose but a celebration of it as the fountain-head of the stream of English prose writing.

In the Preface to her *Chapters on Old English Literature* (1935) E. E. Wardale states that she intends her book 'to fill the gap between Professor Thomas's valuable, but all too brief account in his English Literature before Chaucer, and longer works, such as those of Stopford Brooke and the chapters in the first volume of the Cambridge History' (p. ix). Her choice of title is revelatory, for she does not present a systematic intepretation of the literature but rather a series of illustrations of the texts, chiefly the poetic ones. The result is reasonably thorough, with proper attention paid to the Latin and Germanic sources and analogues, and the significant questions appropriately reviewed. She clings, nevertheless, to an inherited belief that the 'Christian' parts of many poems – the lyrics and *Widsith*, for example – are spurious additions (pp. 29–30 and 71). Her criticism is excessively general and impressionistic, that of a genteel and insipid romanticism: the *Exodus* poet's masterful qualities are his 'handling of crowds' and his 'eye for colour' (pp. 130–1); 'the great merit of the Andreas poet is in his scene painting' (p. 147). Cynewulf, too, excels 'in his pictures, in his scene painting...and, to a lesser extent, in his lyrical passages' (p. 174), but he makes the speeches in *Juliana* and *Elene* too long and he lacks the true gifts of story-telling and character drawing (p. 173). This sort of criticism pervades the Anglo-American school of literary history and has not always served very well the literature it describes.

For the revised fourth edition of James W. Bright's *An Anglo-Saxon Reader* (1935) James R. Hulbert prepared a fifty-page 'Sketch of Anglo-Saxon Literature'. Both sensible and eccentric, his essay is symptomatic of much commentary on Old English verbal art. One is never sure whether he likes or dislikes what he is considering. First he insists that the poems are not 'folk-poems': 'A comparison of any Anglo-Saxon poem with the ballads of later date reveals a formality, a dignity, and at times a courtliness and refinement quite foreign to popular literature' (p. xcii). Further he has no patience with the strain in German criticism that attempts to isolate the ur-Germanic elements in the remaining poetry: 'In fact we have no real knowledge of the origin and early development of Anglo-Saxon style...none of the extant poems antedates the conversion, and...the obvious heathen elements in them are simply the survival in men's thought and feeling of old ideas, which remained side by side with the new religion' (p. xcvi). Alongside these sane and appreciative comments stand reversions to predictable prejudice. Hulbert complains of the 'tiresome religiosity' of *The Seafarer* after line 64 and hopes that the rest was 'added by a monkish scribe and [does] not represent the true mind of the original author' (p. cvi). *Beowulf* is a test case. Discarding the nineteenth-century mythological and historical interpretations, he stresses the view that the poem is comparable to a modern historical novel (p. cix). Although it is episodic and lacks the unity of classical epic, for 'sustained dignity and impressiveness of style, for vivid suggestion of poignant situation and for expression of deep feelings, English literature has no superior to it' (pp. cx–cxi). Hulbert's comments on Cædmon are almost comic: 'It will be observed that though these verses constitute a good hymn, they have no poetic value and hence are just what might be expected from a middle-aged, un-lettered farm-hand who could versify' (p. cxv). And of the 'Cædmonian' *Genesis A* he says that it 'is characterized by the greatest simplicity of mind' (p. cxvii). Cynewulf he dismisses as a 'first-rate craftsman but no poet' (p. cxxi). There is a certain comfort in perceiving how easily he makes such judgements. With similar dispatch but more discernment he sums up Ælfric thus: 'It is not then originality of material, but excellence of form and style which distinguishes Ælfric, and these are really notable. His homilies have a clear structure, are well proportioned, and so articulated that even when Ælfric is using several sources his product seems *one* piece' (p. cxxxi). Hulbert's 'Sketch' is not widely read today, but his idiosyncratic opinions have more than historical interest.

The next major history to be published was Charles W. Kennedy's *The Earliest English Poetry* (1943). But three works in the late thirties and early forties, none a genuine history, should be quickly noticed. W. L. Renwick and H. Orton, in *The Beginnings of English Literature to Skelton, 1509* (1939), provide lists, bibliographies and a very bland commentary which does not even pretend to literary criticism. Theirs is mainly a handbook. H. M. Chadwick's *The Study of Anglo-Saxon* (1941), a lecture written on the eve of his retirement and meant to justify the place of Anglo-Saxon studies in the university, gives a short but perceptive overview. And Gavin Bone in *Anglo-Saxon Poetry* (1943) proffers an intensely personal characterization of the poetry which has the effect of a descriptive survey. He conceives his essay as an apologia for Anglo-Saxon poetry (p. 22) and displays his love of the language, his attraction to the lyric poems and his dislike of the flaccid religious pieces.

Turning to Kennedy's history, we first note its clarity, its careful attention to the recent scholarship, its recognition of the sources and analogues and of their importance, and its sensible resolution of vexed controversies. There is also more information than in most comparable volumes. But the criticism frequently does not rise above the level of plot summary and in general is suffused with a sentimental glow and marked by a tendency towards Christian moralism which together mar its effect and value. Speaking of Cynewulf, for example, Kennedy writes: 'The chief and pervasive addition which the poet makes to the material of his originals is the intimate reflection of his own sensitive and lovable personality' (p. 206). While his idea of the canon is strict and while he rejects all the fantastic aspects of Cynewulf's fictional 'biography', he still believes that we can derive a sense of the poet's 'character' and 'inner life' from the runic 'signatures' (p. 198). He takes, too, a decidedly Christian view of *Beowulf*, though not in any dogmatic or allegorical sense. With special emphasis on Hrothgar's speech as a Christian homily against pride, Kennedy holds 'that the essentially Christian genius of the poem is most clearly perceived not so much in details of Biblical theme and phrasing, as in those passages in which Christian ethics are central in shaping speech and influencing conduct' (p. 89). The most direct statement of his position comes towards the end of his book:

If this earliest English poetry failed to achieve a fusion or reconciliation of these contending forces of temporal and eternal, if it did not always perceive that God's kingdom, if not of this world, still must be fought for here, not without blood and tears, what then? Has any age yet made perfect reconciliation of stubborn worldly fact with the dream which is the substance of things unseen? It will still remain true, I think, for many readers who love this ancient verse, that it stands as a testimonial, even if an imperfect one, of a way of life reborn and reshaped by the life-giving touch of the Christian faith, and the ecclesiastical culture of the medieval Church (pp. 350–1).

Both style and content here expose Kennedy's hushed reverence before the Christian texts of Old English poetry.

Four 'chapters' on the literature should be taken into account before the post-war versions of Anglo-Saxon literary history are examined. The first is the tiny section found in Herbert J. C. Grierson and J. C. Smith's *A Critical History of English Poetry* (1944). Neither its length nor its judgements deserve serious consideration. Its only interest is as a list of the age-old negative criticisms: *Beowulf* is mere folk-lore, and poor folk-lore at that; Cynewulf's poems are totally artificial; the religious poems, apart from *Judith*, are mostly prolix, 'wrapping up the plain words of Scripture in clouds of metaphor, circumlocution, repetition, and pious ejaculation' (pp. 4–5); the riddles have not much merit as puzzles, though some have 'vivid realism' (p. 5). Only *The Battle of Maldon* escapes condescension for its portrayal of 'English courage, the courage never to submit or yield. We heard the note in *Beowulf*: we shall hear it again and yet again in English poetry' (p. 6). Perhaps the date, 1944, explains the pæan of national valour, but the general literary denigration is due not only to lack of sympathy but also to lack of knowledge. The other three chapters form small portions of general histories: 'Learning and Literature in Early England' in F. M. Stenton, *Anglo-Saxon England* (1943), 'Vernacular Literature' in Dorothy Whitelock's *The Beginnings of English Society* (1952) and 'Letters' in Peter Hunter Blair's *An Introduction to Anglo-Saxon England* (1956). Stenton's concerns are plainly historical and not literary. He traces the dual strands of the growth of learning in early England – the classical traditions from the continental scholars and the more artificial Irish scholarship of the fifth and sixth centuries (pp. 176 ff.). He discovers a peasant origin for the Germanic poems and reveals his historian's outlook in his remarks on the gnomic poems: 'they deserve more attention from historians than they usually receive, for there is nothing in literature that approaches so nearly to the authentic voice of the Anglo-Saxon *ceorl*' (p. 198). That he believes in the 'dialogue' theory for *The Seafarer* illustrates that he has slipped behind changes in literary scholarship (p. 198). Hunter Blair's contributions are likewise historical and he does not venture into criticism. Dorothy Whitelock's is certainly the best. She displays a straight-forward awareness of the connections between history and literature as well as a responsiveness to the works. Rejecting the idea that all Old English literature is gloomy, she stresses its inherent Christian optimism (p. 210). And she makes this interesting point about the existence of a pagan heroic poetry transcribed by Christian monks:

The survival into Christian times of the older poetry was aided by the interest which the Anglo-Saxon royal and noble families took in the traditions of the deeds of their ancestors. Bede sent his *Ecclesiastical History* to King Ceolfrith of Northumbria for his criticism because he was well versed in the ancient traditions of his race, and it may be that heroic verse was included among the Saxon songs which King Alfred made his children learn (p. 205).

Dorothy Whitelock's chapter is not meant to be exhaustive but to serve as a brief introduction in an historical work; as such it is accurate and instructive.

The period since the Second World War has been especially productive for Anglo-Saxon literary history. It opens with Kemp Malone's much-praised contribution to *A Literary History of England*, edited by Albert C. Baugh. Published in 1948, Malone's survey could not take into account the theories of the oral–formulaic school, so his remarks on style and oral formula (pp. 20–1) now seem somewhat outdated. However, the major division in his survey is based on a stylistic principle, and here his approach is sure and reliable. He separates Old English into two periods, the 'pre-classical' and the 'classical'. In the pre-classical phase an 'end-stopped style prevailed: every line ended with a syntactical pause and every sentence made either a line or a couplet (i.e., a two-line unit)' (p. 26). In the classical phase enjambment was more frequent and there developed a complex plurilinear unit, which was 'held together, not by uniformities of rhythmical or alliterative pattern, nor yet by uniformities of groupings (i.e., strophic structure), but by the use of run-on lines' (*ibid.*). Most significantly, Malone underscores the centrality of the scops in effecting this change: 'It must not be thought...that the scops were conservators and nothing more. It was they who made the important stylistic shift from pre-classical to classical; the clerics who produced most of the classical poetry extant simply carried on and elaborated a style the basic features of which had already been set by the scops' (p. 47). In his view, Cædmon 'adapted the technic of the scops to his own purposes neatly enough: royal epithets like *ruler, lord, keeper* became epithets for God by qualification with *almighty, eternal, mankind's* and *heaven-realm's*' (p. 60). Beyond these considerations, Malone's contributions seem perfunctory. His handling of the poems, especially the longer texts, is brief, unliterary and given over to plot summary by numbered sections. He concludes with a short chapter on 'Literary Prose', which by definition excludes those works not composed as conscious art forms (p. 96).

Racial identification is also a part of Malone's prospect. On the Anglo-Saxon foundations of the English language lies the basic virtue of Anglo-American civilization (p. 11). But his attitudes are positively benign compared to the reactionary racialism in George K. Anderson's *The Literature of the Anglo-Saxon* (1949). Anderson clearly worships at the altar of British imperialism and its Germanic origins. He thinks a student should trace the recurrent strands in English literature from the earliest time to the twentieth century:

Then will appear the loyalty to king and state, the love of action and adventure, the moral earnestness implicit in the conservative adherence to an established code of conduct, the grimness at need, the persevering and unimaginative plodding and muddling, the near-fatalistic acceptance of life as a somber fight that must be endured to the setting of the sun – all part and parcel of the English approach to living (p. 4).

This political and ideological gush is hardly a suitable basis for literary criticism. In fact, Anderson's philosophy, if it can be so called, comes directly out of the nineteenth-century German school. His view of the people, their culture and their literature reactivates many an obsolete sentiment about the Teutonic English. Their language, for example, was 'typical...of a young Germanic people – harsh, vigorous, muscular, consonantal, given little to sensuousness – aesthetically a poor thing' (p. 13); their literature was primitive, what 'one could expect from a people who lived in a damp climate, in raw sea-driving winds, with more than a happy share of foggy, overcast days in which sunlight too often shone feebly or was lost altogether' (pp. 42–3). These and other notions from the romanticizing, paganizing days of the late nineteenth century (in turn inherited from still earlier times) spill out one after another, adding up to a check-list of clichés. Anderson has not much use for the pseudo-scientific methods of German scholarship, but he embraces fully its neo-paganism. He finds Old English literature 'essentially romantic' (p. 408). He does not seem to like the poetry (a curious fact that applies to many Old English scholars) and he takes every opportunity to criticize its vague, primitive, naive and artless productions. There are old-fashioned stances (*The Wanderer* is non-Christian and the last lines are intrusive (p. 159)) and blatant errors (the inscription 'Cædmon made me' proves that poet's authorship of the verses on the Ruthwell Cross (p. 141)).[10] There is a misguided chapter on 'Old English Literature and the Drama' which attempts to put on more solid ground the old and untenable supposition that there is a source for later medieval drama in the Old English period. Somewhat paradoxically the most successful sections of Anderson's history are his chapters on Old English prose, providing a more adequate treatment than those in other surveys. He describes the narrative of the *Anglo-Saxon Chronicle* as 'spirited', Ælfric's style as 'sonorous', and Wulfstan's *Sermon to the English* as punctuated by a 'rhapsodic refrain' (pp. 295, 317 and 341). Yet, as a whole, his history fails completely to live up to his claim that, however tempted he is to be condescending (p. 411), Old English literature needs no apology.

Apart from R. M. Wilson's *The Lost Literature of Medieval England* (1952) the 1950s saw the publication of only two substantial surveys. In each case Old and Middle English are treated in a single volume: Friedrich Schubel's *Die alt- und mittelenglische Periode*, the first part of his three-volume *Englische Literaturgeschichte* (1954), and Margaret Schlauch's *English Medieval Literature and its Social Foundations* (1956). Wilson considers his work an addition to the usual histories: 'It is hoped that by placing it side by side with the histories of the extant literature a much truer picture of the extent, growth and development of Old and Middle English literature may be gained' (p. vii). By listing the works known to have existed or which can be inferred to have existed he increases the range of our insight into the nature of the literary tradition.

In his volume Schubel divides the history of Old English literature into four periods: (1) the pagan period (449 to the seventh century), (2) the high Anglian period (the seventh and eighth centuries), (3) the age of Alfred (871–99) and (4) the late Old English period (the tenth and eleventh centuries) (p. 12). He remarks that, in the past, literary histories of Anglo-Saxon could be organized only according to genre (he is, of course, not quite correct here), but recent cultural and stylistic studies have made a reliable, if crude, chronological ordering possible (p. 14). Despite his four historical periods his discussion remains primarily generic: he assigns particular types of poetry to each of his epochs. He gives a good and sensible condensation of this well-established German concern, accompanied by the occasional comment on changes in stylistic features.

---

[10] This misreading goes back to George Stephens, *The Old-Northern Runic Monuments of Scandinavia and England* (London, Copenhagen and Lund, 1866–1901), I, 419–20.

The Marxist bias of Margaret Schlauch's history is muted in her section on Old English. While she cautions in her Foreword that she intends the book to give a more realistic portrait of the Middle Ages 'with the help of social and economic history' (pp. xv–xvi), she does not press Marxist dogma at any point. She is most concerned with the 'blind enthusiasm for all medieval culture' that has developed as a reaction to the previous stage of ignorant condemnation, for such idealizations have led some to justify 'systems like the fascist corporate state in Italy' and some others to retreat into the refuge of privatism. She wants her readers, 'students and amateurs', to be properly aware of 'the many aspects of disorder and cruelty and ignorance which existed in the real life of the times' (p. xv). Consequently she provides a reasonably extensive amount of such historical background. But she keeps the social and historical material ancillary to the critical survey and separate from it, aside from noting the effects of class structures on literary forms (hardly the first such notation). There is peasant poetry and poetry of the upper classes, but there are also degrees of artistic merit and these seem curiously (for a Marxist) to have little to do with class. Her treatment is neither exhaustive nor richly detailed, yet within her limits it is thorough. Her background chapters have much value in themselves, although her critical assumptions are often pale and outmoded. Her comments on *Juliana* are typical: 'The devil's speech avowing his destructive role...has a certain dramatic intensity, but in general the poem does not show any great literary independence in the treatment of a familiar type of plot' (p. 59). She gives more than usual space to the importance of Latin sources and Germanic analogues in her discussions of individual poems.

Two guides to Old English literature, one indeed so called, published in the early 1960s, offer concise, basic information, the one for English readers, the other for French. Although David M. Zesmer's *Guide* (1961) has precious little to say about the prose, his handling of Old English poetry is balanced and gives the neophyte a good beginning survey. Marguerite Dubois's *La Littérature anglaise du moyen âge (500–1500)* (1962) is slightly more ambitious, though her excessively schematic structure restricts commentary on any one work to the briefest of encyclopædia entries. Interestingly, she chides her French audience for valuing only the second half of English medieval literature, the part in which they can recognize the influence of French (p. 3). She concludes with an ancient device of neo-classical criticism, a catalogue of (by now familiar) flaws and beauties: Old English is to be faulted for its excessive moralization, coldness, lack of interest in the feminine, a naivety bordering on the absurd, a lack of subtle psychology, an absence of colour and an addiction to death and moroseness; it is to be praised for its strong philosophic and metaphysical probings, its vivid realism, its unexcelled religious fervour and lyrical enthusiasm, its nature poetry and its grand spectacle (pp. 81 ff.). These qualities are certainly questionable both as truths in themselves and as 'goodnesses' and 'badnesses'.

As if to compensate for the myriad histories which ignore Old English prose, Stanley B. Greenfield begins his *Critical History of Old English Literature* (1965) with an examination of the prose tradition. He traces its development from its source in the Latin writers, Bede, Alcuin, Aldhelm and the hagiographers, to its last flourishings in Ælfric, Wulfstan and the miscellaneous prose pieces of the early eleventh century. His approach to the prose is careful and meticulous, though his descriptions remain more factual and informative than analytical. He reserves his critical powers for the poetry, the subject which comprises the bulk of his history and which, one feels, ignites his greater interest. The section on prose strikes the reader as a duty performed, the section on poetry as a labour of love. His survey of the poetry was the first to apply the principles of the New Criticism and still stands alone in this respect. He concentrates on style, imagery and structure, and his criticisms abound in a generous sympathy for the poems as literature. Even when plot summary becomes necessary he does not rest content with a reductionist version but offers a critical perspective as well. In keeping with the New Critical methods he often uses his dissection of a specific item to discover a unity where none has been found before. *Guthlac A* offers a good illustration: '[This poem] receives scant notice in most literary histories, but despite its primitivism it has a unity and focus that suggest the craftsman at work to good effect. From beginning to end there is emphasis upon the virtuous individual vs. the sinful crowd, upon earthly transience vs. heavenly permanence, upon ineffectual words vs. significant deeds' (p. 119). Because he steadfastly refuses to place himself above the literature so that he may condescend (a trap into which all but a few have fallen), he succeeds in an uncommonly powerful way. His history has been rightly influential in arousing new fascination with the aesthetics of Old English poetry. If parts now seem thin or in need of revision, this is because subsequent work has followed his lead and has developed his original hints. The book's historical impact and significance are enhanced, not impaired, by this imitation.

Quite in contrast to Greenfield's work is Ewald Standop's survey in his and Edgar Mertner's *Englische Literaturgeschichte* (1967). Although based on the most recent scholarship, it proceeds nearly without critical commentary. It is up-to-date factually but does not disturb settled judgements. Also published in the same year was C. L. Wrenn's *A Study of Old English Literature*, a volume of great import which should be read in conjunction with Greenfield's, for the two are complementary. Wrenn offers fuller information on historical and cultural contexts, along with more detail on manuscripts, sources and Anglo-Saxon scholarship, and his criticism belongs to no party, a fact which is both an advantage and a fault. While his generally unbiased approach to the literature allows him to avoid the excesses of some predecessors, it also produces a pallid criticism that does not venture beyond comfortable impressionism. Some passages are 'vivid'; too many poems are dismissed as having not much 'literary merit'. A gentlemanly realism in combination with a subdued classicism still imbues most academic critical theory. Wrenn's study is to be praised for its clarity and sound judgements on controversial matters but not particularly for its literary insights.

From knowledge of the scholarship of J. E. Cross one would have expected him to bring the Christian Latin backgrounds to the fore in his contribution, on the Old English period, to *The Middle Ages*, edited by Whitney F. Bolton (1970), the first volume of the Sphere History of Literature in the English Language. To a slight extent this turns out to be the case. Certainly his discussion of *Beowulf* directly raises the possibility of an Augustinian interpretation, but he stresses only that it 'bears reading' from this point of view (p. 51) and he acknowledges that the whole question is open to debate. In fact his essay suffers because he does not press his own concerns and exploit his own expertise enough. The field at large could well profit from a history so conceived and Cross's knowledge makes him a natural choice as author. Occasional flashes of such background material come through, it is true; for example, he unlocks the symbol of *The Phoenix* with a fourfold interpretation modelled on patristic exegesis (p. 37). But in the main he alternates between a superficial repetition of the standard ideas and the odd detail in a poem that has struck him. These sparks are frequently of genuine interest, though within the confines of his short essay they inevitably remain undeveloped. The final effect must be disconcerting for the student who has neither a consistent plot summary to guide him nor the knowledge to catch some of the more illuminating, though cryptic, allusions. When depending solely on the vocabulary of literary criticism to describe a work (and not on the terms of exegesis) Cross relies on the threadbare lexicon ultimately derived from late-nineteenth-century realism and its dramatic assumptions. And even when he recognizes that the creation of a living drama is not the poet's task, he censures him for not having chosen that mode: 'But in [*Juliana*] the imaginative possibilities are neglected in order to reflect the moral nature of the Latin account' (p. 33). At base, Cross does not project much enthusiasm for Anglo-Saxon poetry; he too often finds it desperately poor (p. 20).

Surveys of historical and theological backgrounds do not ordinarily bring the literature into very sharp focus, no matter how good their authors' intentions. This runs true throughout the active period of Anglo-Saxon literary history. So Milton McC. Gatch, in *Loyalties and Traditions* (1971), deserves more than casual praise for having performed such an exercise with success. He wants 'above all, to dispel the notion that Anglo-Saxon literary culture was barbaric or primitive by stressing the sophistication, traditionalism, and learning which lie behind the writings' (p. xiii). It is a mark of the state of Anglo-Saxon studies that he should still have found this an urgent need. Sections of the book are now dated; as the wave of 'relevance' has ebbed in academic circles, so has the requirement to connect the existential 'sense of alienation' in Old English literature with its modern parallels (p. 22). However, Gatch's strong emphasis on the thorough-going Christianness of late Anglo-Saxon literature and his reminder that the Germanic past was remote indeed for a tenth-century Englishman are still timely for many general readers and specialists alike.

In 1971 Karl Göller published his *Geschichte der altenglischen Literatur*, in a series of basic texts for students of Anglistik and Amerikanistik. The question of relevance, raised by Gatch in America, also resounded in Germany, and Göller opens with a chapter headed 'Warum studiert man heute noch Altenglisch?' His reply is not as imaginative as Gatch's; he finds it sufficient to maintain that historical literature should be studied historically (p. 8). Göller's scholarship is current, though his organization by genre, his reference to the wisdom poetry as a 'lower' category (p. 54) and his intense concern with source, origin and generic history place him entirely within the German tradition and connect him specifically with Heusler. His preference for Old English elegiac poetry leads him into a consideration of the minutiae of scholarship; his aesthetic judgements seem all too often coloured by the last critical article to have appeared. But his introductory survey is not intended to be a complex critical study and it succeeds as a well-informed preliminary to a sustained reading of the works.

Another survey in German published in the same year, Frederick Norman's 'Altenglische Literatur' in L. E. Schmitt's *Kurzer Grundriss der germanischen Philologie bis 1500*, directly counters Schubel's premises. Norman insists that a chronologically ordered history of Anglo-Saxon literature is impossible and that therefore the divisions must be generic (p. 117). However, he expends no little effort in trying to establish dates for specific poems, not always successfully. Some of his interests are simply old-fashioned: it is unusual at this date to find a scholar debating the question of whether Cynewulf composed the riddles (Norman decides he did not (p. 138)); and it is hardly more fashionable to complain that *Beowulf* is 'poorly composed' (p. 145). Prose he treats summarily.

Two British studies remain for review and both are histories of the poetry alone. T. A. Shippey, in his *Old English Verse* (1972), dispenses with much of the paraphernalia of the ordinary survey. He frees himself from dates, manuscripts and excessive concern with sources, historical backgrounds and influences, permitting himself instead some extended analysis of specific poems to demonstrate their peculiar subtlety. He believes that 'Old English poetry stubbornly resists the current of modern criticism. It does not try to reach what we would recognise as a goal; though consistent and regular, it is, by any of our standards, odd' (p. 12). He attempts 'to explore the hidden and probably unconscious principles of composition behind Old English verse' (pp. 15–16). What emerges is a promising set of individual aperçus, the products of a good critical mind encountering these old poems. His method resembles the kind of close reading associated with the New Criticism, despite his warning that Old English poetry resists such an approach. But since he finds all meaning in context, syntax and style and ignores thematic, allegorical or typological explanations, he must certainly be classified more with the New Critics than with the exegetes. His lament for the break-up of the Old English poetic tradition in the eleventh century allows him to describe that tradition as representing something outside the individual poetic temperament, best seen as a whole state of mind (pp. 189–90). We might be hard put to say precisely just what that state of mind means to him, but the notion itself and the multiple ways it informs his analyses require our common assent.

Although Derek Pearsall announces that in his *Old English and Middle English Poetry* (vol. 1 of The Routledge History of English Poetry (1977)) his attention will be directed 'to matters of provenance and audience, so as to provide as much information as possible on poetry as a social phenomenon as well as an artistic one' (p. xi), he rarely fulfils this plan. Instead he offers a reading of Old English poetry that is at once interesting and disappointing. He gives much space to the late, neglected works and to the relation between poetry and poetic prose in the eleventh century when both forms were about to undergo abrupt mutations caused by internal and external forces. And he puts the Germanic spirit even further behind him than Gatch does: 'England has no poetry but that of the Christian tradition... and the Germanic heritage, when it emerges in Anglo-Saxon poetry, emerges re-shaped, absorbed, chastened, in a form quite distinct from survivals elsewhere of the pagan, heroic, Germanic past' (p. 1). All the same, Pearsall is averse to making Anglo-Saxon poetry merely 'a series of addenda to the *Patrologia Latina*' (p. 2). In many ways his is an iconoclastic effort – first banish neo-paganism; then be wary of the allegorizers; next watch out for the romanticizers: 'it is not a romantic imagination, as if often assumed by those who seek, for instance, nature-feeling in Anglo-Saxon poetry' (p. 13). Of oral–formulaic theory he makes short work, although he concedes that it 'has not been a complete waste of time' (p. 17). No one need be particularly sad to see these shibboleths, these hackneyed ideas, pass from our critical idiom. In their place, however, Pearsall sets only his own personal evaluations, and these are often idiosyncratic or just as archaic as the platitudes he has demolished. Hence the disappointment. What boots it to learn that rhetorical elaboration in *Exodus* 'runs loose into hectic extravagance, dissolving into desperate, lurid, empty, isolated gestures' (p. 36)? Or to reassert that the inherent simplicity of design in the saints' lives inhibits 'interesting literary development, whatever language they are written in' (p. 40)? To allot the riddles six and a half lines of print and call them 'a perverse encyclopaedia' (p. 51) is plainly irresponsible.

Pearsall's success and failure show clearly the break with the past that the Anglo-Saxon literary historian can now make. We are in a better position than our predecessors have ever been to analyse the literature, both poetry and prose, without preconceptions. To our inherited philological base we have added a much improved technical understanding, encompassing advances in palaeography and in the study of sources and cultural backgrounds. Aided by historians, archaeologists, art historians and anthropologists, we can penetrate more deeply the interrelationships of literature and society. With increased knowledge of related literatures – Latin, continental Germanic, Celtic and Scandinavian – we can make better informed comparisons with them. The myths, those hoary offspring of misinformation, are thus now exposed to a reasonable, factual vision of the Old English literary milieu. The extant corpus and chronology of Ælfric's prose and of Wulfstan's are reliably established. We are well on the way towards separating the prose of King Alfred from that of his contemporaries and towards separating the prose of any of his contemporaries from that of the others. The cultural resources of the prose of his time are more clearly discerned. We have a growing understanding of the course of vernacular preaching. The cultural background of the Old English Martyrology, perhaps mid-ninth-century, is gradually emerging. Such clarifications have great value. We need no longer be partisans of paganism or of Christianity; we need not be nationalistic or idealistic or condescending. We are not now plagued – or should not be – by the non-questions and heated controversies of the far and recent past: by a supposed Cædmonian corpus or Cynewulfian school, by oral-formulaic or allegorical dogmas. Finally, beyond the field of Anglo-Saxon studies proper, critical theorists are improving the tools at the critic's disposal. The literary historian who can exploit all these resources in a sustained, responsive and intellectually rigorous criticism is awaited.[11]

[11] I should like to express my great appreciation of the generous and painstaking assistance Peter Clemoes and Stanley B. Greenfield have given to the writing of this essay. I should like also to thank Professors Greenfield and Fred C. Robinson for allowing me to use parts of their forthcoming bibliography. This has greatly facilitated the task of tracing the many volumes.

Bibliography for 1980

CARL T. BERKHOUT, MARTIN BIDDLE, T. J. BROWN,
PETER A. CLAYTON, C. R. E. COUTTS and
SIMON KEYNES

This bibliography is meant to include all books, articles and significant reviews published in any branch of Anglo-Saxon studies during 1980. It excludes reprints unless they contain new material. It will be continued annually. The year of publication of a book or article is 1980 unless otherwise stated. There is a separate section for onomastic studies for the first time. The arrangement and the pages on which the sections begin are as follows:

C.T.B. has been mainly responsible for sections 2, 3 and 4, T.J.B. for section 5, S.K. for section 6, P.A.C. for section 7, C.R.E.C. for section 8 and M.B. for section 9. Most of section 9 has been compiled by Mrs Fiona Gale. References to publications in Japan have been supplied by Professor Tsunenori Karibe. Peter Clemoes has been responsible for co-ordination. The co-ordinating editing has been done mainly by Dr J. D. Pickles.

. The following abbreviations occur where relevant (not only in the bibliography but also throughout the volume):

AAe *Archaeologia Aeliana*
AB *Analecta Bollandiana*

AC	*Archæologia Cantiana*
AHR	*American Historical Review*
AIUON	*Annali, Istituto Universitario Orientale di Napoli: sezione germanica*
AntJ	*Antiquaries Journal*
ArchJ	*Archaeological Journal*
ASE	*Anglo-Saxon England*
ASNSL	*Archiv für das Studium der neueren Sprachen und Literaturen*
ASSAH	*Anglo-Saxon Studies in Archaeology and History*
BAR	British Archaeological Reports
BBCS	*Bulletin of the Board of Celtic Studies*
BGDSL	*Beiträge zur Geschichte der deutschen Sprache und Literatur*
BIAL	*Bulletin of the Institute of Archaeology* (London)
BN	*Beiträge zur Namenforschung*
BNJ	*British Numismatic Journal*
CA	*Current Archaeology*
CCM	*Cahiers de civilisation médiévale*
DAEM	*Deutsches Archiv für Erforschung des Mittelalters*
EA	*Études anglaises*
EconHR	*Economic History Review*
EEMF	Early English Manuscripts in Facsimile
EETS	Early English Text Society
EHR	*English Historical Review*
ELN	*English Language Notes*
EPNS	English Place-Name Society
ES	*English Studies*
FS	*Frühmittelalterliche Studien*
HZ	*Historische Zeitschrift*
IF	*Indogermanische Forschungen*
JBAA	*Journal of the British Archaeological Association*
JEGP	*Journal of English and Germanic Philogy*
JEH	*Journal of Ecclesiastical History*
JMH	*Journal of Medieval History*
JTS	*Journal of Theological Studies*
LH	*The Local Historian*
MA	*Medieval Archaeology*
MÆ	*Medium Ævum*
MLR	*Modern Language Review*
MP	*Modern Philology*
MS	*Mediaeval Studies*
MScand	*Medieval Scandinavia*
N&Q	*Notes and Queries*
NChron	*Numismatic Chronicle*
NCirc	*Numismatic Circular*
NH	*Northern History*

NM	*Neuphilologische Mitteilungen*
OEN	*Old English Newsletter*
PA	*Popular Archaeology*
PBA	*Proceedings of the British Academy*
PMLA	*Publications of the Modern Language Assocation of America*
PQ	*Philological Quarterly*
RB	*Revue bénédictine*
RES	*Review of English Studies*
SBVS	*Saga-Book of the Viking Society for Northern Research*
SCBI	Sylloge of Coins of the British Isles
SCMB	*Seaby's Coin and Medal Bulletin*
SM	*Studi Medievali*
SN	*Studia Neophilologica*
SP	*Studies in Philology*
TLS	*Times Literary Supplement*
TPS	*Transactions of the Philological Society*
TRHS	*Transactions of the Royal Historical Society*
YES	*Yearbook of English Studies*
ZAA	*Zeitschrift für Anglistik und Amerikanistik*
ZDA	*Zeitschrift für deutsches Altertum and deutsche Literatur*
ZVS	*Zeitschrift für vergleichende Sprachforschung*

1. GENERAL AND MISCELLANEOUS

Acobian, Richild, ed., *Festgabe für Hans Pinsker zum 70. Geburtstag* (Vienna, 1979)

Ando, Shinsuke, 'In Memoriam Dr Fumio Kuriyagawa', *Poetica* (Tokyo) 9 (1978), 1–8

Arnold, Ronald, and Klaus Hansen, 'Die wissenschaftlichen Veröffentlichungen Martin Lehnerts 1975–1979', *ZAA* 28, 170–1

Aubrun, Michel, 'Caractères et portée religieuse et sociale des "Visiones" en Occident du VIe au XIe siècle', *CCM* 23, 109–30

Berkhout, Carl T., 'Old English Research in Progress 1979–1980', *NM* 81, 278–85
'Old English Bibliography 1979', *OEN* 13.2, 39–64

Collins, Rowland L., ed., 'The Year's Work in Old English Studies – 1979', *OEN* 14.1, 15–81

Connor, Patricia, 'The Bede Monastery Museum', *Illustrated London News* August 1979, p. 44

Cooke, W. G., '"Firy Drakes and Blazing-Bearded Light"', *ES* 61, 97–103

Dietrich, Sheila C., 'An Introduction to Women in Anglo-Saxon Society (c. 600–1066)', *The Women of England from Anglo-Saxon Times to the Present: Interpretive Bibliographical Essays*, ed. Barbara Kanner (Hamden, Conn., 1979), pp. 32–56

Foote, Peter, 'Gabriel Turville-Petre, 1908–1978', *PBA* 64 (1980 for 1978), 467–81

Gransden, Antonia, 'Antiquarian Studies in Fifteenth-Century England', *AntJ* 60, 75–97

Gray, Basil, 'Sir Thomas Kendrick', *Burlington Mag.* 122, 194–5

Hansen, Klaus, 'Professor Dr Martin Lehnert zum 70. Geburtstag', *ZAA* 28, 169–70

Hetherington, M. S., *The Beginnings of Old English Lexicography* (privately distributed by author, College of Charleston, South Carolina)

Page, R. I., 'Bruce Dickins', *SBVS* 20 (1978–9), 4–5

'Bruce Dickins, 1889–1978', *PBA* 64 (1980 for 1978), 341–57 [with bibliography]

Rubey, Daniel, 'Identity and Alterity in the Criticism of J. R. R. Tolkien and D. W. Robertson, Jr.', *Lit. Rev.* 23, 577–611

Short, Ian, 'On Bilingualism in Anglo-Norman England', *Romance Philol.* 33, 467–79

Szarmach, Paul E., ed., *Old English Newletter* 13.1–2 (Binghamton, N.Y., 1979–80)

Thomas, Charles, 'The New Insularity: On British Protohistory', *Encounter* 54.5 (May), 65–71 [review of recent publications on Anglo-Saxon history, culture and archaeology]

Tighe, Chris, 'Treasures of the Exquisite Bede', *Sunday Times Mag.* 25 May, p. 87

Turner, D. H., *et al.*, *The Benedictines in Britain* (London) [British Museum exhibition catalogue]

Whitelock, Dorothy, *From Bede to Alfred. Studies in Early Anglo-Saxon Literature and History* (London) [collected papers]

Wilson, David M., 'The Art of the Vikings', *Apollo* 111, 315–18

Yeager, Robert F., 'Some Turning Points in the History of Teaching Old English in America', *OEN* 13.2, 9–20

2. OLD ENGLISH LANGUAGE

[Admoni, V. G.] *Istoriko-tipologicheskaia morfologiia germanskikh iazykov* (Moscow, 1978)

Allen, Cynthia L., 'Movement and Deletion in Old English', *Ling. Inquiry* 11, 261–323

'*Whether* in Old English', *Ling. Inquiry* 11, 789–93

Amati, Antonietta, 'Analisi contrastiva delle congiunzioni anglosassoni e latine nella versione dei Vangeli', *Annali della Facoltà di Lingue e Letterature Straniere* (Università di Bari) n.s. 6 (1978 for 1975), 141–203

Amos, Ashley Crandell, *Linguistic Means of Determining the Dates of Old English Literary Texts*, Med. Acad. Books 90 (Cambridge, Mass.)

'Dictionary of Old English: 1979 Progress Report', *OEN* 13.2, 21–2

Antonsen, Elmer H., 'The Graphemic System of the Germanic fuþark', *Linguistic Method: Essays in honor of Herbert Penzl*, ed. I. Rauch and G. F. Carr (The Hague, Paris and New York, 1979), pp. 287–97

Arngart, O., 'Middle English *hogt*', *NM* 81, 258–9 [OE *hātan*, *heht*]

see sect. 8 (three entries)

Bambas, Rudolph C., *The English Language: its Origin and History* (Norman, Okla.)

Bammesberger, Alfred, 'On the Gloss to Matthew 26.8 in the Lindisfarne Gospels',

Linguistic and Literary Studies in honor of Archibald A. Hill III, ed. Mohammad Ali Jazayery *et al.*, Trends in Ling., Stud. and Monographs 9 (The Hague, Paris and New York, 1978), 9–12

Beiträge zu einem etymologischen Wörterbuch des Altenglischen: Berichtigungen und Nachträge zum Altenglischen etymologischen Wörterbuch von Ferdinand Holthausen, Anglistische Forschungen 139 (Heidelberg, 1979)

'Die westgermanischen Entsprechungen zu urgerm. **uz(−)*', *BGDSL* 101 (1979), 30–5

'Vieil irlandais *sacart* et vieil anglais *sacerd*', *Études celtiques* 16 (1979), 187–9

see sect. 3*biii* (two entries)

Bately, Janet, see sect 3*c* (second entry)

Bauer, Gero, 'Zum Problem der Rekonstruktion von "Lautwerten" in älteren Englisch', *Festgabe für Hans Pinsker*, ed. Acobian, pp. 16–32

Bennett, Paul A., 'English Passives: a Study in Syntactic Change and Relational Grammar', *Lingua* 51, 101–14

Bennett, William H., 'The Germanic Reflex of Indo-European /ə/ in Originally Medial Syllables', *Linguistic and Literary Studies in honor of Archibald A. Hill* III, ed. Mohammad Ali Jazayery *et al.*, Trends in Ling., Stud. and Monographs 9 (The Hague, Paris and New York, 1978), 13–18

Bierbaumer, Peter, *Der botanische Wortschatz des Altenglischen, III. Der botanische Wortschatz in altenglischen Glossen*, Grazer Beiträge zur englischen Philologie 3 (Frankfurt am Main, Bern and Las Vegas, 1979)

'Aspekte der altenglischen Glossenforschung', *Festgabe für Hans Pinsker*, ed. Acobian, pp. 33–50

Brøndegaard, Vagn Jørgensen, 'Ein angelsächsischer Pflanzenname: *openars(e)*', *Sudhoffs Archiv* 63 (1979), 190–3

Brown, Jane Hetherington, and Linda Ehrsam Voigts, see sect. 5

Burrow, J. A., 'Laʒamon's *Brut* 10,642: *wleoteð*', *N&Q* 27, 2–3 [OE *wlitigian*]

Cerasano, S. P., 'The Computer in the Meadhall: Standardizing Anglo-Saxon', *Assoc. for Lit. and Ling. Computing Bull.* 8, 111–24

Cercignani, Fausto, 'Proto-Germanic */i/ and */e/ Revisited', *JEGP* 78 (1979), 72–82

'Early "umlaut" Phenomena in the Germanic Languages', *Language* 56, 126–36

Coates, Richard, see sect. 8 (first entry)

Connolly, Leo A., 'The Rune ᛇ and the Germanic Vowel System', *Amsterdamer Beiträge zur älteren Germanistik* 14 (1979), 3–32 [OE *ēoh*]

'*ē₂* and the Laryngeal Theory', *BGDSL* 101 (1979), 1–29

Corso, Louise, see sect. 3*bii*

Dekeyser, Xavier, 'Some Considerations on Voicing with special reference to Spirants in English and Dutch: a Diachronic-Contrastive Approach', *Recent Developments in Historical Phonology*, ed. Jacek Fisiak, Trends in Ling., Stud. and Monographs 4 (The Hague, Paris and New York, 1978), 99–121

De Roo, C. H., 'Old English *sele*', *Neophilologus* 64, 113–20

see sect. 3*bii*

Doane, A. N., see sect. 3*biii*

Dresher, Bezalel Elan, 'The Mercian Second Fronting: a Case of Rule Loss in Old English', *Ling. Inquiry* 11, 47–73

Fischer, Olga, 'A Comparative Study of Philosophical Terms in the Alfredian and Chaucerian Boethius', *Neophilologus* 63 (1979), 622–39

Godden, M. R., see sect. 3*c*

Greenfield, Stanley B., and Fred C. Robinson, see sect. 3*a*

Hasegawa, Hiroshi, see sect. 3*bii* (first entry)
see sect. 3*biii* (first entry)

Häseler, Heinz-Bernhard, *Die Pertinenzrelation: die Entwicklung ihrer Wiedergabe in der englischen Sprachgeschichte*, Beiträge zur Anglistik 2 (Grossen-Linden, 1977)

Hellberg, Staffan, 'Vikingatidens *víkingar*', *Arkiv för Nordisk Filologi* 95, 25–88

Hetherington, M. S., see sect. 1

Hogg, Richard M., 'Old English Palatalization', *TPS* 1979, 89–113

Hogg, Richard M., and Mary Brennan, 'English Language', *Year's Work in Eng. Stud.* 58 (1979 for 1977), 12–45

Hollifield, Patrick Henry, 'The Phonological Development of Final Syllables in Germanic', *Die Sprache* 26, 19–53 and 145–78

Horgan, D. M., 'Old English Orthography: a Short Contribution', *ES* 61, 385–9
'Patterns of Variation and Interchangeability in some Old English Prefixes', *NM* 81, 127–30

Huld, Martin E., 'English *witch*', *Michigan Germanic Stud.* 5 (1979), 36–9

Ide, Mitsu, '*Factum esse* and *wesan geworden*', *Metropolitan* (Tokyo Metropolitan Univ.) 23 (1979), 17–45 [in Japanese]
'*Wæs Geworden*', *Metropolitan Ling.* (Tokyo Metropolitan Univ.) 3 (1979), 1–25

Insley, John, see sect. 8

Kahlas, Leena, 'Old English "everyone"', *Papers from the Scandinavian Symposium on Syntactic Variation*, Stockholm Stud. in Eng. 52 (Stockholm), 125–32

Koike, Kazuo, 'A Linguistic Approach to Old English Conversation in Ælfric's *Colloquy*', *Obirin Stud. in Eng. Lit.* (Obirin Univ.) 19 (1979), 197–213

Korhammer, Michael, 'Altenglische Dialekte und der *Heliand*', *Anglia* 98, 85–94
see sect. 5

Kuryłowicz, Jerzy, see sect. 3*bii*

Leavitt, Jay A., J. Lawrence Mitchell and Eric Inman, 'KIT and the Investigation of Old English Prose', *Assoc. for Lit. and Ling. Computing Bull.* 8, 1–14

Le Duc, Gwenäel, 'Une glose en Anglo-Saxon glosée en Brittonique', *Études celtiques* 16 (1979), 261–2 [Angers, Bibliothèque Municipale, 477]

Lehnert, Martin, *Altenglisches Elementarbuch*, 9th ed. (Berlin and New York, 1978)

Lenerz, Jürgen, 'Zur Beschreibung eines syntaktischen Wandels: das periphrastische *do* im Englischen', *Sprachstruktur, Individuum und Gesellschaft. Akten des 13. Linguistischen Kolloquiums, Gent 1978*, ed. Marc Van de Velde and Willy Vandeweghe, Linguistische Arbeiten 76 (Tübingen, 1979) 1, 93–102

Loyn, H. R., 'The Norman Conquest of the English Language', *Hist. Today* 30 (April), 35–9

McCord, Laura R., see sect. 3*c*

Miedema, H. T. J., 'Breg, Reg and Green Cheese is Old English and Old Friese', *Liber Amicorum Weijnen*, ed. J. Kruijsen (Assen), pp. 180–7

Milani, Celestina, 'Anglico-Celtica', *Rendiconti dell'Istituto Lombardo, Classe di lettere e scienze morali e storiche* 112 (1978), 286–96 [Corpus Glossary]

Mitchell, Bruce, 'The Dangers of Disguise: Old English Texts in Modern Punctuation', *RES* 31, 385–413

Mitchell, Bruce, and Allison Kingsmill, 'Prepositions, Adverbs, Prepositional Adverbs, Postpositions, Separable Prefixes, or Inseparable Prefixes in Old English? A Supplementary Bibliography', *NM* 81, 313–17

Mizutori, Yoshitaka, *The English Language: a Historical Reader* (Tokyo) [OE, pp. 2–25]

Mogami, Takebumi, 'The Anglo-Saxon Obsolete Words in Laȝamon's *Brut*, I', *Bull. of the Faculty of Education of Kanazawa Univ.* 28, 35–49

Moisl, H., 'Celto-Germanic *wātu-/wōtu-* and Early Germanic Poetry', *N&Q* 27, 98–9

Mōri, Hidetaka, 'Grammatical Gender in Old English, I, Nouns', *Thought Currents in Eng. Lit.* (Aoyama Gakuin Univ.) 52 (1979), 35–50

'Grammatical Gender in Old English, II, The Definite Article', *Thought Currents in Eng. Lit.* (Aoyama Gakuin Univ.) 53, 1–9

Morrison, Stephen, see sect. 3*bii*

Nielsen, Hans F., 'The Earliest Grouping of the Germanic Dialects', *Arkiv för Nordisk Filologi* 94 (1979), 1–9

Niwa, Yoshinobu, 'The Relationships of Old English Verbal Particles to their Latin Originals in the *Vespasian Psalter*', *Stud. in Lang. and Culture* [Jnl of the Lang. Center of Nagoya Univ.] 2.1, 1–27 [in Japanese]

Odenstedt, Bengt, 'The Loveden Hill Runic Inscription', *Ortnamnssällskapets i Uppsala Årsskrift* 1980, 24–37

Ono, Shigeru, 'The Old English Equivalents of Latin *cognoscere* and *intelligere*: the Dialectal and Temporal Distribution of Vocabulary', *Jnl of Social Sciences and Humanities* 136 (1979), 1–49 [in Japanese]

Ono, Shigeru, and Toshio Nakao, *History of English I*, Outline of Eng. Ling. 8 (Tokyo) [in Japanese]

Page, R. I., 'OE. *fealh*, "harrow"', *N&Q* 26 (1979), 389–93

Peeters, Christian, 'The Retrospective Point of View in Comparative Linguistics', *General Ling.* 20, 95–8

Phillips, Betty S., 'Old English *an ~ on*: a New Appraisal', *Jnl of Eng. Ling.* 14, 20–3

Roberts, Jane, see sect. 3*bii*

Ross, Alan S. C., 'The Correspondent of West Saxon *cweðan* in Late Northumbrian and Rushworth One', *NM* 81, 24–33

Ross, Alan S. C., and Ann Squires, 'The Multiple, Altered and Alternative Glosses of the Lindisfarne and Rushworth Gospels and the Durham Ritual', *N&Q* 27, 489–95

Sasabe, Hideo, see sect. 3*bii*

Schabram, Hans, see sect. 3*bii*

Schendl, Herbert, 'Zur Chronologie des Wandels /xs/ zu /ks/ im Altenglischen', *Festgabe für Hans Pinsker*, ed. Acobian, pp. 157–74

Seppänen, Aimo, 'Possessive Pronouns in English?', *Studia Linguistica* 34, 7–22

Shimose, Michiro, see sect. 3*bii*

Short, Ian, see sect. 1

Smirnitskaia, O. A., see sect. 3*bii*

Stanley, Julia Penelope, and Cynthia McGowan, 'Woman and Wife: Social and Semantic Shifts in English', *Papers in Ling.* 12 (1979), 491–502

Steponavičius, A., 'Istoriia perednikh ogu'lennykh monoftongov v drevneangliĭskikh i sredneangliĭskikh dialektakh', *Lietuvos TSR Aukštųjų Mokyklų Mokslo Darbai: Kalbotyra* 29.3 (1978), 56–67 [the development of front rounded monophthongs in OE and ME dialects]

Stockwell, Robert P., 'Motivations for Exbraciation in Old English', *Mechanisms of Syntactic Change*, ed. Charles N. Li (Austin and London, 1977), pp. 291–314

Stuart, Heather, see sect. 5

Sugahara, Shunya, 'An Inquiry into Old English Negation', *The Ronso* [Bull. of the Faculty of Letters of Tamagawa Univ.] 15 (1974), 31–63 [in Japanese]

'On Duplicationalism: centering on *The Seafarer*', *The Ronso* [Bull. of the Faculty of Letters of Tamagawa Univ.] 16 (1975), 189–212 [in Japanese]

'Considerations on the Linguistic Phenomena in the OE Poem *The Seafarer*', *The Ronso* [Bull. of the Faculty of Letters of Tamagawa Univ.] 17 (1976), 189–207

'Observations on Old English Gender', *Tamagawa Rev.* 1 (1976), 8–10 [in Japanese]

'Considerations on the Linguistic Phenomena in the OE Conversation: *Ælfric's Colloquy*', *The Ronso* [Bull. of the Faculty of Letters of Tamagawa Univ.] 18 (1977), 33–58

'*Ælfric's Colloquy*: its Character and Linguistic Structure', *Tamagawa Rev.* 2 (1977), 10–14 [in Japanese]

'*The Wanderer*: the Relationship between Word Formation and Word Meaning', *Tamagawa Rev.* 3 (1978), 47–51 [in Japanese]

'Old English Phonology; on Intervocalization', *The Ronso* [Bull. of the Faculty of Letters of Tamagawa Univ.] 20 (1979), 373–90

'On *The Seafarer*: its Vocabulary and Cultural Phase', *Tamagawa Rev.* 4 (1979), 36–8 [in Japanese]

'Observations on the Old English Word *Wulf*', *Tamagawa Rev.* 5, 77–83 [in Japanese]

Talentino, Arnold V., see sect. 3*bii*

Tops, Guy A. J., 'The Origin of the Germanic Dental Preterit: Von Friesen Revisited', *Recent Developments in Historical Phonology*, ed. Jacek Fisiak, Trends in Ling., Stud. and Monographs 4 (The Hague, Paris and New York, 1978), 349–71

Val'dman, K. N., 'Oproshchenie drevneangliĭskikh sushchestvitel'nykh', *Vestnik Leningradskogo Universiteta* 1979, no. 14.3, 89–95 [simplification of OE compound substantives]

Voetz, Lothar, *Komposita auf -man im Althochdeutschen, Altsächsischen und Altniederfränkischen*, Monographien zur Sprachwissenschaft 3 (Heidelberg, 1977)

Voyles, Joseph B., 'Reduplicating Verbs in North-West Germanic', *Lingua* 52, 89–123

Wagner, Norbert, 'Der Name der Stellinga', *BN* 15, 128–33 [OE *steal(l)*, *gestealla*]

Wenisch, Franz, *Spezifisch anglisches Wortgut in den nordhumbrischen Interlinearglossierungen des Lukasevangeliums*, Anglistische Forschungen 132 (Heidelberg, 1979)

3. OLD ENGLISH LITERATURE

a. General

Amos, Ashley Crandell, see sect. 2 (first entry)

Brown, Jane Hetherington, and Linda Ehrsam Voigts, see sect. 5

Greenfield, Stanley B., and Fred C. Robinson, using the collections of E. E. Ericson, *A Bibliography of Publications on Old English Literature from the Beginnings to the End of 1972* (Toronto, Buffalo and London)

Ikegami, Tadahiro, 'The Society and Literature of the Anglo-Saxons', *A History of English Literature*, ed. B. Sato (Tokyo, 1978), pp. 18–26 [in Japanese]

'The World of Anglo-Saxon Literature', *Stud. in Lang. and Cultures* (Univ. of Tsukuba) 5 (1978), 1–16 [in Japanese]

Mitchell, Bruce, see sect. 2

Niles, John D., ed., *Old English Literature in Context: Ten Essays* (Cambridge and Totowa, N.J.)

Robinson, Fred C., 'Old English Literature in its Most Immediate Context', *Old English Literature in Context*, ed. Niles, pp. 11–29 and 157–61

Shippey, T. A., 'Old English Literature', *Year's Work in Eng. Stud.* 58 (1979 for 1977), 46–67

Simpson, John Mack, 'Sapientia et Fortitudo: the Drama of Athalsteinn', *Jnl of Indo-European Stud.* 7.1–2 (1979), 113–20

Szarmach, Paul E., see sect. 5

Whitelock, Dorothy, see sect. 1

b. Poetry

i. General

Foley, John Miles, 'The Viability of the Comparative Method in Oral Literature Research', *The Comparatist* 4, 47–56

'Hybrid Prosody and Single Half-Lines in Old English and Serbo-Croatian Poetry', *Neophilologus* 64, 284–9

Kabell, Aage, *Metrische Studien, I: der Alliterationsvers* (Munich, 1978)

Kühnel, Jürgen B., *Untersuchungen zum germanischen Stabreimvers*, Göppinger Arbeiten zur Germanistik 209 (Göppingen, 1978)

Lehmann, Ruth P. M., 'Contrasting Rhythms of Old English and New English', *Linguistic and Literary Studies in honor of Archibald A. Hill* IV, ed. Mohammad Ali Jazayery *et al.*, Trends in Ling., Stud. and Monographs 10 (The Hague, Paris and New York, 1979), 121–6

Moisl, H., see sect. 2

Opland, Jeff, *Anglo-Saxon Oral Poetry: a Study of the Traditions* (New Haven and London)

'From Horseback to Monastic Cell: the Impact on English Literature of the Introduction of Writing', *Old English Literature in Context*, ed. Niles, pp. 30–43 and 161–3

'Southeastern Bantu Eulogy and Early Indo-European Poetry', *Research in African Literatures* 11, 295–307

Sato, Noboru, 'A Play on some Runic Letters in *Beowulf* and Ruthwell Cross Inscription', *Otsuka Rev.* 16, 1–9

Steblin-Kamenskiĭ, M. I., *Istoricheskaia poëtika* (Leningrad, 1978) [collected papers on OE, ON etc.]

ii. '*Beowulf*'

Anderson, Earl R., 'Formulaic Typescene Survival: Finn, Ingeld, and the *Nibelungen-lied*', *ES* 61, 293–301

Andersson, Theodore M., 'Tradition and Design in *Beowulf*', *Old English Literature in Context*, ed. Niles, pp. 90–106 and 171–2

Bammesberger, Alfred, 'Three Beowulf Notes', *ES* 61, 481–4

Bjork, Robert E., 'Unferth in the Hermeneutic Circle: a Reappraisal of James L. Rosier's "Design for Treachery: the Unferth Intrigue"', *Papers on Lang. and Lit.* 16, 133–41

Bremmer, Rolf H., 'The Importance of Kinship: Uncle and Nephew in *Beowulf*', *Amsterdamer Beiträge zur älteren Germanistik* 15, 21–38

Brown, Alan K., 'The Firedrake in *Beowulf*', *Neophilologus* 64, 439–60

Clover, Carol J., 'The Germanic Context of the Unferþ Episode', *Speculum* 55, 444–68

Corso, Louise, 'Some Considerations of the Concept of "nið" in *Beowulf*', *Neophilologus* 64, 121–6

Dahood, Roger, 'A Note on Beowulf 1104–8a', *MÆ* 49, 1–4

Damon, Phillip, 'The Middle of Things: Narrative Patterns in the *Iliad*, *Roland*, and *Beowulf*', *Old English Literature in Context*, ed. Niles, pp. 107–16 and 172–3

De Roo, Harvey, 'Two Old English Fatal Feast Metaphors: *ealuscerwen* and *meoduscerwen*', *Eng. Stud. in Canada* 5 (1979), 249–61

Edwards, Paul, 'Art and Alcoholism in *Beowulf*', *Durham Univ. Jnl* 72, 127–31

Eliason, Norman E., 'The Burning of Heorot', *Speculum* 55, 75–83

Foley, John Miles, '*Beowulf* and Traditional Narrative Song: the Potential and Limits of Comparison', *Old English Literature in Context*, ed. Niles, pp. 117–36 and 173–8 see sect. 3*bi* (first entry)

Hardy, Adelaide, 'Historical Perspective and the *Beowulf*-Poet', *Neophilologus* 63 (1979), 430–49

Hart, Thomas Elwood, 'Tectonic Methodology and an Application to *Beowulf*', *Essays in the Numerical Criticism of Medieval Literature*, ed. Caroline D. Eckhardt (London and Lewisburg, Pa.), pp. 185–210

Hasegawa, Hiroshi, '*Wyrd* in *Beowulf*', *Central Education Rev.* (Nihon Univ.) 12 (1976), 50–8 [in Japanese]

'The Sutton Hoo Ship-Burial and *Beowulf*', *Annual Rev. of Science* (Nihon Univ.) 26, 131–6 [in Japanese]

Hume, Kathryn, 'From Saga to Romance: the Use of Monsters in Old Norse Literature', *SP* 77, 1–25

Jorgensen, Peter, 'The Gift of the Useless Weapon in *Beowulf* and the Icelandic Sagas', *Arkiv för Nordisk Filologi* 94 (1979), 82–90

Kabell, Aage, 'Unferð und die dänischen Biersitten', *Arkiv för Nordisk Filologi* 94 (1979), 31–41

Koike, Kazuo, 'The Sword in *Beowulf*', *Obirin Stud. in Eng. Lit.* (Obirin Univ.) 20, 125–48 [in Japanese]

Kuryłowicz, Jerzy, 'Linguistic Fundamentals of the Meter of *Beowulf*', *Linguistic and Literary Studies in honor of Archibald A. Hill* IV, ed. Mohammad Ali Jazayery *et al.*, Trends in Ling., Stud. and Monographs 10 (The Hague, Paris and New York, 1979), 111–19

Lord, Albert B., 'Interlocking Mythic Patterns in *Beowulf*', *Old English Literature in Context*, ed. Niles, pp. 137–42 and 178

Moore, Bruce, 'The Thryth-Offa Digression in *Beowulf*', *Neophilologus* 64, 127–33

Morrison, Stephen, '*Beowulf* 698a, 1273a: "frōfor ond fultum"', *N&Q* 27, 246–8

Nagler, Michael N., '*Beowulf* in the Context of Myth', *Old English Literature in Context*, ed. Niles, pp. 143–56 and 178–81

Niles, John D., '*Beowulf* 431–2 and the Hero's Civility in Denmark', *N&Q* 27, 99–100

Nitzsche, Jane C., 'The Structural Unity of *Beowulf*: the Problem of Grendel's Mother', *Texas Stud. in Lit. and Lang.* 22, 287–303

Opland, Jeff, see sect. 3*bi* (three entries)

Puhvel, Martin, '*Beowulf*' *and the Celtic Tradition* (Waterloo, Ontario, 1979)

Reynolds, William, 'Heroism in *Beowulf*: a Christian Perspective', *Christianity and Lit.* 27.4 (1978), 27–42

Riley, Samuel M., 'The Contrast between Beowulf and Hygelac', *Jnl of Narrative Technique* 10, 186–97

Roberts, Jane, 'Old English *un-* "very" and Unferth', *ES* 61, 289–92

Sasabe, Hideo, '*Medudream* in *Beowulf*', *Rev. of Eng. Lit.* (Kyoto Univ.) 40 (1979), 1–18 [in Japanese]

Sato, Noboru, '*Beowulf* and Sophocles' *Oedipus Tyrannus*', *The Ronso* [Bull. of the Faculty of Letters of Tamagawa Univ.] 20, 353–71
see sect. 3*bi*

Schabram, Hans, '*Stonc, Beowulf* 2288', *Festgabe für Hans Pinsker*, ed. Acobian, pp. 144–56

Schrader, Richard J., see sect. 4

Shimose, Michiro, 'A Variety of Expressions for "Death" used in *Beowulf* – Chiefly on their Figurative Use', *Jnl of Kumamoto Junior College* 59 (1978), 25–50 [in Japanese]

Short, Douglas D., '*Beowulf*' *Scholarship: an Annotated Bibliography*, Garland Reference Lib. of the Humanities 193 (London and New York)

Smirnitskaia, O. A., 'Sinonimicheskie sistemy v *Beovul'fe*', *Vestnik Moskovskogo Universiteta* ser. 9, filologiia 5, 44–57 [synonym systems in *Beowulf*]

Talentino, Arnold V., 'Fitting *guðgewæde*: Use of Compounds in *Beowulf*', *Neophilologus* 63 (1979), 592–6

Tripp, Raymond P., Jr, 'The Restoration of *Beowulf* 2781a: *Hāt ne forhogode* ("Did Not Despise Heat")', *MP* 78, 153–8

Tuso, Joseph, *et al.*, 'The Teaching of *Beowulf*', *OEN* 13.2, 23–7

Warren, Lee A., 'Real Monsters, Please: the Importance of Undergraduate Teaching', *Jnl of General Education* 31 (1979), 23–33

Wright, Louise E., '*Merewioingas* and the Dating of *Beowulf*: a Reconsideration', *Nottingham Med. Stud.* 24, 1–6

iii. Other poems

Alexander, Michael, trans., 'Seven Old English Riddles', *Agenda* 17.2 (1979), 6–9 'Eight Old English Riddles', *Agenda* 18.2, 66–9

Anderson, Earl R., 'The Speech Boundaries in *Advent Lyric VII*', *Neophilologus* 63 (1979), 611–18

Bammesberger, Alfred, 'Zum syntaktischen Aufbau von Bedas Sterbespruch', *Münchener Studien zur Sprachwissenschaft* 37 (1978), 5–9 'Die syntaktische Analyse von *Exodus* 1–7a', *Festgabe für Hans Pinsker*, ed. Acobian, pp. 6–15

Bjork, Robert E., 'Oppressed Hebrews and the Song of Azarias in the Old English *Daniel*', *SP* 77, 213–26

Boenig, Robert E., '*Andreas*, the Eucharist, and Vercelli', *JEGP* 79, 313–31

Braekman, Willy L., 'Notes on Old English Charms', *Neophilologus* 64, 461–9

Bzdyl, Donald G., '*Juliana* 559–563a', *N&Q* 27, 100–1

Chase, Christopher L., '*Christ III, The Dream of the Rood*, and Early Christian Passion Piety', *Viator* 11, 11–13

Conner, Patrick W., 'The Liturgy and the Old English *Descent into Hell*', *JEGP* 79, 179–91

Crossley-Holland, Kevin, trans., *The Exeter Book Riddles* (Harmondsworth, 1979) [orig. publ. by Folio Soc., 1978]

Dane, Joseph A., 'The Structure of the Old English *Solomon and Saturn II*', *Neophilologus* 64, 592–603

De Roo, Harvey, see sect. 3*bii*

Doane, A. N., '*Elene* 610a: "rexgeniðlan"', *PQ* 58 (1979), 237–40

Earl, James W., 'The Typological Structure of *Andreas*', *Old English Literature in Context*, ed. Niles, pp. 66–89 and 167–70

Fukui, Hideka, 'Two Anglo-Saxon Battle Poems', *Jnl of Otemae Women's Univ.* 1 (1967), 23–43 [*Battle of Brunanburh* and *Battle of Maldon*]

Giraudo, Anna, 'La formula anglosassone delle 9 erbe', *Aevum* 54, 283–6

Göbel, Helga, *Studien zu den altenglischen Schriftwesenrätseln*, Epistemata, Würzburger wissenschaftliche Schriften, Reihe Literaturwissenschaft 7 (Würzburg)

Greene, Jesse Laurence, 'Indo-European Social Tripartism in Book 1 of the Caedmonian Paraphrase', *Jnl of Indo-European Stud.* 6 (1978), 263–78

Greenfield, Stanley B., 'Old English Riddle 39 Clear and Visible', *Anglia* 98, 95–100

Hall, J. R., 'The Old English *Exodus* and the *Antiquitates Judaicae*: More Parallels', *ASNSL* 216 (1979), 341–4

Hasegawa, Hiroshi, '*The Riddles* and Runes', *General Education Rev.* (Nihon Univ.) 13 (1977), 51–60 [in Japanese]

'*Spræce* in *The Battle of Maldon*', *Papers on Lang. and Lit.* (Nihon Univ.) 25 (1977), 109–20 [in Japanese]

'*Wulf and Eadwacer*', *Stud. in Stylistics* 26 (1979), 56–69 [in Japanese]

Hieatt, Constance B., 'Divisions: Theme and Structure of *Genesis A*', *NM* 81, 243–51

Hill, Thomas D., 'The *virga* of Moses and the Old English *Exodus*', *Old English Literature in Context*, ed. Niles, pp. 57–65 and 165–7

'Bethania, the House of Obedience: the Old English *Christ II*, 456–67', *N&Q* 27, 290–2

'Bread and Stone, Again: *Elene* 611–18', *NM* 81, 252–7

Hollowell, Ida Masters, 'Was Widsið a *scop*?', *Neophilologus* 64, 583–91

Kanayama, Atsumu, '*The Battle of Maldon*: a Japanese Translation', *Jnl of the Osaka Univ. of Foreign Stud.* 29 (1973), 179–89

'*Judith*: a Japanese Translation', *Jnl of the Osaka Univ. of Foreign Stud.* 31 (1974), 19–30

'*Elene*: a Japanese Translation, 1', *Osaka Gaidai Eng. and Amer. Stud.* 9 (1975), 151–62

'*Elene*: a Japanese Translation, 2', *Jnl of the Osaka Univ. of Foreign Stud.* 36 (1976), 17–28

'*Elene*: a Japanese Translation, 3', *Jnl of the Osaka Univ. of Foreign Stud.* 39 (1977), 79–100

'*The Dream of the Rood*: a Japanese Translation', *Osaka Gaidai Eng. and Amer. Stud.* 11 (1979), 147–54

Kerling, Johan, 'Another Solution to the Critics' Riddle: *Wulf and Eadwacer* Revisited', *Neophilologus* 64, 140–3

Klinck, Anne L., 'Female Characterisation in Old English Poetry and the Growth of Psychological Realism: *Genesis B* and *Christ I*', *Neophilologus* 63 (1979), 597–610

Koziol, Herbert, trans., 'Zwei Gedichte der Sachsenchronik', *Festgabe für Hans Pinsker*, ed. Acobian, pp. 109–13 [*Battle of Brunanburh* and *Death of Edward*]

Kretzschmar, William A., Jr, 'Anglo-Saxon Historiography and Saints' Lives: Cynewulf's *Elene*', *Indiana Social Stud. Quarterly* 33.1, 49–59

Kühnel, Jürgen B., see sect. 3*bi*

Lehmann, Ruth P. M., see sect. 3*bi*

Letson, D. R., 'The Homiletic Nature of Cynewulf's Ascension Poem', *Florilegium* 2, 192–216

Lucas, P. J., see sect. 5

Luria, Maxwell, 'Why Moses' Rod Is Green', *ELN* 17, 161–3 [*Exodus*]

McKill, L. N., 'The Offering of Isaac and the Artistry of Old English *Genesis A*', *The Practical Vision: Essays in English Literature in honour of Flora Roy*, ed. Jane Campbell and James Doyle (Waterloo, Ontario, 1978), pp. 1–11

Nelson, Marie, 'Sound as Meaning in Old English Charms, Riddles, and Maxims', *The Twenty-Seventh Annual Mountain Interstate Foreign Language Conference*, ed. E. Zayas-Bazán and M. Laurentino Suárez (Johnson City, Tenn., 1978), pp. 122–8

Niles, John D., 'The *Æcerbot* Ritual in Context', *Old English Literature in Context*, ed. Niles, pp. 44–56 and 163–4

Olsen, Alexandra Hennessey, 'Guthlac on the Beach', *Neophilologus* 64, 290–6

Orton, P. R., 'Disunity in the Vercelli Book *Soul and Body*', *Neophilologus* 63 (1979), 450–60

Pàroli, T., 'Il *Cristo* i anglosassone: tematica e struttura', *Annali, Istituto Universitario Orientale di Napoli, Studi nordici* 22 (1979), 209–54

Roberts, Jane, ed., *The Guthlac Poems of the Exeter Book* (Oxford and New York, 1979)

Robinson, Fred C., see sect. 3*a*

St-Jacques, Raymond C., 'The Cosmic Dimensions of Cynewulf's *Juliana*', *Neophilologus* 64, 134–9

Sakai, Tsuneo, 'On the Anglo-Saxon Poem *Christ*', *Katahira* 15 (1979), 5–25 [in Japanese; on the authorship of the so-called Cynewulfian poems]

Sato, Noboru, see sect. 3*bi*

Schneider, Karl, '*The Husband's Message* – eine Analyse', *Studien zur englischen Philologie: Edgar Mertner zum 70. Geburtstag*, ed. Herbert Mainusch and Dietrich Rolle (Frankfurt am Main, Bern and Cirencester, 1979), pp. 27–49

Schrader, Richard J., see sect. 4

Schulze, Fritz W., 'Germanischen Bindungen verglichene compositio in Tacitus *Germania*', *Studien zur englischen Philologie: Edgar Mertner zum 70. Geburtstag*, ed. Herbert Mainusch and Dietrich Rolle (Frankfurt am Main, Bern and Cirencester, 1979), pp. 11–25 [*Widsith*]

Shields, John C., '*The Seafarer* as a *Meditatio*', *Studia Mystica* 3.1, 29–41

Spamer, James B., 'The Old English Bee Charm: an Explication', *Jnl of Indo-European Stud.* 6 (1978), 279–94

Stevick, Robert D., 'Geometrical Design of the Old English *Andreas*', *Poetica* (Tokyo) 9 (1978), 73–106

'Mathematical Proportions and Symbolism in *The Phoenix*', *Viator* 11, 95–121

Thundy, Zacharias P., '*Afrisc meowle* and the Old English *Exodus*', *Neophilologus* 64, 297–306

Vickrey, John F., 'Concerning *Exodus* Lines 144–145', *ELN* 17, 241–9

Weise, Judith A., 'Ambiguity in Old English Poetry', *Neophilologus* 63 (1979), 588–91 [*Juliana* 1–2a]

Wells, Richard, 'The Old English Riddles and their Ornithological Content', *Lore and Lang.* 2.9 (1978), 57–67

Yerkes, David, 'The Full Text of the Metrical Preface to Wærferth's Translation of Gregory', *Speculum* 55, 505–13

c. Prose

Baker, Peter S., 'The Old English Canon of Byrhtferth of Ramsey', *Speculum* 55, 22–37

Bibliography for 1980

Bately, Janet M., *The Literary Prose of King Alfred's Reign: Translation or Transformation?* (London) [inaugural lecture]
'The Compilation of the Anglo-Saxon Chronicle, 60 BC to AD 890: Vocabulary as Evidence', *PBA* 64 (1980 for 1978), 93–129
Clemoes, Peter, *The Chronology of Ælfric's Works*, OEN Subsidia 5 (Binghamton, N.Y.) [corrected reprint of 1959 article]
see sect. 5
Dalbey, Marcia A., '"Soul's Medicine": Religious Psychology in the Blickling Rogation Homilies', *Neophilologus* 64, 470–7
Dietrich, Julia, 'The Liturgical Context of *Blickling Homily X*', *Amer. Notes and Queries* 18, 138–9
Fischer, Olga, see sect. 2
Godden, M. R., 'Ælfric's Changing Vocabulary', *ES* 61, 206–23
Jeffery, C. D., 'The Latin Texts Underlying the Old English *Gregory's Dialogues* and *Pastoral Care*', *N&Q* 37, 483–8
Koike, Kazuo, see sect. 6
Langefeld, Brigette, 'Die lateinische Vorlage der altenglischen Chrodegang-Regel', *Anglia* 98, 403–16
Leavitt, Jay A., J. Lawrence Mitchell and Eric Inman, see sect. 2
Le Duc, Gwenaël, *Vie de Saint-Malo, évêque d'Alet. Version écrite par le diacre Bili (fin du IXe siècle). Textes latin et anglo-saxon avec traductions françaises*, Dossiers du centre régional archéologique d'Alet, no. B (1979) [the Life of St Machutus in London, BL Cotton Otho A. viii, fols. 7–34, and Otho B. x, fol. 66]
McCord, Laura R., 'Morris's Translation of *hleahtras* in Blickling Homily IV', *N&Q* 27, 488–9
Manabe, Kazumi, 'On Ælfric's Prose', *Ling. Science* (Kyushu Univ.) 15, 36–47 [in Japanese]
Matsui, Noriko, 'A Comparison of the Concepts of Nature between the Boethian Original and King Alfred's Version of *De Consolatione Philosophiae*', *Rikkyo Rev.* (St Paul's Univ.) 40, 15–46 [in Japanese]
Oetgen, Jerome, 'A Proposed Correction in Ælfric's Homily "In Natale unius Confessoris" (CH II, 43)', *Neophilologus* 63 (1979), 619–21
Roman, S. M. J., 'St Basil the Great and Aelfric in the Light of the *Hexaemeron*', *Analecta Ordinis S. Basilii Magni* 10 (1979), 39–49
Sauer, Hans, 'Zwei spätaltenglische Beichtermahnungen aus Hs. Cotton Tiberius A.III.', *Anglia* 98, 1–33
see sect. 5
Vassallo, Antonina Maria, ed. and trans., *Be gescēadwīsan gerēfan* (with appendix by Patrizia Lendinara), Università di Palermo, Facoltà di Lettere e Filosofia, Quaderni di Filologia Germanica 1 (Palermo)
Wenisch, Franz, see sect. 2
Yerkes, David, see sect. 3*biii*
see sect. 5

4. ANGLO-LATIN, LITURGY AND OTHER LATIN ECCLESIASTICAL TEXTS

Boenig, Robert E., see sect. 3*biii*

Campbell, James, see sect. 6

Clemoes, Peter, see sect. 5

Conner, Patrick W., see sect, 3*biii*

Crehan, Joseph H., 'The Theology of Eucharistic Consecretion: Role of the Priest in Celtic Liturgy', *Theol. Stud.* 40 (1979), 334–43

Cristiani, Marta, *Dall'unanimitas all'universitas da Alcuino a Giovanni Eriugena: lineamenti ideologici e terminologia politica della cultura del secolo IX*, Istituto Storico Italiano per il Medio Evo, Studi Storici 100–2 (Rome, 1978)

Davis, R. H. C., L. J. Engels *et al.*, see sect. 6

Deug-Su, I., 'L'Opera agiografica di Alcuino: la *Vita Willibrordi*', *SM* 3rd ser. 21, 47–96

Dietrich, Julia, see sect. 3*c*

Folz, Robert, 'Saint Oswald roi de Northumbrie: étude d'hagiographie royale', *AB* 98, 49–74

Godman, Peter, 'Alcuin's Poetic Style and the Authenticity of *O mea cella*', *SM* 3rd ser. 20 (1979), 555–83

Göller, Karl Heinz, and Jean Ritzke-Rutherford, see sect. 6

Hartzell, K. D., see sect. 5

Higgitt, John, see sect. 9*i*

Jeffery, C. D., see sect. 3*c*

Jones, Charles W., ed., *Bedae Venerabilis Opera, VI: Opera Didascalica, 3*, Corpus Christianorum Series Latina 123C (Turnhout)

Kelly, Joseph F., see sect. 6 (first entry)

Kerlouégan, François, 'Une liste de mots communs à Gildas et à Aldhelm', *Études celtiques* 15 (1976–8), 553–67

Koike, Kazuo, see sect. 6

Korhammer, Michael, see sect. 5

Langefeld, Brigitte, see sect. 3*c*

Lapidge, Michael, 'St Dunstan's Latin Poetry', *Anglia* 98, 101–6

— 'The Revival of Latin Learning in Late Anglo-Saxon England', *Manuscripts at Oxford: an Exhibition in memory of Richard William Hunt (1908–1979)*, ed. A. C. de la Mare and B. C. Barker-Benfield (Oxford), pp. 18–22

Law, Vivien A., 'The Transmission of the *ars Bonifacii* and the *ars Tatuini*', *Revue d'Histoire des Textes* 9 (1979), 281–8

McNally, Robert E., '"In Nomine Dei Summi": Seven Hiberno-Latin Sermons', *Traditio* 35 (1979), 121–43

McNamara, Martin, 'Ireland and Northumbria as Illustrated by a Vatican Manuscript', *Thought* 54 (1979), 274–90 [Vatican Pal. lat. 68]

Martin, Laurence T., 'The Earliest Version of the Latin *Somniale Danielis*', *Manuscripta* 23 (1979), 131–41

Matsui, Noriko, see sect 3*c*

Morris, John, see sect. 6 (second entry)

Nelson, Janet L., 'The Earliest Surviving Royal *Ordo*: some Liturgical and Historical Aspects', *Authority and Power. Studies on Medieval Law and Government*, ed. Brian Tierney and Peter Linehan (Cambridge), pp. 29–48

O'Keeffe, Katherine O'Brien, 'The Use of Bede's Writings on Genesis in Alcuin's *Interrogationes*', *Sacris Erudiri* 23 (1978–9), 463–83

Olsen, Glenn W., 'Reference to the *Ecclesia Primitiva* in Eighth Century Irish Gospel Exegesis', *Thought* 54 (1979), 303–12

Ray, Roger, 'Bede's *Vera Lex Historiae*', *Speculum* 55, 1–21

Reynolds, Roger E., *The Ordinals of Christ from their Origins to the Twelfth Century*, Beiträge zur Geschichte und Quellenkunde des Mittelalters 7 (Berlin and New York, 1978)

Richards, M. P., 'Liturgical Materials for the Medieval Priory of St Neots, Huntingdonshire', *RB* 90, 301–6

Rosenthal, Joel T., 'Bede's *Ecclesiastical History* and the Material Conditions of Anglo-Saxon Life', *Jnl of Brit. Stud.* 19.1 (1979), 1–17

Sauer, Hans, see sect. 5

Schrader, Richard J., 'Caedmon and the Monks, the *Beowulf*-Poet and Literary Continuity in the Early Middle Ages', *Amer. Benedictine Rev.* 31, 39–69

Serralda, Vincent, *La Philosophie de la personne chez Alcuin* (Paris, 1978)

Shields, John C., see sect. 3*biii*

Stuart, Heather, see sect. 5

Tenhaken, Hans P., *Das nordhumbrische Priestergesetz. Ein nachwulfstanisches Poenitential des XI. Jahrhunderts*, Düsseldorfer Hochschulreihe 4 (Düsseldorf, 1979)

Thomson, Rodney M., 'The Reading of William of Malmesbury: Further Additions and Reflections', *RB* 89 (1979), 313–24

Tolomio, Ilario, trans., *Pseudo-Girolamo, Cassiodoro, Alcuino, Rabano Mauro, Ratramno, Incmaro, Godescalco. L'anima dell'uomo. Trattati sull'anima dal V al IX secolo* (Milan, 1979)

Troncarelli, F., 'Per una ricerca sui commenti altomedievali al De Consolatione di Boezio', *Miscellanea in memoria di Giorgio Cencetti* (Turin, 1973), pp. 363–80

Turner, D. H., *et al.*, see sect. 1

Verey, Christopher D., T. Julian Brown and Elizabeth Coatsworth, see sect. 5

Vollrath, Hanna, see sect. 6 (first entry)

5. PALAEOGRAPHY, DIPLOMATIC AND ILLUMINATION

Angell, I. O., 'A Mathematical Appreciation of Celtic Art', *Science and Archaeology* 21 (1979), 15–22

[Anon.] 'The Codex in Britain', *Book Collector* 28 (1979), 183–98 [review article, largely on J. J. G. Alexander, *Insular Manuscripts, 6th to the 9th Century*, and Elżbieta Temple, *Anglo-Saxon Manuscripts 900–1066*]

Bammesberger, Alfred, see sect. 2 (first entry)

Bischoff, Bernhard, 'Deutsche Karolingische Skriptorien in den Handschriften des Erzbischofs Laud', *Manuscripts at Oxford: an Exhibition in memory of Richard William Hunt (1908–1979)*, ed. A. C. de la Mare and B. C. Barker-Benfield (Oxford), pp. 15–17

Brown, Jane Hetherington, and Linda Ehrsam Voigts, 'University of Glasgow, Hunter MS. U.3.2., f. 210^v', *OEN* 14.1, 12–13 [corrupt text of OE charm on endleaf]

Brown, T. J., 'Late Antique and Early Anglo-Saxon Books', *Manuscripts at Oxford: an Exhibition in memory of Richard William Hunt (1908–1979)*, ed. A. C. de la Mare and B. C. Barker-Benfield (Oxford), pp. 9–14

Byrne, F. J., *A Thousand Years of Irish Script. An Exhibition of Irish Manuscripts in Oxford Libraries* (Oxford, 1979)

Clemoes, Peter, *Liturgical Influence on Punctuation in Late Old English and Early Middle English Manuscripts*, *OEN* Subsidia 4 (Binghamton, N.Y.) [corrected reprint of 1952 edition]

Davies, Wendy, see sect. 8

Faulkes, Anthony, see sect. 6

Ford, Deborah, see sect. 8

Forsberg, R., see sect. 8

Gamber, Klaus, 'Fragmentblätter eines Regensburger Evangeliars aus dem Ende des 8. Jahrhunderts', *Scriptorium* 34, 72–7

Hartzell, K. D., 'An English Antiphoner of the Ninth Century?', *RB* 90, 234–48 [Rouen, Bibliothèque Municipale, 26 (A. 292)]

Higgitt, John, 'Glastonbury, Dunstan, Monasticism and Manuscripts', *Art Hist.* 2 (1979), 275–90

Jeffery, C. D., see sect. 3c

Kelly, Joseph F., see sect. 6 (first entry)

Ker, N. R., *Medieval Manuscripts in British Libraries. II. Abbotsford to Keele* (Oxford, 1977)

Keynes, Simon, *The Diplomas of King Æthelred 'The Unready' 978–1016: a Study in their Use as Historical Evidence*, Cambridge Stud. in Med. Life and Thought 3rd ser. 13 (Cambridge)

Korhammer, Michael, 'Mittelalterliche Konstruktionshilfen und altenglische Wortstellung', *Scriptorium* 34, 18–58

Langefeld, Brigitte, see sect. 3c

Lapidge, Michael, see sect. 4 (second entry)

Le Duc, Gwenäel, see sect. 2

Lucas, P. J., 'On the Blank Daniel-Cycle in Ms Junius 11', *Jnl of the Warburg and Courtauld Institutes* 42 (1979), 207–13

McNamara, Martin, see sect. 4

Meyer, Marc A., see sect. 6

Milani, Celestina, see sect 2

Nordenfalk, Carl, 'Another Look at the Book of Kells', *Festschrift Wolfgang Braunfels*, ed. Friedrich Piel and Jörg Traeger (Tübingen, 1977), pp. 275–9

Padel, O. J., 'The Text of the Lanlawren Charter', *Cornish Stud.* 7 (1979), 43–4 [P. H. Sawyer, *Anglo-Saxon Charters* (London, 1968), no. 1207]
Rella, F.A., 'Continental Manuscripts acquired for English Centers in the Tenth and Early Eleventh Centuries: a Preliminary Checklist', *Anglia* 98, 107–16
Ross, Alan S. C., and Ann Squires, see sect. 2
Sauer, Hans, 'Zur Überlieferung und Anlage von Erzbischof Wulfstans *Handbuch*', *DAEM* 36, 341–84
Stuart, Heather, 'A Ninth Century Account of Diets and *Dies Aegyptiaci*', *Scriptorium* 33 (1979), 237–44 [Leiden, Bibliotheek der Rijksuniversiteit, Voss. Lat. F. 96A]
Szarmach, Paul E., 'The Scribe of the Vercelli Book', *SN* 51 (1979), 179–88
Tite, Colin G. C., 'The Early Catalogues of the Cottonian Library', *Brit. Lib. Jnl* 6, 144–57
Tripp, Raymond P., Jr, see sect. 3*bii*
Turner, D. H., *et al.*, see sect. 1
Verey, Christopher D., T. Julian Brown and Elizabeth Coatsworth, with an Appendix by Roger Powell, *The Durham Gospels* (*Durham, Cathedral Library, MS A. II. 17*), EEMF 20 (Copenhagen)
Yerkes, David, 'The Chapter Titles for Book 1 of Gregory's *Dialogues*', *RB* 89 (1979), 178–82

6. HISTORY

Asakura, Bun-ichi, 'The Monastic Reforms of Tenth-Century England', *Cultural Stud.* (Notre Dame Seishin Univ.) 4.1, 29–40 [in Japanese]
Barlow, Frank, 'The English Background', *Essays on St Boniface*, ed. Reuter, pp. 13–29
'The King's Evil', *EHR* 95, 3–27
Bately, Janet, see sect. 3*c* (second entry)
Bennett, P. E., 'Encore Turold dans la tapisserie de Bayeux', *Annales de Normandie* 30, 3–13
Bilikowska, Krystyna, see sect. 9*c*
Bonner, Gerald, '"The Holy Spirit Within": St Cuthbert as a Western Orthodox Saint', *Sobornost* n.s. 1.1 (1979), 7–22
Boyer, Régis, ed., *Les Vikings et leur civilisation: problèmes actuels* (Paris and The Hague, 1976)
Boyle, Alexander, 'St Cadroe in Scotland', *Innes Rev.* 31.1, 3–6
Bromwich, Rachel, and R. Brinley Jones, ed., *Astudiaethau ar yr Hengerdd/Studies in Old Welsh Poetry*, cyflwynedig i Syr Idris Foster (Cardiff, 1978) [includes articles on the *Gododdin* etc. in Welsh and English]
Campbell, James, *Bede's 'Reges' and 'Principes'*, Jarrow Lecture, 1979 (Jarrow)
Clanchy, M. T., *From Memory to Written Record: England 1066–1307* (London, 1979)
Clark, Cecily, 'Notes on a *Life* of Three Thorney Saints, Thancred, Torhtred and Tova', *Proc. of the Cambridge Ant. Soc.* 69 (1980 for 1979), 45–52
Coates, Richard, see sect. 8 (second entry)
Cormican, John David, 'Asceticism in Medieval Irish Monasticism', *North Dakota Quarterly* 48.1, 53–61

Cox, Barrie, see sect. 8

Cramp, Rosemary, *The Background to St Cuthbert's Life*, Durham Cathedral Lecture 1980 (Durham)

Davies, R. R., *Historical Perception* (Cardiff, 1979)

Davis, R. H. C., 'William of Jumièges, Robert Curthose and the Norman Succession', *EHR* 95, 597–606

Davis, R. H. C., L. J. Engels *et al.*, 'The *Carmen de Hastingae Proelio*: a Discussion', *Proceedings of the Battle Conference on Anglo-Norman Studies II · 1979*, ed. R. Allen Brown (Woodbridge), pp. 1–20

Dietrich, Sheila C., see sect. 1

Duby, Georges, *The Three Orders. Feudal Society Imagined* (Chicago and London)

Dyer, Christopher, *Lords and Peasants in a Changing Society. The Estates of the Bishopric of Worcester 680–1540* (Cambridge)

Faulkes, Anthony, 'The Genealogies and Regnal Lists in a Manuscript in Resen's Library', *Sjötíu Ritgerðir. Helgaðar Jakobi Benediktssyni* (Reykjavík, 1977), pp. 177–90 [genealogies in London, BL Cotton Tiberius B. v]

Finlay, Ian, *Columba* (London, 1979)

Fletcher, Eric, 'The Influence of Merovingian Gaul on Northumbria in the Seventh Century', *MA* 24, 69–86

Fleuriot, Léon, *Les Origines de la Bretagne. L'Émigration* (Paris)

'Les évêques de la "Clas Kenedyr", évêché disparu de la région de Hereford', *Études celtiques* 15 (1976–8), 225–6

Folz, Robert, 'Naissance et manifestations d'un culte royal: Saint Edmond, roi d'Est-Anglie', *Geschichtsschreibung und geistiges Leben im Mittelalter: Festschrift für Heinz Löwe*, ed. Karl Hauck and Hubert Mordek (Cologne and Vienna, 1978), pp. 226–46

see sect. 4

Göller, Karl Heinz, and Jean Ritzke-Rutherford, 'St Oswald in Regensburg: a Reconsideration', *Bavaria Anglica, I. A Cross-Cultural Miscellany presented to Tom Fletcher*, ed. Otto Hietsch (Frankfurt am Main, 1979), pp. 98–118

Graham-Campbell, James, see sect. 9*a* (second entry)

Graham-Campbell, James, and Dafydd Kidd, see sect. 9*a*

Gransden, Antonia, 'The Benedictines and the Writing of English History', *Hist. Today* 30 (November), 49–50

Greenaway, George, 'Saint Boniface as a Man of Letters', *Essays on St Boniface*, ed. Reuter, pp. 33–46

Grinda, Klaus, 'Die Hide und verwandte Landmasse im Altenglischen', *Untersuchungen zur eisenzeitlichen und frühmittelalterlichen Flur in Mitteleuropa und ihrer Nutzung*, ed. Heinrich Beck *et al.*, Abhandlungen der Akademie der Wissenschaften in Göttingen, Philol.-hist. Klasse, 3rd ser. no. 115 pt 1 (Göttingen, 1979), 92–133

Harvey, Sally P. J., 'Recent Domesday Studies', *EHR* 95, 121–33

Higgitt, John, see sect. 5

see sect. 9*i*

Hodges, Richard, 'State Formation and the Role of Trade in Middle Saxon England', *Social Organisation and Settlement: Contributions from Anthropology, Archaeology and Geography*, ed. David Green, Colin Haselgrove and Matthew Spriggs, BAR International ser. (Supplementary) 47 (Oxford, 1978), pt ii, 439–53

Holdsworth, Christopher, 'Saint Boniface the Monk', *Essays on St Boniface*, ed. Reuter, pp. 49–67

Humble, Richard, *The Saxon Kings* (London)

Kapelle, William E., *The Norman Conquest of the North: the Region and its Transformation, 1000–1135* (London and Chapel Hill, N.C.)

Kelly, Joseph F., 'Books, Learning and Sanctity in Early Christian Ireland', *Thought* 54 (1979), 253–61

'The Decline of Irish Monasticism in the Face of Benedictinism in the Early Middle Ages', *Amer. Benedictine Rev.* 31, 70–87

Keynes, Simon, see sect. 5

Koike, Kazuo, 'A Study of English Social Conditions before the Norman Conquest: Focusing on Ælfric's *Colloquy*', *International Culture* (Obirin Univ.) 1, 163–96 [in Japanese]

Kurosawa, Eiji, *A History of England: Ancient and Medieval*, rev. ed. (Tokyo) [in Japanese]

Loyn, Henry, 'The Scholarship of Monasticism', *Hist. Today* 30 (November), 48–9

McNulty, J. Bard, 'The Lady Aelfgyva in the Bayeux Tapestry', *Speculum* 55, 659–68

Martin, E. A., see sect. 8

Meyer, Marc A., 'Land Charters and the Legal Position of Anglo-Saxon Women', *The Women of England from Anglo-Saxon Times to the Present: Interpretive Bibliographical Essays*, ed. Barbara Kanner (Hamden, Conn., 1979), pp. 57–82

Miller, M., 'Consular Years in the *Historia Brittonum*', *BBCS* 29, 17–34

Morris, John, ed., *Domesday Book. 8: Somerset*, ed. Caroline and Frank Thorn (Chichester), and *29: Rutland*, ed. Frank Thorn (Chichester)

ed. and trans., *Nennius. British History and the Welsh Annals*, Arthurian Period Sources 8 (London and Totowa, N.J.)

Nelson, Janet L., see sect. 4

Ó Corráin, Donnchadh, 'High-Kings, Vikings and other Kings', *Irish Hist. Stud.* 21 (1978–9), 283–323 [review article on Alfred P. Smyth, *Scandinavian Kings in the British Isles 850–880* (Oxford and New York, 1977)]

Olsen, Glenn W., 'St Boniface and the *Vita Apostolica*', *Amer. Benedictine Rev.* 31, 6–19

Orme, Nicholas, 'The Church in Crediton from Saint Boniface to the Reformation', *Essays on St Boniface*, ed. Reuter, pp. 97–131

Payer, Pierre J., 'Early Medieval Regulations concerning Marital Sexual Relations', *JMH* 6, 353–76 [penitential discipline]

Piroth, W., ed. F. Leeson, see sect. 8

Radford, C. A. Ralegh, see sect. 9*b*

Ray, Roger, see sect. 4

Renna, Thomas, 'The Idea of Peace in the West, 500–1150', *JMH* 6, 143–68

Reuter, Timothy, ed., *The Greatest Englishman: Essays on St Boniface and the Church at Credition* (Exeter)

'Saint Boniface and Europe', *Essays on St Boniface*, ed. Reuter, pp. 71–94

Robson, H. L., 'Benedict Bishop of Wearmouth', *Antiquities of Sunderland* 26 (1974–6), 34–46

Rollason, D. W., 'The Date of the Parish-Boundary of Minster-in-Thanet (Kent)', *AC* 95 (1979), 7–17

Rosenthal, Joel T., see sect. 4

Savelo, K. F., *Rannefeodal'naia Angliia* (Leningrad, 1977) [early (and pre-)feudal England]

Seeberg, Axel, 'Five Kings', *SBVS* 20 (1978–9), 106–13 [the five who supposedly died with Eric Bloodaxe, king of York, in 954]

Sladden, John Cyril, *Boniface of Devon: Apostle of Germany* (Exeter)

Stafford, Pauline A., 'The "Farm of One Night" and the Organization of King Edward's Estates in Domesday', *EconHR* 33, 491–502

Stout, Adam, 'How Berkshire was Born: the Battle of Benson (AD 779)', *Country Life* 167 (13 March), 742–4

Taylor, Christopher, see sect. 9c

Thompson, E. A., 'Gildas and the History of Britain', *Britannia* 10 (1979), 203–26

'Procopius on Brittia and Britannia', *Classical Quarterly* 30, 498–507

Torrey, Archer, 'The Gregorian Missionary Methods', *Missiology* 8, 99–103

Turner, D. H., *et al.*, see sect. 1

Vollrath, Hanna, 'König Edgar und die Klosterreform in England: die "Ostersynode" der "Vita S. Oswaldi auctore anonymo"', *Annuarium Historiae Conciliorum* 10 (1978), 67–81

'Gesetzgebung und Schriftlichkeit. Das Beispiel der angelsächsischen Gesetze', *Historisches Jahrbuch* 99 (1979), 28–54

Whitelock, Dorothy, see sect. 1

Wilson, David M., ed., *The Northern World: the History and Heritage of Northern Europe AD 400–1100* (London)

see sect. 9a

Winterbotham, J. J., *Hackness in the Middle Ages* (Hackness)

Wise, Terence, *1066: Year of Destiny* (London, 1979)

Wood, Michael, 'Brunanburh Revisited', *SBVS* 20, 200–17

Woodruff, Douglas, *The Life and Times of Alfred the Great* (London, 1974)

Workman, Roy, 'Aelfwine's Gifts', *Suffolk Rev.* 4 (1979 for 1978), 280–2

7. NUMISMATICS

Archibald, M., and D. Nash, 'The Coins', *Excavations at Melbourne Street, Southampton, 1971–76*, Council for Brit. Archaeology, Research Report 33, ed. Holdsworth, pp. 72–3

Becker, C. J., 'Some Anachronistic Danish Coins in the Names of Æthelred and Cnut', *SCMB* 1980, 335–40

Bendixen, Kirsten, 'Møntcirkulation i Denmark fra Vikingetid til Valdemarssøn-nerne', *Aarbøger for Nordisk Oldyndighed og Historie* 1978, 155–90 [with English summary]

Berg, Karin, 'Enkelte bektraktninger I tilkyntning til fenomenet sekundær behand-ling [Some Reflections on the Phenomenon of Secondary Treatment]', *Meddelelser fra Norsk Numismatisk Forening* 2, 25–31 [with English summary]

Blackburn, Mark, 'Some Early Imitations of Æthelræd II's Long Cross Type', *NCirc* 88, 130–2 [the 1910 Digeråkra, Gotland, hoard concealed *c.* 1000]

Blackburn, Mark, and Michael Dolley, 'The Hiberno-Norse Element of the List Hoard from Sylt', *BNJ* 49 (1980 for 1979), 17–25 [some 770 coins and fragments; Hiberno-Norse coins represent 88 per cent of the hoard, buried *c.* 1002–3]

Blunt, C. E., 'Some Doubtful St Peter Hoards', *BNJ* 49 (1980 for 1979), 12–16 ['Derbyshire'; 'Boxmoor'; Lancashire 1734; Sir Simonds D'Ewes]

Dolley, Michael, 'Roger of Wendover's Date for Eadgar's Coinage Reform', *BNJ* 49 (1980 for 1979), 1–11

'The Hiberno-Norse Element in the 1924 Ingelöse Hoard from Skåne', *Coin Hoards IV 1978*, ed. M. Jessop Price (London), pp. 157–9 [over 2000 Viking Age silver coins]

'The Neglected Norwegian Dimension to the 1848 Coin-Hoard from Bradden Mountain (Isle of Man)', *Meddelelser fra Norsk Numismatisk Forening* 2, 15–24 [the hoard consists of twenty-two coins representing eleven English mints]

'Some Insular(?) Imitations from the 1030s of Contemporary English Pence of Cnut', *NCirc* 88, 86–8 [the 1874 Kirk Andreas, Isle of Man, hoard concealed in the 1040s]

'The Minimal English Content of the 1973 Dorow Find (Mecklenburg/Pom-mern)', *SCMB* 1980, 82–4 [the English coins run from the 960s to the 990s]

'Ephippiorum Artifex Vindicatus', *SCMB* 1980, 107 [supports J. C. Sadler (*SCMB* 1979, 390)]

Dolley, Michael, and Tukka Talvio, 'A Thirteenth *Agnus Dei* Penny of Æthelræd II', *BNJ* 49, (1980 for 1979), 122–5 [penny of Leicester mint found in the Maidla, Estonian Republic of the USSR, hoard of 1974, buried in the early 1060s]

Gilmore, G. R., and D. M. Metcalf, 'The Alloy of Northumbrian Coinage in the Mid-Ninth Century', *Metallurgy in Numismatics* 1, ed. D. M. Metcalf and W. A. Oddy, R. Numismatic Soc. (London), 83–98

Hall, Richard A., 'Numismatic Finds from the Excavations of Viking Age York', *SCMB* 1980, 371–3 [discusses especially the unique obverse die of the St Peter type, with sword, *c.* 920]

Harris, E. J., 'Broken Coins as a Guide to Mint Practice', *SCMB* 1980, 179–81

Herschend, F., 'Om vad silvermynt från Gotlands vikingatid kan vara uttryck för – en idéartikel', *Fornvännen* 74 (1979), 217–26

McShane, James, 'Viking Ingots found at Mungret, Co. Limerick', *Irish Numismatics* 76, 164–5 [seven silver ingots and nine Anglo-Saxon pennies found *c.* 1840]

Malmer, Brita, ed., *Catalogue of Coins from the 9th–11th Centuries Found in Sweden* XVI, *Dalarna, pt 1: Falun-Rattvik*, Museum of National Antiquities (Stockholm)

Philpott, Robert A., 'The History of the First Swedish Coinage', *Coins and Medals* 17.1, 13–15 and 17

Price, M. Jessop, ed., *Coin Hoards IV 1978* (London), pp. 104–6 [British hoards nos. 339–51, from *c.* 645 (Crondall) to *c.* 1050 (Dunbrody, Co. Wexford)]

Coin Hoards V 1979 (London), pp. 102–3 [British hoards nos. 271–8, from *c.* 650 (sceattas) to *c.* 1075–80 (Beddington Park)]; pp. 138–9 [Swedish hoards nos. 403–5; Smiss, with 123 English; Eskiltuna, with seventy-seven Anglo-Saxon; Sanda, with 101 Anglo-Saxon and one Hiberno-Norse]

Robinson, P. H., 'A Further Small Parcel of Coins from the Oulton Hoard (1975)', *BNJ* 49 (1980 for 1979), 125–7 [coins of Edward the Confessor, Harold II and William I]

Scarfe, Norman, 'Raedwald's Queen and the Sutton Hoo Coins', *Proc. of the Suffolk Inst. of Archaeology and Hist.* 34.4, 251–4

Sydney, John, 'The Horndon Mint', *Coins and Medals* 17.7, 13 and 15 [discussion of the mint (in Essex) and the unique penny of the 'sovereign' type of Edward the Confessor]

Talvio, Tukka, 'A Parcel of Coins from Cuerdale in the Reichel Collection', *NChron* 7th ser. 20, 188–91 [fifteen Northumbrian Viking pennies once in the collection of Jakob Reichel (1778–1856) of St Petersburg]

Wahlgren, Erik, 'The Norse Coin from Maine: Philology and Navigation', *Meddelelser fra Norsk Numismatisk Forening* 1, 24–30

Walker, Martin, 'Proof that the Die was Cast in York', *NCirc* 87, 400 [the St Peter's Pence die]

8. ONOMASTICS

Addison, William, *Understanding English Place-Names* (London, 1978)

Arngart, Olof, 'Again, the Place-Name Oundle', *N&Q* 26 (1979), 389

'The Hundred-Name Wayland', *Jnl of the EPNS* 12 (1979–80), 54–8

'Barstable: Further Notes towards an Explanation', *Namn och Bygd* 68, 10–18

Barrow, Victoria, 'Early Anglo-Saxon Settlement in Leicestershire and Rutland – the Place-Name and Archaeological Evidence', *Trans. of the Leicestershire Archaeol. and Hist. Soc.* 53 (1977–80), 54–63

Bilikowska, Krystyna, see sect. 9*c*

Cameron, Kenneth, 'The Meaning and Significance of Old English *walh* in English Place-Names' (with appendices: Malcolm Todd, 'The Archaeological Significance of Place-Names in *walh*', and John Insley, 'The Continental Evidence: OHG *wal(a)h*, OSx *walh*'), *Jnl of the EPNS* 12 (1979–80), 1–53

Clark, Cecily, 'Battle *c.* 1110: an Anthroponymist Looks at an Anglo-Norman New Town', *Proceedings of the Battle Conference on Anglo-Norman Studies II · 1979*, ed. R. Allen Brown (Woodbridge), pp. 21–41

Coates, Richard, 'Old English *steorf* in Sussex Placenames', *BN* 14 (1979), 320–4

'On the Alleged Frankish Origin of the Hastings Tribe', *Sussex Archaeol. Collections* 117 (1979), 263–4

'Methodological Reflexions on Leatherhead', *Jnl of the EPNS* 12 (1979–80), 70–4

'A Phonological Problem in Sussex Place-Names', *BN* 15, 299–318

Coutts, C. R. E., 'Bibliography for 1977–78', *Jnl of the EPNS* 12 (1979–80), 75–82

Cox, Barrie, 'Aspects of Place-Name Evidence for Early Medieval Settlement in England', *Viator* 11, 35–50

Davies, Wendy, 'The Orthography of Personal Names in the Charters of the Liber Landavensis', *BBCS* 24, 553–7

Faull, Margaret L., 'The Use of Place-Names in Reconstructing the Historic Landscape; Illustrated by Names from Adel Township', *Landscape Hist.* 1 (1979), 34–43

'Place-Names and the Kingdom of Elmet', *Nomina* 4, 21–3

Fellows Jensen, Gillian, 'The Manx Place-Name Debate: a View from Copenhagen', *Man and Environment in the Isle of Man*, ed. Peter Davey, BAR Brit. ser. 54 (1978), 315–18

'The Name Coppergate', *Interim* [*Bull. of the York Archaeol. Trust*] 6.2 (1979), 7–8

'On the Study of Middle English By-Names', *Namn och Bygd* 68, 102–15

'Common Gaelic *áirge*, Old Scandinavian *érgi* or *erg?*', *Nomina* 4, 67–74

Ford, Deborah, 'A Note on a "Grant by Aethelbald, King of Mercia, to Ealdorman Cyneberht, of Land at Stour in Ismere, Worcs."', *Jnl of the EPNS* 12 (1979–80), 66–9

Forsberg, R., 'An Edition of the Anglo-Saxon Charter Boundaries of Berkshire', *SN* 51 (1979), 139–51

Forster, Klaus, 'Reflections on a Reverse Dictionary of English Place-Names', *Nomina* 4, 78

Fraser, I., 'Gaelic and Norse Elements in Coastal Place Names in the Western Isles', *Trans. of the Gaelic Soc. of Inverness* 50 (1976–8), 237–55

Gelling, M., 'Norse and Gaelic in Medieval Man: the Place-Name Evidence', *Man and Environment in the Isle of Man*, ed. Peter Davey, BAR Brit. ser. 54 (1978), 251–64

Higham, M., 'The "Erg" Place-Names of Northern England', *Man and Environment in the Isle of Man*, ed. Peter Davey, BAR Brit. ser. 54 (1978), 347–55

Hind, J. G. F., '*Elmet* and *Deira* – Forest Names in Yorkshire?', *BBCS* 28, 541–52

'The Romano-British Name for Corbridge', *Britannia* 11, 165–71

Insley, John, 'The Etymology of the First Element of Woodsford, Dorset', *Jnl of the EPNS* 12 (1979–80), 59–65

Jones, B. L., and T. Roberts, 'Osmund's Air: a Scandinavian Place-Name in Anglesey', *BBCS* 28, 602–3

Jönsjö, Jan, *Studies on Middle English Nicknames, I: Compounds*, Lund Stud. in Eng. 55 (Lund, 1979)

Knobloch, Johann, 'Wimbledon. Über das Bedeutungserlebnis geographischer Namen', *BN* 13, 1–3

Lockwood, W. B., 'On the Early History and Origin of the Names Orkney and Shetland', *Namn och Bygd* 68, 19–35

McGarvie, M., *The Bounds of Selwood*, Frome Hist. Research Group, Occasional Papers 1 (1978)

McKinley, R. A., 'Social Class and the Origin of Surnames', *Genealogists' Mag.* 20.2, 103–11

MacQueen, J., 'Pennyland and Davoch in South-Western Scotland: a Preliminary Note', *Scottish Stud.* 23 (1979), 69–74

Markey, T. L., 'Nordic tveit-/tved-Names and Settlement History', *Onoma* 22 (1978), 47–83

Martin, E. A., 'St Botolph and Hadstock: a Reply', *AntJ* 58 (1979), 153

Megaw, B., 'The Manx "Eary" and its Significance', *Man and Environment in the Isle of Man*, ed. Peter Davey, BAR Brit. ser. 54 (1978), 327–43

'Note on "Pennyland and Davoch in South-Western Scotland"', *Scottish Stud.* 23 (1979), 75–7

Megaw, M., 'Norseman and Native in the Kingdom of the Isles', *Man and Environment in the Isle of Man*, ed. Peter Davey, BAR Brit. ser. 54 (1978), 264–314

Mills, A. D., *The Place-Names of Dorset II*, EPNS 53 (Cambridge)

Piroth, W., ed. F. Leeson, 'Where Our Anglo-Saxon Ancestors may have Come From', *Sussex Family Historian 1980*, 183–5

Rivet, A. L. F., and Colin Smith, *The Place-Names of Roman Britain* (London, 1979)

Roberts, Jane, see sect. 3*bii*

Rumble, A. R., 'Hamtvn *alias* Hamwic (Saxon Southampton): the Place-Name Traditions and their Significance', *Excavations at Melbourne Street, Southampton, 1971–6*, ed. Holdsworth, pp. 7–20

Sandred, Karl Inge, 'En ny tidskrift för namnforskning i Storbritannien', *Ortnamns-sällskapets i Uppsala Årsskrift* 1980, 58–63 [review article on *Nomina* 3, ed. Peter McClure; with English summary]

Seltén, Bo, *The Anglo-Saxon Heritage in Middle English Personal Names: East Anglia 1100–1399* II (Lund, 1979)

Smith, Colin, 'The Survival of Romano-British Toponymy', *Nomina* 4, 27–40

Thomas, C., 'Place-Names of Scilly: Where was "Terengores"?', *Devon and Cornwall Notes and Queries* 34 (1978), 25–7

Thomson, R. L., 'The Interpretation of some Manx Names', *Man and Environment in the Isle of Man*, ed. Peter Davey, BAR Brit. ser. 54 (1978), 319–25

Wagner, Norbert, see sect. 2

Werner, K. F., 'Liens de parenté et noms de personne. Un problème historique et méthodologique', *Famille et parenté dans l'Occident médiéval*, ed. G. Duby and J. Legoff (Rome, 1977), pp. 13–18 and 25–34

9. ARCHAEOLOGY

a. General

Addyman, P. V., 'Vernacular Buildings Below the Ground', *ArchJ* 136 (1979), 69–75

[Anon.] 'Wiltshire Archaeological Register for 1976–7', *Wiltshire Archaeol. Mag.* 72–3 (1977–8), 207

Balkwill, C. J., 'Archaeological Finds, 1978', *Proc. of the Suffolk Inst. of Archaeology and Hist.* 34.3 (1979), 213–17

'Archaeology in Suffolk', *Proc. of the Suffolk Inst. of Archaeology and Hist.* 34.4, 289–92

Brown, A. E., 'Chelverdescote Again', *Northamptonshire Past and Present* 6.4, 185–6

Cameron, Kenneth, see sect. 8

Couchman, C. R., 'The Work of the Essex County Council Archaeological Section, 1978', *Essex Archaeology and Hist.* 11 (1979), 32–77

Council for British Archaeology, *Brit. Archaeol. Abstracts* 13 [abstracts articles on all periods published between 1 July 1979 and 30 June 1980]

Eddy, M. R., 'Excavations in Essex 1978', *Essex Archaeology and Hist.* 11 (1979), 101–10

Farley, Michael, 'Archaeological Notes from Buckinghamshire County Museum', *Records of Buckinghamshire* 20.4 (1978), 662–4

Fletcher, Eric, see sect. 6

Graham-Campbell, James, *Viking Artefacts: a Select Catalogue* (London)
The Viking World (London)

Graham-Campbell, James, and Dafydd Kidd, *The Vikings* (London)

Harvey, Sally P. J., see sect. 6

Hewett, Cecil A., *English Historic Carpentry* (London and Chichester) [ch. 1, 'The Anglo-Saxon Period']
'The Implications of Pre-Conquest Carpentry in Essex', *Archaeology in Essex to AD 1500*, Council for Brit. Archaeology, Research Report 34 (London), 108–12

Jones, D., 'The Yorkshire Archaeological Register: 1979', *Yorkshire Archaeol. Jnl* 52, 183–4

Martin, Edward A., 'Archaeological Excavation in Suffolk, 1979', *Proc. of the Suffolk Inst. of Archaeology and Hist.* 34.4, 293–6

Minnitt, S., and B. J. Murless, 'Somerset Archaeology, 1978', *Somerset Archaeology and Nat. Hist.* 123 (1979), 89–90

Morris, John, see sect. 6 (first entry)

Rawes, B., ed., 'Archaeology in Gloucestershire no. 3, 1978', *Trans. of the Bristol and Gloucester Archaeol. Soc.* 97 (1979), 126–30

Spratt, D. A., ed., *The Archaeology of Cleveland* (Middlesbrough, 1979)

Webster, Leslie E., 'Medieval Britain in 1979: Pre-Conquest', *MA* 24, 218–36

White, A. J., ed., 'Archaeology in Lincolnshire and Humberside, 1979', *Lincolnshire Hist. and Archaeology* 15, 67–91

Whittingham, A. B., 'Norwich Saxon Throne', *ArchJ* 136 (1979), 60–8

Wilson, David M., *Economic Aspects of the Vikings in the West – the Archaeological Basis*, 2nd Félix Neubergh Lecture (Gothenburg)

b. Towns and other major settlements

Addyman, Peter V., 'Excavating Viking Age York', *Archaeology* 33.3, 14–22
'The City of York in Viking Times', *Illustrated London News* March 1980, pp. 50–5

Barker, Katherine, see sect 9e

Boddington, A., 'Excavations at 48–50 Cannon Street, City of London, 1975', *Trans. of the London and Middlesex Archaeol. Soc.* 30 (1979), 1–38

Bourdillon, J., 'Town Life and Animal Husbandry in the Southampton Area, as Suggested by the Excavated Bones', *Proc. of the Hampshire Field Club and Archaeol. Soc.* 36 (1979), 181–91

Bibliography for 1980

Burcaw, George Ellis, *The Saxon House. A Cultural Index in European Ethnography* (Moscow, Idaho, 1979)

Carver, M. O. H., ed., 'Medieval Worcester: an Archaeological Framework', *Trans. of the Worcestershire Archaeol. Soc.* 3rd ser. 7

Colyer, Christina, and M. J. Jones, 'Excavations at Lincoln: Second Interim Report: Excavations in the Lower Town 1972–8', *AntJ* 59 (1979), 50–91

Cunliffe, B., *Excavations at Bath 1950–1975*, Council for Rescue Archaeology in Avon, Gloucestershire and Somerset, Excavation Report 1 (1979)

Hall, Richard, 'Sites Review: Coppergate', *Interim [Bull. of the York Archaeol. Trust]* 6.4, 25–35; 7.1, 12–20; and 7.2, 15–21

Hinton, D. A., and R. Hodges, 'Excavations in Wareham, 1974–5', *Proc. of the Dorset Nat. Hist. and Archaeol. Soc.* 99 (1977), 42–83

Hinton, D. A., and I. P. Horsey, 'Excavations in East Street, Wareham', *Proc. of the Dorset Nat. Hist. and Archaeol. Soc.* 100 (1978), 124–6

Hodges, R., 'Trade and Urban Origins in Dark Age England: an Archaeological Critique of the Evidence', *Berichten van de Rijksdienst voor het Oudheidkundig Bodemonderzoek* 27 (1977), 191–216

Holdsworth, Philip, ed., *Excavations at Melbourne Street, Southampton, 1971–76*, Council for Brit. Archaeology, Research Report 33 (London)

'Introduction: Saxon Southampton', *Excavations at Melbourne Street, Southampton, 1971–76*, ed. Holdsworth, pp. 1–3

King, E., 'The Town of Peterborough in the Early Middle Ages', *Northamptonshire Past and Present* 6.4, 187–95

Martin, Edward A., 'Suffolk Archaeological Unit Excavation 1978', *Proc. of the Suffolk Inst. of Archaeology and Hist.* 34.3 (1979), 218–19 [Ipswich]

Milne, G., 'Saxon Botolph Lane', *The London Archaeologist* 3.16, 423–30

Peake, J. C., Margaret Bulmer and Janet A. Rutter, 'Excavations in the Garden of no. 1 Abbey Green, Chester, 1975–77: Interim Report', *Jnl of the Chester Archaeol. Soc.* 63, 15–38 [sub-Roman and late-Saxon occupation]

Radford, C. A. Ralegh, 'The Pre-Conquest Boroughs of England, Ninth to Eleventh Centuries', *PBA* 64 (1980 for 1978), 131–53

Reece, R., 'Town and Country: the End of Roman Britain', *World Archaeology* 12.1, 77–92

Rodwell, W., see sect. 9e

Saunders, C., and A. B. Havercroft, 'Excavations in the City and District of St Albans 1974–6. 1. Excavations within the Saxon 'Burh' of Kingbury, 1976', *Hertfordshire Archaeology* 6 (1979 for 1978), 1–77

Tatton-Brown, T., et al., *Topographical Maps of Canterbury, A.D. 400, 1050, 1200, 1500 and 1700* (Canterbury [1979])

Wallace, P., 'The Archaeological Significance of Wood Quay, Dublin', *An Cosantoir [Irish Defence Jnl]* May 1979, pp. 141–7

c. Rural settlements, agriculture and the countryside

Alcock, Leslie, 'Refortified or Newly Fortified? The Chronology of Dinas Powys', *Antiquity* 54, 231–2

Barrow, Victoria, see sect. 8

Bilikowska, Krystyna, 'The Anglo-Saxon Settlement of Bedfordshire', *Bedfordshire Archaeol. Jnl* 14, 25–39

Briscoe, Teresa, 'Some Anglo-Saxon Finds from Lakenheath and their Place in the Lark Valley Context', *Proc. of the Suffolk Inst. of Archaeology and Hist.* 34.3 (1979), 161–9

Canham, R., 'Excavations at Shepperton Green 1967–1973', *Trans. of the London and Middlesex Archaeol. Soc.* 30 (1979), 97–124

Chapelot, J., 'Le Fond de cabane dans l'habitat rural Ouest-Européen: état des questions', *Archéologie Médiévale* 10, 5–57

Chibnall, A. C., *Beyond Sherington: the Early History of the Region of Buckinghamshire lying to the North-East of Newport Pagnell* (London, 1979)

Cramp, R., and C. Douglas-Home, 'New Discoveries at the Hirsel, Coldstream, Berwickshire', *Proc. of the Soc. of Antiquaries of Scotland* 109 (1977–8), 223–32

Davies, S. M., 'Excavations at Old Down Farm, Andover. Part 1: Saxon', *Proc. of the Hampshire Field Club and Archaeol. Soc.* 36 (1979), 161–80

Dix, Brian, 'Excavations at Harold Pit, Odell, 1974–1978: a Preliminary Report', *Bedfordshire Archaeol. Jnl* 14, 15–24

Drewett, P. L., 'An Excavation at Selmeston, East Sussex, 1978', *Sussex Archaeol. Collections* 117 (1979), 240–4

Drury, P. J., *Excavations at Little Waltham, 1970–71*, Council for Brit. Archaeology, Research Report 26 (London, 1978)

Dyer, Christopher, see sect. 6

Edwards, K. J., and I. Ralston, 'New Dating and Environmental Evidence from Burghead Fort, Moray', *Proc. of the Soc. of Antiquaries of Scotland* 109 (1977–8), 202–10

Fowler, Elizabeth, *et al.*, *Earlier Medieval Sites (410–1066) in and around Bristol and Bath, the South Cotswolds and Mendip*, Bristol Archaeol. Research Group (Bristol)

Freke, D. J., 'Excavations in Tanyard Lane, Steyning, 1977', *Sussex Archaeol. Collections* 117 (1979), 135–50

Gray, Stephen P., 'Searching for Saxon Boundaries', *Country Life* 167 (6 March), 678–80

Jones, M. U., 'Saxon Sunken Huts: Problems of Interpretation', *ArchJ* 136 (1979), 53–9

Orme, Nicholas, see sect. 6

Orton, C., 'Excavations at 32 Burleigh Avenue, Wallington, 1921 and 1976', *Surrey Archaeol. Collections* 72, 77–82

Reece, R., see sect. 9*b*

Reed, Michael, *The Buckinghamshire Landscape* (London, 1979)

Rollason, D. W., see sect. 6

Saunders, A. D., 'Lydford Castle, Devon', *MA* 24, 123–86 [Saxon burh]
Stafford, Pauline A., see sect. 6
Taylor, Christopher, 'The Making of the English Landscape – 25 Years On', *LH* 14, 195–201
Toller, H. S., 'An Interim Report on the Excavation of the Orsett "Cock" Enclosure, Essex: 1976–79', *Britannia* 11, 35–42
Williams, F., 'Excavations at Marefair, Northampton, 1977', *Northamptonshire Archaeology* 14, 38–79
Winterbotham, J. J., see sect. 6

d. Pagan cemeteries and Sutton Hoo

Biddle, Martin, ed., *The Roman Cemetery at Lankhills*, Winchester Stud. 3 (Oxford, 1979) [includes post-Roman material]
Craddock, J., 'The Anglo-Saxon Cemetery at Saxonbury, Lewes, East Sussex', *Sussex Archaeol. Collections* 117 (1979), 85–102
Hasegawa, Hiroshi, see sect. 3*bii* (second entry)
Kerr, N., 'A Pagan Anglo-Saxon Cremation Burial from Sancton, Yorkshire', *Yorkshire Archaeol. Jnl* 52, 169–71
Reynolds, Nicholas, 'The King's Whetstone: a Footnote', *Antiquity* 54, 232–6 [Sancton, Yorkshire]
Saunders, P. R., 'Saxon Barrows excavated by General Pitt Rivers in Merrow Down, Guildford', *Surrey Archaeol. Collections* 72, 69–75
Scarfe, Norman, see sect. 7
Schaedla-Ruhland, Susanne, 'Remarks on the Burial Customs of Sutton Hoo', *Archaeol. Advertiser* Spring 1980, pp. 81–5
Stjernqvist, B., 'The Sutton Hoo Ship Burial: a Frame of Reference for Archaeological Analyses', *Meddelanden från Lunds Universitets Historiska Museet* n.s. 3 (1979–80), 61–7
Williams, D. E., and P. R. Payne, 'Three Burials from St Margaret's Street Rochester', *AC* 95 (1979), 284–6

e. Churches, monastic sites and Christian cemeteries

Aldsworth, F. G., 'The Mound at Church Norton and the Site of St Wilfrid's Church', *Sussex Archaeol. Collections* 117 (1979), 103–7
Barker, Katherine, 'The Early Christian Topography of Sherborne', *Antiquity* 54, 229–31
Campbell, J., 'The Church in Anglo-Saxon Towns', *The Church in Town and Countryside*, ed. Derek Baker, Stud. in Church Hist. 16 (Oxford, 1979), 119–35
Christie, H., O. Olsen and H. M. Taylor, 'The Wooden Church of St Andrew at Greensted, Essex', *AntJ* 59 (1979), 92–112
Cowie, T. G., 'Excavations at the Catstone, Midlothian 1977', *Proc. of the Soc. of Antiquaries of Scotland* 109 (1977–8), 166–201 [early Christian cemetery]

Durham, Brian, 'Traces of a Late Saxon Church at St Mary's, Aylesbury', *Records of Buckinghamshire* 20.4 (1978), 621–6

Hall, D., and P. Martin, 'Brixworth, Northamptonshire – an Intensive Field Survey', *JBAA* 132 (1979), 1–6

Hare, M., 'The Anglo-Saxon Church and Sundial at Hannington', *Proc. of the Hampshire Field Club and Archaeol. Soc.* 36 (1979), 193–202

Hauglid, R., 'Features of the Origins and Development of the Stave Churches in Norway', *Acta Archaeologia* 49 (1978), 37–60

Hewett, Cecil A., see sect. 9a (two entries)

Morris, Richard, *Cathedrals and Abbeys of England and Wales: the Building Church, 600–1540* (London, 1979) [gazetteer with plans]

Oman, Charles, 'Security in English Churches, A.D. 1000–1548', *ArchJ* 136 (1979), 90–8

Parsons, D., 'A Dated Timber Fragment from Brixworth Church, Northampton-shire', *JBAA* 133, 30–6

'Brixworth and the Boniface Connection', *Northamptonshire Past and Present* 6.4, 179–83

Radford, C. A. Ralegh, 'The Church of St Peter, Wootten Warwen', *ArchJ* 136 (1979), 76–89

Redknap, Mark, 'Excavation at Iona Abbey, 1976', *Proc. of the Soc. of Antiquaries of Scotland* 108 (1979 for 1976–7), 228–53

Rodwell, W., 'Wells: the Cathedral and City', *CA* 73, 38–44

Stones, J., 'Brixworth Church: Nineteenth and Earlier Twentieth Century Excava-tions', *JBAA* 133, 37–63

Taylor, Harold M., 'The Anglo-Saxon Church at Wing in Buckinghamshire', *ArchJ* 136 (1979), 43–52

f. Ships and seafaring

---

g. Sculpture on bone, stone and wood

Bailey, Richard N., *Viking Age Sculpture in Northern England* (London)

Hare, M., see sect. 9e

Horn-Fuglesang, Signe, *Some Aspects of the Ringerike Style. A Phase of 11th-century Scandinavian Art* (Odense)

MacGregor, Arthur, 'A Pre-Conquest Mould of Antler from Medieval Southamp-ton', *MA* 24, 203–5

Moltke, E., 'King Harald's Mishandlede Jellingsten', *Kuml* 1979, 205–17

Trench-Jellicoe, R., 'A New Chi-Rho from Maughold, Isle of Man', *MA* 24, 202–3

Tweddle, Dominic, 'Putting on the Style', *Interim* [*Bull. of the York Archaeol. Trust*] 7.2, 22–8 [two bone trial pieces]

Whittingham, A. B., see sect. 9a

Bibliography for 1980

h. Metal-work and other minor objects

Brown, K. R., 'Dating of some Frankish Rings in the Metropolitan Museum of Art', *Bonner Jahrbücher* 179 (1979), 251–8

Collis, John, and Birthe Kjølbye-Biddle, 'Early Medieval Bone Spoons from Winchester', *AntJ* 59 (1979), 375–91

Evison, V., and D. C. Mynard, 'A Saxon Spearhead from Haversham, Bucks.', *Records of Buckinghamshire* 20.3 (1977), 350

Goudge, Cherry E., 'Late Saxon Leather Sheaths from Gloucester and York', *AntJ* 59 (1979), 125–7

Green, B., 'Two Ninth-Century Silver Objects from Costessey', *Norfolk Archaeology* 37.3, 351–3

Hall, Richard, 'A Pictish Penannular', *Interim [Bull. of the York Archaeol. Trust]* 6.4, 36–8

Haslam, Jeremy, 'A Middle Saxon Iron Smelting Site at Ramsbury, Wiltshire', *MA* 24, 1–68

Heslop, T. A., 'English Seals from the Mid Ninth Century to 1100', *JBAA* 133, 1–16

Hinton, David A., 'The Bronze, Iron, Lead and Wood', *Excavations at Melbourne Street, Southampton, 1971–76*, ed. Holdsworth, pp. 73–5

'The Bone and Antler Objects', *Excavations at Melbourne Street, Southampton, 1971–76*, ed. Holdsworth, p. 77

Morris, Carole A., 'A Group of Early Medieval Spades', *MA* 24, 205–10 [wooden separate-bladed shovels]

Owen, O., and R. Trett, 'A Viking Urnes Style Mount from Sedgeford', *Norfolk Archaeology* 37.3, 353–5

Platt, H. M., 'Preserved Worms on an Anglo-Saxon Brooch', *Jnl of Archaeol. Science* 7.3, 287–8

Reynolds, Nicholas, see sect. 9d

Seaby, Wilfrid A., and Paul Woodfield, 'Viking Age Stirrups from England and their Background', *MA* 24, 87–122

Speake, George, *Anglo-Saxon Animal Art and its Germanic Background* (Oxford and New York)

Walton, Penelope, 'A Silk Cap from Coppergate', *Interim [Bull. of the York Archaeol. Trust]* 7.2, 3–5

Webster, L., 'A Gold Pendant from Northwold', *Norfolk Archaeology* 37.3, 350

i. Inscriptions

Connolly, Leo A., see sect. 2 (first entry)

Hasegawa, Hiroshi, see sect. 3biii (first entry)

Higgitt, John, 'The Dedication Inscription at Jarrow and its Context', *AntJ* 59 (1979), 343–74

Odenstedt, Bengt, see sect. 2

Sato, Noboru, see sect. 3bi

j. Pottery and glass

Briscoe, T., 'Anglo-Saxon Pot Stamps', *CA* 72, 15

Brooks, Catherine M., 'Torksey Ware', *Interim* [*Bull. of the York Archaeol. Trust*] 6.4, 39–42

'The Stamp of Luxury', *Interim* [*Bull. of the York Archaeol. Trust*] 7.2, 41–2 [Badorf ware]

Clack, P. A. G., and K. Kilmurry, 'A Stamford Ware Lamp from Saddler Street, Durham City', *AAe* 5th ser. 8, 163–4

Evison, Vera I., *A Corpus of Wheel-Thrown Pottery in Anglo-Saxon Graves* (London, 1979)

Hills, Catherine, 'Anglo-Saxon Chairperson', *Antiquity* 54, 52–4 [pottery figure]

Hodges, Richard, 'The Pottery', *Excavations at Melbourne Street, Southampton, 1971–76*, ed. Holdsworth, pp. 40–59

Hunter, John, 'The Glass', *Excavations at Melbourne Street, Southampton, 1971–76*, ed. Holdsworth, pp. 59–72

Keen, L., 'Late Saxon Pottery from St Peter's Church, Shaftesbury', *Proc. of the Dorset Nat. Hist. and Archaeol. Soc.* 99 (1977), 129–31

k. Musical instruments

---

10. REVIEWS

Addison, William, *Understanding English Place-Names* (London, 1978): Peter McClure, *Lincolnshire Hist. and Archaeology* 14, 62

Addyman, Peter, and Richard Morris, ed., *The Archaeological Study of Churches*, Council for Brit. Archaeology, Research Report 13 (London, 1976): G. P. Fehring, *MA* 24, 281–4; C. A. R. Radford, *AntJ* 59, 164–5

Alexander, J. J. G., *Insular Manuscripts, 6th to the 9th Century*, Survey of Manuscripts Illuminated in the Brit. Isles 1 (London, 1978): see [anon.] in sect. 5; John Beckwith, *Apollo* 109, 328

Andersson, Thorsten, and Karl Inge Sandred, ed., *The Vikings* (Uppsala, 1978): John McNeal Dodgson, *Nomina* 4, 86–7; Edward R. Haymes, *Scandinavian Stud.* 52, 442–3; Wolfgang Laur, *BN* 15, 189–91

Antonsen, Elmer H., *A Concise Grammar of the Older Runic Inscriptions* ('Tübingen, 1975): Joseph Wilson, *Scandinavian Stud.* 52, 65–8

Bacquet, Paul, *L'Étymologie anglaise* (Paris, 1976): Horst Weinstock, *Anglia* 98, 436–9

Bailey, Richard N., *Viking Age Sculpture in Northern England* (London): James Graham-Campbell, *TLS* 7 March, p. 262

Bambas, Rudolph C., *The English Language: its Origin and History* (Norman, Okla.): Catherine von Schon, *Lib. Jnl* 105, 2328

Baugh, Albert C., and Thomas Cable, *A History of the English Language*, 3rd ed. (Englewood Cliffs, N.J., 1978): Joseph B. Trahern, Jr, *JEGP* 78, 242

Bell, Martin, 'Excavations at Bishopstone', *Sussex Archaeol. Collections* 115 (1977): T. C. Champion, *MA* 24, 270–1; R. Leech, *Britannia* 11, 429–31; G. J. Wainwright, *AntJ* 59, 146–7

Beresford, M. W., and J. K. S. St Joseph, *Medieval England. An Aerial Survey*, 2nd ed. (Cambridge, 1979): Peter S. Gelling, *N&Q* 27, 357

Bessinger, J. B., Jr, ed., *A Concordance to the Anglo-Saxon Poetic Records* (Ithaca, N.Y., and London, 1978): Joseph B. Trahern, Jr, *JEGP* 78, 242–4

Biddle, Martin, ed., *Winchester in the Early Middle Ages*, Winchester Stud. 1 (Oxford and New York, 1976): Christian Peeters, *Scriptorium* 34, 173–4

Bierbaumer, Peter, *Der botanische Wortschatz des Altenglischen* III (Frankfurt am Main, Bern and Las Vegas, 1979): E. G. Stanley, *N&Q* 26, 566

Bolton, W. F., *Alcuin and 'Beowulf': an Eighth-Century View* (New Brunswick, N.J., 1978): M. R. Godden, *RES* 31, 325–8; Margaret E. Goldsmith, *N&Q* 27, 246–8; Thomas D. Hill, *JEGP* 78, 408–9; Martin Stevens, *MLQ* 40, 412–15; C. Patrick Wormald, *Speculum* 55, 770–3

Boyer, Régis, ed., *Les Vikings et leur civilisation: problèmes actuels* (Paris and The Hague, 1976): Antonio Ivan Pini, *SM* 3rd ser. 19, 1048–51

Brandon, Peter, ed., *The South Saxons* (Chichester, 1978): E. Christiansen, *EHR* 95, 193–4; Cath[e]rine Hills, *LH* 13, 500–1; F. H[ockey], *Revue d'Histoire Ecclésiastique* 75, 484–5; J. N. L. Myres, *AntJ* 59, 453–4

Brooke, Christopher N. L., *London 800–1216: the Shaping of a City* (London, 1975): Jean-Philippe Genet, *Annales: Économies, Sociétés, Civilisations* 35, 318–19

Brown, David, *Anglo-Saxon England* (London and Totowa, N.J., 1978): Paul Everson, *Lincolnshire Hist. and Archaeology* 14, 64

Brown, R. Allen, ed., *Proceedings of the Battle Conference on Anglo-Norman Studies I · 1978* (Ipswich and Totowa, N.J., 1979): David R. Bates, *History* 65, 288; Joe Hillaby, *LH* 14, 170–1

Bruce-Mitford, R. L. S., *Aspects of Anglo-Saxon Archaeology: Sutton Hoo and other Discoveries* (London, 1974): Detlev Ellmers, *Germania* 58, 238–40

Bruce-Mitford, Rupert, *et al.*, *The Sutton Hoo Ship-Burial* I (London, 1975): Detlev Ellmers, *Germania* 58, 235–8

The Sutton Hoo Ship-Burial II (London, 1978): Vera I. Evison, *AntJ* 60, 124–7; J. N. L. Myres, *EHR* 95, 607–11

Calder, Daniel G., ed., *Old English Poetry: Essays on Style* (Berkeley, Los Angeles and London, 1979): Allen J. Frantzen, *Cithara* 20.1, 60–4; Donald K. Fry, *Lib. Jnl* 105, 510

Campbell, A. P., ed., *The Tiberius Psalter* (Ottawa, 1974): Peter Bierbaumer, *Anglia* 98, 179–85

Chibnall, A. C., *Beyond Sherington: the Early History of the Region of Buckinghamshire lying to the North-East of Newport Pagnell* (London, 1979): George Caspar Homans, *Speculum* 55, 542–3

Chickering, Howell D., ed. and trans., *'Beowulf': a Dual-Language Edition* (Garden City, N.Y., 1977): George Clark, *Speculum* 55, 779–83; T. A. Shippey, *YES* 10, 234–5

Clemoes, Peter, *et al.*, ed., *Anglo-Saxon England 6–8* (Cambridge, 1977–9): W. A. Chaney, *Church Hist.* 49, 101 [7]; W. A. Chaney, *Church Hist.* 49, 483–4 [8]; Cecily Clark, *ES* 61, 456–7 [6]; André Crépin, *EA* 33, 342 [7]; A. J. Frantzen, *Cithara* 20.1, 60–4 [8]; T. F. Hoad, *RES* 31, 196–7 [7]; H. R. Loyn, *JEH* 31, 217–18 [7]; Julian Munby, *BIAL* 17, 150 [7]; E. G. Stanley, *ASNSL* 216, 404–7 [7]; Barbara A. E. Yorke, *Lit. and Hist.* 6.2, 258 [7]

Coombs, Virginia M., *A Semantic Analysis of Grammatical Negation in the Older Germanic Dialects* (Göppingen, 1976): Elmar Seebold, *Anglia* 98, 120–1

Darby, H. C., *Domesday England* (Cambridge, 1977): Karl Schnith, *DAEM* 36, 325

Doane, A. N., ed., '*Genesis A*': *a New Edition* (Madison, Wisc., and London, 1978): [Anon.] *Choice* 15, 1664; Stanley B. Greenfield, *JEGP* 78, 244–8; Edward B. Irving, Jr, *Speculum* 55, 104–6; Bruce Mitchell, *RES* 31, 198–200

Dornier, Ann, ed., *Mercian Studies* (Leicester, 1977): G. R. J. Jones, *Jnl of Hist. Geography* 6, 209–10; Alfred P. Smyth, *EHR* 95, 194

Down, Alec, *Chichester Excavations III* (Chichester, 1978): A. P. Detsicas, *AntJ* 59, 142–4

Drewett, P. I., ed., *Archaeology in Sussex to AD 1500. Essays for Eric Holden*, Council for Brit. Archaeology, Research Report 29 (London, 1978): J. Alexander, *Geographical Jnl* 146, 294–5; F. Thompson, *Britannia* 11, 437; M. Welch, *MA* 24, 278–9

Drury, P. J., *Excavations at Little Waltham, 1970–71*, Council for Brit. Archaeology, Research Report 26 (London, 1978): P. Leman, *Revue du Nord* 247, 947

Dubois, Jacques, and Geneviève Renaud, ed., *Édition pratique des martyrologes de Bède, de l'Anonyme lyonnais et de Florus* (Paris, 1976): Michel Huglo, *Scriptorium* 33, 118–19; Benedicta Ward, *MÆ* 49, 104–5

Els, T. J. M. van, *The Kassel Manuscript of Bede's 'Historia Ecclesiastica Gentis Anglorum' and its Old English Material* (Assen, 1972): Klaus R. Grinda, *Anglia* 98, 175–8

Evison, Vera I., *A Corpus of Wheel-Thrown Pottery in Anglo-Saxon Graves* (London, 1979): E. Christiansen, *EHR* 95, 891; Richard Hodges, *MA* 24, 271–2

Farley, Michael, 'Saxon and Medieval Walton, Aylesbury: Excavations 1973–4', *Records of Buckinghamshire* 20, 153–290: G. Beresford, *MA* 24, 279–80

Farrell, Robert T., ed., *Bede and Anglo-Saxon England: Papers in honour of the 1300th Anniversary of the Birth of Bede*, BAR Brit. ser. 46 (Oxford, 1978): H. Chickering, *Speculum* 55, 559–65

Fellows Jensen, Gillian, *Scandinavian Settlement Names in the East Midlands* (Copenhagen, 1978): Margaret Gelling, *Nomina* 4, 79–83; Fred C. Robinson, *Speculum* 55, 117–18

Finnegan, Robert Emmett, ed., '*Christ and Satan*': *a Critical Edition* (Waterloo, Ontario, 1977): Raymond St Jacques, *Eng. Stud. in Canada* 6, 244–6

Frank, Roberta, and Angus Cameron, ed., *A Plan for the Dictionary of Old English* (Toronto, 1973): Frank-G. Berghaus and Franz Wenisch, *Anglia* 98, 439–47

Fullerton, G. Lee, *Historical Germanic Verb Morphology* (Berlin and New York, 1977): Thomas W. Juntune, *Canadian Jnl of Ling.* 23, 154–8

Gatch, Milton McC., *Preaching and Theology in Anglo-Saxon England: Ælfric and Wulfstan* (Toronto and Buffalo, 1977): A. P. Campbell, *Eng. Stud. in Canada* 6, 94–5; J. Dutka, *Renaissance and Reformation* 16, 95–7; M. R. Godden, *ES* 61, 553–5; Frederick Hockey, *Revue d'Histoire Ecclésiastique* 75, 444–5; Richard C. Payne, *MP* 77, 404–6

Gelling, Margaret, *Signposts to the Past: Place-Names and the History of England* (London, 1978): Gillian Fellows Jensen, *Midland Hist.* 5, 93–4; Peter McClure, *Lincolnshire Hist. and Archaeology* 14, 62; A. D. Mills, *MÆ* 49, 167–70; T. Tatton-Brown, *JBAA* 132, 102–3

The Early Charters of the Thames Valley (Leicester, 1979): Colin Chase, *Albion* 12, 175–6; Joe Hillaby, *LH* 14, 170–1; Eric John, *Agricultural Hist. Rev.* 28, 129

Gneuss, Helmut, *Die 'Battle of Maldon', als historisches und literarisches Zeugnis* (Munich, 1976): D. G. Scragg, *ASNSL* 216, 408–9

Gretsch, Mechthild, supplement to *Die Winteney-Version der Regula S. Benedicti*, ed. Arnold Schröer, repr. (Tübingen, 1978): Henry Hargreaves, *Scriptorium* 34, 177–8

Grinda, Klaus R., *'Arbeit' und 'Mühe': Untersuchungen zur Bedeutungsgeschichte altenglischer Wörter* (Munich, 1975): Angus Cameron, *MÆ* 49, 163–4

Hall, R. A., ed., *Viking Age York and the North*, Council for Brit. Archaeology, Research Report 27 (London, 1978): Ingmar Jansson, *MA* 24, 274–5

Hassall, A. G., and W. O. Hassall, *Treasures from the Bodleian Library* (London and New York, 1976): Iu. R. Ul'ianov, *Srednie Veka* 43, 364–6

Hawkes, S. C., D. Brown and J. Campbell, ed., *ASSAH* 1, BAR Brit. ser. 72 (Oxford, 1979): A. Dierkens, *L'Antiquité Classique* 49, 654–5

Healey, Antonette di Paolo, ed., *The Old English Vision of St Paul*, Speculum Anniversary Monographs 2 (Cambridge, Mass., 1978): F. Hockey, *Revue d'Histoire Ecclésiastique* 75, 460; Paul E. Szarmach, *Speculum* 55, 580–1

Hill, David, ed., *Ethelred the Unready: Papers from the Millenary Conference*, BAR Brit. ser. 59 (Oxford, 1978): Richard W. Pfaff, *Speculum* 55, 581–2

Hope-Taylor, Brian, *Yeavering: an Anglo-British Centre of Early Northumbria*, Dept of the Environment Archaeol. Reports 7 (London, 1979): R. N. Bailey, *AAe* 8, 169–71; R. Cramp, *Antiquity* 54, 63–5; P. A. Rahtz, *MA* 24, 265–70

Humble, Richard, *The Saxon Kings* (London): Tudor Edwards, *Tablet* 234, 903–4

Hunter Blair, Peter, *An Introduction to Anglo-Saxon England*, 2nd ed. (Cambridge, London and New York, 1977): Kurt-Ulrich Jäschke, *HZ* 230, 148–9; H. R. Loyn, *JEH* 31, 256; Angelika Lutz, *Anglia* 98, 482–4

Hutterer, Claus Jürgen, *Die germanischen Sprachen: ihre Geschichte in Grundzügen* (Budapest and Munich, 1975): Horst H. Munske, *Zeitschrift für Dialektologie und Linguistik* 47, 189–91

Jäschke, Kurt-Ulrich, *Wilhelm der Eroberer: sein doppelter Herrschaftsantritt im Jahre 1066* (Sigmaringen, 1977): Erich Hoffmann, *HZ* 230, 155–6

[Jones, Charles W., *et al.*, ed.] *Bedae Venerabilis Opera, I: Opera Didascalica*, Corpus

Christianorum Series Latina 123A (Turnhout, 1975): Henri Silvestre, *Bulletin de Théologie Ancienne et Médiévale* 12, 573

Jones, Charles W., ed., *Bedae Venerabilis Opera, VI: Opera Didascalica, 2. De Temporum Ratione Liber*, Corpus Christianorum Series Latina 123B (Turnhout, 1977): Henri Silvestre, *Bulletin de Théologie Ancienne et Médiévale* 12, 573–4

Kapelle, William E., *The Norman Conquest of the North: the Region and its Transformation, 1000–1135* (London and Chapel Hill, N.C): G. W. S. Barrow, *History* 65, 462–3; E. Fawcett, *Brit. Book News*, pp. 509–10; A. Z. Freeman, *Hist.: Reviews of New Books* 8, 151; Donald K. Fry, *Lib. Jnl* 105, 199; D. J. A. Matthew, *TLS* 15 August, p. 920; M. R. Powicke, *AHR* 85, 1181

Kennett, David H., *Anglo-Saxon Pottery* (Aylesbury, 1978): R. Hilary Healey, *Lincolnshire Hist. and Archaeology* 14, 20

Ker, N. R., *Medieval Manuscripts in British Libraries. II, Abbotsford to Keele* (Oxford, 1977): Jean F. Preston, *Review* (Univ. of Virginia) 1, 223–31

Keynes, Simon, *The Diplomas of King Æthelred 'the Unready' 978–1016. A Study in their Use as Historical Evidence* (Cambridge): D. P. Kirby, *Brit. Book News*, p. 701; Henry Loyn, *TLS* 14 November, p. 1307

Kimmens, Andrew C., ed., *The Stowe Psalter* (Toronto, Buffalo and London, 1979): Peter C. Erb, *Religious Stud. Rev.* 6, 329

Laing, Lloyd, and Jennifer Laing, *Anglo-Saxon England* (London, Henley and Boston, 1979): [Anon.] *Choice* 16, 1628 and 1630; Philip Rahtz, *History* 65, 101–2; Tom Shippey, *Manchester Guardian Weekly* 29 April 1979, p. 22

A Guide to the Dark Age Remains in Britain (London, 1979): Philip Rahtz, *History* 65, 102

Lang, James, ed., *Anglo-Saxon and Viking Age Sculpture and its Context*, BAR Brit. ser. 49 (Oxford, 1978): Howell Chickering, *Speculum* 55, 559–65

Lapidge, Michael, and Michael Herren, trans., *Aldhelm. The Prose Works* (Cambridge and Totowa, N.J., 1979): Jacques Fontaine, *Revue des Études Latines* 57, 588–90; Peter Hunter Blair, *Tablet* 233, 578

Lehnert, Martin, *Altenglisches Elementarbuch*, 9th ed. (Berlin and New York, 1978): Josef Vachek, *ZAA* 28, 66

Lucas, Peter J., ed., *Exodus* (London, 1977): Edward B. Irving, Jr, *Anglia* 98, 170–5; Hans Sauer, *BGDSL* 102, 139–43; T. A. Shippey, *MLR* 75, 616–18

Luecke, Jane-Marie, *Measuring Old English Rhythm: an Application of the Principles of Gregorian Chant Rhythm to the Meter of 'Beowulf'* (Madison, Wisc., 1978): Ralph W. V. Elliott, *AUMLA* 52, 307–9; Donald K. Fry, *Speculum* 55, 143–7; Columba Kelly, *Jnl of the Amer. Acad. of Religion* 47, 705–6

Luiselli Fadda, A. M., ed., *Nuove omelie anglosassoni della rinascenza benedettina* (Florence, 1977): R. Bracchi, *Salesianum* 41, 545; R. Derolez, *ES* 61, 283–6; Domenico Pezzini, *Aevum* 54, 359–60

McClure, Peter, ed., *Nomina* 3 (Hull, 1979): see Sandred, Karl Inge, in sect. 8

Malmberg, Lars, ed., *Resignation*, Durham and St Andrews Med. Texts 2 (Durham and Fife, 1979): Allen J. Frantzen, *Speculum* 55, 872

Malone, Kemp, ed., *Deor*, rev. repr. (Exeter, 1977): J. S. Ryan, *AUMLA* 52, 309–10

Manabe, Kazumi, *Syntax and Style in Early English. Finite and Non-Finite Clauses* c. *900–1600* (Tokyo, 1979): [Anon.] *Amer. Speech* 55, 72–3

Markey, Thomas L., *A North Sea Germanic Reader* (Munich, 1976): Bela Brogyanyi, *Anglia* 98, 434–6

Meyvaert, Paul, *Benedict, Gregory, Bede and Others* (London, 1977): A. de Vogüé, *Revue d'Histoire Ecclésiastique* 74, 245–6

Morris, John, ed. and trans., *Nennius. British History and the Welsh Annals* (London and Totowa, N.J.): Nancy W. Nolte, *Albion* 12, 305–6

Needham, G. I., ed., *Ælfric, Lives of Three English Saints*, rev. repr. (Exeter, 1976): J. S. Ryan, *AUMLA* 52, 309–10

Niles, John D., ed., *Old English Literature in Context: Ten Essays* (Cambridge and Totowa, N.J.): Basil Cottle, *Brit. Book News*, pp. 761–2

Ohlgren, Thomas H., ed., *Illuminated Manuscripts: an Index to Selected Bodleian Library Color Reproductions* (New York and London, 1977): Iu. R. Ul'ianov, *Srednie Veka* 43, 364–6

O'Sullivan, Thomas D., *The 'De Excidio' of Gildas: its Authenticity and Date*, Columbia Stud. in the Classical Tradition 7 (Leiden, 1978): Eric John, *Welsh Hist. Rev.* 10, 239–40

Parkes, M. B., and Andrew G. Watson, ed., *Medieval Scribes, Manuscripts and Libraries: Essays presented to N. R. Ker* (London, 1978): Norman Davis, *N&Q* 26, 564–6; Karen Gould, *Jnl of Lib. Hist.* 15, 94–7; Robert Pope, *The Library* 6th ser. 2, 87–91; J. E. Sayers, *Jnl of the Soc. of Archivists* 6, 366–7

Pearce, Susan M., *The Kingdom of Dumnonia. Studies in History and Tradition in South-Western Britain AD 350–1150* (Padstow, 1978): Leslie Alcock, *MA* 23, 272–3; Eric Christiansen, *EHR* 95, 399; Peter S. Gelling, *LH* 14, 106–7

Pearsall, Derek, *Old English and Middle English Poetry* (London, Henley and Boston, 1977): Przemysław Mroczkowski, *ES* 61, 457–62

Phythian-Adams, Charles, *Continuity, Fields and Fission: the Making of a Midland Parish* (Leicester, 1978): Christopher Taylor, *Midland Hist.* 5, 94–5

Piroth, Walter, *Ortsnamenstudien zur angelsächsischen Wanderung: ein Vergleich von -ingas, -inga- Namen in England mit ihren Entsprechungen auf dem europäischen Festland* (Wiesbaden, 1979): Margaret Gelling, *Nomina* 4, 84–5

Platt, Colin, *The English Medieval Town* (London and New York, 1976): Edith Ennen, *HZ* 230, 676–8

Puhvel, Martin, *'Beowulf' and the Celtic Tradition* (Waterloo, Ontario, 1979): [Anon.] *Choice* 17, 390; Jacqueline Simpson, *Folklore* 91, 250

Rahtz, Philip, *Excavations at St Mary's Church, Deerhurst, 1971–73*, Council for Brit. Archaeology, Research Report 15 (London, 1976): C. A. Ralegh Radford, *AntJ* 59, 164–5

Raw, Barbara C., *The Art and Background of Old English Poetry* (London, 1978): Daniel G. Calder, *MP* 78, 73–5; R. F. S. Hamer, *MÆ* 49, 103–4

Reuter, Timothy, ed., *The Greatest Englishman: Essays on St Boniface and the Church at Crediton* (Exeter): Cecil Northcott, *Contemporary Rev.* 237, 53

Reynolds, Susan, *An Introduction to the History of English Medieval Towns* (Oxford and New York, 1977): Jean-Philippe Genet, *Annales: Économies, Sociétés, Civilisations*

35, 295–6; Robert Gottfried, *Jnl of Interdisciplinary Hist.* 9, 530–2; Michael Richter, *HZ* 230, 157

Rigg, A. G., ed., *Editing Medieval Texts: English, French, and Latin written in England* (New York and London, 1977): Manfred Görlach, *Anglia* 98, 479–82; Ludovico Lazzeri, *SM* 3rd ser. 19, 1096; O. S. Pickering, *ASNSL* 216, 379–81; E. C. Ronquist, *JEGP* 79, 235–7

Rivet, A. L. F., and Colin Smith, *The Place-Names of Roman Britain* (London, 1979): S. S. Frere, *Britannia* 11, 419–23

Roberts, Jane, ed., *The Guthlac Poems of the Exeter Book* (Oxford and New York, 1979): V. J. Scattergood, *Brit. Book News*, p. 442

Salu, Mary, and Robert T. Farrell, ed., *J. R. R. Tolkien, Scholar and Storyteller: Essays in Memoriam* (Ithaca and London, 1979): J. R. Hall, *JEGP* 79, 148–50

Sauer, Hans, ed., *Theodulfi Capitula in England* (Munich, 1978): Frank Barlow, *EHR* 95, 892; D. M[isonne], *RB* 89, 339–40

Savelo, K. F., *Rannefeodal'naia Angliia* (Leningrad, 1977): A. R. Korsunsky, *Srednie Veka* 43, 346–8

Sawyer, P. H., ed., *Medieval Settlement. Continuity and Change* (London, 1976): Janet Roebuck, *Jnl of Interdisciplinary Hist.* 9, 527–9

  From Roman Britain to Norman England (London and New York, 1978): David R. Bates, *Welsh Hist. Rev.* 10, 100–1; Kenneth E. Cutler, *Speculum* 55, 174–6; Margaret Gelling, *Jnl of Hist. Geography* 6, 340–1

  ed., *Charters of Burton Abbey*, Anglo-Saxon Charters 2 (London, 1979): Robert Fossier, *Bibliothèque de l'École des Chartes* 138, 153–4; Antonia Gransden, *EHR* 95, 650–1; F. H[ockey], *Revue d'Histoire Ecclésiastique* 75, 485; Simon Keynes, *JEH* 31, 213–17

Sawyer, P. H., and I. N. Wood, ed., *Early Medieval Kingship* (Leeds, 1977): Anton Scharer, *Mitteilungen des Instituts für österreichische Geschichtsforschung* 88, 186–7; Hanna Vollrath, *HZ* 230, 660–2

Scardigli, Piergiuseppe, and Teresa Gervasi, *Avviamento all'etimologia inglese e tedesca* (Florence, 1978): T. L. Markey, *Colloquia Germanica* 13, 177–9

Scragg, D. G., *A History of English Spelling* (Manchester and New York, 1974): Josef Hladky, *Studia Anglica Posnaniensia* 12, 198–9

Seltén, Bo, *Early East-Anglian Nicknames: Bahuvrihi Names* (Lund, 1975): Martin Lehnert, *ZAA* 28, 66–7; Karl Schneider, *BN* 15, 102–3

  The Anglo-Saxon Heritage in Middle English Personal Names: East Anglia 1100–1399 II (Lund, 1979): Gillian Fellows Jensen, *N&Q* 27, 546–7

Shippey, T. A., '*Beowulf*', Stud. in Eng. Lit. 70 (London, 1978): George Clark, *Speculum* 55, 779–83; E. G. Stanley, *RES* 31, 67–8

Sladden, John Cyril, *Boniface of Devon: Apostle of Germany* (Exeter): Cecil Northcott, *Contemporary Rev.* 237, 53

Smyth, Alfred P., *Scandinavian Kings in the British Isles 850–880* (Oxford and New York, 1977): John D. Bu'Lock, *AntJ* 60, 128; R. Destellirer, *Tijdschrift voor Geschiedenis* 92, 88–9; Kurt-Ulrich Jäschke, *HZ* 230, 149–53; R. W. McTurk, *SBVS* 20, 231–4; Janet L. Nelson, *Jnl of the Soc. of Archivists* 6.4, 230–1; see Ó Corráin, Donnchadh, in sect. 6

Swanton, Michael, ed. and trans., *Beowulf* (Manchester and New York; 1978): Ralph W. V. Elliott, *AUMLA* 52, 307–9; Christine E. Fell, *RES* 31, 68–9

Sweet, Henry, *A Second Anglo-Saxon Reader, Archaic and Dialectal*, 2nd ed., rev. T. F. Hoad (Oxford, 1978): George Clark, *Speculum* 55, 779–83

Szarmach, Paul E., and Bernard F. Huppé, ed., *The Old English Homily and its Backgrounds* (Albany, N.Y., 1978): [Anon.] *Choice* 16, 393; Allen J. Frantzen, *Cithara* 20.1, 60–4; Domenico Pezzini, *Aevum* 54, 356–9

Talvio, Tukka, *The National Museum, Helsinki, and other Public Collections in Finland: Anglo-Saxon, Anglo-Norman, and Hiberno-Norse Coins*, SCBI 25 (London, 1978): M. A. S. Blackburn, *NChron* 7th ser. 20, 226–7; H. E. P[agan], *BNJ* 49, 129; I. Stewart, *EHR* 95, 893

Taylor, H. M., *Anglo-Saxon Architecture* III (Cambridge and New York, 1978): Stephen Gardner, *Speculum* 55, 847–9; Simon Keynes, *JEH* 31, 347–8; Hans Erich Kubach, *Kunstchronik* 32, 466–74; C. H. Lawrence, *Architectural Rev.* 165, 315; Charles B. McClendon, *Jnl of the Soc. of Architectural Historians* 39, 316–17; Janet L. Nelson, *History* 65, 287; C. A. Ralegh Radford, *AntJ* 60, 128–32

Temple, Elżbieta, *Anglo-Saxon Manuscripts 900–1066*, Survey of Manuscripts Illuminated in the Brit. Isles 2 (London, 1976): see [anon.] in sect. 5; Thomas H. Ohlgren, *Speculum* 55, 178–80

Voitl, Herbert, *et al.*, ed., *The Study of the Personal Names of the British Isles* (Erlangen, 1976): Rosemarie Gläser, *ZAA* 28, 282–3; Hans Sauer, *Anglia* 98, 447–50

Watson, George, ed., *The New Cambridge Bibliography of English Literature, I: 600–1600* (Cambridge, 1974): Johan Gerritsen, *ES* 61, 466–7

Whitelock, Dorothy, ed., *English Historical Documents* c. *500–1042*, Eng. Hist. Documents 1, 2nd ed. (London, 1979): Peter Hunter Blair, *TLS* 9 May, p. 524; R. W. Pfaff, *Speculum* 55, 878

Williams, John H., *St Peter's St, Northampton: Excavations 1973–1976* (Northampton, 1979): D. Parsons, *Northamptonshire Past and Present* 6, 236–7

Williamson, Craig, ed., *The Old English Riddles of the ' Exeter Book'* (Chapel Hill, N.C., 1977): Jackson J. Campbell, *MP* 77, 315–17

Winterbottom, Michael, ed. and trans., *Gildas. The Ruin of Britain and other Works* (Chichester, 1978): C. A. Ralegh Radford, *AntJ* 60, 123–4

Witney, K. P., *The Jutish Forest: a Study of the Weald of Kent from 450 to 1380 A.D.* (London, 1976): Joan Thirsk, *EHR* 95, 399–400

Yerkes, David, *The Two Versions of Waerferth's Translation of Gregory's Dialogues: an Old English Thesaurus* (Toronto, Buffalo and London, 1979): Geoffrey Russom, *Speculum* 55, 878–9

Zettel, Horst, *Das Bild der Normannen und der Normanneneinfälle in westfränkischen, ostfränkischen und angelsächsischen Quellen des 8. bis 11. Jahrhunderts* (Munich, 1977): Bernard S. Bachrach, *Speculum* 55, 613–15; Harald Neifeind, *HZ* 230, 153–5

Index to volumes 6–10

Volume numbers in italic precede page numbers

Abactor glossary, *7*.28
Abbo of Fleury: Byrhtferth draws on works of, *10*.124, 125, 140; writes *Passio S. Eadmundi* while at Ramsey, *10*.115
Abbo of St Germain: poem by, *8*.201n; sermon by, *8*.259
Abingdon, *7*.67; bequests of Wulfric to, *10*.154; body of St Vincent translated to, *7*.66, 91; gifts from Ælfhere and family to, *10*.159, 166
abra (Latin = 'handmaid'), OE glosses on, *6*.78, 79, 82, 86
Abstrusa glossary, *7*.29
acanthus leaves, in Carolingian art, *6*.164; Anglicized forms of, *6*.162, 164, 165
Acca, bishop of Hexham, *8*.25n; *10*.98; Bede's *De Die Iudicii* dedicated to, *10*.116n, 121
Acha of Deira, mother of St Oswald, *8*.37, 38, 43–4
achaten, stone alleged in *Physiologus* to be used for finding pearls, *7*.24; mentioned in OE Lapidary, *7*.47, 50–1
acrostics, Latin
    (1) ADALSTAN/JOHANNES, *9*.64, 72–3, thought to refer to King Athelstan, *9*.73–4, the form 'Adalstan' indicating speaker of Old German dialect, *9*.74–7, possibly John the Old Saxon, *9*.79–80; written on the occasion of the ceremony involving the child Athelstan, arranged by his grandfather Alfred? *9*.80–1
    (2) ALFRED/ALFRED (two), possibly also by John the Old Saxon, *9*.81–3
ad Herennium, earliest surviving Latin treatise on style, *6*.62–3
Adam and Eve, Book of (5th- or 6th-c. Ethiopian), *8*,147n, 153n
adamant, *7*.30; mentioned by Augustine, *7*.45, and Pliny, *7*.45–6, and in *Physiologus*, *7*.24; reputed to be soluble in he-goat's blood, *7*.21, 23, 25
Adamnan: criticizes nuns of Coldingham for making and wearing fine garments, *8*.220; MSS of *De Locis Sanctis* by, *8*.295; prose style of, *6*.54, 72, 73
Adda, king of Bernicia, *8*.48
Adémar of Chabannes, MS written and illustrated by, *7*.240n
Ado of Vienne, dating in *Chronicle* by, *8*.186
Adso, OE translation of *De Antichristo* by, *8*.249
Advent (*Christ I*): Latin Advent antiphon as source

of *Advent* x, *6*.240n; damaged passage in *Advent* II in MS, *9*.137, (previous readings) *9*.138–43, (restoration) *9*.143–54, (revised text and translation) *9*.154–5; literary historians on *Advent* VII, *10*.207
Æbba, St, *see* Edor, St
æcerbot charm (11th-c.): pagan ritual to promote fertility of fields, adapted to Christian use, *6*.213–21
Ælfgar, outlawed earl, in slave-raid on Hereford, *9*.111
Ælfgifu, St, mother (*recte* grandmother) of King Edward the Martyr, *7*.65
Ælfgifu (Emma), wife of Æthelred II, then of Cnut, *10*.182, 183; clothes worn by, in illustrations, *8*.196, 215, 217, 219; gifts to Ely from, *9*.132
Ælfheah, bishop of Wells, *6*.143
Ælfheah, ealdorman of central Wessex, brother of Ælfhere, *10*.144, 147–8; buried at Glastonbury, *10*.170n; described as kinsman by Kings Eadred, Eadwig and Edgar, *10*.145n; Edgar grants lands to, *10*.158; estates of, *10*.150–1, 152–3; friendship of, with Ælfsige, bishop of Winchester, *10*.149; makes gifts to Abingdon, *10*.154, and Glastonbury, *10*.167; sons of, *10*.170; will of, *10*.149–51; as witness to charters, *10*.157–8
Ælfheah, St, bishop of Winchester, *6*.143; *7*.65; *9*.84; *10*.149; buried at Old Minster, Winchester, *7*.71
Ælfhere, ealdorman of Mercia, *10*.143, 155–60; buried at Glastonbury, *10*.167; described as kinsman by Kings Eadred and Eadwig, *10*.145n; Edgar grants lands to, *10*.158; estates of, *10*.156; family of, *10*.144–6, 147; and murder of King Edward, *10*.170; and re-emergence of Mercian consciousness, *10*.164–6; relations of, with Evesham, *10*.168–9; strife between Æthelwine of East Anglia and, *10*.160, 165, 166; witness to will of his brother Ælfheah, *10*.150
Ælflæd of Deira, second abbess of Whitby, *8*.38, 39, 40, 43
Ælfric, abbot of Eynsham: *Colloquy* by, *10*.209; commonplace book of, *10*.141, 142; *De Temporis Anni* by, *6*.22, 28; *10*.132; on elephant's howdah, *9*.250–1; identification of works of, on stylistic grounds, *9*.241; includes computus among

Index

Æthilberht, bishop of Hexham, *8*.21

Agapetus II, pope: letter from, mentioning watermills, *6*.21n

Agobard, acquainted with Jewish language and mystical lore, *8*.158n

Aidan, St, bishop of Lindisfarne, *7*.65, 74n; *8*.42, 43; Bede on, *7*.1; body of, translated to Glastonbury, *7*.66, 71, 84, 92

air reconnaissance: discovery of AS settlements by, *10*.191–9; in research on AS farming, *9*.265, 267–8

Alain de Lille, prose style of, *6*.74

Alban, St, *7*.62, 74n, 76n, 83; buried at St Albans, *7*.64, 87; limbs of other saints in tomb of, *7*.81

Alchmund, bishop of Hexham, *10*.98

Alcuin: acquainted with poems of Venantius Fortunatus, *8*.292–5; *Dialectica* by, *10*.10; on Eanbald II, archibishop of York, *8*.25n; MSS of *Super Genesim* by, *10*.7, 14; now thought not to be author of Supplement to Gregorian Sacramentary, *6*.238n; on Offa's purge to secure kingdom for his son, *8*.20, 28; passages in letter by, used by Wulfstan in *Sermo Lupi*, *6*.176; poems by, *10*.35, 37; recalls AS conquest of Britain, *9*.237; substitutes Ham for Cain in commentary on Genesis, *9*.194; refers to adamant in simile, *7*.22–3, 24; *Virtues and Vices* by (OE translation of), *8*.248, 257, 261

Aldfrith, king of Northumbria, son of Oswiu, *9*.226n; an illegitimate child, *8*.27; struggle over succession to, *8*.28

Aldgytha, St, buried at Stortford, *7*.71

Aldhelm, St, abbot of Malmesbury, bishop of Sherborne, *7*.65; acquainted with Damasus's poem on St Paul, *10*.34; on behaviour of British priests, *7*.8; books brought to Malmesbury by, *10*.1–2, 8, 14; buried at Malmesbury, *7*.95; knowledge of works of, shown by Byrhtferth, and in first part of *Historia Regum*, *10*.113; Lactantius quoted by, *10*.15; literary historians on, *10*.205, 211; MS of *De Metris* by, at Malmesbury, *10*.15, 18; prose works of, all in form of letters, *6*.54

prose style of: alliteration in, *6*.41, 46, 67; characteristics of, *6*.39–46; compared with that of Irish and continental writers, *6*.46–62; features of, found in works of other writers, *6*.73–6; place of, in ancient tradition of rhetorical amplification, *6*.68–70; rhythmic endings of clauses and sentences in, *6*.71–3

references by, to garments, *8*.203n, 204n, 212n, 216, 222, to St James in Spain, *7*.78, and to Theodore's school at Canterbury, *7*.18; reminiscences of verse of Venantius Fortunatus in works of, *8*.288–9; riddles by, *6*.76; *7*.25, 27n; *10*.113, (MSS of) *7*.256; *9*.72

Aldhelm (poem), bilingual verse in, *9*.252

Aldred, glossator of Durham Ritual, *9*.241, and of Lindisfarne Gospels, *8*.201; *9*.241

alectorius, mineral mentioned by Solinus, *7*.47, 48

Alexandria: computation of date of Easter made at, using 21 Mar. for equinox, *7*.2, 3

alexandrius, mineral mentioned in OE Lapidary, *7*.48, 49

Alfred, ætheling, son of Æthelred II, *8*.5; taken captive by Godwine, *9*.111

Alfred, king, son of Æthelwulf, succeeded his three elder brothers, *8*.2, 22; anointed in Rome as a child by Pope Leo IV, *8*.21; *9*.79–80, and has similar ceremony arranged for his grandson Athelstan, *9*.80–1; *Historia Regum* on, *10*.111; literary historians on writings of, *10*.202, 209, 217, 224; and Guthrum make agreement not to harbour each other's runaway slaves, *9*.107; operas, plays and poems about, *9*.227n, 236–7, 238; referred to, in reign of his brother Æthelred, as *filius regis*, *8*.11, and as *secundarius*, *8*.1–2, 22, 24; on his ships, *6*.261; subordinates himself to the law of the land (in his will), *9*.232; summons to England Grimbald of St Bertin and John the Old Saxon, and learns from them, *9*.77–8; uses Offa's law code in drawing up his own, *10*.163

prose translation of psalms by, *9*.240, 248; lexical agreements between accepted works of Alfred and, *10*.77–94; lexical differences between works not by Alfred and, *10*.71–7

translation by, of Boethius's *De Consolatione Philosophiae*, *8*.4, 191, (*Metres* in, into prose and verse) *9*.240; *10*.69; quoted by Longfellow, *10*.209

translation by, of Gregory's *Pastoral Care*, *10*.69; *chlamys* translated *mantel* in, *8*.212; John the mass priest thanked for help with, *9*.77–8, 83; OE term for mill-weir in, *6*.23–4; variations between two MSS of, *9*.213–15, (lexical) *9*.215–17, (syntactical) *9*.217–21; verse prologue and epilogue of, *9*.240

alga (Latin = 'seaweed'), OE glosses on, *6*.78, 79, 82, 85, 87

Alhflæd of Deira, *8*.43n

Alhfrith, king of Deira, son of Oswiu, *8*.43n, 47n

Alhred, king of Northumbria, descended from Ida, *8*.16

allegory, in OE poetry, *9*.260

alliteration: in Aldhelm's prose, *6*.41, 46, 67; in continental writings, *6*.49, 66, 70; recognition of, as structural principle of OE verse, *10*.206

alnus (Latin = 'alder-tree'), OE glosses on, *6*.78, 80, 83, 86

alpha (represented by *A*), symbolizing Christ?: on coins, *7*.169–70; with *omega*, on coins, *7*.170, and on charters, *7*.172n

Index

Index

Index

Kent *(cont.)*
6.19, 22, 26; Jutes in, *8*.313; tidal mills in, *6*.24;
legends from, in first part of *Historia Regum*,
10.98

Kenticisms, in OE Lapidary, 7.34, 54

'Kentish Royal Legend', on saints' resting-places,
7.70, 73–4, 83, 85

Ker, W. P., *The Dark Ages* (1897), *Epic and Romance*
(1897) and *English Literature: Medieval* (1922) by,
10.219–20

kings, Anglo-Saxon: choosing of successors by,
8.18–19, fighting and manoeuvring over succession, *8*.27–9, and removal of competing successors, *8*.19–20, 30; consecration of, *8*.20–1;
10.185–8, could sanction a usurpation, *8*.27;
institutionalized 'heir to the throne' not found
among, *8*.24, 33; nobility and, *8*.30–1; trend
towards stress on legitimacy of, *8*.26–7; *see also*
coronation charters, coronation oaths

kingship, depending on descent from founder of
dynasty, *8*.15–18

Kirkpatrick, John (writing *c*. 1700), on early Norwich, 7.176–7

Körting, Gustav, *Grundriss der Geschichte der englischen Literatur* by (1887), *10*.217–18

Lactantius: *De Opificio* by, quoted by Aldhelm,
10.15; William of Malmesbury's copy of works
by, *10*.11, 15, 18

lacunar (Latin = 'fretted ceiling'), OE glosses on,
6.78, 79, 84, 86

ladders of AS construction, in churches, 7.207,
209–10, 214

laeti, peoples deliberately settled by Romans in
depopulated areas, *8*.300, 304; supposed burials
of, in N. France and Belgium, *8*.301, 303

Lambarde, William, *Archaeonomia* by (1568), 9.229,
231

Lambert of St Omer, *8*.59

Lambeth Bible, *10*.17

Lambeth Psalter, *blot/hlyta* translating *sortes* in,
6.93–4

landgable rents for Norwich (1397–1626), information about form and extent of town from,
7.184–7

Lanfranc: involved in suppression of slave trade?
9.113; *Monastic Constitutions* by, 6.241

Lankhills, near Winchester, late Roman cemetery
excavated at, *8*.306, 308

Lantfred of Winchester: on reconstruction of Old
Minster at Winchester, 6.243; on stealing of a
slave woman, 9.108

lap-dovetails, mitred, in AS carpentry at Sompting,
7.218, 220, 229

Lapidary, Old English, 7.9, 19, 31–2, 34; compared
with glossaries, 7.35–41; sources of first half of,
Epiphanius, 7.41–2, Pliny, 7.42–5, and unknown

(ultimately) Greek, 7.42; sources of second half
of, Augustine, 7.45–7, 54, and Solinus, 7.47–54;
text and translation of, 7.32–3

lapidary writings, 7.9–10; by classical authors,
7.10–11; in exegetic tradition, 7.20–5; in medical
tradition, 7.11–20; terminology of, in AS England, 7.25–30; traditions of, in AS society, 7.30–1

lapis indicus (stone thought to cure dropsy), in
Physiologus, 7.24

Latin language: in early OE dictionaries, 9.249;
literary historians on effects of, on OE literature,
10.215; possible difference in AS and Old French
pronunciation of, 9.69

Latin poems concerned with Athelstan:
(1) beginning *Carta dirige gressus*, on Athelstan's deeds, 9.83–6; attempted restoration of,
9.88–90; circumstances of composition of,
9.90–2; metrical form of, 9.87–8; Peter, clerk on
Athelstan's staff, as author of, 9.90, 92–3; two
versions of, 9.86–7

(2) beginning *Rex pius Ædelstan*, in gospel
book presented by Athelstan to Christ Church,
Canterbury, 9.93–4

(3) praising Athelstan, quoted by William of
Malmesbury, 9.63–4; dating of, by diction,
9.64–5, by rhyme scheme (indicating speaker of
Old French), 9.66–9, and by use of polysyllables,
9.65–6; Peter of Malmesbury suggested as
author of, 9.69–71

see also acrostics *and under* Leland

Latin prose style: of Aldhelm, 6.39–46, (compared
with that of contemporary Irish and continental
writers) 6.46–62, (ancient tradition of rhetorical
amplification in) 6.62–70; of first part of *Historia
Regum*, resembles that of Byrhtferth of Ramsey,
10.98–9

Latin-speaking people, place-names as evidence for
contact of Anglo-Saxons with, 6.12–13

Latin verse, MSS of collections of, 7.235

law, of Anglo-Saxons: of God and man,
transgressions against, and need for restoration
of, stressed in *Sermo Lupi*, 6. 181, 182, 190;
history of study of, 9.231–4; MS collections of
texts, 7.234, 235; Mercian, West Saxon and
Danelaw, *10*.163; use of vernacular in, 9.232–3,
234

Leander, prose style of, 6.75

leap year, in Byrhtferth's *Enchiridion*, *10*.134

Lebor Gabâla (12th-c. Irish), on monsters as descendants of Ham, 9.194

legal memory, limits of, *10*.179

Legatine Synod (786), on legitimate birth of kings,
8.27

Legouis, Émile, *Histoire de la littérature anglaise* by
(1924), *10*.229–30

Leiden Glossary, 6.82, 85, 87, 88; 7.28–9, 38; *8*.206;
compared with OE Lapidary, 7.35–7

Index

Index

Sihtric, Scandinavian king of York, enters into alliance with Athelstan, *9*.91

silver: spoons and bowls of, in Sutton Hoo ship burial, *6*.254–5

Simeon of Durham, *see* Symeon

Simon and Jude (Thaddeus), Sts, source for Cynewulf's account of, *8*.169–70

Sisebut, king of Spain: prose style of, in letter to king of the Lombards, *6*.58–9, 65; rhythmic endings in writings of, *6*.72, 73

'slaughter', OE word for (*wæl*) in 'weapon' compound words in *Beowulf*: *wælsceaft*, *8*.132, 133, 134, 137; *wælseax*, *8*.137; *wælsteng*, *8*.132, 134, 138

slave trade, *9*.99; from Bristol to Ireland, *9*.112–13; from England, to Denmark under Cnut, *9*.110, to Low Countries, *9*.105, to Marseilles and Rome, *9*.104, and to Rouen, *9*.109; by Frisians, *9*.102, 105; by Jews, *9*.105–6; outlawed in England (1102), *9*.113, but continued longer in Ireland, *9*.114; supplying Roman Empire, *9*.100; by Vikings, *9*.106–7, 108

slaves: in AS England, *9*.99, and Roman empire, *9*.100; bequeathed by Wynflæd, *8*.197, 204n, 222; Britons as, *9*.101–2; female, as grinders of corn, *6*.27; in law code of Æthelberht of Kent, *9*.99; redemption of, *9*.104; sale of Christians as, among sins of nation reproved by Wulfstan, *6*.189–90; selling of children as, *9*.103; stealing of, *9*.108; toll paid to Crown on sale of, *9*.113; war captives as, *9*.102–3; word *wealh*, formerly meaning 'a Celt', came to be used for, *9*.107

Snell, F. J., *The Age of Alfred* by (1912), *10*.226–7

sods, from four sides of field: cutting, blessing and moistening of, in *æcerbot* charm, *6*.215, 217

soil conditions, of Sutton Hoo ship burial, compared with those of AS cemetery at Mucking, with respect to presence of phosphate from interred bodies, *6*.258–9

Solinus, Caius Julius, *Collectanea Rerum Memorabilium* by, *7*.10–11; corrupt text and uncouth Latin of, *7*.54; on minerals, *7*.31, not used by 7th-c. glossator concerning jewels in Apocalypse, *7*.41, used for OE Lapidary, perhaps via Damigeron, *7*.47–53

Solomon and Saturn (prose), *9*.194; *10*.209, 217

Solomon and Saturn (verse), *8*.157n, 160

Somerset: estates in, owned by Ealdorman Ælfheah, *10*.150, 152, and by Ealdorman Ælfhere, *10*.156

Somner, William: OE dictionary by (1659), *9*.235; publishes Ælfric's *Grammar*, with *Glossary* (not Ælfric's), *7*.164

Sompting, Sussex, St Mary's church at: expert carpentry of AS pyramidal spire of ('Rhenish helm'), *7*.214, 216–26; framing of upper floor in

tower of, *7*.226–7, 228; holes in walls of tower of, for square put-logs, *7*.227

sortilege: Christian church in AS times attempts to suppress, *6*.92; implied not random selection, but ascertaining the will of the gods, *6*.92–3

Soul and Body (OE poems): *6*.107–8, 110; use of *sylf* in, *9*.205

South Elmham, Suffolk: holes in masonry of ruined church at, for triangular put-logs, *7*.210, 227

Southwell, *7*.63n, 66, 67; body of St Eadburg enshrined at, *7*.63, 89

Spain: slaves taken from, by Vikings, *9*.106; survival of slavery in, and transmission to New World, *9*.100n

spears, in AS pagan graves, *8*.321

OE words for, in *Beowulf*: *æsc*, *daroð*, *gar*, *wudu*, *8*.129, in compounds *æscholt*, *garholt* ('forest of spears'), *8*.130–1, 134, 140, and *bongar* ('killer spear'), *8*.129–30, 134; also *sceaft*, *8*.131, (in compounds) *8*.132, 133, 134, *stend*, *8*.132, (in compounds) *8*.132, 134, 138, and *eaforspreot* ('barbed throwing spear'), *8*.129, 134, 135

specificity of description, in Aldhelm's prose style, *6*.45, and in *Sermo Lupi*, *6*.194–5

Speculum Historiale, used by writer of saga of Edward the Confessor, *6*.236

Spelman, Sir Henry, *9*.233; on Norwich as arising from *Venta Icenorum*, and on name (1600), *7*.175–6

Spelman Psalter, *7*.224n

Sphaera Apulei, magical–medical text, iconography of personified Vita and Mors in, *6*.167–8

Spong Hill cemetery: number of graves excavated at, *8*.318; pottery from, *8*.309, 317, 326

Sprouston, Roxburghshire, AS settlement at, discovered by air reconnaissance, *10*.191–6, pls. I, IIa, IIb, IV; compared with that at Old Yeavering, *10*.196–9

Stamford Bridge, Battle of: in saga of Edward the Confessor, *6*.231–3

Standop, Ewald, and E. Mertner, *Englische Literaturgeschichte* by (1967), *10*.240

Stenton, F. M., 'Learning and Literature in Early England' by (1943), *10*.235–6

Stephanus, prose style of, *6*.56–7

Steyning, *7*.67, 68; St Cuthman buried at, *7*.93

Stigand, bishop of Winchester, archibishop of Canterbury, presents roods to Winchester and Canterbury, *9*.132

Stone, Sts Rufinus and Wulflad buried at, *7*.72

Stortford, St Aldgytha buried at, *7*.71

Stowe Psalter, *9*.248

Sulpicius Severus: prose Life of St Martin by, used by Venantius Fortunatus, *8*.287

Summons to Prayer, bilingual verse in, *9*.252

sundial (*horologium*), known to Bede, *7*.5